Redemption of the Executioner

Redemption of the Executioner

(An Officer's Spiritual Journey Through Georgia's Death Row)

By: Robert L. Allen

Xulon Press

Xulon Press
2301 Lucien Way #415
Maitland, FL 32751
407.339.4217
www.xulonpress.com

Printed in the United States of America.

ISBN-13: 9781545616642

References

- **Murderpedia.org**
- **Wikipedia – List of people executed in Georgia (U.S. State)**
- **Georgia Execution Tapes – Georgia Department of Corrections**
- **Attica Prison Riot – Wikipedia**
- **New Mexico State Penitentiary Riot - Wikipedia**

Acknowledgements

- **Names used by Permission**
- **Other names changed to protect Identify**

Song Titles

- **The Winner takes it all – Abba**
- **Leader of the Band – Dan Fogelberg**
- **Once Upon a Time – Frank Sinatra**
- **You Are, Say You, Say Me – Lionel Richie**
- **Behind Blue Eyes – The Who**
- **And when I die – Blood, Sweat and Tears**
- **I will Remember you – Amy Grant**
- **In Too Deep – Genesis**
- **99 – Audio Adrenaline**
- **Oceans – Hillsong United**
- **Hero – Mariah Carey**
- **Other names used are part of a public record**

Dedication

This book is dedicated with love and respect to Lord Jesus Christ. If not for his grace and Mercy, I would not be alive today.

For the memory of my parents: Bill and Ruby Allen, Thank you, Daddy for showing me how a good man should live and Thank you Mother for showing me the meaning of unconditional love.

For my children: Leighanne, Tracey, Kimberly and Miki. Though you didn't grow under my heart, you grew in it. Jesus said, " Therefore if any man be in Christ, he is a new creature: old things are passed away; behold, all things are become new." Because of that promise, I am excited about the possibilities.

For my Grandchildren: Alex, Nicholas, Dylan, Harley, Rayleigh, Sophia and Chloe. My heart is big enough to hold you even if my arms never do.

Introduction

"And I looked, and behold, a pale horse;
And his name that sat on him was death and hell followed with him...
- Revelation 6:8
(King James Version)

Death, the very word strikes fear in most people and conjures up images of the four horsemen of the apocalypse with death sitting on the pale horse as the grim reaper comes to steal precious life away. Then there is the fear of the unknown and the question that has plagued mankind for centuries; what happens when we die? Is it only oblivion as some suggests or is there something more? There are those who believe that this life is all there is and when we die, that is the end of all we know. Others believe that this life is only a part of our existence and that eternal life in heaven or hell waits for us. All my life I felt as if there was something more than just this existence. I always felt as though something or *someone* was there. Even in my darkest hour, when I thought my life was over and I didn't believe in anything, there seemed to be a presence with me and a still, small voice that said, *"I'm here and you are not alone."*

When I think of death, my mind always takes me back to 1985. I was a twenty five year old correctional officer working for the Georgia Department of Corrections at the Georgia Diagnostic and Classification Center near Jackson, Georgia. It was the state's most modern maximum-security prison at that time. It was also the home of "H" house; known to the outside world as "death row." I had been assigned there for nearly four years.

It was midnight and I was in charge of security at the front entrance this cool January night. A helicopter from the Department of Public Safety circled overhead. There were many lights surrounding the entrance as though a Hollywood production were about to take place. There was also quite a collection of law enforcement personnel assigned to the entrance and fellow members of the prison staff were also present. Troopers from the Georgia State Patrol surrounded the entrance along with their mobile command post. Rangers from the Department of Natural Resources were present and one of their boats patrolled the small river that flowed adjacent to the institution. Butts county sheriff's deputies were present along with City police officers from the nearby small town of Jackson, Georgia.

Directly behind the perimeter fence, there was an area partitioned off for those opposed to the death penalty to demonstrate and on the opposite side was an area for those who

supported capital punishment. They gazed across the fence at each other, but no words were spoken until the news media arrived. TV stations from Atlanta arrived with their live broadcast vans. They were looking for any comment from the two opposing groups and they were not disappointed. Everyone wanted a chance at his or her fifteen minutes of fame.

Those opposed to the death penalty burned candles, held hands or comforted each other in some manner as if they were attending a funeral for a friend. Those who supported the death penalty yelled now and then as if they were at an outside party and held signs using the name of a popular music artist of the day yet slightly used out of context, "Shock-a-con." It was an obvious reference to what was about to take place here tonight. I looked around in amazement at the circus that unfolded in front of me.

We were all present for the execution of Roosevelt Green, Jr. I had known Green personally for the four years that I worked on death row. I had known *of him* several years prior to that. Roosevelt Green was convicted of the brutal rape and murder of a young college student named Teresa Carol Allen. It was a sad case for everyone involved with Teresa Carol Allen paying the ultimate price.

One night in December 1976, Green and his accomplice robbed a convenient store in Cochran, Georgia, took Ms. Allen as a hostage and headed north to Monroe County, Georgia. They took turns raping her on the one-hour trip there. Their final destination was a dirt road less than a mile from where I lived at that time. According to Green, when he left to gas the vehicle, his accomplice shot Ms. Allen with a high-powered rifle at close range. When he returned, they both dumped her body in a wooded area like a discarded bag of trash. This execution was personal for me because her body was discovered so close to my home. Our last names were the same so my parents followed the story in the local newspaper and it therefore became an interest for me.

Green and I had many altercations through the years in H-house. I often wondered if he ever considered my name when he looked at the nametag on my uniform and wondered if Teresa Carol Allen and I were related. As far as I knew, we were not. If the thought ever crossed his mind, he never said so. I considered myself a professional and I tried not to let my name or the circumstances of his crime affect my working relationship with him or any of the other inmates on death row. I never pushed the button causing the death of an inmate who sat in the electric chair, but I was their executioner just the same. I was part of the process that led to their deaths. The inmates themselves saw all the officers of H-house that way and let us know it every chance they got. Those of us assigned to staff the U.D.S (under death sentence) unit were specially selected. We were there from the moment they arrived in H-house right up until the time they were escorted to the holding cell adjacent to the electric chair. They were completely segregated from the rest of the prison population and we kept them in our custody at all times. Whenever an inmate moved from H-house to any other part of the institution, we moved with them, step for step as escort officers. We were with them for visitation, medical appointments any movement what so ever and remained with them until they returned to H-house. We brought them their food trays, made sure they received haircuts, showers and attended to any other personal needs. We were more than just their keepers. In a strange sort of way, we became family to many of these men.

It was against departmental policy for any officer assigned of H-house to actively participate in the last phase of the execution. We had worked with some of these men for years and became quite intimate with some of them so it therefore became our responsibility to take them from their cell, prepare them for execution and escort them to the holding cell inside of the execution chamber and turn them over to men they did not know just hours before they were scheduled to die. I had escorted Green on his "last mile" only a few hours before. Now I stood outside in the cool night air and watched as all these people gathered for the end of his life. I participated in three other executions and there was no love lost between Green and me, but this execution seemed to affect me personally. Was it just her name and the fact that she died so close to my home or was it something deeper? Maybe even spiritual. I had a connection with Roosevelt Green and Teresa Carol Allen that none of these people out here could possibly understand. I shook my head as I watched them cry for or curse at a man that none of them knew. There was no one to weep for *her* and to think about how her family felt on that fateful night in 1976. I also wondered if by some miracle he were released tonight, would any of them volunteer to take him home with them.

I was watching and listening to the crowds as each was making their case to the media as to why he should die or why he should live when suddenly the crowd went silent. All heads turned toward the institution at the set of vehicle headlights that appeared. The long black vehicle was slowly moving toward the front entrance. As it approached, for a moment, it felt as if time stood still and there was no air to breathe. No one said anything. Instinctively, I looked at my watch and noted the time as one am. With no announcement to any of us outside, Roosevelt Green had died in Georgia's electric chair. As the hearse got closer, the pro death penalty crowd began to cheer. There was only silence from the anti-death penalty side. After what seemed like an eternity, the vehicle was at the gate and a Butts county sheriff's cruiser was waiting with blue lights on to escort Roosevelt Green on his last ride away from the Georgia Diagnostic Center and to a local funeral home where he would be prepared for burial. I was certain that his body was still warm from the 2,000 volts of electricity that had passed through him only moments before. I had a strange feeling inside, though I had experienced this same procedure before.

As the hearse passed by me I immediately thought about the family of Teresa Carol Allen. They had chosen not to attend his execution tonight. I wondered if they knew he was dead yet or did they want to know? I wondered if they had simply chosen to let this night pass by. After all, none of this was going to bring back their daughter. I thought about Teresa Carol Allen. I wondered if in the grand design of the spiritual realm she was aware that *he had joined her*. My struggling faith had me asking all sorts of questions and none that I would receive an answer to here tonight.

My mind drifted back to the first time I saw a picture of Teresa Carol Allen. At that time, I was the unit clerk for Lieutenant Bill Treadwell, the unit manager of H-house. One of my duties was to inspect all incoming and outgoing mail of the inmates on death row. Sometime before his execution order arrived, Green had sent out his trial transcript. While inspecting the file, I came across a picture of Teresa Carol Allen in death. It was a Xerox copy and of poor quality, but I saw all I needed. She was lying on an autopsy table and I could see that one side of her face appeared to be missing where the bullet had exited. I could tell that she had once been a pretty girl, but a rifle blast took care of that. I once heard a line from a movie, "Nothing much surprises me anymore except what people do to each other." That was my thought here. Then she was discarded like so much trash.

I felt a rush of anger come over me as I looked toward the demonstrators. With that image forever burned in my mind I immediately asked, *"You came to cry for a man who was capable of that?* My faith in God took another blow. I looked toward the night sky as if God himself would hand me down an answer that I could understand, but received only silence. I tried to consider it all. She was working to put herself through college. I could imagine her in school talking with her friends about the parties and the weekends that she would never see. I imagined her smiling at the boys she would never meet and the dates she would never come to know. The husband and the children she would never have. I tried to imagine what her mother was feeling tonight. The loss and the fact that she would never see her baby again and the cold hard truth was that what happened here tonight would change none of that.

Roosevelt Green must have loved someone at some point in his life and they had loved him in return. He had a mother who loved him just has Teresa Carol Allen had a mother that loved her. His mother was in fact, present here tonight for his execution. She was there at that moment to give him life and now she was here to see it end. Somewhere along the way something had gone terribly wrong. What could possibly drive a person to treat another human being the way that Green and his accomplice had treated her? Again, I had no answers. God remained silent tonight.

I reflected back to the comments I used to hear my fellow officers make in H-house that there should be an electric couch instead of an electric chair so that we could execute more than one at a time. They would quote the bible with verses like, "and eye for an eye." I wondered if any of them could even say where that scripture was located in the bible and if they knew what came before or followed that scripture. I also wondered if they really meant it or were they acting like a scared young child walking in the forest all alone, whistling as though everything was alright, all the while afraid of what might be lurking in the shadows. Death was here tonight to claim the life of Roosevelt Green and no one could deny his presence. It is the presence that strikes fear in seasoned veterans and causes men to look over their shoulders for a presence that one can feel, but cannot see.

With Green's body gone, the circus was over. One by one they all cleared the front entrance until I was alone. I was dropped off at the front Tower of the institution to turn my weapon in to the tower officer. On the drive home, I was alone with my thoughts of the night's events and my challenged spiritual feelings. I finally made it home and walked straight into my daughter's room. She was there, sweet little Kimberly, sleeping. I also thought about my twin daughters, Leighanne and Tracey who weren't here with me tonight. Their worlds were untouched by the hardness of what happened tonight and the tragedy of Teresa Carol Allen's life and death and of her family's anguish and I wanted to keep it that way for as long as I could.

I thought about Teresa Carol Allen's parents and the fact that they could no longer participate in precious moments like this with her. I watched Kimberly's chest rise and fall with life sustaining breath. I leaned in and kissed her on the cheek and headed to my own bed. I lay my head down on the pillow, closed my eyes and waited for the demons to come. There were images of life and death and the angel of death coming for his latest victim. I saw images of an inmate's last walk, my participation and walking past the electric chair to leave him in a cell to wait for his death. I lay in the silence of the night and thought about the fact that in the morning, Roosevelt Green would be gone and Teresa Carol Allen would not magically appear alive from the grave. Her parents would be just as alone in the morning light as they were in the dark. I felt emptiness inside. Not at the loss of a convicted murderer and rapist, but at the loss of my understanding of it all. Good or bad, there was

a connection between Roosevelt Green, Teresa Carol Allen and I that would not allow me to rest easy tonight. Did Green and I meet at the end of his life for spiritual reasons? Had God arranged the meeting? If so, did I fulfill my part in all of this? It opened up a whole new avenue of questions. As my spirituality came under attack, I drifted off to sleep.

A war between good and evil began. The battleground would be my life and as the lines on the map moved from side to side, everyone I loved would be caught up in it. My friends, my family and my children would end up as the victims. The next few years of my life would see me in the midst of the angel of death in ways I would prefer to avoid. I had the attention of something evil and it would invade my mind and body and very nearly claim my life. I was in a battle for my very soul.

“Having received authority from the chief priest; and when they were put to death, I cast my vote against them.

The Apostle Paul
Acts 26:10

Chapter 1

And Moses said unto the Lord, O my Lord, I am not eloquent, neither heretofore, nor since thou hast spoken unto thy servant: but I am slow of speech and of a slow tongue. And the Lord said unto him, who hath made man's mouth? Or who maketh the dumb or deaf or the seeing, or the blind? Have not I the Lord? Now therefore go and I will be with thy mouth and teach thee what thou shall say.

- Exodus 4: 10, 11, 12
(King James Version)

It was a cold, rainy night in Macon, Georgia when I first received the message. I was working as a front desk monitor at the Salvation Army facility for women. Everyone was long since asleep and I had stepped outside, leaned up against the wall to watch and listen to the rain fall as I contemplated the past few years of my life. It wasn't a voice in my ear or even in my mind, but more of warm feeling that swept through me when God visited. It was a feeling like someone was watching and caused me to stand erect and look around to see whose eyes were on me. As I stood away from the wall, I looked, but I knew no one was there. I looked down at my watch. It was past midnight and I was alone. I looked out to the rain again, but the feeling persisted. I knew *He* was here.

Through the years, life taught me that deep down in the human soul there is a place that only God himself can occupy. I spent so many years of my life trying to fill that void inside with money, cars, motorcycles, boats, women and people in general. I tried anything I could to combat the terrible emptiness inside me only to end up right back where I started. It was there, when my mind lost all hope and my heart had given up, that God met me. There is a supernatural force there and help that is available to anyone and activated with three very powerful words; *"God, help me,"* and I have always heard the same response, *"I am here and you are not alone."*That place God occupied seemed empty for so long, but I always heard those comforting words from him. There is no strength of my own in that place, but tonight as I looked in that place, He was there staring back at me. As I reflected about the way I lived my life, I knew I should have been dead several years ago. While my faith was challenged on many levels, I still believed in God and His son Jesus Christ. Even with my weak faith I found myself praying to him and asking that if there was any chance of me going to heaven that he would please take me.

In the last few weeks I was so distraught I was contemplating suicide. I tried that solution before with no success and tonight I found that I didn't have the courage to make another attempt. It was then that my mind started to hear a song. All of my life, music has been a constant companion. I believe it was a spiritual gift God gave to me so that whenever any stressful moment occurred in my life, I would hear the message he was trying to give me. Tonight, with the rhythm of the rain, the words formed in my mind to hear his message tonight. It seemed to be in response to the hopeless feeling I was feeling tonight and his message came through loud and clear. The song *"Hero"* by Mariah Carey was so very plain. It speaks of the hopelessness that I was feeling, but to look inside. That's where hope seemed to be hiding. But, it wasn't me. It's that place inside us all that God occupies. That is where hope lies. It sent cold chills down my back and I dared feel a glimmer of hope. I looked around and then skyward as though I was going to see God looking down at me. I needed to hold on to that feeling so I could at least try to see a vision of what he wanted me to do. In my mind's eye, I could almost see God looking back at me. Then I heard the words, *"You have a message to write for me."*

With those feelings within me, I wondered what message could I write that would inspire anyone. Then I recalled the moment God revealed his plan for Moses to speak to pharaoh concerning the children of Israel. Moses had the same feeling that I had here tonight. *Who am I?* He was a murderer on the run from his past. I hadn't killed anyone, but I certainly was on the run from my past. If God spoke through Moses, maybe he could speak through someone like me. As the rain fell, I began to look back into my life at all that I accomplished all that I experienced, all that lost, the people I hurt and the tragedy that my life had become. But, I also knew that God had his hand on me through it all. Being alive here tonight to hear his voice was all part of his plan somehow. As the rain fell and my mind took me back to the beginning.

It was June 1972 and our family just moved to Monroe County, Georgia. My Father was offered a job by his Texaco representative to open a brand new gas station there. It was the days before convenient stores and self service gas pumps. My father also had an aunt there who deeded some property to him. I was the youngest of five children. My oldest sister, Billie, was Daddy's daughter from a previous marriage and was married with children of her own. My oldest brother, Don, was living alone. My middle sister, Rachel, was married with a child and living in Warner Robins, Georgia. My middle brother, Rusty, recently quit school and was living at home, so he, mother and daddy and I moved to a brand new home.

Daddy and mother stopped attending church a few years before. I don't know why and they never spoke about it, but I knew that they both were members of a church and believed in God. Once we moved, they decided that I needed to attend church. So, I was sent to church, but never taken to church. I just turned thirteen years old and believed in God, but I wasn't sure about the whole church thing. The local Baptist church was the home church of my great Aunt Elberta. She was my father's aunt by marriage. All my grandparents died by the time I was seven years old and she was the closest thing to a grandmother I ever knew. Now I was going to church with Aunt Elberta and listening to the fire and brimstone sermons of this Baptist preacher. Within a few months, I was scared to death of God. Whether from curiosity or fear, I continued on. One Sunday, the preacher had an alter call and I wasn't sure what to do. I heard him say, "If you'll make the first step, God will make the rest." I stepped forward and found I could not stop walking and made my way to the

front. He prayed for me and then the church secretary came over to ask me if I wanted to join the church by transfer of letter or by baptism. I had no clue what a transfer of letter was, but I had never been baptized so I chose the latter.

The following week I was baptized and became a member of the church without any family attending the service. I wasn't really sure what I was supposed to be doing. I didn't feel any different. I was just going through the motions. One particular Sunday a guest preacher was delivering the message. I remember he told this elaborate story of God appearing to him in some manner and it frightened me. I was an average teenager going through puberty and now my nights were filled with visions of God appearing to me, in my room at night, to condemn me for all my thoughts. I was just about ready to dispense with God altogether. But, he had other plans.

God in his wisdom knows what we need when we need it. I still remember the very first time I heard the voice of God. There were no loud claps of thunder, lightning bolts or a burning bush. He chose to speak of love through someone I loved very dearly so that his message would be received the way he intended me to hear it. I went to bed as usual and was lying in the dark about to drift off to sleep. My door opened and my mother appeared and sat down on my bed without turning on the light. As I looked up, I could only see her silhouette. She began," I want to talk to you for a minute." I started to sit up in the bed to face her, but she put her hand on my leg for me to remain still. "I want you to think about going to school to become a preacher. You know, you can't bargain with God because you don't have anything to offer." Then she said good night and walked out of my room without saying anything else.

I was stunned. I still try to imagine the look on my face because I know I was lying there with my jaw open. It was way out of character for my mother. I kept a prayer journal and thought maybe she found that. But, then I remembered that I had never had any thought what so ever of becoming a preacher let alone making any written remarks about it. In fact, in the preceding days I had thoughts of giving up on God altogether. Tonight I found that God wasn't going to give up on me. But, becoming a preacher was an entirely different matter. I was very shy and withdrawn and the thought of standing in front of people delivering the word of God never crossed my mind and actually terrified me. As I contemplated what just happened, I drifted off to sleep.

My mother and I never talked about her night time visit, though she did lead me spiritually quite often. I believe that God was speaking to me in a way that I could understand and receive His love. She once told me, "Bobby, you can go outside, get down on your knees and be as close to God as you are in any church." It stuck with me. To this very day, outside in nature is where I feel my strongest connection to God and where I often offer my prayers to him. Mother was a true southerner from south Alabama in every sense of the word and many considered her a "hick."But, she was full of spiritual wisdom and God used her to reach me.

In 1973 I began to lose interest in church. My parents sensed it and they didn't pressure me to continue. I still prayed every day and read the bible, but the condemnation I was feeling from the church frightened me away. I preferred my mother's method of reaching God and that was outside in nature. I spent the evenings after school outside and that's where I would communicate with God. I hadn't grown much in the past few years, but the summer of 1973 I began change. Muscles started to appear and I was growing tall. That same summer, Bruce Lee became a household name and his movies hit the big screen so my

parents took me to the local drive in to see "Enter the Dragon." I was absolutely mesmerized by the things I saw him do. That was all it took. I began to buy any magazine I could get my hands on about the subject. There was always a section that demonstrated techniques and I started to practice on my own. I practiced at night in the front yard under the security light and found that I had a natural ability to perform the techniques and quickly became a fanatic.

When I was with my father at his station, I practiced on his used tire rack and anywhere else I could throw a punch or a kick. It drove him crazy. He assumed it was just a phase I was going through and I would soon outgrow it and he could hardly wait. In 1973 there weren't many martial arts schools in middle Georgia, but I did manage to find a class through some schoolmates at the Y.W.C.A in the city of Macon. It was only once a week on Saturdays, but it was a chance to learn from a real instructor. Over my Father's objections, Mother made sure I made the class.

My Father was a no nonsense kind of man who was raised during the great depression and he thought that my interest in martial arts would never take me anywhere. In time, he saw that I was very serious and he relaxed about it a bit. He would give me that little smile from the corner of his mouth and shake his head at times and that was all the approval I would receive from him. In turn, it allowed me to relax a bit. I still remember my first class on that Saturday morning. I performed the techniques so well, the instructors found it difficult to believe that I had never had any instruction. It all seemed rather natural to me. I was never interested in any type of sports in school because I was so shy. It was difficult for me to participate in any of the team sports for fear that I wouldn't be good enough. But, I finally discovered a God given ability that I could claim as my own. I was tall, limber and fast. I performed the techniques so well in fact that one of the students said, "Stop doing it so perfect!" I finally found something that I could do well. It felt good to be praised for my ability. Somewhere in my childhood I developed low self esteem issues. I was the youngest child and I wasn't close to my brothers. We had no common interest. They were interested in fast cars and girls. I had no interest in cars and because I suffered from low self-esteem, I was too shy to talk to girls. I had no self-confidence and no idea where it stemmed from. I only knew I felt inferior to everyone else. I never felt as though I measured up to either of my brothers and they made no effort to make me feel comfortable. Maybe it was because they had the car thing in common with our father and I could not relate. I loved my father and desperately wanted to seek his approval in anything I did. I simply had no interest in working on cars in any form. I know he wanted better things for his children, but he just couldn't fathom anything happening with my choice in martial arts. He just tolerated it. Mother was the real support behind my new fascination. I practiced often and I became stronger and faster. I was in my early teen years and starting to think about my future so I formed a plan. I would continue to study martial arts and receive a black belt. Later, I wanted to join the U.S. Army and become a soldier. After my service, I would become a police officer and open my own martial arts school. I focused on my plan and prayed about it at night as I worked out outside under the security light in the front yard.

I went to school during the day and worked for my father in his service station business in the evenings and weekends. When business was slow, I would work out on the side of the building. I was quiet and shy in school and only a small group of friends. My body was changing and I started to get looks from the girls in school. Occasionally I would get a message from someone that a girl was interested in me, but I was too shy to do anything about it. I stayed in my own little world where I felt comfortable, but alone.

In the summer of 1975 a karate school opened in our little town of Forsyth. Up to this point, I only attended a class at the Y.W.C.A. Now, I had a chance to study at a real martial arts school from a master and closer to home. I jumped at the chance. The instructor accepted my rank as a green belt and in a matter of months; I became one of the top students of the Budo Kai School of Shorin-Ryu Karate. I trained daily and was so diligent, that the instructor gave me a key to the school. I only had two other interests at that period in my life. I played the trumpet in the school band and was a regular at the local skating rink every Friday and Saturday night. I also fell in love for the very first time in my life (or so I thought) with the daughter of the owners of the skating rink. Her name was Charla and I adored her. I just didn't have any experience with girls. I believed in God and respected Charla so much that no thought ever crossed my mind of attempting any type of sexual relationship with her. I was ridiculed by some of the guys in school. They made comments like, "You should love her enough to have sex with her." I chose instead to allow my faith to guide me and I didn't feel that having sex was the right choice for me at my age. Besides, with my shyness, it was all I could do to hold hands during a couple skate with Charla and I decided that was enough for now.

Martial arts and music were the only two places in my life that I felt comfortable and in control. Eventually it caught up with me because Charla broke up with me. Later I was told by a mutual friend that she had said, "Karate is all that Bobby cares about." It hurt me, but it made me take notice of things. I was becoming consumed by martial arts. Even mother once made an observation that my diet had changed. I had read about Bruce Lee's diet in several books and without noticing it, I began to follow his eating habits. I continued my martial arts training, playing music, working for Daddy and hanging out at the skating rink on the weekends. My schoolwork started to suffer mostly because I just wasn't interested. I had a lot of trouble with math. I was so shy that rather than ask for help, I would just take the bad grades. I was barely hanging on and going through the motions. I was trying to survive long enough to graduate so I could join the Army, then become a police officer and open my martial arts school. I finally met a friend that shared the same interest as me. Charles Johnson joined the Budo Kai School and we quickly became friends. He was a loner just like me. But, we both had a passion for the martial arts. I told him about my plan. The army, law enforcement and opening a school of my own. He liked the idea and decided to make it his plan as well.

In 1976, my parents bought a motorcycle for me and Charles went down the next week and bought the same motorcycle. We were inseparable that summer. He was originally from Columbus, Georgia and we made several trips there. We traveled all through the west Georgia area of Pine Mountain. It was the area where President Franklin Roosevelt had built his "Little White House" because it was so close to Warm Springs, Georgia where he went for polio therapy. He subsequently died there and the entire area was made into a national park. Charles and I visited often. Looking back, it was one of the happiest times of my life and he was a devoted friend.

That same year, a female classmate became very ill. Deedee Anderson and I were in the same homeroom class together. Her illness took a turn for the worst. She developed leukemia and was sent to Houston, Texas to seek help from a prominent hospital. Her illness was so serious in fact, that she was placed in a germ free environment known as a "bubble." She was dating a friend of mine and I had once had a crush on her younger sister. I remember that we would look at each other and smile, but that was the extent of our interaction. It became a very big deal in school. The town and the school held several fund raising functions for her. A reporter from Macon took an interest in her and he ran a series of stories about her. At one point, a picture was posted on the bulletin board at school showing Deedee in her germ-free bubble. I don't know why I took such an interest in her. We weren't close by any means. She seemed to capture a place in my heart and I knew I wouldn't forget her.

Charles and I grew closer. We continued to study martial arts together and make our weekend motorcycle trips. We had a brotherly relationship that I was never able to cultivate with my own brothers. He was a year ahead of me in school and graduated in 1976. My schoolwork continued to suffer to the point that I just no longer cared to continue. Over my parent's objections, I quit when Charles graduated. We decided to follow our plan of joining the army together. During the summer, we went together to see a recruiter. We joined the army on the "delayed entry program." We were sworn into the U.S. Army Reserve in June 1976, but would not report for active duty until December of that year.

We decided to enjoy our next few months of waiting together. We weren't the partying type, but we did have a few close friends, so we got an apartment together so we could have some fun. That summer, we had friends over and practiced martial arts together. My parents accepted Charles as another member of the family. We had family outings together and Charles was a big part of that. We continued to make our motorcycle trips to the mountains. My life was off to a great start. The plan I conceived in my mind as a teenager was going to come true and now I had a true partner to share it with.

Charles wasn't really into the skating thing, but I had made many friends there and I was very close with the owners. Every now and then, I would stop by to visit though I rarely skated anymore. On one such trip, I noticed a crowd in the concession area. There was a party being held for someone. There was nothing unusual about that, but this turned out to be a special welcome home party. As I walked closer to the crowd, I saw how special it truly was. I had almost forgotten her. She was thin, pale and very frail looking. When our eyes met, I recognized her immediately. She smiled through thin lips, but it was her. The words formed on her lips, "Hey Bobby." I smiled and waved across the room at her. She was surrounded by dozens of her friends, but none that I was close with. She seemed to be engulfed in them. We lost our gaze so I continued over to the benches to have a seat. I was looking out at the skaters to see if I recognized anyone else. I was there only a few minutes and then I felt a touch on the shoulder as she said, "You weren't going to say hi?" I looked up at Deedee Anderson standing there with her hands on her hips. I smiled and said, "Well, you looked a bit overwhelmed back there." She didn't waste any time. She moved my arm to one side and sat right down in my lap. She lost a lot of weight and I could feel her bone digging into my leg. We never had any type of relationship that would lead either of us to expect such a move on her part. Apparently her brush with death made her bold. As I studied her features, her eyes burned deep into mine. I asked her how long she had been back and she responded, but I really don't remember what she said. It was good to see her *alive!* We talked for a bit about what she had been through in Texas and what she had been up to since she was home. I found that the newspaper reporter was still following her story and rightfully so. Though she was definitely not out of the woods, she was home and here with her family and friends. She made me promise to call or come see her. I told her I would, though I wasn't sure I ever would see her again. I was about to join the army and I didn't know what my future held. We said goodbye and she walked away looking over her shoulder and then she was engulfed by her friends again. I filed her face away in my memory.

The Karate closed so Charles and I continued to train on our own. Between that, our home parties and our frequent motorcycle trips, the summer passed by quickly. We left the apartment and Charles moved back home with me. Before we knew it, December had arrived and we were at the bus station in Macon, Georgia headed for Fort Jackson, South Carolina. We would spend the night in Atlanta and after a few minor medical test, we would be on our way to basic training. Mother was in tears, of course. Daddy was there and ever the brick wall he always was. He very seldom ever displayed emotion. As I looked at him, my memory took me back to the first day I told him I had joined the army. With no expression, he looked across from the dinner table and said, "That ain't a big thing." My heart sunk. He wanted me to join the Air Force, but my test scores were not high enough and the Air Force was being very selective because it was peacetime.

Now my father, my hero, stood facing me squarely as a man. His youngest child was about to leave the nest. He asked me if I had money and I told him what I had in my wallet and he said, "No, you're going to need more than that." He reached in to his wallet and handed me several folded bills. I thanked him and he shook my hand. I gave one last hug to mother, then Charles and I set out for an adventure. We boarded the bus and headed for Atlanta. The next couple of days were a blur to me. I just remember being on the bus from Atlanta to Fort Jackson and the bus was very quiet. I suspect that everyone was deep in thought about what was about to happen. I remember that my first girlfriend, Charla, had given several pictures to me and I kept them in my wallet. We remained friends and I was still in love with her. I pulled them out, stared at them and had an uneasy feeling in my stomach. I put the picture away and stared out the window. Without any conscience thought, Deedee Anderson's face appeared in my mind. She was my age and I couldn't imagine that kind of heavy burden in my life, especially at our age. I prayed silently for her and hoped that she would completely recover. As I gazed out the window, I drifted off to sleep.

We finally arrived at the reception station of Fort Jackson, South Carolina. The next few days went by really fast. There were test, and a lot of paperwork to fill out. I found time for a short phone call to mother and daddy and found out that I was more homesick than I realized. But, I had Charles and that was a little bit of home. We even bunked side by side. After all the tests were complete, we transferred to the training brigade known as "tank hill." It was late in the evening and we were loaded onto what can only be described as a cattle trailer. With all of our belongings in a duffle bag, we were "herded" into the trailer where there was only room to stand. It was a short trip to tank hill. When we arrived, we all got a real education on just how much our life changed. The doors opened and the drill sergeants started their routine. Yelling and barking orders, we were hurried off the trailer and gathered into platoons. It was all a blur and total confusion. After a few hours of yelling, we were assigned bunks, the lights turned out and we were left alone with our thoughts. I was fortunate enough to get a bottom bunk, but in order for us to remain together, Charles had to take the bunk above me. It seemed as though we had just closed our eyes and the lights were on again and the yelling started for the day. In the next few days, we learned that army life was about routines. There were always late nights and early mornings. Everything

in between seemed to be mind games intended to see how we would react. Finally, our drill sergeants told us exactly what basic training was about. In six weeks, they had to appear before the Battalion Commander and say they would take us in to combat. That was the meaning behind the mind games.

It was tough, but Charles and I adjusted. That is, until a day came when we were chosen for special duty in the armory. Several of us from 2nd platoon, Alpha Company, were taken to the armory to help the corporal in charge move some weapons racks around. One private and I were told to move a rack from one area to another. We did as we were instructed, but apparently it wasn't what the corporal wanted. With no warning, he walked over to the private and me and struck us both in the mouth and simply said, "You aren't going to endanger my life!" I was in shock because I had no idea what he was talking about. I never reported the incident, but the other private did, but nothing was done about it. Charles was there, but didn't get hit. But, it was enough for him to decide that he didn't want any part of this army we had joined. He decided to try for a medical discharge. When we first joined, Charles almost didn't qualify because he had flat feet and an issue with his toes. After careful consideration, he was accepted. Now, he intended to use that issue as a way out. In a matter of days, he was out of the platoon and I was alone. I felt betrayed. I was 17 years old, homesick and in a strange place. My best friend, who was like a brother to me, just abandoned me at the first sign of trouble. I wanted to run as far away as I could as fast as I could. I felt totally isolated from anyone who cared about me.

I would see Charles from to time on the way to the chow hall, but I wasn't allowed to speak to him. When any of us moved alone around the company area, we were required to run, never walk. Now, I noticed that Charles was walking with a limp that he had not had a few days before. It was an obvious attempt to make his condition seem worse that it was. I was confused about my feelings. I felt angry at what he was doing and also hurt that he would abandon me like this when I needed him the most. One week later Charles was gone from the company area. I could only assume that he had been moved to a different area or was discharged. I tried to focus on my current situation and what lay ahead. It was getting close to Christmas and we were informed that we would all be going on Christmas leave. I tried to remain optimistic and upbeat because I knew I would be going home soon. The training was tough and I was lonely without my friend, but I decided to stick it out.

We were given a two-week Christmas leave and instructed to dress in the green class-A uniform. There were countless inspections by the drill sergeants, executive officer and company commander. Since we were new, they wanted to insure that we represented the U.S. Army in a positive light. I was given a bus ticket while others, which were from across the country, went by airline. After changing locations on the base several times, I finally made it to the bus terminal in Columbia, South Carolina. After a brief stop in Atlanta to change buses, I was on my way home. When I made it to the bus that would carry me home, I almost collapsed from exhaustion. It was more mental stress than physical. I had only been away from home about a month, but during that time a lot had happened. The biggest shock was having my best friend desert me. I relaxed knowing that in a few short hours I would be home with my family. The bus turned on to I-75 headed south and I was asleep before we left Atlanta. I woke up just in time to see the lights of Forsyth, my home. There was no stop over there, so my trip would end in Macon. Five miles south of Forsyth, I saw Daddy's gas station in the moonlight. It was about two in the morning and the station was closed, but

I could see lights which I used to practice under when I worked there. I smiled because I was almost home.

The bus pulled into the greyhound station in Macon and I stepped off and claimed my bags. It was only a month, but it seemed like an eternity since I was here last. I walked out front and directly across the street was a Krystal restaurant. After eating army food for a month, I was ready for some civilian food. It was nearly three am and I knew it would take mamma and daddy about thirty minutes to get dressed and make the trip to Macon. I made the call to let them know I had arrived and then made my way to the Krystal. After receiving my order, I sat down and stared out the window as I ate. It was quiet and the streets were empty. I made short work of the three hamburgers that I ordered so I went outside to wait for my parents and reflected back on the past month of my life. I took a long, deep breath of the cool December air. Macon was as much home as Forsyth and it felt good to be in familiar surroundings. I smiled as I thought of the things Charles and I had done this past summer. But, the smile quickly left my face as I remembered what he had done just a few short weeks ago. The lights of a car shined in my face and it brought me back to the present. Mother was out of the car first and hugged me and smiled. Daddy stayed in the car, but I could tell he was glad to see me. He was ever the brick wall of non-emotion that he always was and smiled.

We talked on the way home and because of the long bus ride; we were there before I knew it. I grabbed my bag from the car and walked into the house. Nothing had changed much except now mother had a new puppy. I smiled as I thought that maybe it was her way of dealing with my absence. It was still very early so we decided that catching up could wait until the sun was up. I said good night and went to my bedroom. I turned on the light and smiled again as I surveyed my old room and it was just as I left it. Last time I was here, Charles was sharing this room with me. The smile disappeared from my face.

I undressed, turned out the light and slid into the bed. The sheets were cool and it felt so good after a month on the bunk bed at Fort Jackson. I smiled as I closed my eyes and drifted off to sleep. I dreamed of Fort Jackson and basic training. My life was so regimented in the last month and I was used to rising early, but probably from exhaustion I slept until I saw the sun coming through my window. It felt good to be home with my parents and we used the morning to catch up. They both knew that I was unhappy in the army and about what Charles had done. I tried to remain positive about the situation, but I knew that I had to return in a couple of weeks and it made me uneasy to think about it. I tried to focus on the day and the time I had to share with my family. I could at least spend Christmas with them and I felt at ease. The next few days I rode with Daddy when he made his rounds at the stations he managed. I could sense daddy's pride as he was showing off his son, home on leave from the army. I tried to play the role for his sake and not tell anyone the truth of how I really felt. I hated my experience in the army so far and still felt hurt because my best friend had abandoned me. But, true to my form, I kept it all inside. Without realizing it, I was developing a pattern that would follow me all my life. Whenever I felt any emotional pain, I kept it inside. I was always careful to keep the outside polished and smiling, so that no one would see what was happening on the inside.

I still can't remember how the connection was made, but Charles found out I was home. He came by to see me. It was subtle, but I could sense the tension between us when we embraced. It wasn't the brotherly love that I had experienced with him just this past summer. He told me that he was now engaged to be married and I tried to appear happy for him. Inside, I felt a deep feeling of resentment and jealousy. Not only had he left me alone at Fort Jackson, but now he had someone special in his life and I had no one. Again, I kept it all inside. Charles was having a New Year's party at the home of his new family and invited me. He also had someone he wanted me to meet. I wasn't sure how to take that. I wondered if this was his attempt to make things "right" between us. There was no way I could begin any kind of relationship at this point in my life. I would be in South Carolina or God knows where and he knew it. If this was his attempt to make him feel better about leaving me, I wasn't buying into it. However, because I wasn't any good at confrontation in any form, I accepted his invitation.

New Year's Eve arrived and I dressed in my uniform. I wanted to display my colors and I'm still not sure why. I'm not even really sure why I went because I knew that Charles and I had grown apart as friends. The friendship we had back in the summer just wasn't there anymore. He arrived to pick me up and brought his fiancé with him and the girl he wanted me to meet. My mother insisted we all pose for pictures. That angered me as well. My parents had accepted Charles as part of the family and he had abandoned them too. Now we were posing for pictures like nothing was wrong. A couple of pictures and we were on our way.

When we arrived, several of them had already been drinking. Charles mixed a drink for me and I accepted it hoping to ease the tension I was feeling. I downed it very quickly and it worked all too well. I started to feel warm inside. In a matter of minutes, things didn't seem quite so bad. I asked for another drink. If that one made me feel better, the next one should make me feel very good. I don't know how many I had, I just kept drinking. My thinking started to change. I no longer felt resentment toward Charles. I made up my mind that I would finish what I started without my best friend with me. I didn't need him or anyone. I could do this on my own. I decided I would stay in the army and make something of my life and make my parents proud. As I continued to drink I realized I found a new friend. What I didn't realize is that I found a new coping skill that would follow me for a long time.

The warm feeling persisted and I looked around the room. I saw the girl that Charles introduced me to talking with another guy. I smiled and said to myself, "No problem." I took another drink and she disappeared from my thoughts, too. If I drank more, maybe they would all disappear. In a matter of hours, they did. I recall waking up on a sofa at some point, but that was it. I don't remember speaking to Charles and it was the last time I would see him for a while.

I came to in the bathroom at home and my sister-in-law, who was staying with my parents, was helping me out of my clothes. I have a vague recollection of my brother, Rusty, looking at me from the bathroom door. Apparently I collapsed in the bed and then awoke when I saw the sun coming through the window. Daylight had found me and all the resentments, fear and anger were right back with me along with a really good hangover. As I lay in the bed trying to compose myself, I realized that I was to return to Fort Jackson later today. All the negative feelings came rushing back at once. Nothing had changed; my feelings were merely interrupted for a while.

I got to my feet and heard the sound of scrubbing coming from the bathroom. As I walked down the hall, I saw mother in the bathroom scrubbing an area of my uniform pants. Apparently I vomited on them the night before without realizing it. She was doing all she could to remove the stain. I had to catch a bus in a few hours and was totally unprepared. She looked up when she saw me in the doorway, but said nothing and I felt ashamed. The night before, I was all charged up on making her proud of me. Now she was here cleaning up the mess I made like a child.

Later in the day my parents drove to Atlanta for me to catch the bus. All the negativity I encountered at Fort Jackson was there waiting for me and I wanted no part of it. My heart was here with my family and now that my best friend had deserted me, I did not wish to return. But, I had no choice and I knew it. I hugged my mother, shook my father's hand and boarded the bus. I had a long lonesome ride ahead.

I finally arrived back on "Tank Hill" and army life resumed again. While I was settling in, I stared at the top bunk that Charles occupied a few weeks ago. I felt a pain deep in my chest. I felt betrayed and I could tell it was going to stay with me for quite a while. I finished unpacking and tried to ignore it. Once everyone reported back, the yelling started again and it was business as usual. Night came quickly and it was a welcome relief from the drill sergeants. I slid into my bunk and immediately thought about my bed at home. I closed my eyes and welcomed sleep.

Charles was gone and out of my life all together. Apparently, the brotherly love had a limit for him. It was an experience in learning that relationships, no matter how close they might be, always came to an end. I felt alone, but decided to stick to the plan. I was in the army now and phase two of the plan would be next, becoming a police officer. Then it would be my martial arts school. Whatever it took, I was going to make it to that goal. It was now "my" plan again and not "our" plan as Charles assured me it would be. It was also the beginning of putting walls around my heart to insure that no one would hurt me. Trust turned into a word I learned to fear. In the coming days I found I had no motivation to continue what I started and all I wanted was to leave.

I left the army in February 1977. Even at that young age, my depression showed its head and it was the beginning of a narrow path down the long road of mental illness. The army recognized it as well and discharged me for that reason. Different forms of mental illness started to peak its head out and would take a foothold in my life in the years to come. My world would become a series of walls that I subconsciously built around my mind and my heart to keep people out. The end result would prove to be difficult and very nearly destroy me.

After I returned home, my parents allowed me some time to readjust to home. Then daddy let me to go back to work with him at his gas station. I was glad to be back at home where I was loved and accepted. But, deep inside I knew I let my family down. Daddy once said that he didn't want me following in his footsteps. He wanted something better for me and I wanted better for myself. Though he was sometimes sparing with his praise, my father was a wonderful man who always provided for his family.

One morning, daddy had me go to the side of the building to sort some used tires and load them on a trailer. As I was throwing tires, I had one of those moments of clarity that we sometimes get in our lives. I was seventeen years old, a high school dropout and not off to a very good start on my plan. It made me shudder. I stopped, took a deep breath and looked around. A car pulled up to the gas pumps and I saw daddy go out to wait on the customer. He was 56 years old and if I wasn't careful, that would be me in 39 years. I wasn't ashamed of him by any means; I just wanted to be the one who made him proud for all his hard work. I looked toward heaven and said a silent prayer for God's help.

I worked for daddy during the day and rode my motorcycle in the evenings. Riding in the open air gave me a sense of freedom. Whenever I needed some peace, I would go for a ride. I often thought of Charles and our rides we used to share. I hated to admit it, but I missed him. He had come by for one brief visit a few days after I came home, but things weren't the same. There was a distance between us. I don't know if he felt it, but I sure did. Now, I only thought about him on my motorcycle rides.

One spring day, I was returning home from a ride and just enjoying the smell of the blooming flowers. I was in no particular hurry and just enjoying the ride when I drove up behind a white car that caused me to slow down. I could see two girls in the car and I could tell they were looking in the rearview mirror and talking to each other. I was just about to pull around them when they started to motion for me to pull over. It wasn't a car I recognized, so I paid no mind to them. As I drove around a white bag flew out of the car and came my way. I slowed and stayed behind them. I assumed it blew out of the car. Then, a paper cup came whisking by. Ok, now I figured out they were trying to get my attention. They continued to point. Then, they slowed to pull over so I thought I would play along and pull in behind them.

I put the kick stand down on my bike and removed my helmet as they exited from both sides of the car. I saw the driver first. She closed the door and stood there with her hands on her hips for a moment. Then she started toward me. I didn't recognize her at first, but slowly the face became familiar. The last time I saw her, she was pale and very thin. Now, I looked at this beautiful, shapely young woman walking toward me. But, the smile was still the same. Deedee Anderson walked up to me and said, "I was wondering if I was going to have to jump out of the car to get your attention!" My first thought was my hair. It was 1977 and most guys were still sporting long hair and mine had not grown back yet. I rubbed my head, but she didn't seem to care.

She was already reaching for me as she asked, "You going to give me a hug or what?" Her personality was still the same. I was still sitting on my bike, but I hugged her back. The rider with her was her sister, whom I had a crush on a few years ago. She was talking, but I was focused on the way Deedee looked. She was not at all the frail young girl I remembered from last summer. The color returned in her face, she had a head full of hair and she gained some weight. I studied her as she told me what she had been up to the last few months. She asked me what happened with my army and I told her that it just hadn't worked out as I planned. We talked a bit longer as she wrote her phone number down and made me promise to call her. I told her alright, though I wasn't sure I would. I was still the shy teenager I was in school. I still wasn't comfortable around girls. She hugged me again and said, "You better!" Then she and her sister returned to the car. When she drove out, she had her arm in the air waving.

I sat there for a moment looking at her number and contemplating my next move. As I stuck the paper in my pocket, I looked up from the parking lot at the building in front of me. It was the skating rink that I visited so often a few years ago. I fastened my helmet and remembered that the last time I saw Deedee was here. I smiled, looked up to the sky and said, "Ok, Lord, I hear you." I pulled onto the road and headed home already trying to gather the nerve to call Deedee later. Charla had been the only real girlfriend I ever had and that was mostly just skating and holding hands. I had only one date the entire time I was in school. I had such a low opinion of myself that I never even called the girl again because I was sure that she didn't like me. Now, maybe I had another chance. I needed something positive to happen in my life and maybe this was it.

I didn't call for a couple of days because I was simply afraid. Fear had controlled so much of my life up to this point. It's just one of those issues in my life that was there, but I could not explain it and had no idea where it started. I was the youngest of my family and as a child; I had seen violence in my family. My parents had argued a lot when I was a young child. In fact, I found out many years later that they very nearly divorced.

I recalled a time when I was six years old. Daddy was away from home and I didn't understand what was happening. On one occasion, I was outside playing in the front yard and I remember daddy came out of the house crying. He leaned down and with tears streaming down his face, cupped my face in his hands, kissed me and said, "I love you, baby." Then he got in his car and drove away. It was very confusing for me. I would remember the rest of my life that it was the only time that my father actually said the words, "I love you." It proved to be one of the most precious moments of my life.

Another time, I would see my oldest brother, Don, arguing with my father. I don't even remember what the argument was about. I only know that it all ended with Don striking daddy with his fist across the face and it knocked him to the floor. My sister, Rachel, hugged my father and pushed him away because he said that if he got his hands on Don, he would kill him. I ran to my bedroom and buried my face in the pillow and made a vow that I would never live my life like this. In that same time period, my brother, Rusty, would argue with Don and he broke a chair in half and use the handle to threaten to hit Rusty with it. I witnessed my mother and my sister, Rachel, get into a slapping match. Another time, I would see Rusty attack Rachel and attempt to strangle her until she got the upper hand and ended up on top of him. Rusty would bully me like a coward, picking on me because I was smaller. Maybe it was his way of releasing his anger because he could never do anything with Don. It continued until my teenage years when I eventually outgrew him and started to study martial arts.

Later, Rusty would become a very serious drug user and terrorize my parents and me on his violent outrages. He would steal from my parents and threaten me constantly. I don't know why, but daddy always seemed to protect Rusty. I always assumed he was daddy's favorite. I saw the difference in the way he treated us. On one of Rusty's violent drug induced fits, he passed out on the kitchen floor. Daddy leaned over him and said, "If I could take your place, I would." He meant it because that was the kind of man he was. He was sparing with words, but always the provider and the protector. Though the words weren't there, his family was imbedded deep in his heart.

Because Rusty knew that he was daddy's favorite, he used it to his advantage. Don and Rusty worked for daddy in his business just as I did. On one occasion, Rusty used a wire clothes hanger to "fish" some money out of the drop slot of the floor safe at work. Daddy had to suck it up and replace the money. He did so, but never confronted Rusty about it. The only reason I knew about it was because I overheard he and mother talking about it. It hurt daddy and I could see it in his face. I suspected that was one of the reasons why daddy hardly ever smiled. Again, he was the protector. On one occasion, Daddy's business partner told him, "Bill, your boy's are going to take everything you make."

One of Rusty's last schemes very nearly landed him in jail and hurt my father to the core. He and a couple of his friends decided to stage a mock robbery at a self serve gas station where his friend worked. The friend was taken to the bathroom and one of them hit him in the back of the head to appear as though he had been robbed. They all three split the money. When the police got involved, one of the friends admitted what happened. Rusty and his other friend had to leave the state to avoid prosecution. Though he eventually returned home, mother and daddy had to help rescue him from that episode. It made me more determined to succeed in my life. That was one reason I felt like such a disappointment to my parents when my army career failed.

I had a feeling that my inner fear stemmed from those moments in time. Seeing my family tear each other apart and not be able to do anything about it was a very hard thing to witness. Also seeing what my brothers did to my parents and knowing that I wasn't doing anything with my life made me feel shame and guilt. I wanted to do more to help them and ease their minds. I wanted to be a hero for them. I felt the need to rescue them even if they didn't necessarily think they needed to be saved. Maybe they were just doing what good parents do. But, I know they deserved more.

Now, here I was years later afraid to even pick up a phone and call a girl for fear of rejection. I decided that a first step had to be made, so this was it. It reminded me of that Sunday in church, years earlier, when the pastor said, "If you'll make the first step, God will make the rest for you." I walked back to my parent's room where I knew I could have some privacy. There was a phone by their bed and I knew I would be undisturbed. I sat down on the bed and did nothing for a few minutes. Then I looked over at the large mirror and saw my reflection. I laughed as I realized how ridiculous I looked. Looking at the number, I took a deep breath, let out a sigh and picked up the phone.

I quickly dialed the number, but hung up before it could ring. I looked at the mirror, laughed and said to my reflection, "This is silly!" I picked up the phone again and dialed and it rang before I could hang it up. Now my heart was pounding as I went through all the reasons why she would say no to me even though I realized that she gave me the number and told me to call. While my mind was racing, a female voice picked up the phone. I actually managed to speak, "May I speak to Deedee, please?" "Hold on," was the reply. I heard the voice yell for Deedee. My heart beat faster and my breaths were short. I dared not look in the mirror else I would burst out in laughter at how ridiculous I looked or either hang up the phone in fear.

While my mind continued to race, another voice came on the phone, "Hello." It was her. "Hi, Deedee, it's Bobby". "Oh, hey," was the response. My fear had me frozen. Mercifully, she started first, "It's about time you called me," she said playfully. We talked for several minutes and I was surprised at how well I did. We actually made a date for the following weekend and then said goodbye. When I placed the phone down, I looked over at my reflection in the mirror, smiled and said, "You did it."

My mind continued to race all week long about where we should go and what we would do. I wasn't used to dating. By the time the weekend came, I had myself convinced that she wouldn't like me at all after this date. My lack of confidence was sickening to me at times.

I caused myself so much unnecessary anxiety. It was Friday night and I said a prayer and left it in God's hands. I picked Deedee up at her house and we went to Macon. I honestly can't remember what we did because I was so nervous. I know that she was very sweet, patient and kind.

I do remember the end of the night because I had been dreading it all night long. The closer we got to her house, the quieter I became. I was so nervous. It had been a while since I kissed a girl and ironically, the last girl I kissed was Deedee's sister. As I recall, the word got back to me that I wasn't such a good kisser. I had no experience at it. Now, I would have to wait to see how this night would end and what the verdict would be. Finally that magic moment arrived and we stood alone at her door. She was looking in my eyes and I know she could sense how nervous I was. She made the first move and our lips touched. It all seemed rather natural as though we had done it a thousand times. She smiled, told me she had a wonderful time and said good night. I drove home with a smile on my face and thought things were going to change for the better in my life.

Deedee and I continued to see each other and our relationship grew. Before I knew it, we were together for a year. It was now 1978 and she was growing stronger with each day. She was still required to make annual trips to Texas for her checkups, but she was told that she could look forward to a so called "normal" life. We began to make long term plans. She was now working at the local hospital as a switchboard operator. Since we were talking about our future, I decided that I needed to look at a career move.

A high school friend was working at a local industrial plant and making decent money. He offered to help me get hired. It would mean better pay and a job with benefits, like health insurance. I accepted his offer, applied and was hired in a very short time. Deedee wasted no time telling me that she wanted us to get married as soon as possible. We talked about it and decided that since we were both working fulltime jobs and spent all of our free time together, it seemed like it was the right move. I loved Deedee, but felt a little uneasy. I recently turned nineteen and she was only eighteen. I just wanted to be sure we were making the right decision. She was very persistent, and we decided to make the step.

We married in June of 1978 in a small family ceremony at her parent's home with our family and closest friends around us. I chose my father as my best man. He was after all, the best man I knew. Her reporter friend who had followed her story wanted to photograph the wedding. He also wrote an article about it in his weekly column. We didn't have a lot of money, so we took a short honeymoon in a nearby town over the weekend and then it was back to work for the both of us the following Monday. Her parent's home was an old two story Victorian style house. The upstairs was like an apartment so we moved there. I worked the midnight shift at the plant while she worked mostly evenings at the hospital. We talked about having a family at some point, but with her past medical problems and money being so tight, we didn't make any immediate plans.

Hugh Tillman was another friend I made at the karate school. In fact, had he not married shortly after high school, we may very well have joined the army together. Charles just happened to come along when Hugh married his high school sweetheart, Kay. We remained friends, but we weren't as close as we had been in school. He was married and I was single. Now, that we were both married and working at the same place, we rekindled our friendship. We would all get together on the weekends, Hugh, Kay, Deedee and me. They also had a baby daughter. We got together on the weekends and mostly sat around playing cards and drinking.

In November of 1978, it was time for Deedee's annual checkup in Houston, Texas. She and her mother would fly to Texas and stay with and aunt who lived near the hospital. It would be our first time apart as husband and wife. It felt strange for her to be away now that we were married. It was only a few days, but we had been together every day since June. This trip would prove to be very special. Deedee called me from her aunt's home the night of her check up. It was good to hear her voice and she was glad to hear mine. She told me that they had done the usual lab work. Her blood tests showed no signs of the leukemia and the Doctor said that everything appeared normal to him and that she would not have to return for her annual checkups. As far as he was concerned, she was cured. It was cause for celebration to be sure. But, she wasn't finished. "There was one small thing the blood test did show." Ok, here it comes, I thought. She continued, "Remember we talked about having a family some day?" "Yeah, they don't think it's a good idea, do they?" I asked. "Well, it's a little late for that because I'm pregnant!" She dropped the bomb on me.

I was totally caught off guard. "That's wonderful, sweetie, how does the doctor feel about that?" I asked as I held my breath. "He says there is no reason why we shouldn't expect anything other than a normal pregnancy!" As she replied, I let out my breath as easy as I could. I knew that there was a concern because of all the chemotherapy she had received. I smiled in spite of that. I looked over my shoulder at Deedee's two sisters and then looked over to see Mr. Anderson, Deedee's dad, washing dishes at the kitchen sink. Deedee was the oldest of the family and been through so much. The fact that she was even alive was a miracle. I decided to make the announcement. "Deedee's pregnant." I said. Her sisters were overjoyed, but it was Mr. Anderson I watched. He stopped moving for a moment, looked at me and then resumed his duties.

I wasn't sure how to take it. Mr. Anderson and I had our differences, but he was a good man. I knew his first thought would be for Deedee's welfare and rightfully so. He and I had a small conflict when Deedee and I first married. He wanted to treat me like one of his children and not in a good way. I wasn't having any part of it. It was severe enough that Deedee and I had moved out for a few days. In time, we made peace with each other, but things were never the same again. Now, we just tolerated each other. In my mind, I always had the idea that he never thought I was good enough for Deedee. Now things were in a whole different light. I was now going to be the father of his grandchild.

I started to think in a different way. Deedee and I were going to be parents now and that caused me to think about where I was in my life. I was nineteen years old and working in a textile plant with probably no future. I had taken the test to receive my G.E.D. so at least I had rectified that situation. But, I lost sight of my dream and the future I wanted. I still had it in my mind to become a police officer some day and open my martial arts school. I just thought I would have more time. Now, things were happening so fast. Deedee and I had only been married a few months. Now we were about to bring a new life into the world. I needed to provide a future for us.

When Deedee returned home, I wasted no time. I told her how I was feeling. I wanted to revive my plans and asked her how she felt about it. She didn't even hesitate when she said,

"I will support and help you in whatever you decide to do." She was a wonderful woman and a devoted wife. I in turn wasted no time in making some plans. Since I had no background in law enforcement, I decided my best shot at getting into the law enforcement field was to have some training under my belt. I focused on my martial arts training first and I knew exactly where to start.

I went to Macon to visit a local Martial Arts school. It was owned and operated by a Korean master whom I had met through my instructor at the Budo Kai School in Forsyth a few years earlier. The master taught the Korean art of Taekwondo. He assisted my instructor with several demonstrations and I was aware of his ability. I observed one of his classes and approached him after he was finished teaching to introduce myself. As he shook my hand, he said he remembered me. I told him that I wanted to join his class and without hesitation, he accepted me and even told me that I could keep the green belt I earned from my previous instructor. I thanked him and started home. I was excited and felt a new sense of hope at the prospect of studying the martial arts again and more importantly, making my dream come true.

When I first began the class at the Taekwondo Academy, I discovered just how much I didn't know. I was taught to use my hands more than my feet. But, I was very limber and kicking came natural to me. At the Budo Kai School, I was admonished for kicking so high. Now I was studying Taekwondo and the master encouraged high kicks. It felt good to be able to do what came natural to me. He took notice and worked with me. The first few classes were hard. I became winded very easily, so much that the master told me that I would not be able to keep up with the advanced class. His comment only made me more determined to work harder.

I continued to work nights at the plant, practice on my own in the evenings and attend class three to four times a week. I was becoming a fanatic again. I had a natural ability with the Martial Arts. It was an area I was praised in and given my low self esteem, I craved the attention. I was soon in the advanced class and some of the black belts took notice of me and took me under their wing. When I entered the advanced class, I was a green belt which was an intermediate rank. I watched the other members of the class. There were several red belts which is the rank before black belt. I began to train along side of them and used them to gauge my progress.

Deedee continued to work nights at the hospital and she was gaining a lot of weight. Though I was working nights and training in the evenings, I tried to make every doctor's appointment with her. After what she had been through as a teenager, we both wanted to make sure she was remaining healthy. It was her fifth month of pregnancy and time for one such visit. I worked the night before, but got up early for the appointment. It was all pretty much routine at that point, so I remained in the car to sleep while she went inside. I closed my eyes and fell asleep very quickly. Day time sleep just was not the same as night sleep and with my schedule, I needed all I could get.

I immediately awoke when the car door opened. It seemed as though she had just left. I was rubbing my eyes and just instinctively asked how it went. I didn't receive an answer right away and immediately thought the worst. "I knew I should have gone in with you!" I sat up straight trying to compose myself. "What's wrong?" I asked. I looked over and she simply smiled and said, "Oh nothing, they just did another sonogram." Then she asked,

"Would you like to see?" I sighed with relief and said, "Of course." I took the picture and looked. I could never make heads or tails of these things. In those days, they just weren't very clear.

I looked at the strange image and said, "Well, that looks like a beak right there." She laughed and slapped me across the arm. "No, silly, look right here!" I still couldn't make anything out and cut my eyes over at her. She said playfully, "You're so stupid!" She took the picture from me and moved close to me. "That's our baby right there," she said. I looked at the picture, pointed to the image and then looked at her and asked, "Right here?" She smiled and said yes. She pointed to the other image and said, "That's our baby, too." "Man that's a huge kid," I said. She smiled shook her head and said, "No, you don't get it." She pointed again and said, "That's our *other* baby." My lack of sleep was indeed affecting my brain. Then it hit me. I looked at her and that big beautiful smile was ear to ear. "You're kidding," was all I could manage to say. Then she grabbed me, hugged me and said, "We're having twins, baby!"

We smiled all the way home. This was indeed big news. With all Debbie's treatments and chemotherapy, we weren't sure she would ever be able to get pregnant or even if she should. Now we were blessed in a very big way and were excited to tell our families. They were, of course, all excited to here the big news. The twins came from Deedee's side of the family. She had twin cousins, but as far as I knew, this was a first for my family. My mother was overjoyed and even my father couldn't contain his excitement. He smiled more than I had noticed in many years.

It made me more determined than ever to finish what I started and fulfill my dream. More importantly, it wasn't just my dream anymore; it was Deedee's dream and now the future for our children. I trained even harder in my spare time and attended more classes. Debbie worked a while longer, but she was gaining a lot of weight. In time, the doctor made her stop working and rest as much as possible. Now I was the only one working and our families had to help out financially. Deedee was as dedicated as I was to my training and was adamant that I did not stop attending the taekwondo academy, no matter what the cost.

I turned 20 years old in July of 1979. I looked around at our friends and most of them were about to graduate college or were starting a career. We were about to become parents and I was the only one working and not in a profession I wanted. I looked around at some of the men at work. Some had been there since high school and were close to retirement. They rarely smiled as they performed their duties. They must have had dreams at some point. At break time I watched and listened to one man as he referred to the plant as, "This damn place!" As I watched him curse his life, I shuddered as I thought of that being me in twenty years. It seemed more like they were living out a prison sentence than working a job. I promised myself that this was *not* going to be my life.

At the end of July, Deedee started to have major pain. We made the regular appointments, but also started making trips to the hospital. Finally, late one evening in the first week of August, we made the last trip to the hospital and they kept her. It appeared she was in labor, but was not properly dilated to give birth. She agonized all through the night and the doctor kept checking on her. On his last visit he said that this continued he would have to do an emergency cesarean section. My mother held the vigil with me all through the night. Deedee's mother stayed long enough for mother and me to go home shower and change. Once we returned, she was gone and made us promise to call if things changed.

Early the next morning, they all returned. Finally the doctor decided that Debbie wasn't going to dilate and scheduled the "C" section. In 1979, husbands weren't allowed in the delivery room for that procedure. But, it wasn't long before a nurse called for me. With butterflies in my stomach, I walked over to the door. And she said, "Congratulations Mr. Allen. Everything went fine and you have two beautiful, healthy daughters." I let out a deep sigh. She smiled and said, "They will be in the nursery in just a few minutes." I came back and made the announcement to our families and the waiting room erupted in a cheer. We all went over to the window and waited. I watched in amazement as I saw my daughters for the first time.

I remember when my nieces' and nephews were born. My mother and other family were saying how beautiful they were. I smiled but thought to myself, *"There's nothing beautiful about that!"* Now my babies were here and it all suddenly made sense to me. This was flesh of my flesh and blood of my blood and they were absolutely the most beautiful creatures I had ever seen. Deedee and I already decided on names and I took one look at them and just knew which names to give them. One daughter was born minutes earlier and looked exactly like me. She had blondish brown hair like me and was longer than her sister. Then I looked over and saw our other baby girl. She was smaller and had Deedee's hair color and facial features. I looked back to our first daughter and said, "That's Leighanne." Then I looked over and pointed to our second daughter and said, "That's Tracey."

In just a few more minutes they brought Deedee out and I walked over to her, kissed her on the forehead and said, "They're beautiful Deedee." Once she was settled in her room, they brought the girls into her. Maybe it's just the miracle of birth or a gift from God himself, but she knew exactly what to do with the girls and looked so natural holding them. As I watched her, I was both excited and concerned. I thought back to that night in the break room at work and listening to the men curse their lives. I wanted so much more for her and these two beautiful little girls. I also thought how unprepared I was for all of this.

As it turned out, the birth of our daughters was more than a personal blessing, it was a miracle. Not only for Deedee as a survivor, but we were told that it was the first multiple birth for a surviving leukemia patient. The newspapers came to photograph Deedee and the girls and the story went out across the country. Letters and support begin to pour in from everywhere. When we arrived home, we had a plentiful supply of disposable diapers, formula and all sorts of donations. I even received gifts from a friend in my childhood who read about the story. The more attention we received, the more nervous I became. I felt as though the world was watching me and I felt the pressure of measuring up to everyone's expectations of what I should be. It was the inadequate feelings from my childhood. The low self esteem returned to visit me. I decided to combat it with overindulgence.

I focused all my energy into my training at the taekwondo academy. I watched our girls grow as I trained on a daily basis. I was getting fast and accurate. I entered tournaments and started winning. I begin to rise in rank. One year later, I looked around at my peers. When I entered the class, I was a green belt and there were several students with red belts. They were now ready to test for black belt and I was ready to test with them. My instructor was already grooming me to teach. He began to have me lead the class in stretching exercises. I felt I had arrived.

My attendance was poor at the plant where I worked. I was so focused on training, that I just lost interest in the job. As a result, I was terminated after two years. I took it as a blessing in disguise because I had such a fear of ending up like the men with whom I worked. Deedee and I discussed the possibility of opening a school of our own. Our girls were almost a year old now and I was ready to make the move. Since my instructor's school was in Macon, I began looking for a place in our little town of Forsyth. I found a building that was perfect for a school. It turned out that it was owned by one of my school friends. As the girls crawled around on the big open floor, Debbie and I worked on the building. Finally everything was set and we had a grand opening. We signed a few people the first day and most of my clientele were friends of mine from school.

I couldn't afford to advertise anywhere other than the local newspaper. Forsyth was a small town and although it was just after the martial arts craze that Bruce Lee created, taekwondo still had not caught on. I was getting nervous. I had a family to think about. I wondered if I had been too hasty in my decision to open a school. Deedee and I talked about it and decided that we just couldn't afford to keep the school open on our own. So after only a few short months, we reluctantly closed the school. It sickened me because now I was back at square one.

I had taken out an insurance policy when the girls were born and for some reason, my insurance agent had taken a liking to me and he offered me a job. I was no salesman by any means, but I was determined not to return to an industrial plant. I had to do something very quickly, so I took the job. I was assigned a route and with the help of my manager, I made three hundred dollars in about fifteen minutes one day. It still wasn't for me, but I knew I had to work. I felt my dreams slipping away from me again.

One of my students from the Taekwondo School had been a friend in high school. We weren't close, but Dave Harris seemed to like me. He was employed at the nearby maximum security prison in Jackson, Georgia. He thought my abilities as a martial artist might be an asset to the prison. He gave me an application to fill out when he was a student of mine. Once again, my low self esteem took over and I decided in my mind that they would never be interested in me. I filled out the application, he returned it for me and I dismissed the idea.

But, God did for me what I could not do for myself. I received a computer print out from the state of Georgia. I was prequalified as a Correctional Officer at the Georgia Diagnostic and Classification Center in Jackson, Georgia. I felt the butterflies come again. I dared to allow myself a glimmer of hope. My dreams thus far had failed. I wanted to be a soldier and that failed. I wanted to have my own martial arts school and that also failed. This was the third part of my dream now dangling in front of me. I wanted to be a police officer, but maybe this was a means to an end. Though technically not police work, it was in the law enforcement field.

I talked with Deedee about it and once again, she was the devoted wife. She was behind whatever I wanted to do. I picked up the phone and called the number provided. I talked with a girl in the personnel department. She scheduled an interview for me. I hung up the phone and was overcome with excitement. Deedee was excited as well and hugged me. I went into where the girls were playing. They were about to have their first birthday. When they saw me, they both smiled and reached for me. I picked up Leighanne and then Tracey. They were so innocent. No matter what was going on in my life, I could hold them and feel unconditional love. They had no idea of the struggles we faced and it made me want to put an invisible blanket of protection all around them. Deedee and our girls deserved nothing less. I thought to myself, *"This has got to work!"*

I left the girls to play and walked outside. I looked up to the sky at the beautiful afternoon. I offered another of my foxhole prayers to God. I felt ashamed because lately the only time I prayed to Him was when I needed something. I wondered where he was when I made all those bad decisions. But then, maybe that was the key. He was there, but I followed my own decisions and then blamed him when my plans fell through. I never really consulted him when I made those decisions. I just made them and then conveniently blamed him when everything flopped.

I tried to mentally prepare for the interview that was scheduled. I continued to work the insurance job and never told them about the interview. I prayed for strength. Finally the interview day arrived. Because I hated confrontation on any level, I decided to lie and call in sick rather than ask for a day off. That morning I went into the girl's room to gather strength for why I was doing this. I kissed them, then Deedee and started the thirty minute trip to the prison. It was located just off of I-75 in near Jackson, Georgia.

I prayed on the drive. I couldn't decide; was my gut wrenching with butterflies or fear? I hated my lack of confidence. Every time a new situation or opportunity presented itself, I spent most of my energy convincing myself why it wouldn't work. By the time I reached the exit where the prison was located, I was a nervous wreck. I approached the entrance and saw two white brick walls on either side of the driveway and drove past. I still needed a few more minutes to gather my nerve. I turned around in a driveway just down from the entrance and stopped. Finally, I turned the car around and approached the entrance again. Now, I could see the letters on the walls. On one side it read, "Georgia Department of Corrections." On the other wall it read, "Georgia Diagnostic Center." I couldn't turn away again. I turned the wheel to the right and pulled in.

There was an unoccupied guard shack to my left. I drove slow as I continued down the wide road. It wasn't what I expected at all. A long road lay ahead of me. On each side of the road the grass was trimmed very neatly. I approached a speed break in the road. There was a driveway to the right and two beautiful two story homes facing each other. Once over the speed break I continued on. Again on the right, I saw a beautiful lake. This looked more like a state park where one might take their family for an outing. On one side of the lake I saw a mobile home compound and several mobile homes on the lakeside. Another speed break and there was another brick home. There were still no gates or bars to be seen.

I finally came upon a curve in the road and that's where the "state park" image stopped. In front of me was a very tall tower. Now, it was starting to look like a prison. Once I drove around the curve, I saw a set of tall, dual chain length fences, topped with barbed wire surrounding a huge building. I looked ahead at the parking lot and another tall tower sat in the middle of the parking lot and faced the building.

I turned into a parking space and switched the car off. Again, I had to gather my nerve. I opened the door and proceeded toward the huge tower. The officer in the tower saw me approaching and opened the window of the tower, peered down at me and asked, "May I help you?" I shielded the sun with my hand and yelled back up, "I'm here for an interview." He pointed toward the building. I walked over and saw a large, green iron bar gate. I turned to look at him again. He nodded as he pointed and I heard the gate make a low buzz and then there was a click. When I pushed the gate inward, I was surprised how heavy it was. "Be sure to close it behind you and let it slam," he yelled. I walked through and pushed the gate closed behind me. I started to take a step, but turned when I heard a loud "Clank" as the heavy gate closed behind me. It occurred to me that I was now locked inside.

I turned to walk inside and a long dimly lit tunnel lay before. As I walked I figured out that I was underground and that the prison was on top. I remembered from the drive in that the prison seemed to be built on a hill of sorts. In my mind, I could see that the tower officer was able to see the prison from his high position. I could hear the echo of my footsteps in the tunnel as I walked toward the light at the end. I was the only one in the tunnel and it gave me an uneasy feeling. Every prison movie I ever saw came flooding back in my mind. I walked alone with my thoughts, listening to my footsteps. Finally, after what seemed like an eternity, I reached the light and discovered that it was a stairway that led up the main building.

There were two flights of stairs and then I was in daylight again. There was an African American female officer sitting at a desk. She asked, "May I help you?" She was polite, very professional and there was no doubt that she was in charge. "I'm here for an interview," I replied. "What's your name," as she reached for the phone. I gave her my name and she made a call. I looked around and took notice that I was in an administrative area. There was a glass partition with a door behind her, but no sign of the prison itself. She pushed a clip board over to me and had me sign my name on visitor's log in sheet.

She hung up the phone and looked at me again, "Have a seat and someone will be with you in just a moment." I sat down on a set of padded benches against the wall. It gave me a chance to compose myself. I wasn't sure what to expect and I wanted to make a good impression. I thought about the last couple of years. After the army I only had to be concerned with myself. Now I had a family to think about and I needed this to work. More importantly, I wanted it to work. I was making myself more nervous with my thoughts.

In a few minutes, a man appeared in the hallway from the set of offices down the hallway. "Mr. Allen, I'm Mr. Morgan, the personnel manager." He stuck his hand out and I stood to accept it. I didn't know what a personnel manager was supposed to look like, but Mr. Morgan looked like a high school principle. He was very humble, with gray hair and glasses. He invited me to his office and offered me a chair. He sat behind his desk and we began to converse. We talked about my past employment and he asked me about my interest. I took the opportunity to plug my martial arts background. I figured that would be my best selling point and he was most interested.

After only a few minutes he said, "Will you excuse me for a minute?" I nodded and smiled. He walked out the door and down the hallway. I hadn't attended too many job interviews, but I knew enough to know that asking me to wait was a good thing. I figured if he wasn't interested, he would have dismissed me and I was correct. He was back in a few minutes and said, "I'd like you to meet our assistant Superintendent," as he motioned me toward the door. It was a positive sign. He took me to the next office over. "This is Mr. Kenneth Parish, the Assistant Superintendent of Security," he said and smiled.

Kenneth Parrish was a middle aged man with a very neat appearance. He was retired from the Army and it showed. He wore a short sleeve, white shirt with a tie and neatly pressed trousers. Though he was in civilian clothes, it still presented the appearance of a uniform. He had a gray receding hair line and wore glasses. He offered his hand and smiled. I took his hand and introduced myself. He motioned toward a chair and went right to work as he sat at his desk. Apparently, Mr. Morgan had told him all he needed to know about me.

He told me about the prison security staff of which he was in charge. He was very careful to say that his staff were not "guards" instead they were "Correctional Officers" and pointed out that there was a difference. He said that would be made clear to me in the weeks to come. I smiled inwardly at his inference.

He went on to tell me that the prison was referred to as an institution, that prisoners were called inmates. He said that an institution was like a city in itself and that his officers were the police force of this city. He further stated that there were several different divisions of this unique "city" and that the Superintendent or (warden) was the mayor of this city making him the police chief here. It amazed me at how complex this all was. My only knowledge of prisons was from movies and that they were just designed to hold prisoners.

After he finished his presentation, he looked at me and asked if I had any questions for him. I smiled and said, "You covered everything so well, I wouldn't know where to start." He smiled in return. Then he got up from his desk and took me back to Mr. Morgan's office and told me to have a seat. In a few minutes, Mr. Morgan reappeared and asked, "Is he done with you already?" It was a rhetorical question because he didn't wait for an answer. He walked out of the office again. As I sat alone trying to get a sense of it all, I overheard Mr. Morgan and Mr. Parrish talking in the hallway. "So, what do you think?" It was Mr. Morgan. "Yeah, I like him," was the reply from Parrish. I smiled broadly and looked up toward the ceiling.

I sat a while longer and then Mr. Morgan returned. "Okay, Bobby, you have one more person to meet." I followed him past Mr. Parrish's office to the end of the hallway. The door was open, but I could see the sign on the door that stated, "Walter Zant, Warden and Superintendent." The title had a significance that I would be made aware of later. He motioned me to a chair. As I sat down, I took notice of my surroundings. I was sitting in an outer office and there was a lady sitting at a desk. Apparently this was the warden's secretary. She was on the phone and smiled at me when she saw me take a seat. Mr. Morgan waited until she was done and then asked, "Is he busy?" She excused herself and walked to an "inner office." I heard muffled voices and then she returned. She looked at Mr. Morgan and said, "He can see him now."

Mr. Morgan went in first, apparently to set the stage for me. He was back in just a few seconds. He looked at me and then ushered me toward the office. I walked into a large office with a conference table to my left. The man behind the desk studied me as I walked in. I was being assessed. As I approached his desk, he stood and I had a chance to assess him. He was short and had cold, blue eyes. I remember thinking that he resembled Robert Conrad of the TV show, "The Wild, Wild West." When I reached his desk, he put out his hand as he spoke, "I'm Walter Zant." I took his hand and clenched it firmly, but never let my eyes leave his gaze. I allowed him to sit first before I took my seat.

He picked up a form from his desk and studied it. Apparently it was my application. He read through it briefly before looking over the top of the paper at me. He said, "You know, you'll have to cut your hair." My hair had grown over my ears and almost down to my shoulders. "That won't be a problem," I replied. He studied the application again. Then he stood and stuck out his hand again and said, "We'll be glad to have you." I shook his hand firmly, but still maintained the gaze. "Thank you, sir," I replied and turned to walk back to the outer office of the secretary. The decision was made before I went in there. It was just

a formality to meet the superintendent. Mr. Morgan smiled as I reappeared and then he went back into Mr. Zant's office retrieved my application and we went back to his office.

Once we returned to his office, he explained the process of being hired. There would be a physical examination and fingerprints for a background check. I had to supply a birth certificate and a few other documents. He told me that new employees began on the first or fifteenth of each month. It was the first week of August, so I would start work on August 15th. He asked if I had any questions about anything that transpired. I was trying to contain my excitement about the whole situation. My mind was going in a thousand different directions. I told him I couldn't think of anything so he shook my hand and told me to call him when I had my documents ready and the physical examination completed.

As I approached the front desk to leave the female officer pushed the clip board back over to me so I could sign out. As I was writing, she smiled and said, "Welcome aboard." I looked at her name tag and then replied, "Thank you, Officer Rogers." Apparently information traveled fast around here. It was the beginning of a friendship between her and me. I turned and made my way down the stairs and then to the long tunnel that lay ahead of me. Going out, knowing I was hired, the tunnel didn't have the sinister look as it did when I walked in. I was alone now, so I made no effort to contain the smile that came to my face. I heard the lock click on the Iron Gate. The officer saw me approach before I reached the gate. As I was walking toward my car, the fear and anxiety were gone that I had felt when I drove in.

The first two phases of my childhood plan, being a soldier and owning my martial arts school failed. This was actually the second phase of the plan I made when I was thirteen years old. I thought that things were looking up and I would find my place in the world. As I drove down the long driveway I thought about Deedee and the Girls. I could make a life for us now. I thought about my mother scrubbing my uniform pants four years ago in the bathroom at home. I recalled my father shaking my hand at Fort Jackson, S.C. the day he took me home. Maybe I could still make them both proud of me.

Chapter 2

"Hide me from the plots of evil men, from the crowd of evildoers."

- Psalms 64:2
(New English Translation)

I had to get a complete physical examination including a chest x-ray and once completed, I returned to the prison. At that time, they fingerprinted me and ran my name and information through the National Crime Information Computer. I later learned that this was known as the *NCIC*. Georgia had its own version called the *GCIC* and I would be entered there as well. I was cleared in a few days and instructed to report at 6:00 am, Saturday 15 August.

When Deedee and I went to bed on the night of the 14th, I was a raw case of nerves. It was a mixture of excitement and anxiety. I was excited to finally have a new career, but nervous because I had no idea what to expect. I tossed and turned the entire night, but finally drifted off to sleep. When the clock sounded, it was time to start my new adventure.

Deedee got up with me and waited patiently as I showered and got dressed. The only instruction I was given was to dress casually. It was August, so I wore blue jeans and a short sleeve shirt. Once I was dressed, Deedee and I peered in at the girls as they slept. I stepped inside and gave both Leighanne and Tracey a kiss. I wanted to remember why I was doing all of this. My little family was here and I wanted to enjoy every moment of it.

Daddy and mother were still asleep as well so it was just Deedee and I. We walked to the back door and as I reached for the door, Deedee grabbed my arm and looked into my eyes. She could sense my uneasiness and gave me that big smile and said, "You'll do fine, I know it. I'm so proud of you." Then she put her arms around me, kissed me and pushed me toward the door. I opened the car door and sat inside. My stomach was alive with butterflies. I cranked the car and looked up at Deedee and she blew me a kiss. Then I started my journey.

I left Forsyth and drove north on I-75. I was still nervous, but not as uneasy because I already had the job. Now I was anticipating what the day would hold. My only view of a prison was the same as most of the civilian population; what I saw in the movies. There was no other image to compare. I turned the radio on just to calm myself. At least the sound of

another voice would help me to get out of my mind where my fear lived. It worked, because before I realized it I was at the exit where the prison was located.

I turned in and again took notice of the beauty of the place from the road. Even further down the road toward the fences wasn't a bad view. But then, I was looking at this from the outside and I didn't have to live here. It was an early Saturday morning and there was no movement in the parking lot. I found a parking place rather easily and assumed it was because it was a weekend. I made my way to the main tower and the officer already spotted me and opened his window to speak. "You can go on in, they're expecting you." I heard the motor buzz on the giant Iron Gate. I knew what to do this time so my hand was already reaching for the gate as I approached it. Once inside, I pushed the gate behind me. Once again there was that loud clanging sound when it closed. It was a sound that I would never become comfortable with and I would find out later that most of the other officers felt the same. It was like an alarm that signaled to you to be on guard because you were now locked inside.

I made my way up the tunnel and to the stairwell. This time at the top of the stairwell there was no one to greet me. Officer Rogers was not yet on duty. The day I was fingerprinted, I was instructed on where to report. I made my way to the glass door and through the visiting room that was empty. The night-lights were still on so the lighting was dim. Ahead I saw a set of yellow colored gates like the huge Iron Gate at the entrance. There was a final glass partition just before I reached the gate. It was still relatively quiet. I opened the glass door and my perception changed immediately. All my senses came alive at once.

The first thing I noticed was the smell; a musty scent of perspiration. Then there was the muffled sound of voices far away, almost as if I was in a warehouse. As I approached the gate, I heard a click and the Iron Gate began to slide to the right. I heard the hum of the electronic motor. It moved ever so slowly and finally opened just far enough for me to walk through. I surveyed the scene to make a mental note of my surroundings. Training from the army was brief, but it was still there and my instincts took over.

As soon as I was through the gate, it immediately closed behind me. As I looked around I saw that I was in a holding area. There were four gates. There was one behind me, one to my left, another to my right and finally one directly in front of me. Also inside this "holding area" I saw and officer's station. It was partially inside the area I was in. It was completely enclosed in very thick glass. My instincts told me it was bulletproof glass. The lights were dim and the glass had a slight reflection to it, but I could see the officer standing inside at what appeared to be a control station. This station was known as 'Control One." It was the nerve center of the entire institution. I found out later that there was a full armory in the back. This was also the location of the institution's base radio and the main switchboard.

As I approached, I saw several knobs on the console in front of him. I could only see the top half of him because the panel concealed his legs. There was a small porthole and I could tell this is where we were to communicate. I observed him as I approached. He was in his thirties, with a military style haircut. His blond hair fell across his forehead. No expression that I could detect, but he appeared to be expecting me. Officer Charles Kindle pointed to the gate directly in front of me and said, "Lieutenant Folds is expecting you in the chow hall." These were military terms of which I was familiar. I nodded and his hand reached for a button on the control panel and the gates begin to move. That was my signal to walk forward. Officer Kindle and I would become friends and develop a friendship as we served together.

I walked through the gate and started down a long, wide corridor that was empty and as I walked I could see yet another set of yellow gates at the end. I started to hear the low hum of conversation and the rattle of pots and pans. When I arrived there, I saw that it was the same design as the area I just left, "Control one." An officer's station enclosed in bullet-proof glass and four gates in all directions. There was an officer inside and as I approached I heard the click of the electronic gate. This was "Control Two." Not nearly as sophisticated as "control one" and it's only purpose seemed to be to control traffic.

The officer looked at me and the pointed to one of the other gates as it began to open. I felt almost like a lab rat being led through a maze. I walked through the gate and saw several uniformed officers standing in the hallway beside a large open door. That's when I figured out where the noise was coming from. It was the inmate-dining hall. At my approach, the group of officers looked at me with no real enthusiasm then all looked at the elder of the group. I noticed the chevrons on their collars. It was all military style rank. The one who spoke first had a set of silver bars on his collar; a lieutenant.

"You must be Allen," he asked. I saw his nametag, but there was no mistaking who he was. "Yes," I replied. "I'm Lieutenant Folds, first shift supervisor," as he offered his hand. A brief shake and it was business as usual. The other officers nodded at me, but said nothing. I could tell this was routine for them even though it was all new to me.

I was the only one out of place because I wore civilian clothes. He looked to one of his subordinates and said as he nodded his head, "Alright, show him how it's done." With that, an officer motioned with his finger to follow him as he walked toward the wide open door that appeared to be on a track and slid to the left side. Once inside, the inmates in the serving line eyed me with little interest. It was my first real contact with any of them. The Officer and I walked to the center of the huge room.

There were rows of tables with inmates in white jump suits seated. They were busy eating and paid no mind to the officer or me. This apparently was routine for them. I looked around at the sea of white all around me. There were easily 100 or more inmates in this huge room. The officer and I stopped about halfway in the room. He began to explain the feeding procedure to me. The Inmates entered the room from a door in the rear, followed a line around the edge of the dining hall and up to the serving line. The first officer was stationed at the silverware station and observed as each inmate took a fork, spoon and a plastic tray. They continued through the line and were served. Then they exited the serving line and walked toward us and he instructed them where to sit. They all moved through with little direction because they'd done it many times before.

Once they were seated they began eating immediately. As this was happening, I saw another officer standing in another isle giving commands to stand and exit the dining hall. The inmates stood and walked toward yet another side door as they dumped their trays in a small window where a set of hands grabbed their trays. There I saw another officer watching to ensure that each inmate turned in a set of silverware. Then they exited through the door. It was like a well-oiled machine through the entire process.

After a few minutes, the officer I was assigned with, looked at me and said; " Do you think you got it" I looked at him and nodded my head more as a reflex than actually acknowledging his question. Then he pointed to the large, sliding green doors and said, "See those doors?" I replied yes this time. He continued, "Those doors have slam locks which means they don't require a key to lock them. " I looked directly in his eyes. "Don't get too far away from them. If anything goes down, they will slam those doors and secure the chow hall and everyone in here." There was no smile on his face.

Then he gave me a pat on the back and said, "Ok see you in a little while" and walked away. I was left alone in the middle of this large room in a sea of white. It was only then that I realized how ridiculous I must look. I was dressed in blue jeans and a short sleeve shirt. I still had not cut my hair. I felt utterly alone in a room full of people. I looked around and counted the officers in the room. There were only five including me and I was not in a uniform. Three of the officers were stationed at doors. The officer directing the inmates to stand and I were the only two actually in the dining hall. I felt uneasy. I reflected on the movies I'd seen and it was always the dining hall where trouble seemed to start and officers were outnumbered.

I wasn't sure if this was another test or if this was regular procedure. It really didn't matter because this was not a movie. It was reality and I was in the middle of it. I reverted back to my training and stood firm with no emotion on my face. I continued to direct the inmates where to sit and made eye contact with them to demonstrate that I had no fear, even though I felt uneasy inside. They showed no outward emotion that anything was different from their normal routine. I suspected it was because of the other uniformed officers standing in the area.

My mind was working overtime and before I knew it, the last row of inmates had entered and the officer closed the rear entrance door. He came and stood by me and only nodded to acknowledge me. Once the last of the inmates finished eating and were instructed to stand, it was over. The officer patted my back and motioned for me to follow him to the front of the dining hall where the wide doors led into the corridor. There was the lieutenant standing with several officers as if they were in a huddle waiting for the next play. My escort and I joined the group. Lieutenant Folds begin to issue orders as he read from a pad in his hand. Apparently, that was the playbook for the day. Finally, it was time for my assignment. He looked at an officer and said, "Take Allen down to F house and let him work with Ramirez. The other officers smiled and then looked at me. My escort said, "Follow me."

We walked to "Control 2" and waited for the gates to open, then walked down a long corridor. The noise of the dining hall was fading away as we approached another set yellow gates that were pushed to one side. Above the gates I saw "F" Cellhouse printed on the metal frame. We entered a huge room and it was just as I had seen in most prison movies. There were rows of cells on either side of us. There was an upper and lower tier. We walked through an open area and I noticed a set of open bay showers on each side. Once we passed that we stopped at a high desk and chair like you might find at a loading dock at a warehouse. It was painted bright red. Even though I didn't understand the system yet, I could tell that these colors had meaning.

Behind the desk on the wall were a phone and two large panels. My escort put his hands in his pocket and even though he said nothing, I could tell we were waiting for someone. I didn't feel comfortable having my hands disabled in my pockets, so I crossed my arms over my chest as we waited. Finally I heard loud talking on the opposite side of the room where we stood. It immediately reminded me of basic training at Fort Jackson. The voice was getting louder and I could tell someone was walking toward us. In a moment, he appeared around the corner with a clipboard in his hand and two inmates following behind and still barking orders. He paid no mind to either the officer or me standing by his desk. Once he approached, he dropped the clipboard on the desk and finished his sentence. The inmates acknowledged what he said and then quickly disappeared. Finally he looked to the officer and then to me.

My escort spoke first, "This is Mr. Allen." Officer Ernest Ramirez looked at me and put his hand out and said, "Mr. Allen," as we shook hands I detected the strong Spanish accent. Then he picked up his clipboard and was off again barking orders to a group of inmates. My escort looked at me, smiled and said, "Good luck." Then he walked away back up the corridor from which we came. I was left alone at the desk as I studied my surroundings.

I saw 2 solid red doors to my right. Both were closed and I was sure that they were locked. I looked behind me and saw another large yellow gate like the one through which I entered, only this one was closed and locked. I looked above the gate and saw "H-Cellhouse" printed on the frame. As I looked through the bars and down the corridor I could tell that it was different from "F" Cellhouse. I saw a row of offices and through the windows I could see officers moving. As I studied the area, the loud voice returned from the opposite side.

Officer Ramirez was back and just as before, he threw the clipboard on the desk. I sensed that it was something he did many times before. He surveyed the entire area and then looked over to me. He smiled slightly and said, "I'm sorry about before, but the mornings are always so busy." I returned the smile and said, "No problem." Then he asked, "Have they shown you anything at all?" I smiled again and said, "Well, they made sure I knew what the middle of the dining hall is like." He returned the smile and shook his head. I could tell it was all an inside joke. Apparently this is what they did with all "new hires" just to see what type of reaction they would get. Then he started again, "Well, let me give you the real tour." He began to explain the entire operation of the institution to me.

The Diagnostic center is a processing center for those leaving county jails and entering the state prison system. There are two types of inmate classifications here, "Diagnostic" and "Permanent." The diagnostic inmates stay only 6 weeks for testing and classification. They are assessed to determine what institution is best suited for them to serve their time. They undergo many physical examinations. While housed here, they wear a solid white jumpsuit and black brogan boots. The term "permanent" referred to those who would serve their time here at the diagnostic center. They wear a white button down shirt with dark blue collar and dark blue stripe down the center of the shirt. White trousers to match with a solid blue stripe down either side of the outside of the legs.

He was very careful to point out that the population was to be called "inmates" and not prisoners. All prisons in the state are called "Institutions." The only apparent reason was to modernize the department. He carefully laid out the rest of the institution for me. There were 8 main housing units called "Cellhouses." They were lettered A thru H. In addition there are three open style dormitories. Each cell house has 126 individual cells and they looked exactly like the cells I'd seen in any prison movie. A single bunk attached to one wall and a combination toilet and sink at the rear of the cell. Every Cellhouse has an upper and lower tier. All cell houses resembled each other with the exception of "H" Cellhouse. It was the unit adjacent to "F" Cellhouse and was behind a locked gate, though I didn't know why at the time.

He began to explain the color-coding of the institution. Grey is the standard color of the housing units including the inmate cells. Yellow indicates caution and inmates could proceed through those gates with permission. Red indicates that inmates have no access to those areas or either must be escorted. As he talked I looked over at the cross gate that lead to "H" Cellhouse. He didn't bother to explain, but my interest was aroused.

As he talked we walked over to the two gray panels on the wall located behind his desk. He reached in his pocket and produced a large key. He opened one panel and I saw a display of buttons and above each button was a red light. Each button and light represented a cell. If the light was on, the cell door be was closed. If the light was out, the cell was open. The button only opened the door. The door had to be physically closed by the inmate or an officer. Also inside the panel was a large key ring with keys for many other doors inside the Cellhouse. There were only two keys that remained out of the panel box. The key in his hand opened the panel box, but also would open each individual cell. The second key was tucked away under his belt at his waist. I was about to ask what it was for, but an inmate walking in the Cellhouse interrupted us. He was obviously a kitchen worker because he wore a disposable white paper hat and a white plastic apron.

He pointed toward the yellow gate behind us and said, "I need to get back to death row." Officer Ramirez produced the key from his belt and walked over to the gate. He opened the gate and allowed the inmate to pass through and then closed it again and pulled on it to make sure it was locked. So, there it was. I knew that death row was here at this institution and now I knew its location. I started my first day off less than a few feet away from some of the most notorious men in the State of Georgia. I felt a sudden rush of adrenaline, not fear, but excitement.

I turned again to give my attention to Officer Ramirez. He was on the phone talking. After a brief conversation, he produced the key from his belt and handed it to me and said, "You might as well make yourself useful while I take care of something." He handed the key toward me and as I reached for it, his grip tightened on it before he released it so that we were both now holding it. He looked in my eyes and said, "If you hear a bell ring over that gate, open the gate, wait for the traffic to cross through and then make sure it is locked again." I sensed the seriousness of what he was telling me. Once he was sure that I understood him, he released the key and it was now in my control. I felt the adrenaline again and looked at the key as if I had been handed the key to a forbidden entrance. I turned and looked down the hallway. Those that were housed there required a locked cross gate inside of a maximum-security prison, surrounded by dual fences and guarded by several gun towers. I was excited, but nervous of the unknown that was back there.

While I reminisced, I heard the bell ring. It brought me back to the present and I remembered Ramirez's instructions. I walked over the gate not quite knowing what to expect. In just a moment they appeared. I saw the inmate first. He was dressed in the "permanent" inmate attire. He wore a white shirt and trousers with the blue stripes on the legs and blue

collar. There was nothing sinister looking about him. But, his escort signaled the difference. There was an officer walking behind him and slightly to the right of the inmate. On his right hip, attached to his belt he wore a black nightstick about 24 inches long. On his left hip was a handcuff case. He was very careful to keep about an arms distance reach away from the inmate. They walked almost in step together.

As they approached the gate, my gaze caught that of the inmate for only a moment. As he looked into my eyes, I felt as though there was something missing. It was almost like looking at a painting and noticing something missing, but not knowing what it is. It was a brief interchange that seemed like an eternity because of my fascination with my location. Then it became clear to me. There seemed to be no life in his eyes. A cold chill ran down my back as I realized I was exchanging glances with a convicted murderer.

Once through the gate he looked ahead again and the officer never acknowledged my presence. I could tell his focus was on the inmate. Once they cleared the gate, I pushed it closed as I was instructed. Once I heard the loud "clank" I pulled on the door to ensure it was locked. They disappeared up the corridor out of "F" Cellhouse.

I returned the key to my pocket and waited for Officer Ramirez to return. In just a matter of minutes before I heard the voice first, then the man himself returned from around the corner. Again, he dropped his clipboard on the desk. He looked around for a few seconds as if going over a mental checklist in his mind to ensure that everything was in its proper place. He turned to me and we continued my education of the maximum-security world.

I asked him if all Cellhouses were the same. He further schooled me on the prison lingo. He said they used the term "House" when referring to Cellhouses. So "F" Cellhouse was now "F" house. He went on to explain that "C" and "D" houses had 63 cells and only half capacity housing units. Furthermore "C" house was the unit designated for those with mental disorders. "D" house also housed the disciplinary isolation cells. He told me I would hear more about that during my training sessions.

I spent the rest of the morning with Officer Ramirez as he enlightened me on the proper procedures for supervising a Cellhouse. It was an awesome responsibility and the officers were greatly outnumbered. I could see that it took a special person to maintain control of this many men. Officer Ramirez definitely had the personality for this work. He had a commanding presence. Later that morning things began to quiet down and we had a chance to talk about our personal lives. Then it became clear why he had the skills for this job. He told me that he was retired from the U.S. Army. I shared a bit of my past about Deedee and the girls. Because of my youth, I didn't want him to think I was entirely unskilled, so I told him about my martial arts background.

It sparked his interest and told me he had a son enrolled in a karate class in the nearby town of Jackson. The class was held at the town's National Guard armory and the instructor was a young man who was also a security officer at a nearby industrial plant. He suggested I visit the school. I told him that once I was settled into the job a bit, I would stop by, observe the class and give him my opinion of the instructor. He smiled at the thought. Even though it was a minor thing, it was common ground for us.

The rest of the morning went by really fast as Ramirez took me around "F" house and explained the morning process of operating a Cellhouse. Once we were back at the desk we sat down as he explained the importance of counts. There were multiple counts held in

a twenty-four hour period to ensure that all inmates were accounted for. He attempted to show me a count sheet that would be turned in after a count was performed. His very thick accent was difficult to understand certain aspects of it. I mostly nodded my head. When he attempted to get me to actually fill out a count sheet, it was too much for me. I couldn't take it all in. He seemed to sense my frustration and backed off.

It was now close to lunchtime. The phone on the wall rang and he looked down at his watch. After answering the phone, he took me over to one of the large locked panel boxes on the wall. He pointed an explained the row of lights again. They represented one row of cells called a "Range." There were eight ranges in a Cellhouse with approximately fifteen cells on each range for a total of one hundred and twenty six cells. There was one button for each range that would release all the cells. That was the procedure for "chow call."

He allowed me to press the release button and the inmates from one of the lower tiers immediately exited their cells, closed the doors and made a single file line. I could tell it was routine for them and they paid no mind to me. Ramirez had me go to the beginning of the line and count them as he gave the signal for them to start walking up the corridor. It was the same procedure for the other seven ranges. The procedure was so organized that by the time the last range disappeared up the hallway, the first range sent out was now returning from the chow hall. It was smooth and orderly like clockwork.

After chow call, things were quiet and I could sense this was normal weekend operation. Ramirez and I talked through the afternoon and at 2:00 pm, I could see and hear the gates opening up the corridor at Control two. I saw other officers walking to F house. I looked at Ramirez and he was already anticipating my question and said, "Shift change."

I saw a rather large, round officer walking toward F house. Once at the desk he gave a huge grin and introduced himself, "Hi, I'm Jerry Cahn." I couldn't help but smile as I shook his hand. He looked like a black Santa Claus as he grinned. He sat his belongings down on the desk and he and Ramirez exchanged information. Next they both walked over to the panel box on the wall. Ramirez opened the panel and gave Officer Cahn the keys. He counted each key and then recounted. Then Ramirez gave Cash the two keys he kept on his belt. The key for the panel box and the key for the H house gate. Cahn, in turn, handed Ramirez a small metal chip.

When they returned to the desk, Cahn explained that the keys never left the cell house and that each officer was issued a "key chit." The key chit was placed in control one on a hook marked for each cell house. The relieving officer gave his chit to the control room, retrieve the chit of the officer to be relieved and then once the briefing was over between the two officers, the key chit was given to the officer relieved. Once the key chit was passed, the officer was properly relieved.

Ramirez looked at me, offered his hand and said, "Officer, it's been a pleasure." I shook his hand and a felt a surge of pride. It was a title that I wanted for a long time and even though it was only my first day, he had bestowed it on me. I felt as though I belonged to a special group. As I looked around at my surroundings I thought, "This is something special." Not everybody gets to do something like this.

After Ramirez left, I turned my attention to Officer Cahn. He was looking over his clipboard. After a few minutes, he turned his attention to me and asked some of the same questions as Ramirez. There wouldn't be another feeding period until early evening and I would be gone by then. We just sat there talking. I liked this guy immediately. He was very friendly and I could tell he had the respect of every inmate in the Cellhouse. He didn't "bark" orders like Ramirez. He had a calmer way about him. Neither style was wrong, but it gave me insight how things were done here. I could see that everyone had to develop their own style of dealing with the inmates.

Before long, Cahn looked at his watch and said, "Well Bobby, looks like it's your time." It was approaching 4 pm. so he released me. As we shook hands, he gave that big grin. I turned to look at the H house gate as I walked up the corridor, I reflected back on the day when I entered the facility in the morning, I was uncertain of what I was facing and how both the inmates and the officers would accept me. While there was still some uncertainty, the fear had been replaced with something else. Ramirez addressed me as officer and I felt pride; a familiar feeling that I had not felt in a while. The last time was when I put on the uniform of a soldier.

The drive on the way home was different. The butterflies from the morning were gone. I was more relaxed, but a bit excited too. I thought about Deedee and the girls and the future that I might be able to provide them. The smiled reappeared on my face. I thought about mother scrubbing my pants before my return to Ft. Jackson and the guilt and shame I felt at that moment. I thought about Daddy the day they both picked me up to bring me home. I thought about how I never saw one ounce of condemnation in either of their eyes. It just wasn't the type of parents they were. Now I had another opportunity to make them proud and I wanted to redeem myself, for their sake.

The drive home was fast and there was Deedee and the girls waiting for me. Deedee had that big beautiful smile and my two beautiful angels in her arms. The site nearly brought me to tears; the family that I loved so dearly. As I got out of the car, the girls recognized me and they started smiling. When I was at arm's length, they reached for me. I took them both and kissed them as they hugged me. Mother and Daddy were waiting as well and all wanted to know about my day.

Once inside I recapped the day for them. I explained the dining hall without going into too much detail. I didn't want any of them to know how outnumbered we were. I gave a brief description of F house and seeing where death row was located. I felt out of place with my long hair so I drove to the local barber shop and asked for a military style haircut. Afterwards when I looked in the mirror, I thought I looked 10 years younger. It wasn't a look I needed for the Job I had to perform. No matter, I was going to make this work. After Deedee and I put the girls to bed, I walked outside in the night air and offered my prayer to God and asked for the strength I needed to perform my duties. I felt I had a second chance to become the son, husband and father that my family deserved. I knew I'd done all I could do to prepare myself for the career that lay ahead of me. I was determined to succeed as I laid my life down at the foot of the cross.

Chapter 3

"My son, attend unto my wisdom, and bow thine ear to my understanding: that thou mayest regard discretion and that thy lips may keep knowledge"

- Proverbs 5:1, 2
(King James Version)

Deedee was asleep before me because she had the hardest job and that was as a fulltime mother, especially with twin girls. I was finished praying and so I lie in bed looking out the window at the night sky. My parents were so good to Deedee and me. They allowed us to stay in their home at almost no cost to us because things had not started well for Deedee and me. We had plans, but they just had not materialized as we had hoped. My parents were only doing what mothers and fathers do. They opened their home and invited us in with no conditions attached. I was also thinking about my brothers and sisters. I was thinking about my childhood and all that we had been through. I closed my eyes still thinking about our little family and soon found sleep.

My dream took me back to1966. I was six years old and we had just moved from Atlanta to Russellville, Georgia. It was no more than a wide space in the road. It was the tiny little community where my father was born, in a house, in 1920. There was a general store on the corner of the main road that was owned by daddy's aunt and uncle. It was a true country store because just about any item for the home could be found in there. But what I remembered most as a child was the huge glass counter where the candy was kept. It was like a Norman Rockwell scene on an addition of Saturday Evening Post. Across the street was a small one-room building that was used as the courthouse many years before. Other than a few homes scattered around, that was the town.

My sister was the one who cared for me and kept me entertained. I remembered making the trip to the store on hot summer days with her and how our feet would burn as we walked barefoot on the asphalt. However, my brothers quickly learned that if we didn't entertain ourselves; there were no others to play with. We would make up our own games and at times, our own toys.

My oldest brother, Don was the creative one and quite skilled with his hands. On one occasion we were so desperate for fun, that he made several wooden soapbox type cars, put a string around several trees and made an enclosed area. Then he made a sign that said,

"Don's used cars." We each took a turn going to his car lot to purchase a car using Monopoly money. Once purchased, he would push us out to the road and down a small hill and we were on our way. The small road we lived on was paved, but rarely traveled.

It was my brother, Rusty who first talked me into mischief. He once had me go the bottom of that same hill where he had dug up a fairly good size rock. It took both of us to move it. He wanted me to help him move it into the middle of the road so someone would run over it. I had no idea what kind of fun that was supposed to be, but it was the beginning of his mischievous life that would last into his teenage years.

I remember being terrified at the thought. I just knew we would get caught and have to answer to daddy. He convinced me otherwise and I helped him put the rock in the middle of the road. Then we ran back to the woods and waited for a car to drive by and I was terrified out of my mind that whoever drove up, would know we were hiding and walk right over pointing an accusing finger. While we were waiting, the picture of daddy burned in my mind, but we didn't have to wait long. A car drove up and I closed my eyes and held my breath. I heard the car slow down and then stop. I opened my eyes to see the man getting out and walking to the front of his car. I still wasn't breathing, but I saw the man lean over, pick up the rock and throw it in to the trees in front of us. I was praying the entire time that he would not see us.

He returned to his car and drove away. Finally I could breathe. I ran home as fast as I could and left my brother behind. Even at that early age I found that I was not one to go looking for mischief or trouble. It just didn't appeal to me to do anything wrong. I loved my family and everyone paid special attention to me because I was the youngest. Whatever the reason, they took care of me. It was during that time that I noticed a change in my father. Mother and daddy were distant with each other and I noticed that they sometimes argued. One night, my sister and brothers woke me up to say that mother was leaving and was going to walk away. They said we were going to follow her. In my six-year-old mind, my only concern was following her from the side of the road in the brush and falling asleep. They assured me that they would keep me awake. I don't remember her ever leaving and I went back to sleep with no thought about it the next morning.

At some point things got so bad, that daddy left the house for a while. Again my six-year-old mind never processed that mother and daddy had separated. It is sometimes amazing how our minds protect us by not processing some information especially as children. It was during this period that I remember a very special moment in my life. Daddy was home and he and mother again had been arguing. I was outside sitting in the yard playing. Daddy had gone to one of the windows of our mobile home trying to talk to mother. She tried to roll the window shut on his head. Then he was back in the house.

I brushed it off not really knowing what was happening and continued to play in the front yard. In a few minutes the door opened and my father came out with an expression on his face I never saw before. I'd seen him smile and laugh at times, but normally he had this look on his face that let one know that he was all about business. He was crying. I had never seen him cry before and never saw him cry again in his life. He was distraught and there was no mistaking it. He walked directly over to me, looked in my eyes, cupped my face in his hands, kissed my cheek and said, "I love you, baby." With tears in his eyes he got in his car and drove away. It was the only time in my life I ever heard those words from him and it became one of my most precious memories of my father. I still today have no idea

what it was about. I only know that at some point, he returned. I have flashes of memories of us all being in a car and watching my parents together and feeling warm inside because they were happy on that day.

Don was my protector as well. We lived out in the country and one of our favorite places to play was out in an area we simply called, "the woods." There was a small stream that we used to visit. He was going down to the stream and as a little brother will sometimes do, I followed behind him. I remember approaching the stream and stopping by the bank to watch him. Suddenly I felt pain up and down both legs. I was wearing blue jeans and I began to slap my jeans where I felt the pain. He asked me what was wrong and I remember saying "it feels like ants biting me."

The pain got worse and all I remember after that was him throwing me on his back and running home. Once we reached the edge of the yard, he began to scream for mother. She came running out and immediately grabbed me as he told her what had happened. She yanked my pants off and that's when we discovered what had attacked me. There were small yellow jackets all in my pants. I stepped on their nest and they flew up my pants stinging me. By the time they got my pants off, I was already starting to swell. My eyes were almost swollen shut and it was becoming difficult to breathe.

I was taken to the hospital and discovered I had a severe allergy to bee stings. Over the next two days, the swelling would go down and then return. I remember at one point I had to vomit and had trouble catching my breath and awakened with mother's hands on both of my arms, shaking me and crying out to me, "baby, baby?" There is nothing more attentive than a mother with her baby boy in distress. Once I regained conciseness, she just hugged me. I eventually made a full recovery, but found my archenemy was bees.

A that time, my mother was a young countrywoman who didn't have any formal education, but had a lot of spiritual wisdom. I never knew her father (my grandfather) because he died when she was only nine years old. But, she told me that he was a very spiritual man and was in church, with his family, every time the doors were opened. Evidently, his wisdom was passed to her because she always had a way of teaching me things in a way I could understand. She loved her children and that never changed through her life no matter how old we were and her love would prove to be unconditional.

On one such occasion she taught me a life lesson that would follow me for the rest of my life. It was on a trip to the country store and I decided I wanted a snack. It was close to dinner and mother of course, said no because she didn't want it to spoil my meal. Of course I didn't see it that way and decided I wasn't going to speak to her ever again. I pouted all the way home and wouldn't even look at her. Once in the house, I went to the living room and sat on the couch with my arms crossed. This persisted until diner time and I refused to eat. Later, as she was putting the dishes away, I went into the dining room to sit at the table so she could see that I was still not speaking to her.

I sat at the table looking out of the window in my own little world of defiance. Rather than become angry and force me into submission, she decided to teach me a valuable lesson. She walked over and sat down beside me at the table. I still refused to look at her and she began to speak to me very tenderly. "Are you still not speaking to me?" I looked at her, shook my head and then looked out the window. She continued, "I know you're angry with

me, but I want you to think about something. " I still wouldn't look at her. Then she leaned in a little closer, but still not touching me and said very tenderly, "I'm going to the bedroom to iron clothes and I will be gone. What if momma died here tonight and you remembered all the rest of your life that you never spoke to me again." Then she got up and walked into the rear of the house out of my sight.

After she was gone the seriousness of what she said began to burn deep inside me to the point that I thought I was going to be sick. As I started to think about the implications of what she was telling me, tears formed in my eyes. I've often heard that there is a special bond between a son and his mother. Male children are more often closer to their mother's than their father's. I loved my father dearly, but there really was something special between my mother and me. Whatever the reason, I felt so very empty inside and she was just down the hallway out of my sight. I couldn't stand it any longer. I got up from the table and slowly walked down the hallway to my room. I kept looking out of the door toward my parent's room at the light that was shining through the door.

I wanted to go down there so bad just to be sure she was still there. Even though I was only six years old, my embarrassment from my actions had me paralyzed. I sat on my bed trying to decide what to do. Finally my heart was hurting to the point I couldn't take it anymore. I slowly made my way down the hallway and stopped at her door. First I peered in to see her back to me and with iron in her hand. I slowly walked in and eased myself down on her bed. I lay there and watched her for a moment. I'm sure she heard me get on her bed, but never acknowledged me at all. I believe she was allowing me to get comfortable. She turned slightly to look over her shoulder and then returned to her ironing.

Thinking about all she had said, I tried to imagine life without her and I couldn't imagine it at six years old. She was a fixture in my life and I depended on her as much as the air that I breathed. I could feel tears welling in my eyes. She must have figured that I had been there long enough, turned to me and asked softly, "Are you looking at me?" There was a lump in my throat so I simply nodded. She walked over to the bed, held out her arms and asked, "Do you want to love me a little bit?" I jumped into her arms and hugged her and she wrapped her arms around me and squeezed. Then she let me down and with no condemnation for my actions whatsoever and said, "Go tell Rachel to fix you something to eat." My heart was as overjoyed as if she had returned from the dead.

There were so many happy memories from my childhood with my family. In those days, we had to rely on each other because we needed each other. It was what I believed family was always supposed to be. Caring about each other's needs and taking care of one another. I smiled at the thought of my childhood. Slowly my eyes opened and I started to look around at my surroundings. It was my room, but not the room from Russellville in 1966. It was 1980. I looked over and there was Deedee next to me. I had been dreaming. I eased out of the bed and walked into the girls' room. Looking at their innocent faces made me think of my dream about my family and of my mother holding me at six years old. I looked over my shoulder at my parent's bedroom door and smiled.

I walked back to the bedroom and eased back in the bed. Deedee briefly rolled over, smiled, and pulled my arm around her waist and close to her. It had been a long time since I dreamed about my childhood and the innocence I knew at that time. I assumed my first

day behind bars had caused my mind to recall something precious to me. I didn't know at the time, but that was going to prove to be a defense mechanism for me many more times in the future. Tonight was an exercise for the future. My mind was learning to protect me. I smiled and closed my eyes to try and find sleep again. My last thoughts took me back to F house and the cross gate at H house where I saw the dead eyes of a cold-blooded killer. The wings of the angel of death brushed me lightly.

Chapter 4

"Anyone who shows contempt for the judge or the priest who stands ministering there to the Lord your God is to be put to death. You must purge the evil from Israel."

- Deuteronomy 17:12
(New International Version)

Sunday at the Diagnostic Center was mostly a repeat of Saturday. The only exception was that I was instructed to report directly to F house and Ramirez again. Apparently my initiation in the dining hall was complete. I'm not sure if that is what it was, but it seemed really strange for a new employee, in civilian clothes no less, to stand in the middle of the dining hall alone. Ramirez was already well into his morning when I arrived. He greeted me and continued his duties as I waited at the desk. He looked over his shoulder at me as he walked away. He knew something was different about me and it puzzled him. When he returned, he dropped the clipboard on the desk and starred ahead. I could tell he was deep in thought. Finally, he couldn't take it any longer, looked at me and asked, "Did you get a haircut?" I smiled and replied yes. He nodded and then was lost in thought again.

It was visitation day for all the "permanent" inmates and that included those on death row. Again Ramirez handed me the cross gate key leading to H house. After making sure that I understood to unlock the gate only when I heard the bell ring and then close it again once traffic cleared, he handed me the key. I was going to be the keeper of the gate for the day. He disappeared around the corner and I looked down at the key and then to the gate with the markings "H Cellhouse" over it.

My mind wandered back to the year 1976. I remembered the story so well. I thought about the young woman, Teresa Carol Allen, who was discovered only about a mile from my home. I had fleeting thoughts of the trial that took place. I also remembered the escape by one of the accused killers from the Monroe county jail. His name was Roosevelt Green. There was a story that circulated that Green had been allowed to escape only to be killed by someone. That turned out to be false and Green was subsequently apprehended in New York City.

I was intrigued with the whole event because of the brutality of the crime and because her last name was Allen. It made it personal for me even through my time in the Army and the four years since; it was stored in my memory and would resurface from time to time.

Now, it was all too real because Roosevelt Green was somewhere behind that gate. I saw pictures of him in the paper, but I wanted more. I wanted to see him and the face of a kidnapper, rapist and convicted murderer. I felt a rush of adrenaline. My heartbeat increased a bit. I wasn't sure if it was excitement of seeing a monster or anger at the thought of the brutality he caused.

The bell brought me back to the present. I walked over to the gate and waited. Finally the duo of an officer and inmate appeared. Just as the day before, the inmate looked directly ahead and paid no mind to me as he approached the gate. Key in hand, I opened the gate. The officer nodded slightly at me, but no words were spoken. I assumed the inmate was too focused on his visitor to pay attention to me. Once they cleared the gate, I closed the gate and gave it a tug to insure it was locked as I had been instructed.

I looked toward H house one final time. I wanted to go back there, but I didn't quite know how to make the request or even if I could. I turned my attention to F house. There was nothing happening. I walked around a bit and started to take note of the inmates in the cells. I was told that they were usually here for a minimum of six weeks before they were shipped to another institution to begin serving their sentence. Other than meal periods, an occasional chance to go outside on the yard, appointments in the medical or testing departments or occasional gym calls, they were locked in the cells.

To the untrained eye it might not have seemed like much of any punishment. But, if one took the time to study the size of the cell and how much time was actually spent there, it would be a different story. I could only imagine the real prison; inside one's own mind where there is no escape. Time to think about lost opportunities and making the wrong decisions. I looked at the long faces and began to have a little more understanding of what they were feeling. It was definitely prison.

Other than the occasional traffic from H house, it was quiet all morning and into the afternoon. Ramirez chatted away about his time in the army and his retirement. 2 o'clock came really quick and the only thing that really gave it away was the sound of the gates opening at control two. I saw the smile on Officer Cahn's face first as he came walking toward F house. When he arrived he put down his belongings and shook my hand. I could tell that he liked me. It was the same exchange of information between the two officers as the day before. The usual exchange of keys and Ramirez was gone again.

With very little to do, Cahn sat at his desk and I pulled up a chair and we continued where Ramirez left off. He said that starting on Monday; I would report to the training officer and that more than likely I would be assigned to a regular shift until I went to school. He hoped I would get his shift, the second shift. I smiled at the thought of working with him because he was very personable. Four O'clock came fast again because we continued our conversation. We said our goodbyes and he gave me that big grin and said, "I'll be seeing you around," as if he knew something I didn't. Even though this was only the second day, the trip to the front seemed familiar and shorter. Lieutenant Folds was waiting at the stairs for me and instructed me to report Monday morning at eight O'clock. As I walked out of the tunnel, closing the big Iron Gate, even the tower officer waved at me as if he was used to seeing me on a daily basis.

I rested better Sunday night and Monday morning arrived very quickly. As I drove into the institution it was like the first day that I arrived for the interview. The parking lot was full. All of the administrative staff and civilian employees were back to work. I finally found a parking space at the end of the parking lot. The tunnel didn't seem as dark this morning because I was becoming used to it. I reached the top of the stairs and standing by the time clock was short heavyset man with a radio in his hand and he appeared to be expecting me. He looked right at me and asked, "Are you Robert Allen?" When I replied yes, he put out his hand and introduced himself. "I'm Larry Branch, the Training officer." I shook his hand. The he continued, "We are expecting a couple more men and then we'll head to that back."

He was very professional and asked me about the weekend. I took that to mean he didn't work on the weekend. As we chatted 2 more men about my age walked up the steps. He greeted them as well and introduced us all. Then he led us as a group through Control one, down the corridor, through control two. We began walking toward F house where I had worked the weekend. Then he stopped at an unmarked door in the middle of the corridor, produced keys from his pocket and opened the door. He paused to turn on the light and it revealed two rooms. The outer room, which we all entered, appeared to be a small classroom with items hanging on the wall. The inner office was his personal office.

We gathered in his office and sat in chairs in front of his desk as he asked us for personal information. He wanted emergency contact names and numbers for us all. Since we had already been introduced, we each took turns talking briefly about ourselves, our interest and why we wanted to be correctional officers. When it was my turn to speak, I told of my interest in law enforcement, but also of the more important reason now. I told them about Deedee, my girls and that I wanted to make a future for all of them. I didn't realize how in depth I had gone because when I looked up to make eye contact with them, I realized I had said more than they probably wanted to hear. They were all starring at me. I smiled and apologized to them. Mr. Branch returned my smile and simply said, "No apology is necessary."

While he talked, I thought about what the other two men said and probably what any other young man would say in that position. They wanted something different. They wanted a good paying job with some benefits. I wanted that as well, but my motive for succeeding, I suspected, was very different from theirs. My life had not started off according to the plan I laid out and I felt I let down people that I loved even if they never said that. Now, God had given Deedee and me two beautiful little girls and I made it my mission not to make the same mistake with them. I wanted them to grow up proud of their daddy and knowing that I was doing something honorable with my life. As my thoughts returned to Mr. Branch, I felt a bit embarrassed at the things I had said out loud. However, they were things that I meant, took to heart and intended to see through.

Mr. Branch told us that there wouldn't be another school beginning for several weeks. He was going to assign each of us to a regular shift until the next school started. We were finished with our orientation so he sent us to different locations in the facility to finish the day and said he would call us back to his office before the end of the day to give us shift assignments. The orientation lasted all morning and he was about to release us for lunch when he said, "Before you go, I have on last thing to tell you." He took his glasses off and sat back in his chair. He interlaced his fingers and placed his hands across his belly. I studied him for only a second before I surmised that this was something really important so I leaned a little closer then he began.

"Georgia's death row was moved here last month from the state prison at Reidsville. Death row is now located just down the corridor from my office. He pointed toward F house where I worked over the weekend. The unit is called H house, but its not like any other unit of this facility. You will eventually get a chance to see it."

He continued, "I want to explain to you how dangerous this job can be and how desperate the inmates can become." Then he got up from his desk and walked into the classroom and returned with a large wooden board that had all types of instruments attached to it. He explained that these were "contraband" items confiscated from this institution. There were all types of edged weapons and some simply used for stabbing. He saved the most important for last. At the very end of the board was what appeared to be a very old and tattered officer's uniform. However, it was also contraband. He looked around at all three of us for a second and said, "Pay very close attention to what I'm about to tell you about this uniform." He pointed at it and began his story.

The Corrections department had decided that death row should be moved from the state prison at Reidsville, Georgia because it was an old institution and they were concerned about security. The Diagnostic Center was chosen because of its location. It was located in the center of the state and only about fifty miles from Atlanta. The second determining factor was that it was a more modern maximum-security prison.

Apparently there was a plan in place for several months for several of the death row inmates to attempt a daring escape. Once the move was announced, they had to move very quickly because they had no idea what the new institution would look like or how tight the security would be.

In the months before the move was to take place, five of the inmates had devised a plan. Carl Isaacs, Timothy McCorquodale Johnnie Johnson, David Jarrell and Troy Gregg had been in contact with relatives and friends they made. The first plan was to have hacksaw blades mailed into the institution. The prison staff foiled the plan and the blades were intercepted. At that time, the inmates were allowed to have personal items mailed to them and they all chose pajamas. They also obtained some type of dye. The pajamas were dyed the color of the officer's blue uniforms. It was reported that Carl Isaacs became quite an accomplished tailor while in prison. He and the other inmates made their uniforms by hand out of the pajamas. Isaacs talked an officer into allowing him to make an impression on a bar of soap of the officer's badge. Once that was done, they made badges out of cardboard and even put plastic wrapping over them to give them a shiny appearance.

They all sawed through their bars and waited for the right moment to make their move. Unfortunately for Isaacs, he was moved to the Diagnostic Center in the early morning hours of the day they had planned to make their move. However, Jarrell, Gregg, McCorquodale and Johnson had their chance and they took it. The four of them pushed out the bars that had been previously sawed. They crawled out onto a ledge and then down onto the main yard. They were questioned only once by a tower officer. It was reported that McCorquodale shook one of the gates and said, "Security check." Then they were allowed to pass. The four of them eventually made it to the parking lot and got into a car that McCorqudale's aunt had left for them. Four convicted murderers, with death sentences, then drove off the prison property without being stopped.

There was a newspaper reporter from Albany, Georgia that had befriended Isaacs and was to write a book about his crimes. He received a phone call from Troy Gregg who told him he was calling from Jacksonville, Florida. Gregg reportedly told him that they "had to make a move." He also said that they all decided that they couldn't stay at the prison any longer and that they would rather be dead than spend another moment in that place.

Timothy McCorquodale, David Jarrell and Johnnie Johnson were caught five days later in North Carolina. The body of Troy Gregg was found near a lake. One account tells that McCorquodale had beaten him to death for making the call to the newspaper reporter who subsequently notified Corrections officials of the escape. Why they chose to stay together is still a mystery to this day. Law enforcement officials believe that had they split up, they would have had a much better chance of maintaining their freedom. But, no one knows for sure.

The Georgia Bureau of Investigation investigated the newspaper reporter. He was never convicted of any crime. He did go on to write a book about Carl Isaacs's crimes. It was also reported that a homemade uniform was found in Carl Isaacs's cell at The Georgia State Prison at Reidsville. I was told many years later that Isaacs was the mastermind behind the entire ordeal. Many believe that if he had ever made it to the streets, that he would have been smart enough to separate himself from the group and quite possibly remained free.

Mr. Branch then told us why he wanted this to burn into our memories. He said, "These are the type of people that you will be charged with securing to ensure that the citizens of Georgia will be safe." Once he finished, there was an eerie silence for a moment. Mr. Branch being the veteran got everyone back on track. He put the board away and returned to his desk. He produced three slips of paper and said, "These are your schedules for the rest of the day." Then he handed one to each of us. He asked each of us for our clothing sizes. He wrote the information on a sheet of paper. He continued, "After lunch, report to the locations, but be back in my office at 3:30 pm for uniforms and shift assignments." Afterwards, we were dismissed for lunch.

The three of us went to the staff dining room for lunch. It was a quiet walk because we were all lost in thought about what we had just been told. Once we got our food trays, we sat down at a table together. Curiosity was getting the best of us so we all looked at the slips that Mr. Branch gave us to see where we were to be assigned for the rest of the day. Weather by coincidence or design, I was assigned to F house again. Immediately I recalled his story and thought about H house. I would be working just a few steps away from the men he had just described. My adrenaline kicked in again and my heart started to race. I really wanted to go behind that gate to see what lurked back there.

There was small talk at the table for the thirty minutes, but my mind was on H house. After we finished, we all proceeded to our assignments. I walked through the gate at control two and then down the corridor to F house. To my surprise, Ramirez was on duty again. I walked up to his desk and before I could say anything, he looked up and with a smile on his face said, "Hello Officer Allen." It seemed as though he was genuinely glad to see me. He was looking over his roster for the day. As he did that, he explained to me that during the week was when all the medical appointments took place and also the inmates were regularly called out for testing in the counseling area. Once again, he handed me the key for the cross gate to H house. This time, there was no hesitation he simply said, "You know what to do."

He opened one of the gray panel boxes and started to push buttons and as he did so, lights started going out and he began to call out whatever number he pushed. He closed the panel box and disappeared around the corner leaving me alone at the gate. I took advantage of his absence and sat down on his stool. I crossed my arms and waited while observing my surroundings.

I only had to wait a few minutes for the bell to ring signaling to open the gate. I went to the gate to see who would appear. My mind went back to the story I had heard from Mr. Branch and I began to wonder if it might be one of them. Once again, my heart began to race, but this time with anticipation. Could it possibly be one of them? The "permanent inmates" (which included death row) all had cloth name tags sewn above their left shirt pocket. That's how I would be able to tell.

I saw the shadows on the floor approach from around the office corner first. There were two, of course. The inmate was in front and the escort officer trailing slightly behind. I had the key out in my hand and my eyes were sharply focused on the corridor. Then they appeared and my heart jumped. I didn't need to see a nametag. I immediately recognized his face from the newspapers. He was fairly light skinned and he was stockier than I had imagined. As they approached the gate, I put the key in the lock, opened the gate and slid it to the side. He walked closer to the gate and for a moment I was locked in a stare with Roosevelt Green. I'm sure I was of no particular interest to him, but the entire story flooded my mind. As he walked by and up the F house corridor I said her name out loud for the first time since I had read it in the news paper three years before; Teresa Carol Allen. As I watched him walk up the corridor with his escort, my mind took me back to December 1976.

I was in basic training at the time at Fort Jackson, South Carolina, but I remember mother and Daddy telling me about the story when I returned home and that her body had been discovered less than a mile from our home. Daddy and Mother saved the newspapers so I could read the story. I became nauseas as I watched him walk up the corridor, clean, apparently healthy and the citizens of Georgia, including me, were paying for his every need.

He and his escort disappeared around the corner after they cleared the gate at Control 2. I don't know how long I stood there, lost in the memories of December 1976. I was still staring up the corridor when I heard a voice, "Officer Allen, are you alright?" It was Ramirez and he reappeared from around the corner and I never saw him coming. I blinked, shook my head and turned toward him and replied, "Yes, I'm fine." But I wasn't sure if I really was.

I hadn't known *her* personally. But, it was the fact that she was found so close to my home and that we shared the same last name. Now, I was here in this place, face to face with one of her killers. He had an accomplice, but I couldn't recall his name at the moment. It was Green that I remembered. I could still recall the smug smile on his face, from the newspaper, when he was captured in New York City. He was being placed in a police car and had the nerve to smile. I was suddenly filled with rage and it came upon me very unexpectedly. It was not a good thing. I had training in discipline that was supposed to help me process things like this better.

I was working in a place where a temper would not do. The really amazing thing about it all was that this wasn't my nature. I was very laid back and easy going. I had been paid many compliments on my demeanor in the past. It was a character trait that I thought would serve me well working in a maximum-security prison. There were so many different personalities here and I would have to learn to work with them all.

The most astounding thing about it was that I had never laid eyes on Green before today; never uttered a word to him. Now, just the sight of him had made me feel ill and brought on feelings I didn't realize I had about the situation until today. I made a mental note to myself and filed it away telling myself I would deal with this later. Subconsciously, I just made a very big mistake. I would come to find out later that "filing things away" wasn't going to be a good idea in a place like this. I became a master of taking note of things, processing the moment, and then filing it away, always promising myself to deal with it later.

I have heard it said that the human mind is like a super computer in the area of processing information. I've read books on the subject. I've also read that our minds protect us from traumatic situations and information that it perceives as harmful to itself or the body. I suppose it is a self defense mechanism. "Filing away" was my mind's way of protecting me from those moments in my life. That and the false promise I always made to deal with it later. I became a master at it. Filing situations away became easier than filing people away. Stuffing faces away, deep inside, is fine until they decided not to stay there anymore. I don't know if the mind can ever get crowded and full, but I know that the conscious of man can and *will.* When all those people that I stuffed inside decided to revisit me, it became a personal hell.

Today, seeing Roosevelt Green alive, breathing and in good health while Teresa Carol Allen was tortured, shot and left to die like an animal, aroused my anger. So on this day, I stuffed away my first two faces. The face of a young college student I never met and the face of one of her personal demons that just walked past me, still alive. I didn't want to think about them anymore. I filed them away. So I told myself. I stuffed them as far down and away from my thoughts as I could. What I didn't know at the time is that I would have no control over when they decided to revisit me.

Officer Ramirez touched my shoulder and asked, "Are you sure you're alright?" My head snapped over to look at him. I smiled, trying to reassure him and said, "Yes, I was just thinking about something." He smiled back and said, "You looked as though you had seen a ghost." I answered him in my mind, *"maybe I just did."*

I didn't know much about the spirit world other than what I'd been taught in Sunday school or read in books. I was taught that God was spirit therefore that implied there is a spiritual world we cannot see. Ramirez returned to his duties at the desk and his eyes were glued to his clipboard so he paid no attention to me. I slowly turned my head in all directions as inconspicuously as I could. I wondered if *she* had been here to tap me on the shoulder as Green passed by for the first time. Maybe *she* had been here to deliver a message to her namesake. The words formed in my mind. *"Don't forget about me."*

I couldn't forget her. I would not forget her. I also promised myself that if I ever made it to H-house; *they* would not forget her either. But, for the moment, I needed to return to the present. I stuffed it all a little deeper. But, something deep inside said that this was only the beginning of something that I could not let go. I took one more glance up the corridor, took a deep breath and left the chambers of my mind.

I walked over to Ramirez at the desk. He was still studying his clipboard and I asked, "Have you ever worked in H house?" He looked up from the clipboard and said, "No, I

retired from the Army to get away from that kind of duty." I looked at him and asked, "What kind of duty?" He replied, "The dangerous kind." I smiled at him and looked toward H-house. I wanted to go back there. More importantly I wanted to work back there. I had a strange feeling that this was the beginning of a journey that would lead me exactly where I wanted to go. For now, I turned my attention back to Ramirez and F-house.

Ramirez allowed me to be more involved with the inmates, but he kept an ever-watchful eye over me. We walked through the cell house and down each range. He told me that each inmate was issued a set of headphones when they arrived. On the wall of each cell, there were three round plug receptors for the headphones, just like you would find on any stereo system.

He explained that there were three radio stations from which the inmates could choose. Some were propped up on their bunks listening to music. As we walked the ranges and passed by cells it was like passing an art exhibit with each cell representing a different painting. Some were reading, some sleeping. What really caught my attention the most was the inmates that were lying there with no headphones on and no book in their hands. Nor did they appear to be asleep. Those were the inmates lying on their bunks with one arm stretched across their eyes as though blocking out light. That was what I witnessed the most. Then a thought occurred to me, ***"no, they're not blocking out light. They were attempting to block out this place in time where they found themselves."***

The only escape they had was into their own minds and what a tortured existence that must have been. I didn't need to see their faces; it was in their body language. Arm stretched over the face and one foot crossed over the other rocking back and forth. I could only imagine the movie that was playing in their minds. Weather it was remorse for what they had done, regret over being caught or just simply missing a loved one. I looked at the second hand on my watch click by; I could only imagine how slow it was moving for them.

I heard Ramirez talking and pointing, but I wasn't really listening. I was studying these men locked away in their minds. We continued to walk and that's when I saw his face. The lid from the mounted wall locker on the wall was down to form a desk. He was sitting on his bunk; pen in hand on a piece of paper. His left arm was on the desk and his right hand to his chin. I doubted he even noticed me as we walked by. He starred right through me and out the window. He was lost deep in thought.

The face was from my past. Slowly it came from the shadow of my mind and into the light. I remembered him from my freshman year in high school. The only name that formed was "Charles." I couldn't remember his last name, but I remembered his attitude in school. He was only interested in the girls and every teacher new his name and not in a good way. He was constantly in trouble with them in some way. My first thought was, ***"well, that figures."***

I have no idea why he was there, but I didn't need to know. He had graduated from his school days antics and on to something more serious because now he sat inside a cell inside of a maximum-security prison and was being processed to determine where he would serve his time. It was a scary thought because we had classes together. Two young men with the same opportunities, but had taken two very different paths. It was true enough that my path had taken some negative turns, but at least I was on this side of the bars. I felt both humbled and grateful for where my path led me. As we walked by, I tried not to stare at him. I looked slightly over my shoulder as we walked by and then forced my eyes forward.

But, I knew he would be in my mind the rest of the day if I didn't do something. So, with one conscience thought, a third face was stuffed down in the dungeons of my mind.

Ramirez left at 2 pm. and I was with Officer Cahn again. Because it was a regular workday, there wasn't much time for chatting. But, as usual, he gave me that big smile and started about his duties. When 3:30 pm came, I told him I had to meet Mr. Branch for shift assignment and to be fitted for uniforms. He leaned in and said, "I'll be seeing you real soon." Then he winked at me, gave me that big smile and walked away. It wasn't hard to figure out that he knew something I didn't. I smiled and started up the corridor.

I opened the door and saw that I was the last to arrive. There didn't seem to be any problem because Mr. Branch said simply, "Come on in." Once the door was closed, he asked us a little about our day. We all said pretty much the same thing, "it was fine. None of us had any experience so there wasn't really anything else we could say. Apparently it was the standard answer because he said, "That's good," and never looked up from his desk where he was writing. After he finished writing, he looked up and pointed to each of us and gave us a shift assignment. When my turn came, he looked at me and said "Second shift." That was from 2 pm until 10 pm. Then I remembered Officer Cahn telling me he would see me real soon. As it turned out, he did have inside information. Mr. Branch instructed us to report to the officer's classroom fifteen minutes before our shift began for shift briefing. Then he gave us each the Captain's name to which we would report.

He pointed to a corner table in his office to three stacks of uniforms. We were told to find the stack with our name on it. Once we retrieved our uniforms, Mr. Branch said, "We have one more stop to make." We followed him up the corridor to Control 1. Instead of going through the forward gate, we turned right and went through another gate. Just a few feet on the other side of the gate, we saw a set of office doors to the right; our destination.

Mr. Branch made a couple of taps on the door and went right in. There was an inmate at one desk and an officer at another. The inmate was obviously some type of clerk because he was typing on a typewriter. He looked up and went right back to his work. One by one we were called over to the officer's desk. He produced three badges. When it was my turn at the desk, he handed me a badge and had me sign for it. I glanced at it briefly and placed it in my pocket. When we were done, we all walked out of the office with Mr. Branch. He escorted us to the time clock and asked us if we had any questions. The three of us looked at each other and said almost in unison, "No." He assured us that he would always be around if we needed him. Then he shook our hands and said, "Good luck men." Then he released us for the day with our instructions to report for duty at our specified times.

The three of us walked down the tunnel together. We shook hands and wished each other good luck, but we knew that we would see each other when it was time to report for school then went our separate ways. I was in a rush to get to my car. Once inside, I pulled the badge out of my pocket to study it. It was shaped like the state of Georgia. It was obviously used and was a bit dull. The silver had lost a little of its shine. Below the state seal the title was engraved, "Correctional Officer." Just below that was the badge number. It had some weight to it. I smiled as I looked at it and whispered to myself, "You made it." Part of my plan was still alive. I was working in law enforcement.

I learned to sew watching mother through the years. That night, I tailored my uniforms to fit. Then I ironed one and had creases almost sharp enough to cut. Next, I turned my attention to the dull shine on the badge. Someone told me that toothpaste would bring the shine back. I decided to try it. With a little water, the toothpaste worked remarkably well. I dried it and used a soft cloth to bring it to a shine. It glistened in the light. I pinned the badge in the precut holes over the left pocket. I was given silver collar "chevrons" for my rank. There was one stripe for each collar. That was the insignia of a Correctional Officer I. I stepped back and looked. I noticed something missing. Over the right pocket, was supposed to be a nametag and I hadn't been issued one yet.

Everything that was personalized with my name on it was given to me when I left Ft. Jackson. Among those items was a black nametag that simply said "Allen." I went to look through a box where I had placed some of those items. I only had to move a couple of items and there it was. I had a brief flashback of Ft. Jackson from three years earlier. After cleaning it up a bit, I placed it over the right pocket where it belonged. Now, the uniform looked complete. Debbie was sitting in a chair watching me and said playfully, "Why don't you just wait?" The she smiled at me. From the look in her eyes, I could tell she approved. Now I was ready to enter the Institution as a uniformed officer and I was excited.

I arrived the next day at 1:30 pm even though the briefing didn't start until 1:45 pm. It was more training from the army and it would serve me well through the years in my personal life as well as my professional one. The officer's classroom was located adjacent to the visitation area. I had to pass through the officer's locker room on the way. Just outside the classroom were a barbershop and a shoeshine chair. I could tell there would be no excuse for an officer to not be neat and look professional. I peered inside the classroom from the doorway and noticed a few officers already seated and talking amongst themselves. I looked behind me and decided I would enter as well. It was set up just like a classroom in school including wooden desks.

Like most new students in a new environment, I sat in the rear. I wanted to be able to see who ever came though the door and survey the rest of the classroom. Two of the officers talking, looked up briefly and nodded at me. I smiled and nodded back. Over the next fifteen minutes I could hear others outside the classroom talking. Just before 1:45 pm, they all entered as if they received a cue. As I studied the door, I could see why. Two lieutenants and a captain entered the room. One lieutenant held a clipboard and went to a podium. The other lieutenant and the captain stood just to the rear. The lieutenant at the podium greeted us and then went right to work.

The briefing lasted about fifteen minutes with the lieutenant passing along information that was completely foreign to me. He made several announcements one of which reminded all the officers to check the bulletin boards before and after every shift. After the announcements, he looked at the clipboard on the podium and read post assignments. He read off all the cell houses first; A thru H. After each post, he read an officer's name and that was his post for the day. He did the same with the three large dormitories. My new friend, Officer Cahn, was assigned to F house. At the very end of the briefing, the lieutenant called out, "Allen." I responded with a "Yes sir." "You will report to F house with Officer Cahn." I responded again with, "Yes sir." Then he asked if there were any questions. With no reply

from anyone he said, "Stand." There was a rush of chairs shuffling and officers coming to attention and I followed suit.

The Captain walked slowly though the lines; it was an inspection. He was looking at each officer from top to bottom. He checked haircuts, uniforms and shoes for a proper shine. He stopped every now and again to point and mumble something to an officer. I would see the officer's head nod and a crisp, "yes sir." I could feel my chest tightening as he approached me. This was my first inspection since leaving the army three years earlier. No one had prepared me for this. I could only hope that my own discipline concerning the dress code would be suitable for him. He walked slowly by, without saying anything, but I could see him looking at me from the corner of my eye. Before he cleared my peripheral vision I could see his lips tighten and a slight nod from his head. I let out a slight sigh. It appeared that he approved of his new trainee.

After the Captain finished his inspection, everyone gathered their personal belongings and started toward the door. I found Officer Cahn and fell in behind him. The shift change was explained to me earlier and now I would see one first hand. As the first officer reached for the handle on the glass door, the yellow gate of control one began to move slowly to one side and the officers began to form a single line. One by one they filed passed the window and each officer dropped a key chit in a drawer like you might find at the drive thru teller at any bank. As they did that, they called out the location they were relieving. The officers inside control one placed their chit on a hook and retrieved the chit of the officer that was being relieved. That chit would only be surrendered once the briefing had been complete and the keys for the location exchanged.

There was laughter and talking in the group as we all headed down the corridor. It was new to me, but it was second nature to all of them and I could tell they had done it a many times before. Once we cleared control two, some officers split off from the group and turned down another corridor. They were going to relieve the three dormitory officers. Officer Cahn and I continued down the corridor to F house. As we walked down the corridor he asked, "What do you think about being assigned to second shift?" I answered, "If it means working with you, I'm glad it happened." He gave the big grin again and said, "It didn't just happen, you were selected." I was right. He did have inside information. If he had anything to do with it, it meant that he had favor with the "powers that be."

I waited at the desk as he went over the briefing with the officer he was relieving. As soon as he finished and he had possession of the keys, he walked over to me and for the first time acknowledged the fact that I was in uniform. "You look sharp today," and he handed me the key to the cross gate at H house. "Thank you," I said as I took the key. "You look pretty sharp yourself." He laughed and said, "Bull, but thank you for saying that." He turned to walk away. The fact was, Cahn was a big, round man. He wasn't a poster model for anyone wearing a uniform, but he was very much a professional. It wasn't the uniform that gave Cahn his authority it was his commanding attitude. When he was around these inmates there was never any doubt about who was in charge. They respected him and it had nothing to do with the uniform or the badge.

As I looked around I took note of the fact that we were constantly outnumbered. There were no weapons that any one of us could use to maintain control. Cahn became an officer for me to emulate. He walked around giving orders to these inmates and they carried them

out without hesitation and he never once flinched when he turned his back on any of them. He was in control of F house. He knew it and more importantly the inmates knew it. I knew that if I was going to be successful here, I was going to have to have the edge that he possessed. I took mental notes of everything he did and the way he did it.

There was very little traffic from H house. I suspected that most of the appointments of the men on death row were conducted in the morning hours. The only time I opened the gate was to allow a staff member through. The afternoon went by relatively fast. I watched Cahn checking in inmates that returned from appointments with either the counseling section or the medical section. Afternoon gave way to early evening and soon it was dinnertime. The phone on the wall rang and Cahn answered. It was a brief conversation and when he ended the call with a quick, "10-4," I knew it was the signal to send the inmates up the corridor for chow. When he hung up the phone it was confirmed when he yelled, "Chow time!" I heard the inmates rustling in their cells. Cahn went to the panel box on the wall and began the process while I stood by the gate and observed.

One range at a time they left like a well-organized army moving in sync. It was the same on the second shift as it was on the first shift, but under the direction of a new general. Once the last range left, there was silence in the huge cell house. Officer Cahn told me to follow him. We stopped at a cell and he produced a single key; a master key. He inserted the key and with one slight turn, I heard the motor buzz in the panel above the cell. The door opened and we stepped in. He explained that this was the only time a Cellhouse officer had to conduct cell searches and that when I went to school, they would teach me the proper way to conduct cell searches. For the time being he had me observe him.

A diagnostic inmate wasn't allowed to have any personal property. Everything in their possession was a state issued item. When he let down the lid to the wall locker, all I saw were a few pieces of writing paper and a couple of paperback books. The search consisted mostly of looking through the mattress to make sure there were no hidden weapons or any other unauthorized items. He looked under the bed and made a quick visual inspection of the entire cell. Then we were out and on to another. He told me they usually tried to search five cells during "chow time." By the time we were through and made our way back to the officer's desk, the first range of inmates was returning. They went right to their cells and waited. Officer Cash unlocked the panel box and opened all their cells and all knew to enter and close their cell doors. He carefully observed the range and the panel box until there was a red light over each cell that signaled the doors were locked.

I walked with him as we completed the same process until all the inmates were secured in their cells and every light turned red. Then we walked to every range to make sure there were no inmates walking free. In the confusion, it would be easy for an inmate to close a door and remain out. Nothing was left to chance. Once that was completed, we returned to the officer's desk and sat down; Officer Cahn at his desk and me in a chair beside the desk. We both let out a sigh. The afternoons and early evenings could be quite busy. As he studied his paperwork, I thought about the day's events. We had been moving ever since arriving at 2:00 pm. Finally he was done with his paperwork and turned his attention to me.

"What do you think so far?" he asked. I replied, "It's different." He let out a laugh before he continued, "yeah, I'm sure it is." "Do you think you're going to like it?" he asked. I could tell these were the standard questions that were asked of any trainee. "Once I get used to it, yes I do," I replied. "We have had veteran police officers come to work here because they wanted something different," he said. "I think the longest lasted only a month." I studied him for a second before I asked the obvious question, "Why?" He said, "Most of them are used to working alone, relying on their guns at their side and dealing with only one criminal at a time." He continued, "They couldn't handle being outnumbered with no weapon."

I thought about it for a second. It made sense to me. Every police show or movie I had ever watched showed the officer arresting the criminal and putting him in the back of the car. But, that's usually where that story ended. I suppose that even real officers never gave a second thought to how these men were dealt with once they left their eyesight. Here was the real world. Men locked behind bars, waiting for their fate to be decided by a battery of test and examinations and then shipped off to obscurity. It occurred to me that I would likely never see any of these men again. Some of them would probably still be in prison after I retired.

Dusk was upon us and as the sun began to set the natural light from the large windows started to fade. Officer Cahn got up from his chair and said, "Follow me." We walked over to the cross gate that led to the corridor and approached a smaller panel box on the wall. He opened a small door and there were several round dials inside. He pushed one in and held it down as he spun it in a circle. Lights instantly came on. Apparently it worked almost like a dimmer switch in a home. He did it again with other dials and more lights came on. Once that was completed we returned to the officer's desk to continue our conversation and wait for the evening to wind down.

I heard the gates open at control 2 and saw a group of officers walking down the corridor toward F house. Apparently Officer Cahn knew their destination was F house because he got up from his chair and stood by the desk. I took his cue and stood as well. There was a group of three. As they walked closer I could see the batons hanging on one side connected to the baton ring on their belts. When they arrived at the officer's desk, they stopped to talk with Cahn. I could tell they were all friends as they conversed.

Cahn knew they weren't here for F house so he asked, "You guys headed back to H house?" The elder and leader of the group answered, "Yeah, we're going back to shower isolation." Then he looked over at me and continued, "The lieutenant wants us to take Allen." My heart skipped a beat. Ever since laying eyes on the H house cross gate and seeing Roosevelt Green, I wanted to go back there. Now I was going to have the opportunity and I felt apprehensive. The leader of the group asked Officer Cahn, "Do you have a baton he can use?" He answered, "Sure." Then he went over and opened the panel box on the wall and pulled out a long, black nightstick. He walked over and handed it to me. It was heavier than I expected. It was made of a composite material I didn't recognize. There was a black strap that hung from the handle. Officer Cahn held out his hand and said, "Gate key." I handed him the cross gate key for H house. Then he smiled, winked at me and said, "You'll do fine."

As he walked over to the gate, the other three officers drew their batons in unison and held them in their right hands. Because of my training in martial arts, I was no stranger to what I held. We called it by a different name, but the fact was, it was an impact weapon.

When I saw them draw their batons, I instinctively wrapped the black strap over my thumb, allowing it to cross over the back of my hand and then finally gripping it by the handle. Cahn opened the gate and I followed the team, that I was now a part of, through the gate. I looked back only once when the gate slammed shut.

We walked down a short corridor and through a door. The doorway was all I was ever able to see from F house. Once through the door, I saw a set of three small offices to the right side of the corridor. The left side of the corridor was where we walked. As we continued down the small corridor, I saw another cross gate and an officer standing ready with a key. From behind that officer I heard a loud, booming voice yell, "H-2, Lock'em down". I recognized the tone and it was definitely military. As we approached the gate, the officer unlocked the gate and let us through and quickly slammed the gate shut.

As I surveyed my surroundings, I could see that this unit wasn't like any other part of the institution. To my left I could see a red door and it was closed and locked. I saw a pair of eyes staring out of the small observation window, which was covered with a wire mesh. The eyes turned out to be an officer. It was a small control room. Beside that door was another red door with a black iron bar across it. It was a backup in case the lock on the red door ever became compromised. Above the door I saw "H-3;" a housing unit. To my right I saw another red door. Over the door was the inscription, "H-1." As we walked down the corridor, I saw a solid block wall to my left with small observation ports in them. I looked into one and I could see that it was the shower bay for that unit. At the end of the corridor were two more red doors to my left. Again, a pair of eyes peered through one door and over the second red door I saw "H-4." As with H-3, there was a black iron bar over the door.

Directly across the corridor was a sixth red door with the inscription, "H-2." So death row consisted of four separate housing units; H-1, H-2, H-3 and H-4. H-2 appeared to be our destination. I found the source of the thundering voice standing at the H-2 door. He was looking up through the small observation port in the door. On his collar I saw three stripes. He was a sergeant and apparently the supervisor here. He yelled again, "You got'em locked up yet?" I wasn't sure whom he was talking to. I looked around as we waited. Everyone had a baton except the sergeant. The corridor officer had his baton in the metal loop attached to his belt.

As we waited, I took another look around. I had an eerie feeling as though we were in a dungeon. I walked over and peered through the observation port in H-4. On the other side of the door was a wire fence with yet another gate that led directly into the unit. I saw inmates walking around inside. It appeared to be a smaller version of any of the other cell houses. There was an upper and lower tier with a set of steps in the middle of the range. I could tell there were individual cells in there. The lights were dim and I could see the flicker of a television. I wondered where Roosevelt Green was in all of this. I looked to the upper range to see if I could see any movement and catch a glimpse of him. Apparently my movement caught the attention of one of the inmates standing and watching TV. He looked over to the door and returned my gaze. There was no expression on his face. I was almost hypnotized as I watched him.

Then I heard my name, "Allen." I felt my heart leap. I don't know if I physically jumped or not, but I was startled. It brought my attention back to the door at H-2. They had received a signal that they were ready. The corridor officer took his large gate key and tapped on the brass handle of the door. I heard a voice from the other side call out, "Enter." My heart was beating faster as the door opened. I was actually going inside a housing unit. The door opened only to reveal an inner corridor. I looked up and saw where the sergeant had been looking. There was a deck above and completely covered in wire mesh. In front of me was another red door. Then I heard the door behind us slam shut. We were locked in this holding area and I felt uneasy. It was as if I had entered a lower level of the dungeon. I was trapped in "no man's land." I couldn't go forward nor could I return the way I entered. My breaths quickened because I didn't know what was going to happen next. All that was missing was a sign above the door that read, "Abandon all hope, ye who enter here," the sign at the entrance to Hell.

We waited for what seemed like an eternity, but were actually only a few minutes. Finally the voice from above us said, "Alright." Then the red door in front of us clicked and the sergeant pulled the door open. He walked in with no reservations while I was watching all around me. One by one the other officer's filed in the door and each knew exactly where they were going. I was the last to enter and it seemed as though I was entering a forbidden place.

There was a wire fenced in area in the back with a gate large enough for probably two men to fit through. As I walked I observed my surroundings. To my left were the windows, but with a large chain length fence in front of them that started at the floor and went to the ceiling. There were also televisions encased in boxes about halfway up the fence. To my right was a row of cells. I guessed about twenty and an inmate in each one. I observed them, but not making eye contact.

The Sergeant was waking fast like he was on a mission and reached the gate first. He looked back at the control room and waved to the officer there. I heard a buzz and the sergeant pushed the gate open. On the right were three solid doors. The sergeant placed his hand on the handle of the first door and waited impatiently for the rest of us to catch up. Once we were gathered at the door, he peered through the observation port and then unlocked the door with a key. Inside there was a cell door and the inmate standing at the door in nothing but a towel wrapped around his waist and a washcloth in his hand. No matter, one of the officers stepped inside through the doorway and had the inmate strip down and ordered him to pass his towel and washcloth through the bars leaving him nude.

The officer carefully searched the towel and washcloth, but before passing the items back, he had the inmate turn around. Once his back was exposed, the officer had him bend over and spread his buttocks apart. Another officer leaned closer to me and said, "Before any inmate under death sentence is allowed to leave his cell, he must be stripped searched." The officer returned the towel and the sergeant looked toward the control room and yelled, "Open one." I heard the familiar buzz and the door popped open. The inmate pushed the door to the side and walked out. He knew where he was going and walked back toward the entrance with the sergeant and the rest of us walking behind him.

He glanced toward the cells and acknowledged the other inmates as he walked. When we reached the entrance I saw his destination. It was a small shower stall that I didn't notice on the way in. He stepped in and turned on the shower. There was no shower curtain to pull. I saw the other officers assume a relaxed position. I took the opportunity to survey my surroundings a bit more. I looked up and down the row of cells and the faces that were

locked inside. Most were staring straight ahead at the TV and paying no attention to what was happening. They were used to the routine as well.

Only one stood out to me. He was small, thin with an almost bald head. I could tell it was a fresh haircut; a new arrival. One officer saw me looking at him and walked over, leaned in and said, "That's Carl Isaacs, the Alday family murderer." I recognized the name from the newspapers and also from the training officer's story. He was the mastermind of the escape from Georgia State Prison at Reidsville. He was moved the very morning of the escape.

He was a small man and I wondered how he could have killed anyone at his size. Then the thought crossed my mind that a gun can make anyone superior in any situation. I must have starred too long because I could tell he had the feeling that he was being watched. Slowly he dropped his gaze from the TV and his head started to turn in my direction. The eyes were dead. Then slowly a very sinister grin started to form on his lips. I was locked in a staring match with a murderer. The hair stood up on the back of my neck as I started to recall the story.

I was a teenager in May of 1973 when the story first broke. Carl Isaacs, his half brother Wayne Coleman and Coleman's friend George Dungee escaped from a Maryland prison camp. Isaacs was serving a sentence for burglary. Coleman was serving time for robbery and Dungee for failure to pay child support. They drove to Baltimore and picked up Isaacs brother Billy, only 15 years old. They drove south heading to Florida. On May 14, 1973, they were in Seminole county Georgia and their car was almost out of gas. They thought they saw a gas pump behind a rural mobile belonging to Jerry and Mary Alday and stopped to investigate. They discovered there was no pump; however, the trailer was empty, and they decided to burglarize it. Dungee remained in the car while Isaacs and Coleman entered the trailer. While they were inside, Billy Isaacs warned them that two men were approaching in a jeep. Jerry Alday and his father Ned Alday pulled in behind the trailer, unaware that it was being burglarized.

Isaacs met them and ordered them inside at gunpoint. After their pockets were emptied, Jerry Alday was taken to the south bedroom of the trailer while Ned was taken to the north bedroom. Isaacs then shot and killed Jerry Alday, and then both he and Coleman shot and killed Ned Alday. Soon afterward Jerry's brother, Jimmy Alday drove up on a tractor, walked to the back door and knocked. Coleman answered the door stuck a pistol in his face and ordered him inside. He was taken to the living room and forced to lie on the sofa. Isaacs shot and killed him. After Isaacs went outside to move the tractor, which was parked in front of their car, Jerry's wife Mary Alday drove up. Isaacs entered the trailer behind her. Mean while Chester and Aubrey Alday (Jerry's brother and uncle) drove up in a pickup truck. Leaving Coleman and Dungee to watch Mary Alday, Carl and Billy Isaacs went outside to confront the two men, and forced them at gunpoint into the trailer. Once inside, Aubrey was taken to the south bedroom where Carl Isaacs shot and killed him, while Chester Alday was taken to the north bedroom and killed by Coleman. Coleman and Carl Isaacs then raped Mary Alday on her kitchen table.

Afterward they drove to a wooded area several miles away where Mary Alday was raped again. Dungee killed her. They abandoned their car in the woods and took Mary Alday's car, which they later abandoned in Alabama. They stole another car there, and were arrested a

few days later in West Virginia, in possession of guns later identified as the murder weapons, and property belonging to the victims. Later, during an interview, Isaacs admitted shooting Jerry, Ned, Aubrey and Jimmy Alday, raping Mary Alday and burglarizing the trailer. From the look on his face, I had no trouble thinking that it was an admission made out of pure arrogance.

Now here I was in a staring contest with the man who had murdered an entire family. As my subconscious returned to the present, I could see he still had the evil grin on his face. He was the veteran convict and I was the rookie officer. I was amazed later to discover that he was only 6 years older than I. I'm not sure if he was trying to instill fear in me, but I was not intimidated.

I thought back to my church days as a teenager and how I was taught that we are all God's children. I wondered if God was watching the day four of his children wiped out an entire family. I wondered if they were evil or had they allowed themselves to be used by evil? I wasn't sure, but his cold dead eyes continued to look through me and the grin never left his face. I didn't want to be drawn in any further, so I looked away to the inmate in the shower. He was busy yelling out all types of insults about the staff to no one in particular. The steam rose from his shower and I thought all that was missing was the fire and it would be a scene from hell.

Eventually he finished his shower and stepped out and got dressed. He started back toward the isolation cell talking to the inmates in the cells along the way. They seemed to have their own language, like a code. He walked slowly to enjoy the time away from his isolation cell. Finally he reached his destination and walked inside. The sergeant, impatiently, stepped forward and slammed the cell door shut. Then he stepped out and closed the solid door and locked it. He started toward the front entrance and as I followed, I tried to keep my eyes forward away from the cells. As I approached Isaacs's cell, I couldn't keep myself from looking over. He locked eyes with me again. He was getting some sort of enjoyment from our exchange. I assumed because I was new, I was his entertainment for the night. I maintained eye contact with him. He never appeared to blink.

We passed through the red door and another officer closed it behind us. I felt more at ease except now we were back in the hallway in no man's land. The sergeant tapped on the door with his key and in just a moment, the corridor officer outside arrived. He looked through the observation port and then slid his key in the lock to open the door. I felt relieved because it was lighter in the corridor, but I still had the feeling of being in a forbidden place. Without stopping and with no real enthusiasm the sergeant said, "Thanks for your help men." We walked to the gate and waited. The corridor officer made his way to us with the key and unlocked the gate.

We walked through the gate toward F-house. Even in the corridor leading to the cell house there seemed to be more air. It was like I was coming out of a hole into daylight. It was psychological, but felt all too real. The H-house corridor officer rang a bell signaling there was traffic heading toward F-house. Cahn met us at the gate with key in hand. He slid the gate open and smiled. The other officers walked out of the other side of F-house and up the corridor. Cahn let the gate slam behind us. I snapped my head around suddenly to see

him standing there. He reached for the baton that was clenched in my right hand and said, "Let me take that."

He opened the panel box and returned the baton to its hiding place. He turned around, looked me in the eye and asked, "What did you think?" I took a deep breath and said, "Well, it's a different world back there." He smiled and said, "Imagine working back there for eight hours daily." Then he handed me the gate key and walked to the other side of the cell house. I looked down at the key and then back to H-house. There was something different back there. It was a presence that didn't seem to exist on this side of the gate. Looking into the eyes of a murderer tonight confirmed it for me.

Chapter 5

"Yea, mine own familiar friend, in whom I trusted, which did eat of my bread, hath lifted up his heel against me."

- Psalms 41:9
(King James Version)

The next few weeks I settled into the routine of the second shift. A lot of these officers were older, several were retired military and I was one of the youngest officers on the shift, but they seemed to like me. Since I was not yet a certified officer, most of my duties consisted of watching the dining hall at chow time, helping with count time and making security checks of doors in the evenings. These were duties that didn't require me to work directly with inmates on my own. It did, however, give me a chance to get very familiar with the layout of the institution.

Just as I was getting used to the routine of the second shift, a new training class was beginning. In those days, there was no academy. It was a three-week school called Basic Security Training or "B.S.T." The Department leased a building on the campus of the University of Georgia in Athens. We received orders to report to the institution on a Sunday afternoon. The school would not begin until Monday, but we would report a day early to be assigned living quarters. I was both excited and nervous at the prospect. It was a new adventure, but I had not been away from Deedee or the girls over night before, let alone an entire week. I was also nervous about attending a school again. It had been a while since I was in a classroom and high school had not been a pleasant experience for me.

I said goodbye to the girls at home and Deedee drove me to the prison. My fellow officers were waiting when we arrived. The vehicle was already signed out and ready to go. I looked at Deedee and she gave me a reassuring smile and said, "The girls and I will be just fine." I smiled knowing that the look must have been all over my face. I kissed her good bye and grabbed my suitcase from the back seat. The hour and a half ride to Athens was a pleasant drive. East Georgia has very beautiful countryside and the scenery helped to relieve my anxiety. The three of us engaged in small talk now and again. But, I spent most of my time starring out the window and thinking about my family. I had a real opportunity here for a wonderful career and the thought of the school was making me uneasy.

We arrived at the University of Georgia and found the corrections building easily. There was a lot of activity on campus. When we checked in at the desk, we found out why. It was rush week for the University of Georgia. We were advised to be careful and on our best behavior if we decided to venture out in the evening. We were further instructed that most of the students on campus thought that anyone residing in the building were inmates from prison. As I looked around the lobby, I understood why. There were standing displays all around the lobby of the corrections department, but mostly detailing inmates. To anyone entering the lobby, it would appear that anyone living here were inmates.

We were pared up in the dormitory rooms and I was lucky enough to get assigned with one of the men that I came with. We quickly unpacked and decided to explore the campus and see the excitement of the students. My two companions were single and were interested in all the young women walking around. I didn't want to sit alone the first night so I tagged along. It turned out to be quite an experience.

The fraternities were serving free alcohol so we decided to visit each house. It was like a massive party that carried over from one house to another. There were bands outside on the lawn of some of the houses. The three of us were young and relatively in the same age group as the students so no one questioned who we were. We walked from one party to the next and helped ourselves to the free beer and listened to the music.

We were careful not to drink too much because it was our first night and we didn't know what to expect. After a couple of hours we called it a night because we knew this would be going on all week. We returned to the building fairly early. It had been a long time since I was out with any guys drinking so when my head hit the pillow, I was out.

The next morning we gathered in one of the lecture rooms close to the main building. The first part of the morning was used for filling out paperwork and explaining what we should expect in the next few weeks. We were given notebooks and the instructors explained that we would receive material that we should keep and we would be tested on it. I liked the instructors and what they represented. Even from the first day I knew that becoming an instructor is what I wanted to do someday. I had some experience teaching taekwondo and I liked it. Watching these men and women made me realize how much I enjoyed teaching.

The afternoon session was our first class called "Emergency Response." It was a class that was meant to give us an idea of the emergency procedures during a riot. There were two videos for the class. The instructor explained that the department wanted us to know immediately how dangerous our jobs were. There was always be a chance of being taken hostage and they wanted us to see what we could be facing. My mind went to H-house and what would happen if those men ever managed to take over. The officers would become hostages for sure, but with nothing to lose, would be expendable.

The first video was from the riot at Attica prison in New York. The riot took place on September 9, 1971. Approximately one thousand inmates of the twenty two hundred inmates housed there were responding to the death of a black activist inmate who was killed in California's infamous San Quentin prison. The inmates seized control of the prison and took 42 staff members as hostages. Sometime after 8:00 am that morning a group of inmates from what was called 5 company lined up for roll call. They heard rumors that one of their fellow inmates was to remain in his cell and be tortured after being isolated for an assault on a correctional officer. A small group of inmates from that same company said that they too should be locked up and started walking back toward their cells. The remainder of 5 company continued toward the dining hall.

As the protesting inmates were walking past the isolated inmate they were able to free him then rejoined the rest of 5 company and proceeded on their way to the dining hall. A short time later, when the command staff discovered what happened, they changed the scheduling of the prisoners. Instead of going to the yard after breakfast as usual, the prisoners realized they were being led back to their cells. Complaints led to anger and when an officer tried to calm them, he was assaulted and the riot began. The inmates quickly gained control of key sections of the institution, D yard, two tunnels, and the central control room. I thought of our own control room at the Diagnostic Center and what could happen if it were ever seized. There was a full armory, the communications center and keys to every part of the institution. It would be a disaster as I am sure it was on that day. The inmates at Attica took forty-two officers and staff hostage and aired a list of grievances demanding their conditions be met before they would surrender.

There was a list of twenty-seven demands made by the prisoners including better food, better visitation and calling for an end to brutality. The prisoners had demanded that New York Governor Nelson Rockefeller come to hear demands personally, but to no avail. Negations began to break down and the prisoners were ordered to surrender or the state police would retake the prison. When the Governor refused to visit the prison to quell the disturbance, the mood of the prisoners took a turn for the worse. They appeared to be fortifying their positions. Trenches were dug, metal gates were electrified, and gasoline was put in place to be lit in case of a conflict. The prisoners brought four officers to the top of the control center and threatened to slit their throats. Officers in helicopters circling D yard were reporting that the hostages there were being prepared for killing. An official seeing the danger to the hostages ordered that the prison be retaken by force.

On Monday, September 13, 1971 at 9:46 am teargas was dropped into the yard and New York state troopers and soldiers from the New York National Guard opened fire for two minutes non-stop into the smoke. Among the weapons used were shotguns, which led to the killing of hostages and inmates, not involved in the disturbance. By the time the facility had been retaken, nine hostages and twenty-nine prisoners were killed. Four prisoners had been killed who were subject to vigilante killings.

It's one thing to see a movie on TV knowing it is fiction and saying to those around you that it is an awful thing. It's quite another to see actual footage of people dying and then realizing that it could very well be us on any given day when the slightest thing may set someone off who is not quite balanced to begin with. Every time something became more real for me I thought about my family, especially my two beautiful girls. I thought about the men who died in that terrible riot and realized that they had people who loved them and missed them, too.

The instructors told us this riot was used as a model of what not to do. It was part of the reason that states had started to develop their own riot control teams. Georgia has several Tactical squads positioned around the state for just such an occasion. In times of a disturbance, there would be no action by our Governor or the Georgia State Patrol. The jurisdiction would fall on the commissioner of our department and the warden of that particular institution. I overheard one Lieutenant say at our institution that if he were ever taken hostage, he wanted them to come and get him immediately with no time for negotiations and before the inmates to get organized. After what I saw today, I was in complete agreement. I was a rookie but even I could see that prisoners could not be allowed to get organized or fortify their positions. I would prefer to take my chances with armed tactical officers that I worked beside and who had my well being in mind.

The next video was of a recent riot and more graphic. It occurred only six months before in February 1980 at the New Mexico State Penitentiary. The riot was caused by poor housing conditions at the institution and the recent dismissal of educational programs for the inmates. As with many other institutions there was overcrowding and a lack of trained staff. When the riot occurred, there were 1,136 inmates housed in a prison designed for 900. Apparently there were unsanitary conditions and they were served poor quality food. Because there was a shortage of trained staff, officers used inmate informants to obtain information. These inmates were labeled as "snitches" and did not do well in general population. They had to be segregated into protective custody and were at danger from the general population. They would be in grave danger if ever caught out of protection and it proved to be a disaster.

Early on the morning of Saturday, February 2, 1980, two prisoners were caught drinking some homemade liquor by an officer. The two overpowered the officer and took him hostage. Within minutes, four more officers were taken hostage. It was thought that the riot might have been contained at that point, but one officer managed to escape, but in his rush to get away he left behind a set of keys. Soon, the entire dormitory was under inmate control. Using the keys left behind, the inmates captured more officers and released other inmates from their cells. Just as in the Attica riot, the inmates were able to break into the main control center and obtained more keys and also weapons.

Sometime later in the morning, things went terribly out of control. Rival gangs were now at war with each other and murders were being carried out. Some of the most violent inmates from solitary confinement had been released and they were now leading a charge to break into cellblock 4 which housed protective custody. This unit held those labeled as informers. But, the unit also housed inmates who were vulnerable, convicted of sex crimes and those who were mentally ill. It was reported that the plan was to only take revenge on the snitches, but the violence soon got out of control and no one was exempt.

When they reached cellblock 4, they discovered they did not have keys to enter these cells. But, they found blowtorches brought in for a construction project. The inmates used the torches to cut through the cells over the next 5 hours. The inmates locked down begged to be saved, but the State Police had agreed not to enter the prison as long as the officers held hostage were kept alive.

Meanwhile, the inmates were using the two-way radio to tell prison officials what they were going to do to the men in cellblock 4 once they cut through. But, no action was taken. Early the next morning the inmates finally cut through and entered the cellblock. Victims were tortured, decapitated or burned alive. One eyewitness reported that he saw one of the inmate snitches being held up in front of a window. He was being tortured by holding a blowtorch to his face. Next they moved the torch to his eyes, and then his head exploded.

It appeared that the mob mentality had taken over and men were being killed with piping, tools and knives. One inmate was to be hanged.

A rope was tied around his neck and he was thrown over the second tier balcony. He was partially decapitated. He was then pulled down and dismembered. As with most every prison disturbance, fires were set all through the institution. During the first 24 hours of the disturbance, neither the inmates nor the state officials had a spokesperson. The inmates eventually made a list of demands to be met including the issue of overcrowding, better food and reinstate the educational programs. Eventually the officers held hostage were released when the inmates were allowed to meet with reporters. Some officers were protected, but others had been raped or brutally beaten. Eventually negotiations broke down with state officials saying that no concessions had been made.

36 hours after the riot began heavily armed state police officers and National Guardsmen entered the prison to retake control. The prison had been burned out. The official report stated that 33 inmates died. Some overdosed on drugs they got from the pharmacy, but most were brutally murdered. Twenty-three had been housed in the protective custody unit. Some inmates were prosecuted for crimes committed during the riot, but most went unpunished.

It was a lot to take in. I thought about what the officer told me in the chow hall on my first day at the Diagnostic Center. He told me not to get too far from the doors because they would surrender the chow hall if anything happened. This made it all too real. The officers trapped inside had probably seen the Attica film just as I did. I could not even imagine what had gone through their minds when they realized that they were now caught inside at the mercy of very violent men. No one likes to think about the unthinkable happening to him or her. But, the fact remained that this was a real possibility for any of us watching this film here today. Always in these moments I thought about my family.

Now I had something new to think about. How would my family handle the situation if I were ever taken hostage? That thought brought back a memory of a special speaker at my high school. It was the early 1970's during the closing years of the Vietnam War. The assembly took place in the auditorium. He came to the podium in his white Navy uniform. He was an aviator, was shot down over North Vietnam and taken prisoner. I don't recall how long he was held captive, but I still remember the message he brought. He spoke of torture, starvation and how everything was taken from him. As a teenager, it was difficult to fathom the things he described. He described the nights of lying alone almost naked in a very tiny cell.

Then he gave the secret of his ability to stay alive and endure whatever might come is way. He accepted Jesus Christ early in his life and been washed in the blood of a loving savior. As other men lay in the dark and cried from being pushed to the brink of death, he had the peace of knowing that he and his family were taken care of. He said, "When you are beaten, starved, alone, stripped of all material possessions and left alone with only your thoughts and in your underwear, you'd better have something to reach for in your spiritual bag." He did. He was not alone in his cell. He was comforted by THE comforter; the Holy Spirit.

Having accepted this assignment and with a family of my own to take care of, I realized that I needed Jesus Christ in my life now more than ever. If the day ever came that I was taken hostage, beaten, stripped, raped, humiliated before men, I would need to know that my family was alright. I needed to know that I would be alright if I had to make the ultimate sacrifice. I needed to know that I would have a spiritual bag hanging on my side.

I settled into being a student again. My fear began to subside and my anxiety started to go away. The material was covered very well and the tests at the end of each week were multiple choice. That alone allowed me to relax. In addition to written test, there were performance test. We were instructed on the proper use of restraint devices such as handcuffs and leg irons. We were allowed to practice on each other multiple times and evaluated at the end of the class. At the end of the week, we were graded on our general knowledge of the proper way to apply the devices.

The second week was defensive tactics training. We were finally in an area of my expertise. However, it wasn't a martial arts class like I was involved with or taught in the past. They were very careful to explain that this type of training was only to familiarize everyone some techniques and we were encouraged to get into shape and seek other training. The defensive tactics were a variation of some aikido joint locks and taught more as control techniques rather than a way to defend ourselves.

During defensive tactics, we were instructed on the proper use of the baton. They were very careful to teach everyone to stay away from strikes to the head because that was a huge liability for the department. It was very understandable because a strike to the head was a potentially fatal blow. We were taught instead to strike the joints, such as the knee or the wrist. That type of strike would cause a lot of pain with no fatal consequences. Again, we were given ample time to practice on each other during the week before the performance test at the end of the week.

The third week was primarily firearms training. There was a lot of classroom instruction on the legal and illegal use of a firearm. The main weapons used by the department at the time were the .38 caliber revolver and the 12-gauge pump shotgun. We were to be trained further at our own institutions with the Ruger mini 14 high-powered rifle. During the classroom portion of our training, the point was really emphasized on the fact that the Department of Corrections was protected by the "fleeing felon act." Authority was given to a Correctional Officer to use any force necessary (including deadly force) on any inmate attempting to escape custody because any inmate escaping custody of a state correctional facility was a convicted felon in the act of committing another felony, the escape.

The Department of Corrections is charged with protecting the citizens of the state of Georgia from crimes being perpetrated on them. The Instruction was on the gravity of what we had to do. We may have to take the life of another human being even if that person were running away from us. The point was really stressed that no officer is ever to shoot to kill. We are to shoot to stop the person from escaping, even if that included their death. The job I accepted just became surreal. I was saved by Christ many years before and had to ask myself if I could really take a human life. It made me reexamine the job. I justified it away by telling myself that it was no different than a soldier taking a life during war. I knew this was an issue I would have to revisit at a later date. For now, I would just continue the training.

After two days of classroom instruction, we were taken to the firing range of a local institution. We lined up in formation at the firing line and talked through the steps of the firing procedures. This process was called "dry fire," because there was no ammunition in the chamber of the weapon. We repeated these processes several times until the instructors were satisfied that we understood all of the safety procedures very well. Only then were we allowed to go through a live fire course. The first live fire round was for practice only and to allow us to become familiar with handling a loaded weapon. Next we fired three courses of fire and the average of those rounds would be our qualifying score. This was the performance test.

Maybe it was because so much information had been given so fast, but the three-week school had gone by very fast. In those days there wasn't much pomp and ceremony so our graduation day was a matter of passing out certificates in the lobby of the building that was leased. Then we were allowed to go home early on a Friday afternoon. I was quiet on the ride home with many new things to think about. The videos of the riots we saw in the first week were still fresh in my mind. I did not discuss the details of the riot with Deedee or my parents because I didn't want them to worry. But, the images still lay fresh on my mind. I learned so many new things since August 15th, when I was hired. Being left alone in the middle of the dining hall on my first day, visiting H-house and seeing the death row unit and experiencing the coldness there made me realize the gravity of the job I faced.

When we arrived back at the institution to turn in our vehicle and weapons we had checked out for the class, we were informed that our orders with our shift assignments were waiting for us in the control room. I opened my envelope in the parking lot. The lieutenants from the second shift wanted me to apply for the second shift, the shift I trained on prior to going to school. I neglected to make that request and my orders were a posting on the third shift; midnight shift from 10 pm to 6 am. I wouldn't be seeing much of the inmates. They would already be in their racks by the time I got to work each night. I was definitely starting off my career on the bottom of the totem pole. There would be hardly any action on that shift. From what I was told, it was more like a night security job. It was a Friday afternoon; I was given the weekend off and ordered to report for duty Sunday night at 9:45 pm. I arrived at 9:30 am that Sunday evening so I could check out my surroundings and the staff. While working the second shift prior to going to school, I'd met some of the staff as they relieved us at 10 pm. I mostly spoke to them on the way out of the institution. Now I would be working with them side by side.

The institution looked quite different as I drove up that evening. With everything brightly lit up, it really took on the appearance of a forbidden fortress or castle. The parking lot was really bare because there was no administrative staff or civilian staff on duty at night. I knew I was early, but I expected to see more uniforms around. As I approached the entrance, I heard the gate buzz. The officer in the tower could see me, but I couldn't see him because of the bright light shining down. It could have been the scene out of any prison movie. The long dark tunnel seemed especially eerie tonight. Pulling the huge Iron Gate behind me and the slam that followed always gave me a chill. My first thought was of the films I viewed at school. I wondered how many times those deceased officers who were taken hostage had so routinely walked though their entrances not knowing that on that fateful day, they would never walk out again. It was a reality check that I needed to acknowledge because it could happen to me at any time.

The administration area was a little more lighted, but very quiet. As I approached the officer's classroom, I could hear the low mumble of voices. There were other officers already here. As I walked through the Officer's barbershop, I noted an officer sitting in the barber's chair. He wasn't getting a haircut; he was just relaxing in the chair. There were other officers sitting in other chairs around the wall. It looked like the scene from any local barbershop minus the barber. The one sitting in the barber chair seemed to be leading the conversation. As I walked by, he acknowledged my presence with a nod, but never stopped talking. The men sitting around talking were much older than me. I knew from talking with the officers on the second shift that a lot of these men were retired from the military. They looked like a group of night watchmen waiting to punch the clock. I was the outsider here. They weren't rude to me, but they weren't overly friendly either.

I walked into the classroom and looked at the officer's bulletin board. I'd been informed early on that it was my responsibility to keep up with any information that was posted there. I saw nothing new, so I took a chair and contemplated what the shift would be like. I was lost in my thoughts when they entered the classroom and that signaled the supervisor was approaching. The night shift was minus a Captain because the last one had retired and had not been replaced yet. That's when he walked in. Lieutenant Jack Gosse was the senior lieutenant. He was short, with stocky forearms and his uniform was very neatly pressed. He had big silver bars on his collar. Larger than what other lieutenants wore. He was in his late fifties with a short flattop hair cut. One look was all I needed to guess that he was retired military. He had a clipboard in his hand and proceeded directly to the podium at the front of the classroom. All the other officers took their seats. I wasn't the only new officer he had so he took a minute to introduce himself and he introduced us to the group as well. Then he went right to work assigning duties for the shift. I liked him immediately.

I was assigned to dorm 3. It was one of the largest of the three dormitories in the Diagnostic Center. The control rooms for dorms two and three were side by side so I would not be alone. I had never worked a dorm so I felt a little relieved that there would be a veteran officer in the control room with me. Things were much less formal on the night shift. Lieutenant Gosse didn't conduct an inspection before he dismissed us. I followed the officers out of the classroom and toward Control 1. I stood in line as each officer dropped his "key chit" into the metal drawer and retrieved the "key chit" of the officer we were to relieve.

The institution was very dimly lit and there were dark corners to consider .My partner and I arrived at dorms 2 and 3, respectively. There was no talking allowed by inmates during a count. That offense would earn them a trip to the isolation unit and they all knew it. Multiple officers helped with the count because the inmates were counted according to race. In those days, there were no African-Americans, Latinos or Caucasians. One was either black or white. Once count was clear, my partner and I surrendered our key chits for the keys belonging to the dorm.

The dorms easily housed over one hundred inmates in sets of bunk beds all through the unit. After the briefing from the second shift officers, the lights were turned down and that was it. There was some minor paper work, but the majority of the night was a battle to stay awake. After all the training with firearms and defensive tactics, I was now a night watchman. The senior officer with me in the control room adjusted his chair so he could see out into the dorm and propped his legs up on the workbench attached to the wall. I could tell that this was probably a regular assignment for him. I was just trying to adjust to the routine and plan my next move.

The night shift became a hassle because of the drive I made. It wasn't a bad drive during the day, but driving home in the early hours of the morning and fighting sleep became a problem. Deedee and I talked about it and decided that moving to the city of Jackson was a wise decision. It would cut my drive time in half. Deedee was really excited at the prospect of moving our little family to a new town to be on our own. Her father wasn't thrilled with the idea. He was overly protective, but I knew why and I understood. He had nearly lost her to leukemia.

I was on a rotating work schedule. I always had the same hours, 10pm to 6 am, but my off days changed. I worked six days on and three days off. So on my off days, Deedee and I started looking for an apartment in nearby Jackson. We soon found a duplex house just outside of Jackson and on the same road that led to the institution. It was a perfect start. It really wasn't that far from Forsyth, but Deedee and I had never lived too far from our parents. But, it felt really good to move out on our own and begin our life together. We were excited at the adventure. We were barley settled into our new home and Deedee was blessed with a job at a local dollar store. With me working nights and Deedee working days, it wasn't possible for me to keep the girls while she was working. Money was tight, but we did manage to find a young woman to watch the girls during the day. Things were coming together nicely for us. The drive to and from the institution was much easier to make and I didn't dread the drive home so much.

One morning as I was on my way out of the institution, I saw Officer Ramirez in the corridor. He congratulated me on completing the school and asked me if I ever stopped by to see the karate instructor he told me about. I told him I had not because of all the changes my family and I were making. I almost blew him off, but instead I asked him what days the class was held. He told me Tuesday and Thursday nights and I made him a promise that I would check it out and let him know what I thought. The truth was, now that I had a career with a future, I had been giving some thought to training again. I thought about it and on the drive home and decided that maybe this was my sign to begin again. The thought stayed with me at home. Deedee was always asleep when I arrived, so I tried to get undressed as quietly as I could so I wouldn't disturb her or the girls. It wasn't going to happen this morning. I heard a noise coming from the girls' room. I tried to ignore it at first, but then I heard a whimper. One of my daughters had spotted me through the open door. I turned on the hall light so as not to wake the other sleeping beauty. I stuck my head in the doorway and there was Tracey standing in her bed and smiling very broadly at me. She started to jump up and down so I reached over and took her in my arms.

It satisfied her. I had so little time with them; I couldn't resist taking her to our bedroom with me. Apparently she woke her mother up earlier and in an attempt to keep her asleep, she gave her a bottle. Obviously, it didn't work. I reached over and picked up the bottle and brought it with me. I was thinking maybe in our bed, she would take the bottle and go back to sleep. We lay down together and she took the bottle from my hand and I heard the noise of air escaping as she sucked on the nipple. I kissed her cheek and closed my eyes. Deedee never moved. I started to think about visiting the National Guard armory on the coming Tuesday so I could check out the karate class. I was getting a warm feeling inside thinking about the possibility of training again and if things worked out right, maybe even teaching again. Teaching martial arts was my passion and I was very good at it. I smiled as I closed my eyes and stated to fall asleep. It wasn't going to happen. I felt a "whack" across my forehead and as I opened my eyes, I saw a beautiful little round face with a large grin staring at me. Tracey decided that whopping me in the face was very funny to her. I tried my best to look stern and tell her, "Be still, Daddy has to sleep."

I placed the bottle against her lips and lay her back down. I waited for just a second to see if she was going to comply and be still and hopefully drift back to sleep. I lay down and waited to hear the noise from the bottle again. Once the rhythm of the air started, I closed my eyes. Just as I started to think about the karate class again, "whack" across my head. I didn't even bother to lift my head; I just looked over at the beautiful face smiling at me. No way could I be mad at that. I lay her down and tickled her for a second and listened to her giggle. It was a moment in my life that was forever burned into my memory.

Eventually Tracey and I made enough noise and movement that we woke Deedee. Her instinct told her what to do. She smiled, picked up Tracey and said, "Kiss Daddy good night." Then they were off to check on Leighanne and she closed the door behind her. I was left with my thoughts about the coming Tuesday. I wanted to train again especially now that I was working in a place where my physical abilities might be needed. I smiled and fell into sleep.

The following Tuesday was during my scheduled three days off. I talked with Deedee about it and she said she would ask one of her employees at the dollar store about the location of the armory. Even though Jackson was a small town, we still didn't know much about it. The town was laid out much like Forsyth and many other small southern towns. There was a town square with the courthouse right in the middle of the square. Even so, I was only familiar with the road to the prison and the way to Forsyth. It turned out that Deedee's job at the dollar store was on the road to Forsyth. Even more coincidental, Deedee learned that the National Guard armory was on a road right across from her store.

We made the drive together to find the armory so we would be prepared for the trip on Tuesday. All small town armories look the same. This one was located next to the High School. Now I had the location, it was just the wait. I had no one to ask about the class itself so I had no idea what style of martial arts was being taught. Not that it mattered, in my few years as a student, I was exposed to three different styles; Japanese karate, aikido finally received my black belt in taekwondo. It was always exciting to train with someone from another style. I thought about my old friend Charles and the trips we made through the mountains in the summer of 1976. We passed by several martial arts schools that year and stopped at them all to introduce ourselves and talk about the style we studied. It was a pleasant memory and I have to admit, I missed my friend.

I pulled my uniform out of the closet along with my black belt. It was a while since I wore my uniform to an actual class. While at school in Athens, I had happened upon a group of U.G.A. students training in one of the gyms. During the second week, I brought my uniform back and participated in some training with them, but no real class. Even then I did not wear my belt. Now that I was visiting a school, I wanted to make a good impression and look my best. I pulled out the ironing board and pressed it neatly.

On Tuesday evening, I arrived a little early. I didn't like to be late for anything and especially this evening. I wanted to arrive 30 minutes early. I was nervous on the drive over. In the back of my mind was always the thought of what people would think of me. I hated my lack of confidence. I was always second-guessing myself. But, I was going to suck it up tonight so that I could begin training. I was just hoping that this guy would recognize my black belt. Some styles would not recognize the rank of others. I could only hope that he would be as lenient as the instructor in Macon had been in 1979 when I switched from Japanese karate to Korean taekwondo. He allowed me to keep my green belt from the Japanese style I studied.

As we drove in the driveway of the armory, I could already see someone standing outside the door in a white karate uniform. I felt the butterflies in my stomach already. I just loved the martial arts. It was a passion that never seemed to waver in any way. I was excited and as we got closer, I saw the figure leaning up against the guardrail outside the door. He wasn't wearing a colored belt; in fact, he wasn't wearing a belt at all. That was the same tradition that we followed at the school in Forsyth when I was a teenager in high school. That particular style didn't allow one to don the belt until entering the dojo to train. I smiled and immediately thought of my friend Charles and our years before the army.

As I got closer I noticed the posture of the person in the uniform. There was something familiar there. I saw the dark hair and then it all came clear as I parked in front of the armory. There stood my best friend from my past, almost exactly as I remembered him. I said to Deedee, "That's Charles Johnson." The past glory days of our youth and the summer motorcycle rides through the mountains flashed through my mind. There was my brother who had abandoned me in my hour of need at Fort Jackson four years before. But, none of that mattered to me now. I felt a sudden rush of adrenaline. I realized then how much I had missed him. His eyes finally caught mine and it was as if he saw a ghost from his past. In a sense, I suppose he had. The eyebrows raised and he stood up straight from the guardrail. None of what we had been through in the past mattered at that moment. I found my brother again.

It was ironic that we would meet again at a martial arts class. He shared the same passion for the arts that I did and we had a dreamed once of having a school together. All that disappeared after our failed army venture. I made my step into the law enforcement arena and now I was here. My heart wanted to believe that maybe this was a second chance at a forgotten dream I shared with my best friend. Whatever the future held, I prayed that it would be with us together as friends. I got out of the car as quickly as I could and walked up to him and we embraced each other. I held my friend close, but only for a moment because I was afraid that if it lasted any longer, I would be in tears.

We talked for a while and informed each other of our lives over the past 4 years. He was married again and she was here with him tonight. He was a sergeant with a security company at an industrial sight. It wasn't the law enforcement jobs either of us had hoped for, but it was a step in the right direction. I filled him in on my job at the prison and told him I finally earned my black belt and a bit about my failed school in Forsyth. Deedee took the opportunity to brag on her husband and said, "Charles, he is getting so fast." Charles smiled and asked, "Did you bring a Gi?" I replied, "I came to work out." He showed me the men's room and started his class.

I was nervous as I dressed, but excited. I could hear him calling out techniques and it was as familiar as if we were back at the Budo Kai School in Forsyth. I smiled as I remembered our time there together. After I tied my black belt on, I checked myself in the mirror and stepped out onto the floor. When Charles saw me, he stopped the class, called them to attention in Japanese and said, "Turn and bow to Sensei Allen. " It was an incredible honor because I was the visitor here. It is common not to take your eyes off of those in front of you as you bow, but I bowed very low with my eyes to the ground to show my respect, then I observed the rest of the class as he taught. After the class was over Charles introduced me to his wife Sarah, her cousin, Rita and her husband Tony, who was part of the class. We all agreed to meet on another day and catch up. The important thing for me is that I was in touch with my friend again. On the drive home I reminisced of summer motorcycle rides. I missed that and I missed having a best friend. I had hopes of what could come from this meeting. I thought that we could make our plan come together of having a school together.

There was no challenge to the night shift at work. It became boring really fast. I was moved around to different post. The worst assignment was duty in a gun tower. There was nothing but an empty recreational yard to stare into. The towers were equipped with two firearms; a 12 gauge pump shot gun, For close encounters and a high powered rifle with a scope for anything at a distance. Officers assigned to tower duty, were responsible for security around the perimeter of the institution. That included outside as well as inside the fence line. But, our main objective was to prevent escapes. The fence line consisted of two rows of chain length fence around the main building and the recreational yards. In between the fence was an area that resembled a high school track. That was called "no man's" land. Outside the outer fence was an armed officer on patrol in a vehicle. He patrolled the outer campus and the fence line. I know that all the old prison movies sometimes showed someone escaping over the fence, but I couldn't imagine anyone being desperate enough to attempt scaling the fence to gain freedom. It would be suicide and I believe that all these inmates knew it. Even if they didn't know exactly what firearms we had, they were aware that there was significant firepower here.

At the first sign of an escape attempt, the patrol officer would be radioed and would come to that area. There would be no warning shots because as were taught, what goes up must come down. Any officer shooting a warning shot would be responsible for wherever it landed. There would, however, be continuous verbal commands to stop. Once the escapee was on the ground outside the outer fence, we were required to "shoot to stop." That would include any force up to and including deadly force. Besides the tower duty, I was moved from dorm, to cell house to utility duty, which meant helping out other areas of the institution. On midnight shift, that usually meant helping during the 3 am count. It was a master count that included every area. It was also the second time I was allowed to go back to H-house. Death row took on an even more sinister look in the early hours of the morning. My turn as a utility officer finally came early one morning.

I was one of three officers walking through the institution taking count. One by one we went through each cell house walking from cell to cell checking each very carefully with a flashlight. Every now and again we would hear a low grumble under the covers, but they all knew not to say anything because disrupting count was a serious offense. Finally we made it back to my old stomping ground on the second shift, F- house.

Everything seemed different. Our approach to the cross gate at H-house seemed as an entrance to a haunted house exhibit at a theme park. The lights were dim and I could hear our footsteps as we walked closer to the gate. The officer in F-house was waiting and almost on cue, he unlocked the gate allowing us to enter without having to stop. There was no other sound but the sliding of the gate. My heart began to beat faster just as it had done before when I was sent here. The further down the corridor we went, the more sinister it felt. The cross gate was open at H-house when we arrived at the end of the corridor.

This time, they provided the batons before we entered the unit. H-3 was the first unit to be counted and was different from the H-2 unit I had visited before. The black iron bar was removed from the red door and then a slot opened on the door of the officer's control room. A single key was passed to the corridor officer. He placed the key in the lock of the red unit door and opened it and the three of us proceeded inside. We walked down passed a row of chain length fence to the first of two electronically controlled gates. Apparently the officer in the control room knew when we reached the gate because by the time we walked up to it, the door popped open. We stepped inside the "sally port" and an officer closed the door manually. Once the door was secured, the second gate popped open allowing us entry to the unit.

Inside there were two tiers, upper and lower. We started at the bottom and walked the row of cells together. As we were careful to make sure we saw a living, breathing body in every cell. As two of us counted, the third used his baton to check each row of bars to make sure that none were loosened. This was a result of the escape at the Georgia State Prison in July. After we checked each cell carefully and counted each face inside, we went upstairs to repeat the process. Even with the knowledge that each cell was shut and locked, there was the thought in my mind that at any moment, if the system failed, the doors could open and out would come fifty inmates with a death sentence and the three of us would be outnumbered and at their mercy.

It concerned me enough that I look constantly over my shoulder as we walked by each cell. We repeated the procedure in three other units. By the end of the fourth unit, one officer looked at the baton in my hand smiled and said, "Allen, you'd better loosen your grip a bit before you lose circulation in that hand." I hadn't noticed that as I walked through each unit, my grip became a little tighter. We left H-corridor walking toward F-house and as I heard the bell ring to let us through the gate, I couldn't help but look back. The rush I felt was not fear, but adrenaline from excitement. Being in this place put my mind and my body at a heightened sense of awareness. I liked the feeling and it made me even more determined to work on the unit full time.

Charles worked the midnight sift just as I did. It allowed us to spend some time together during the day. We often visited a martial arts supply store in Atlanta. In time, he invited me to be his partner in teaching his classes. It felt so right. I had a career I wanted, my wife and children in a little rented home of our own and I was teaching martial arts again. On the weekends, we would get together with Charles, his wife, her cousin and her husband and hang out at each other's homes. Life was good and I was excited about the way things were going. Our friendship was rekindled and we had some new friends as well. Sarah's cousin, Rita, was pregnant and about to give birth, but I wasn't sure what Charles and Sarah had planned for a family. They never talked about it and I didn't ask. We all became closer friends as the weeks went by.

The class at the armory belonged to Charles, though he had asked me to come in and teach with him. He was the lead instructor and I assisted him. Usually I had the task of taking the class through warm up and stretching exercises which usually lasted about thirty minutes. Once I felt they were ready, Charles would take over and teach the class. I would walk around and observe the class and if I saw someone performing a technique improperly, I would correct them and then continue to observe. I was constantly moving. I had become accustomed to people watching me especially as I demonstrated to a student the proper way to perform a technique.

Tonight I felt something different. Someone was watching me, but it wasn't from the class. Charles was calling commands from the front of the class. I saw a student who needed help and I stopped to assist. Once I was satisfied that the technique was being performed correctly, I started to walk again. As I lifted my head, I saw her looking at me from the side of the class off the main floor. Sarah was watching me very intently. I smiled and continued

to walk, but her smile seemed to have purpose. On my second round around the floor, I noticed she was still looking. She smiled again, but this time she winked slightly at me and my heart sank. Was my best friend's wife flirting with me? I dismissed it as her being overly friendly, but over the next few weeks, I could see a difference in her. The advances became stronger and she wasn't being shy about it. We all gathered at Rita and Tony's house one evening and as I was sitting in a chair, she actually sat down on the floor, took my shoes off and began massaging my feet in front of Deedee and Charles. Deedee looked over at us very strangely, but Charles simply shrugged it off as a crazy thing his wife would do. I wasn't sure what to make of it, but I liked the attention.

Sarah worked at a local bank in town. She had asked me to stop by and say hello if I were ever in town during the day. I avoided it at first, but soon found myself making an excuse to stop by the bank. This particular day, she came out from around the counter and invited me to sit down. She faced me as we sat and I could see her grab her dress and pull it well over her knees as she crossed her legs. We made idle talk for a few minutes and then finally she looked deep in my eyes and said, "You're pretty, Bobby." I know I probably turned pink from embarrassment and I had no idea what to say. I did my best to let it pass by and she didn't pursue it.

I became very uncomfortable during class at the armory. At first, she would only stay around for the beginning of the class and then return later when class was over. Now she was staying for the entire class. I found myself thinking about her at work after my rounds were complete, all my paperwork was done and there was nothing left to do but think. I knew I was headed on bad journey and I felt incredibly guilty. The worst part of it all was that Deedee and Charles trusted the both of us completely. The day came when Charles said that Sarah was going to a nearby town to pick up some packages and asked him if it would be all right if she asked me to come along to help her. I checked with Deedee first to see if she minded and of course, she didn't. Neither of them suspected anything. So I went to Charles and Sarah's house one morning to ride with her to pick up her packages. We took her car, but she asked me to drive. It didn't take long before she had her arm on my back and twirling her fingers through my hair.

I was excited, frightened and ashamed all at the same time. She didn't need any help with packages; it was just to provide a way for us to be alone together. I knew I had no business being here alone with her today and I could have stopped it at any time, but I didn't. Eventually we arrived back at her house and she invited me in. Knowing that I shouldn't be here was not enough to stop me. She stood in the doorway with the door open. It's been the same story since the Garden of Eden, the serpent using Eve to tempt man into sin and Adam following the lust of the flesh and then blaming Eve for enticing him in the first place. It was the blame game with each participant pointing the finger at the other.

My mind flashed back to the year I was baptized as I stood frozen at the pew when the preacher made the alter call. He had said, *"If you will make the first step, God will make the rest."* Here I stood again afraid to make the first step. All I could see were the faces of Charles, Deedee and my girls. It was wrong for me to be here and it wasn't fair to Sarah either that I had accepted her invitation to go along with her. If I had said no, that may very well have been the end of it. Instead, I made the first step as I did all those years ago in church. This time, I had help from a different source. I made the first step and Satan took

all the rest. It was the Garden of Eden all over again. The serpent shows the pleasures of the flesh and then backing away to leave the man and the woman left all alone. It was the same scenario that has played down through the centuries; and so, I walked in to the house and cheated on my wife and my best friend, with his wife.

The following weeks were torture. Everything was different. Deedee and I argued constantly and Charles and Sarah fought. The worst part of it was that Charles was confiding in me about the trouble he was having at home. I wanted to find a hole to crawl in and disappear because I created this mess. My life was unraveling before my eyes and spinning out of control and I couldn't seem to stop it. Finally it all came to a head one night at our house. Deedee and I simply had to have some relief. I don't remember whose idea it was for her to leave, but she got the girls out of bed. Leighanne was sound asleep and Debbie put her in the car seat. Next she came for Tracey and took her from me. As she walked out the door, she stopped with her back to me and whispered in Tracey's ear. That beautiful little girl lifted her head off of her mother's shoulder and looked into my eyes and waved good-bye with her little fingers.

For the sake of one foolish, selfish moment of fleeting pleasure, I destroyed six lives. Not to mention Deedee's family, my family, Sarah's family and Charles' family. The fallout from all of this was going to be terrible for all of us and I blamed myself for it all. I had no idea how I was ever going to look Charles in the eyes again. As far as I knew, he didn't know why his world was collapsing around him. I looked up to attempt a prayer only to find I was too ashamed to talk to my God. I didn't see any scenario where He would want to hear from me. I thought about Debbie driving off with the girls in the back seat and neither of them having a clue of what was happening or how I was destroying the family God created. It was as if I had touched a lever on some piece of machinery and the wheels in the cog started moving and there was no way I could stop them.

I thought about Deedee and all she had been through in her life. She survived a death sentence that was leukemia. We found each other and she saw me as her prince charming and she put her trust and hopes in me for a future. She wanted to make a home with me. I was almost numb with the grief that I felt as that moment. Part of me wanted to run out into the night shouting for her to return with the girls. I saw the headlights from the car start down the road and then looked around at the empty house and how big it seemed now. As always, my love for music always found its place in my mind. It was as much a curse as it was a gift that I could recall lyrics to almost any song I ever heard. They seemed to fit themselves to the situations in my life, just like a movie playing at the theater. Now I saw Deedee's face as the words of "The winner takes it all," by Abba flashed through my mind.

The song of a grieving woman facing the man she loved and knowing their life together has ended. I imagined Deedee saying the words of that song to me. I heard that song before and thought that the lyrics were so sad. I remember thinking to myself, "How could anyone treat someone they loved like that?" Now here was I playing out the lyrics in my life. I walked inside the house and closed the door. I listened for anything that would take my mind away from here, but found only silence. I tried desperately to find a prayer, but found nothing but shame. I crumpled to the floor and put my face in my hands and cried.

Chapter 6

"And God shall wipe away all tears from their eyes; and there shall be no more death, neither sorrow nor crying, neither shall there be any more pain: for the former things have passed away."

- Revelation 21:4
(King James Version)

Work was the only place I didn't feel out of place anymore. My coworkers weren't aware of my personal life and I kept it that way. My parents accepted me because I was their child, but they certainly did not approve of what I had done. Deedee and I divorced and she moved back in with her parents and I moved back in with mine. Charles and Sarah divorced and I heard that he moved back to Columbus, Georgia where he was born. We had made a trip over there a few times as teenagers on our motorcycles, but I never really got to know any of his family.

Sarah and I eventually ended up together and I moved back to Jackson to be closer to work. The truth was that I was so ashamed of myself that I didn't want to be around my parents and be a reminder of how I failed them. My father reminded me that Charles was been my best friend. Everything he said was the truth and it burned into me. I wanted to focus on my career to see if I could redeem myself there.

I continued on the night shift, but I also submitted a letter to be transferred to the day shift. I needed a fresh start. The nights I was on tower duty was pure torture because I had so much time to think. The images of the lives I had destroyed rolled over and over in my mind. Even the nights that I was assigned to Cellhouse duty weren't much help. The paperwork could be done in an hour and then I walked the ranges with a flashlight in my hand and stare out the windows into the darkness. Everything haunted me and I couldn't take the silence anymore. I decided I was going to look for other employment. I had to get off of the night shift.

As human beings we have free will and are given the chance to make choices in our lives. I do believe that. I also learned through the years that God has a plan for our lives and if He has a path planned for us it will materialize no matter how much we try to sabotage it. He has proven it to me time and again. I believe that happened to me and as always, God showed up on time.

I sat down in the classroom and waited for the shift briefing. The Lieutenant walked in and started his announcements. As usual, before he gave out shift assignments he passed out mail to officers. It was usually no more than copies of leave slips. I certainly never got any mail from anyone. Then I heard my name and the Lieutenant held up an envelope. I retrieved it, sat down at my seat and ripped it open. It was from the Deputy Warden of Security; announcing shift reassignments. Some new officers returned from school and changes needed to be made to make room on the night shift for them. My heart started beating faster when I saw my name listed on the letter transferring me to the day shift. My new hours would be 6 am to 2pm. I must have been smiling all the way down the corridor because someone asked me, "What's up with you, Allen?" I smiled and held up my letter, "Good news!" My assignment was F-house and I breezed through the count so I could get the second shift officer out of the Cellhouse. I finished the paperwork quickly, sat down at the officer's desk and propped my feet up. I pulled out my letter and read it again. I smiled as I let it sink in that I was getting off of the night shift.

I had an overwhelming feeling that I was exactly where I was supposed to be. Even with the disastrous decisions I made in the last few months regarding my personal life, I still believed that God had a purpose for my life. It included me being at this job. Now I just needed to atone for the tragic things I had done. I had the desire to make my parents proud of me. Perhaps, even more so after I let them down, my father in particular and the way I hurt him with my adulterous ways. The hardest part of this all was that in his mind, he always considered me the one that never gave him any trouble. I meant to make that up to him anyway I could. Of course, Sarah was thrilled that I was going to be home nights. We were living together and both knew it was wrong because we professed to be Christians. She wanted to be married while in my mind, I still had a tie with Deedee and the Girls. Though we were no longer married, she was the mother of my children. It was a mixture of guilt, shame and conviction in my heart that I had done a terrible thing by leaving my family. Now, here was Sarah wanting to start a family with me. In an attempt to make things right with God, we decided to get married.

Sarah knew a preacher that worked at the funeral home in Jackson. In what was probably a sign of things to come, we married in the chapel of his funeral home. I wondered if this was symbolic of what we were doing in our lives. We were home wreckers and I felt the burden on my shoulders. As a Christian man, it was my responsibility to say "no." That's all it would have taken. Sarah was not a bad person and she came from a very good Christian family. Apparently, she was as lost at the time as I was and we both reached out in a way that human beings do when something is missing. But, having to learn through trial and error that it is really God we both needed. Now the only thing left to do in our young minds was attempt to make it right by getting married and ask for forgiveness. I know I was too ashamed of my actions to approach God and ask him to bless a marriage that began with adultery. For me it was a silent prayer said out of shame and then swept it under the rug as if it could be forgotten.

I turned my attention to my career. It had been several months since I worked during the day and it felt strange. My duties began much the same way as when I first got hired. The first week I was assigned as a utility officer and that meant duty in the dining hall watching inmates come and go. The day shift officers worked breakfast and lunch. It was no one's favorite duty, but it did give me a chance to roam about the prison. My very first day, after morning dining hall duty, I was called to H-house to escort an inmate to the counseling area. Once I cleared the cross gate I was handed a baton and then told to wait in the corridor next to the H-3 unit. An officer finally opened the control room door and handed out an inmate uniform. The officer in charge of the corridor took the clothes and began to search them very carefully under the watchful eye of the sergeant. Once he was certain that there was no contraband in them anywhere, the H-3 officer passed out a key though the slot in the door. The iron bar across the door was removed and the door opened just long enough for the inmate to exit, then quickly closed and the bar placed over the door.

Standing before me was Joseph Mulligan in only his boxers and his socks. He was instructed to remove his socks and they were carefully searched as well. Next he lowered lower his boxers and turned 360 degrees. Once they were assured that he had nothing on him, he was allowed to get dressed. It was the procedure followed anytime and inmate under the death sentence came out of any of the four units to be escorted through the institution. As Mulligan dressed, the sergeant said, "He is never to leave your sight, where he goes, you go." I replied, "Yes, sir."

Once he was dressed he stood at the gate and never acknowledged my presence. He was like a robot programmed for this routine. The corridor officer removed a set of keys from his belt and opened the cross gate. Mulligan walked through and I followed behind him as I had been instructed to escort during school. The officer rang the bell to signal to F-house that we were coming through. I slid the baton in my baton ring on my belt an allowed it to hang at my left side. If I needed it, I would have to cross draw with my right hand. Mulligan was on the right side next to the wall, as all inmates were required to do when they moved through the institution. This kept the baton out of his reach because I walked to his left side and slightly to the rear at an angle.

Once we cleared the F-house cross gate, I relaxed a bit. He was following his routine and paid no mind to me. When we reached the control two gates, he finally looked over at me and asked, "What time you think we will be back on the block?" I had no clue because I didn't even know why we were going to the counseling section. I sensed that he wouldn't settle for an answer like that so I replied, "It shouldn't take too long." He studied my eyes for a second and that was when I took my first real look at him. Just as other inmates I saw from H-house, the eyes were cold and dead. I wondered if it was a trait that all murderers shared. The answer seemed to satisfy him and he nodded as if in agreement with me. Then he turned is head forward and waited for the gate to open. I thought about what I saw in his eyes. More to the point, what I *didn't* see. I hadn't been around a lot of these men, but the ones I made eye contact with seemed to have no life in their eyes. I wondered if that was what was required in a person to be able to take another life. Perhaps, in that respect something was already dead inside them. I didn't know anything about demon possession other than the movies I watched, but I could see that as a possibility.

As he walked beside me his expression was almost lifeless. Most of these men didn't look very intimidating based on stature. I remembered Isaacs from H–2 and the horrendous things he did and he was a very small man. Mulligan was not quite as tall as me and not very muscular. He was an African American, but he had straight hair and slicked straight back. He could almost pass for an American Indian. There was nothing remarkable about him.

But, put a gun in someone's hand and all that changes. It was hard to imagine what kind of rage must live inside a person that could cause them to kill so indiscriminately. Maybe there was no way to understand how a person could get to that point in their life. In the next few moments I was given an insight into the mind of a cold-blooded killer.

There is always an officer stationed at the counseling section to keep control of the inmates that are assembled and waiting. He expected us and pointed to the room where we were to wait. It looked like a classroom from any school. There were desks lined up and a teacher's desk in front. There was a civilian there and I assumed he was the counselor. However, there was a desk set to the side apart from the rest of the class. Mulligan and I both knew that was for him and he went right to it. There was no one else in the classroom except the three of us. Since Mulligan went directly to the desk, there was no need for him to speak. I positioned myself far enough away so that I wouldn't be standing over his shoulder, but close enough that I could react in case something happened. It was deathly quiet for a while and I could see Mulligan looking at the counselor. I could tell he resented being here and probably came just to get out of H-house for a while. It appeared he was sizing up the counselor looking for an opening from which he could attack and found one.

He asked a question about crime and punishment in America. I don't remember what the counselor answered, but I could tell from the look on Mulligan' face that no answer he gave was going to be correct so a debate ensued and it was a battle from that point. There was nothing I could say because Mulligan was not being threatening in any way. He was accomplishing his goal of irritating the counselor, though I have to admit, that the counselor stood his ground and never showed any anger at all. Finally the story came that allowed me to see into the mind of a criminal. Mulligan told the counselor that he (The counselor) could never understand crime and punishment or how unjust the system was because he didn't have any firsthand experience. The counselor told him that he was wrong. He went on to tell the story of how he and his wife had been the victim of a crime. Their car was stolen while they were out shopping. Mulligan wasn't going to allow him to take a stand. Mulligan interrupted, "That young man probably needed your car for something." I snapped my head over to look at him. The counselor asked, "But, how is that fair to me?" Mulligan was ready. "He may have needed your car for an emergency and just didn't have time to ask." I shook my head though he couldn't see me. His sights were on nailing this counselor.

"At the very least he caused my wife and I mental anguish over what he did." Mulligan didn't know what to say. He crossed his arms and looked away as though the counselor was no longer worth is time. So there it was. I had just stepped into the mind of a convicted murderer whose every thought was of his need and whatever it took to get it should be acceptable to anyone. I wondered if this was the thinking process of all of these men in H-house. In fact, maybe it was insight into what every man locked up in this facility might be thinking. I wondered if this is what mankind came to or had it been this way for a very long time? Maybe I was just beginning to see the world in a light to which I wasn't accustomed. I decided that Satan is alive and well on planet earth.

Mulligan remained quiet as the diagnostic inmates entered the room and took seats. He continued to eye the counselor. The counselor passed out some sort of test. Listening to him give instructions about the paper, I could tell it was an aptitude test and a simple one at that. Apparently it offended Mulligan because I heard him chuckle under his breath and then he was up headed toward the door. Since this was my first day and had been given instructions to remain with the inmate, I followed. I had no idea if he was required to stay or not. I followed him out the door and down the corridor back to H-house. He didn't speak on the way back and I could tell he was still bothered by the fact that he couldn't defeat the counselor with his argument.

We arrived in H-house and waited at the gate. There was no need to search Mulligan again because he never left my custody. Once we passed the cross gate, the corridor officer pushed the gate closed and Mulligan was allowed to go right into the H-3 unit. It was my first experience escorting an inmate from death row alone. I liked the feeling of having that authority. I returned the baton to the officer and the sergeant thanked me for helping out. As I walked away I was more determined than ever to work in H-house. I liked the feeling of being a part of something this unique.

Over the next few months, I was assigned to various parts of the institution. Though I was one of the youngest officers in the institution, I could tell that I earned the respect of the rest of the staff and the Captain of the shift seemed to really like me. Lieutenant Gosse from the night shift transferred to the day shift as well and I knew he liked me also. In fact, I once overheard him saying to a senior officer that I was levelheaded. I considered it a genuine compliment coming from him.

I worked as a utility officer for a while. Besides escorting and working the dining hall, it also meant working different Cellhouses on the off days of the officers regularly assigned there. That meant they worked that post through their entire six days. On their three days off I worked their post. I finally received a permanent assignment of my own. D-house was one of the smaller cell houses. It looked like half a cell house with 63 cells rather than the usual 126 in a regular Cellhouse. It also housed the intuitional isolation unit. At the time I was assigned there, it housed a lot of older, more mature inmates. Though most of these men were old enough to be my father, I earned their respect. I did so by adhering to the philosophy taught to me by our training officer; "Inmates are in prison as punishment and not for punishment." I observed other senior officers talking to inmates and they seemed to enjoy talking to the inmates in punitive way. It didn't seem the proper way to me. I found it to be often counterproductive. I treated all these inmates as men. If time came that I needed to adopt a tougher stance, I did so. I let them know I was in charge. I treated them firmly, but fairly and they respected me for that. I was always addressed as "Mr. Allen" or "Officer Allen."

I later discovered that some of these inmates were involved in the riots at the Georgia State Prison many years before. They were well-seasoned men. Now they were under my supervision and seemed to have no problems with that. In fact, one inmate once told me, "Mr. Allen, if anything ever happens here, you give us the keys, we will put you in a cell and I promise you no one will hurt you." It was a sign of respect. The isolation cells were a set of four cells used to discipline those inmates that were habitually a problem in general population. They were regular cells with a solid door in front of them that was kept closed and locked to keep the inmate in total isolation with no TV and no contact with other inmates. They never left the cell for any reason except during shower periods. The amount of time they were kept in isolation depended on the seriousness of the rule infraction. It could be

from 7 days, but no more than 30 days at one time. Some inmates said that they could do that time, "Standing on their heads" and maybe they could. But, I do know I saw some behavior changes over time. So therefore it seemed to be an effective tool.

At least once per shift a supervisor had to come by and inspect each isolation cell to view the inmate in the cell. They stopped by my desk to sign the isolation sheet verifying they observed the inmate was alive and in good health. This particular day it was Captain Meriwether, the senior supervisor. I knew the Captain liked me from our discussions. While he was signing the sheet, I decided to make my move. I asked him how an officer was selected to work in H-house. He said, "I select the personnel for that duty." He continued, "Not everyone can work there and the lieutenant assigned to oversee the unit only stays for a year." I put myself forward and said, "I'd like to work back there, Captain." He looked over the top of his glasses at me and I continued," I think it would be interesting and I believe I would be a good addition back there."

I knew that the Captain was aware of my martial arts training because we had talked about it on occasion. He studied me for a few seconds and then smiled, winked at me and said, "I'll see what I can do." I smiled in return and thanked him. He finished signing the sheets and walked away. After he left, I smiled, nodded my head and said silently, "yes!" I knew the Captain to be a man of his word. I felt excited through the rest of the day. My career seemed to be heading in the right direction or at least in the direction I wanted it to go.

The twins were young enough that they really didn't understand what had happened between their Mother and me. I saw them as often as I could with my schedule. Working six days on and three days off made it tough to see them every other weekend and spend real quality time with them. I felt shame and guilt as I looked at Deedee when I picked them up. She was always very nice to me, but I knew in the back of her mind she harbored a tremendous resentment against me and I deserved it.

Sarah and I rented a house in Jackson from an acquaintance of her family. It was a very small house, but it was only the two of us and we didn't require much room. When the girls were with me, they usually slept on pallet on the floor. During that time I started to notice a change in Sarah. She started dropping hints about a child of her own. I just wasn't ready for that. The pain of all that we caused was just too fresh.

I was trying to focus on my job and find some sense of redemption there. The pain I'd caused was too fresh on my mind to consider having a child. The twins were still so young and I removed myself from their lives by a very selfish act. When I didn't agree with her about having a child, I started to hear comments from her. Walking through the house she would say things like, "The one thing I want, I will never have." That was an attempt to make me feel guilty and the one thing I did not need in my life was more guilt. I was still trying to come to terms with what we had done. I tried to assure her that it wasn't that I didn't want to have a child with her; I just needed to get things back to some sense of normalcy.

That didn't seem to matter to her. She felt like she was missing something and she wanted it now. Her attitude started to change toward the children on their weekend visit. It wasn't just a matter of sensing the change; it was the look on her face. She stopped smiling when they came in and was very distant from them and me through the entire weekend. She became overbearing with them when she felt like she had to discipline them. It was like she was waiting for an opportunity to release how she felt and take it out on them.

I started to get them less after that. Rather than be the father I should have been, I yielded to the pressure I was feeling from her. I wasn't going to see them being overly disciplined because she resented them because she didn't have a child of her own. My life at home changed after I realized what was happening. I started to feel the burden of the decision I made when I decided to cheat. In my heart, I felt I deserved what I was getting, but those two precious little girls did not and I wasn't going to see them be punished for my choices. I died a little inside during that time. I couldn't bring myself to pray any real prayer because I felt as though God didn't want to hear from me. I turned my attention again to my job.

It was the summer of 1981 and my first anniversary with the Department of Corrections. I continued to work D-house and it was getting very monotonous. I didn't like that feeling because this was a maximum-security prison and that kind of feeling can be perceived as weakness. Even though these men in this cell house seemed to like me, they were still prisoners. They were men being held against their will and most of them were career criminals. I needed a change.

Shift briefings were becoming monotonous as well. Nothing ever changed. Sit down; listen to the information being shared. Every now and then a piece of intelligence would be gathered from an inmate informant and that would be shared. Sometimes there would be a policy change, which would be posted on the bulletin board and we would be told to take notice of that. The Captain or Lieutenant would ask for questions and then post assignments were announced. Today it was the captain announcing post assignments. He called out each cell house in order from A through F. When he came to D-house I was surprised when my name wasn't called. I sat up in the chair and gave my attention.

H-house personnel were always called out with their particular assignments such as, H-1, H-2, H-3, H-4 and H-corridor. If there were anyone extra assigned, he would be an escort officer. I smiled when I heard my name called out for H-corridor. When the captain was finished he looked at me and gave a little smile as he shuffled his paperwork together. He had been true to his word to see what he could do. I was officially assigned to Georgia's Death Row. The day felt different already.

In the group headed to H-house was my friend from high school, who had also been a student at my failed karate school in Forsyth. It was Dave Harris who suggested that I apply to the prison in the first place; now we were working together. He was employed about a year longer than I. As we were walking down the corridor he said, "welcome aboard" and patted me on the back. I felt invigorated. I wanted this assignment from the first day I worked in F-house and held the key to the cross gate in my hand. Though my personal life was not what I wanted it to be, my career seemed to be on track.

The first order of business when we arrived was to complete the count. It was mandatory everywhere in the institution, but was so important in this place because in the early morning hours a year ago, five death row inmates walked out of Georgia State Prison in Reidsville. We walked through each unit and carefully checked to see a body. Most of the inmates were beginning to wake because they knew that the breakfast trays would be arriving soon. These men never saw the inside of the dining hall in fact, never left H-house except for a trip to the medical section or visitation and then only under escort.

I was working with Dave and I mirrored every move he made. The main duty of the corridor officer was to secure the cross gate. No one could enter or leave unless he opened the door. Dave explained that the most important issue was to make sure that only one red door was opened at any given time and only one inmate in the corridor. It was a security measure designed to maintain control of the unit. The odds were always to be in our favor.

Even if an inmate were to gain control of the keys in the corridor, he still could not get into any of the housing units. But, the other reason for allowing only one inmate at a time in the corridor was because these men had enemies among themselves. Some even tried to kill while living on death row. It was another insight into the mind of convicted murderers. There was no honor here. It was kill or be killed and it required constant surveillance in each unit to maintain security.

Next the food carts arrived with breakfast. There were four mobile carts designed to keep the plastic insulated trays warm on the trip from the kitchen to H-house. They were pushed by diagnostic inmates working in the kitchen and escorted by a member of the kitchen staff. He came along in case there were any complaints from the inmates or the staff concerning trays. Once the carts were pushed through the cross gate, the diagnostic inmates were dismissed. We then took control of the carts and inspected them for contraband. Once that was done, one by one, they were pushed into the housing units. Once the red doors were secured, the inmates inside would push the carts into the unit and pass the trays out to each other.

Even in the units there were enemies housed together and that meant some inmates could not be let out of their cells at the same time. In order to maintain control and allow everyone a chance to come out of their cells, they were divided into three groups. Each group was allowed out of their cells for two hours starting at 6am. The groups would then rotate through the day until 10 pm when the entire institution was placed on lockdown. The following day, the rotation would begin again where it left off.

After the trays were placed back into the carts, the cart was pushed back to the red door. Once the unit was securely locked, the outer red door would open only long enough to retrieve the food cart. Again, only one red door was open at a time. It was the corridor officer's job to ensure that this procedure was followed. It amazed me because these guys had been doing this so long it went like clockwork. Everything was done with precision and mistakes were not tolerated because men could die.

I observed, but also participated in all the procedures through the day. After the food carts left, there was a little down time to wait for the next procedure. At 8 am three more officers appeared. These were additional officers assigned to the H-house for support and they worked a split shift Monday through Friday from 8 am to 4:30 pm. It was a coveted shift. Once they came in and attended their briefing, it was time for yard call. Dave explained each step to me very carefully.

Each unit was allowed outside in the exercise yard two times per week. It was a privilege, not a right and could be taken away for disciplinary infractions. The H-house exercise yard was a unique place. Besides the outside perimeter fence, the yard was divided into two sections with very high chain length fence and topped with razor tipped wire called "concertina wire." The exercise yard was constructed in front of a gun tower and anytime these inmates were on the yard, the armed vehicle patrol officer was parked facing the exercise yard in case any of the inmates attempted escape. In addition, once all inmates were outside, one of the support officers was stationed outside the door observing in case anything happened, he could radio for assistance or contact the tower or vehicle patrol officer.

When "yard call" commenced, all escort officers were present in the corridor. Inmates were required to pass their clothes through the officer's control room and then passed out to the corridor officers. Once the items were thoroughly searched, the inmate was allowed out in the corridor in his boxers, which were lowered and finally allowed to dress. Next, the outside gate was unlocked and opened and the inmate was now in a "sally port" or holding area. Once the outside door was locked, a button was pushed; opening a gate to the yard and the inmate was now outside. The process was repeated in reverse when the inmates returned from the yard. Nothing was left to chance. The procedure was followed to the letter every time an inmate moved from the cell house.

H-house was operated with military precision. If any officer were found deviating from the procedure in any way, he would not be assigned here again. Now I knew what the Captain meant when he said that not everyone could work here. Inmates assigned here probably studied every move every officer made. In fact, they probably knew the policy and procedures as well as the officers. If anything were done different from the procedure, they would take note of it and perceive it as a possible weak link in the security of this unit. These were men with absolutely nothing to lose and would attempt to gain their freedom any way they could. If that meant killing again, they would kill.

Five cells were searched daily. A list was maintained to be sure all cells were searched. Once every cell in the unit had been searched, the list was repeated but in a different order so that the inmates could not keep track of the schedule of when the search would be conducted. The unit to be searched was locked down and the support officers, called the "split shift," entered the unit to commence the search. The search began with each bar of the cell being hit with a large rubber mallet to ensure that none of the bars were loose or cut. The inmate was strip searched before the door was opened. The sergeant stood outside the cell with the inmate and the remaining officers would do a systematic search of every item in the cell. By the time the cell search was completed, it was time to bring the inmates in from yard call. The entire process was completed in reverse with one inmate at a time coming through the door and strip-searched before returning to his unit. Next it was noon chow call and I could hear the food carts rolling down the hall toward H-house. The same procedure as Breakfast was followed. Again, nothing was left to chance and no short cuts were taken. Step by step the search was done on all 4-food carts.

Once the food carts were retrieved from the units, they were inspected again to ensure that no contraband was leaving H-house. I asked what contraband could be leaving the unit. Dave explained to me that we were looking for possible communication with others outside of H-house. It could be an attempt to get a message out for tools or weapons that could be smuggled in the unit. A weapon didn't have to be gun or a knife; it could be anything that could be fashioned into a weapon once it got back here. I learned that I was going to have to think with a different mind-set to work here.

After the food carts left, there was some down time where we could sit and talk out in the corridor. There wasn't much downtime in H-house Monday through Friday. Dave said the weekends would be slower because all that occurred for H-house was visitation. We only sat for a few minutes before the sergeant came walking down the corridor and said,

"Put them out on the yard." It was time for the afternoon yard call for the other side of the corridor. Now I could see the way the procedure was conducted. On the North side of the corridor, was H-1 and H-2. On the south side, the opposite side of the corridor was H-3 and H-4. One side went in the morning and then the opposite side in the afternoon. The schedule was continually rotated seven days a week. We conducted the yard call procedure once again carefully bringing out one inmate at a time until all that wanted to participate were outside. Conducting each procedure, step by step, made the time pass by quickly.

I remembered the small offices along the wall as we entered H-house. I'd seen civilian employees walking in and out of them all day. After the F-house cross gate, there was a doorway and on the right side of the corridor were three offices on the right before we reached the cross gate at H-house. I hadn't asked about them before, so now that we were just waiting for the second shift to relieve us, I asked Dave. The first office belonged to the Lieutenant, the unit manager. The second office belonged to the unit counselor. He was a civilian assigned fulltime to H-house. The third office was a utility office used as a chapel, interview room and also a barbershop. Three sergeants assigned to H-house for each shift. After 4:30 pm, the sergeants used the Lieutenant's office as a command post. He went on to explain that H-house was a specialized unit that was managed separate from the rest of the institution. The officers were assigned here from the shifts managed in regular population, but were supervised by the commissioned officers assigned here.

Finally I saw a group of officers walking down the corridor toward H-house. It was the second shift officers coming to relieve us. I heard the gate open at F-house, but when they arrived at the Lieutenant's office, they stopped to be briefed by the second shift sergeant. There was a lot to learn down here and I could see that it wasn't like any other duty in the institution. I wanted full time duty here. It gave me the feeling that I could be part of something special and I liked it. I felt proud to be assigned here, just as I felt when I escorted Joseph Mulligan up the corridor. Inmates would move to the opposite side of the corridor as we walked with a look on their face as if to ask, *"Who is that?"* Even other officers took notice when an inmate under the death sentence moved through the institution. I wanted the feeling to continue to counter act that shameful act of taking my best friend's wife. I could sugar coat that any way I chose, but in my heart, I knew it was a sinful act I committed.

I stood by and listened as the first shift officers briefed the second shift officers on the day's events. Every detail of the day was relayed. Nothing seemed insignificant. It was another testimony of the seriousness of this place. After Dave briefed his relieving officer he gave the corridor keys to him and he received his key chit which was left in control one in the morning. The second shift officer's key chit was now on the hook for H-corridor. But, had something not appeared right to the relieving officer, he would not have surrendered the chit. No officer was required to relieve another officer if he felt there was a security violation. That was stressed to us in school.

We walked the corridor toward the entrance then through the gates at control one and through the visitation area, which was empty. There sat Captain Meriwether. The senior supervisor was required to stay until he visually checked to make sure every officer that reported for duty in the morning walked out in the afternoon. It was a requirement for all three shifts. H- house was almost always the last crew to clear the front entrance so as we

came walking through, the captain was getting to his feet and walked with us. He asked me as we walked without looking at me, "Well, what did you think about today?" I didn't even hesitate as I replied, "I liked it." He smiled and gave a little nod of approval and said, "Well, get used to it." I looked over at him at that point as he continued; "I'm assigning you there permanently tomorrow. " He walked away without looking at me.

I wasn't sure if I was smiling because I often tried to mask my emotions in here, but I was sure smiling on the inside. I wanted to tell someone, but I didn't want to act like a school kid. It was an important move to me. My personal life was in the toilet, but my professional life seemed to be talking off. All my coworkers seemed to like me and had no idea what was going on with my life at home. I was successful at masking my emotions here at work of any disappointment or stress I might be feeling. I wanted to make this work so that I might see the look of approval on my father's face again. That look that told me he was proud of his son. I knew he was disappointed and I wanted to rectify that.

On the way down the long tunnel to the parking lot, my mind took me back to a night when I was 16 years old. I had driven to my father's gas station and was on my way back home. I sometimes made the trip for daddy at night for something he had forgotten during the day. There was a stop sign on the little country road that ended at the main road, U.S. 41. At night you could see a long distance in both directions and I could tell there were no cars coming in either direction. I slowed a bit, but then blew through the stop sign as I had done on many occasions. However, there was a Georgia State trooper sitting in the dark with his lights off as I drove through the sign and in a matter of seconds he was behind me with his blue lights on.

I remembered I walked out of the house with no wallet and that meant I had no license. I was mortified! I was only a short distance from our home and I thought I might be able to make it home without stopping. It wasn't happening. The trooper began to flash his lights even with the blue light blaring in the dark. I pulled over to the side of the road and he behind me. In those days, officers asked you to step out of the car and come to them. As I walked to the rear of the car I thought I might vomit at any minute.

He had his flashlight out and in my face as he said, "You know, it would have been nice if you would have stopped at that stop sign back there." It was pure sarcasm.

There was no humor intended. Then he asked the question, "May I see you license, please?" Well, I thought, at least he said please. I knew his polite demeanor wasn't going to save me.

As I opened my mouth to answer I could barely speak because my mouth was so dry. I'm sure I replied in a voice so timid it sounded like a mouse squeaking. "I don't have it on me," I said. He looked up at me and replied; "You know its Georgia law that you have an operator's license on your person anytime you are on the road?" There was no way I could maintain eye contact with him. I looked down the ground as I said, "Yes sir, but I left it at home." "Where do you live?" He asked. I pointed and answered, "Right around the corner." I'm sure he could sense that I was scared out of my wits so he said, "Alright, I'll follow you to your house and you can show me." I got back in the car and started around the corner and immediately saw the lights of our home. I pulled in the driveway and thought "Daddy's going to kill me!" I had this trooper behind me, my father in front of me and no licenses on me. As I parked the trooper pulled in behind me. Daddy could tell there was another car and came to the door.

I looked at the trooper and he motioned to the house for me to get my license. I met daddy and he asked, "What's going on?" I told him as quickly as I could. He frowned and said, "Go get your wallet." He started out the door to talk to the trooper. I ran to the bedroom to get my wallet. It wasn't on my dresser! My heart sunk back down to my feet. I searched frantically everywhere with no luck. "Not tonight," I said to myself. It seemed like an eternity since I walked inside and I knew that they were both waiting. I took a deep breath and headed back outside. Daddy was leaning across the hood of our car talking with the trooper as I approached them. They both looked over at me.

I knew of no easy way to say it so I just blurted it out, "I can't find my wallet." Daddy just looked at me with no expression on his face. The trooper looked at daddy, to me and then back at daddy. "Mr. Allen, does he give you any trouble?" He was following his instincts with compassion. My father was a strong willed man. Life had made him hard, but he had love in him that rarely manifests itself in any physical form. He looked over at me while answering the trooper and said in a calm voice, "Not this one." My heart melted.

I felt a tear welling up in my eye and wasn't sure I could contain it. As teenagers, my brothers were the ones who gave him the most trouble. They experimented with drugs and caused him more financial grief and heartache than anything else. It's not that I was any better than them, I wasn't, but I was just too timid to get out and experience life as they had done and they made some very poor choices in their short lives. But, daddy had always been there for both of them. Tonight, he was here for his youngest son.

As I stood before him, he knew I was scared and he wanted to protect me. The trooper sensed what was happening and said, "Give me your social security number and I'll run you name through the computer." He wrote it down and returned to his car and spoke into his microphone. I heard the radio crackle as it answered him. He came out of the car and said, "You're very lucky, young man." Daddy and I both looked over at him as he continued; "It's very hard to get anything run through the computer at this hour." I don't know why, but I didn't seem surprised. The trooper did though. "Everything checked out." He bid us good night and headed on his way. Daddy simply said, "Go to your bedroom and find your wallet and make sure you have it with you when you go out again." That was all he ever had to say about it. We never spoke of it again.

"Hey Bobby, are you ok?" It was Dave. We reached the gate and I realized I was lost in thought all the way down the tunnel. I blinked and shook my head slightly as I replied, "Yeah, I'm fine." "Ok, see you tomorrow," he replied. I nodded and headed for my car. Thinking about my father made me a little sad because I felt I had let him down. I sat in the car and looked in the rear view mirror. There was a tear in the corner of my eye. Thinking about my parents and the past always caused me to feel that way. It was all brought on by guilt and I carried a full load. I'd always felt things very deeply. I let it all dissipate on the drive home.

The Captain was true o his word. I became permanent staff in H-house. I took notice of the staff and came to the conclusion that Dave and I were probably the youngest two officers in H-house. I worked the corridor post a lot, but was assigned to work the housing units, as well. In each unit there was a set of POST orders to ensure the officer assigned knew exactly what to do. I studied each set of orders very carefully as I was rotated through the various post. I was determined to make an impression and I wanted to learn all I could. Escorting became my favorite duty mainly because it got me out of the unit for a while, but I also liked the attention I received from the civilian staff.

It was not a good idea to become complacent with our duties, but it did become routine. That kind of thinking was exactly what these men counted on. They would wait and observe for any moment that they could capitalize on. Some of these men had incredible personalities and some were charismatic. I wondered if it was that kind of gift that allowed them to gain the confidence of the very people that they murdered. In fact, some of their victims were people they knew personally. Others simply murdered because of a belief they held even if it seemed twisted, prejudiced or perverted. The longer I worked in H-house the better aquatinted I became with the men who were housed here. In dealing with them, I sometimes even had to do research of my own to see just what they had done.

One such inmate was Timothy Wesley McCorquodale. I was working escort duty today and he had visitation with his attorney. I was standing at the H-4 unit door waiting for him to appear. The H-4 officer handed me out his clothes so I could search them. I heard the click of the gate inside the red door. That meant he was in the holding area. The H-4 officer passed the key out. The corridor officer removed the bar off the door and unlocked it. As he walked out he said, "Hello Mr. Allen." I smiled and returned the greeting. As I watched him get dressed I began to consider all that I had learned about him. He was very pleasant to talk to and always very polite in his mannerism. He was also very large. He was approximately 6 '1" and probably weighed over 240 lbs. He looked like an out of shape football player. As a martial artist I could tell that he could do some damage to anyone should he ever decide to get physical. He always addressed me, as "Mr. Allen" and I never heard him disrespecting officers or other inmates. The sheer virtue of his size assured him that he never need do that. There was always a smile on his face.

That was just what appeared on the outside, but there was also a very dark side. McCorquodale was one of the four inmates that escaped from death row at Georgia State Prison in Reidsville in the early morning hours just as the entire unit was being moved to the Diagnostic Center in 1980. Only three were recaptured alive. It was reported that McCorquodale had beaten Troy Leon Gregg to death for making a phone call while they were free. Now the view of a different personality surfaced. I decided to do a little research myself and find out what happened that landed him on death row.

Timothy McCorquodale was once a member of the notorious Outlaw biker gang in Atlanta. He very much fit the part. He was intimidating to look at and from what I read; he could be just as vicious as the reputation for which the Outlaw gang was known. One evening in January 1974, a 17 year old runaway named Donna Marie Dixon and her friend were in a restaurant in an area of Atlanta known as "the strip" when they were approached by a man named Leroy who invited them to the bar for a beer. While in the bar the two girls started to talk with two black men. Leroy left the bar, but later followed the girls to another bar on the strip. He approached their table and accused them of stealing $40 or $50 from him and then giving the money to a black pimp.

At this point, McCorquodale and his girlfriend, Bonnie Succaw, joined them at the table. At the request of Leroy and McCorquodale the girls were taken to the bathroom and searched by Bonnie and a friend. They found no money. McCorquodale and Leroy then called for a cab, and joined by Bonnie, they took Donna Dixon to Bonnie's apartment. They arrived at Bonnie's apartment shortly after midnight and found Bonnie's roommate, Linda, and Bonnie's three year old daughter asleep. Linda joined them in the living room and at that time there was a discussion going on between McCorquodale and Leroy about Donna being a "nigger lover" and that she needed to be taught a lesson.

McCorquodale, after telling Donna how pretty she was, hit her across the face with his fist. When she stood up, he grabbed her by her blouse, ripping it off. He then removed her bra and tied her hands behind her back with a nylon stocking. McCorquodale removed his belt, which was attached to a large belt buckle, and repeatedly struck her across her back with the buckle. Next he took off all her clothing and gagged her mouth with a washcloth and duct tape. Leroy kicked her and she fell to the floor. McCorquodale took his cigarette and burned her on her breasts, her thigh and her navel. He then bit one of her nipples and she started to bleed. He asked for a razor blade and then sliced the other nipple.

Next he called for a box of salt and poured it on the wounds he made on her breast. At this point Linda, who was eight months pregnant, became ill and went into the bedroom and closed the door. McCorquodale then lit a candle and proceeded to drip hot wax all over the young girl's body. He held the hot candle about a ½ inch from Donna's vagina and dripped hot wax on that part of her body. Next he used a pair of surgical scissors to cut around her clitoris. While bleeding from her nose and vagina, Leroy forced her to perform oral sex on him while McCorquodale raped her. Then Leroy raped her while McCorquodale forced his penis in her mouth. McCorquodale found a plastic bottle and placed an antiseptic solution in it. Then forced it inside her vagina and squirted it. She was then permitted to go to the bathroom and was instructed to clean up.

McCorquodale then found a piece of nylon rope and informed Bonnie and her roommate that he was going to kill the girl. He hid in a closet across the hall from the bathroom and when she came out he wrapped the cord around her neck. Donna screamed, "My God, you're killing me!" As McCorquodale tried to strangle her the cord cut into his hands and She fell to the floor. He fell on top of her and strangled her with his bare hands. As he removed his hands, she began to have convulsions. He strangled her again, but this time he pulled her neck up and forward and broke her neck. He covered her lifeless body with a sheet and left the apartment searching for a means to transport her body from the scene.

By this time it was now shortly after 6 am the following morning. She had endured 6 hours of brutal torture and was killed for talking with two black men. McCorqudale's girlfriend sat and watched the entire sick event unfold and did nothing. Some reports stated that she even assisted by retrieving items that Mcorquodale asked for during the rape and torture. McCorquodale soon returned to the apartment and asked Bonnie for a trunk in her room. He and Leroy then tried to place Donna's body inside the trunk. Finding the body was too large for the trunk, Mcorquodale then broke her arms and legs by holding them upright and stomping on them with his foot. After her body was forced in the trunk, it was placed in a closet.

Leroy and McCorquodale then slept most of the day on the couch and left the apartment sometime in the afternoon. The body began to emanate a strong odor and Linda was unable to mask it with deodorant spray so she called Bonnie to ask McCorquodale to remove the trunk from the apartment. Shortly after 8:00 pm McCorquodale arrived at the apartment with a person named Larry. As they attempted to move the trunk from the closet, blood started to spill on the floor of the apartment. McCorquodale placed a towel under the trunk to absorb the blood as they carried the trunk to Larry's car. They dumped her body out of the trunk beside a road. Then they placed the trunk into a dumpster.

As I watched him get dressed, I was careful not to allow my expression to indicate what was racing through my mind. That young girl was only three years older than I when she was brutally killed in 1974. She was just a young teenager. I tried to imagine what evil could influence a human being to kill anyone in that manner especially a young girl. He was smiling and talking to the other officers as he dressed with no regard for me or what was on my mind. I was absolutely horrified of the evil that men can do. I never saw a picture of Donna Dixon, but it became a pattern for me that when I learned of the crimes these men committed, I tried to imagine the face of the forgotten victim. Something stirred inside me as if I were being reminded to do that. McCorquodale himself had said that she was pretty, just before he bashed her across the face. I remembered a feeling I had while training in F-house and thinking of another young victim, Teresa Carol Allen. *"Don't let them forget about me."* It was here again today as her murder ran through my mind. As it always does, music commemorated this moment in time for me. Watching him dress and thinking of her, the music and lyrics of a song from long ago by Frank Sinatra, "Once upon a time" played through my mind as I thought about a 17 year old that I had never met nor would ever meet.

I'd heard the song on TV sung about a fairytale type of love. I had no idea why it made me think about Donna Dixon except that the song described a moment in time that all little girls should experience. A young man professing his love for her, and not the perversion of what she had experienced. It only reminded me of the twisted world in which we live and of how precious is every breath we take. At any moment it could be taken away brutally by someone like Timothy Wesley McCorquodale or is friend Leroy, who was never found.

During an interview with a psychiatrist in 1976 it was reported that McCorquodale could not remember the murder of Miss Dixon, "I cannot believe that I would do them things," he was quoted as saying, " I just don't believe I could do it." Reading that statement made me wonder about the possibilities of what he had done and the brutality of the murder. Even after her death he exhibited signs of cruelty. Just the way he broke her body and stuffed her in a trunk was almost beyond belief. Then reading further how he cooperated with the police when he was questioned. They noticed a spot on his pants and wanted to send them to the crime lab. The report said he readily surrendered his pants to the police. He still had the belt on that he used while beating her. If he really had no recollection of killing her, could it be that he was used by some evil and then abandoned to take the blame? It made me think of others in Bible history. The serpent in the Garden of Eden was said to be one of the most beautiful created, but was cursed by God when it was used by Satan. Cain killed his brother committing the first murder. There are some who believe it was Satan who entered him only to leave after the crime was committed.

The most famous of all is Judas Iscariot, the betrayer of The Lord himself. The Bible speaks of Satan entering him to betray Jesus and then leaving after the deed is done which left Judas alone, in guilt and shame. It was so overwhelming for him that he hanged himself. If it happened then, why couldn't it happen now? In our so-called modern age, people just don't believe anymore. Which brought my mind back to the present and the knowledge that Satan has said his greatest feat would be convincing the world He didn't exist. Maybe he had achieved that. For me to mention any of this to the men I worked with would have brought ridicule and certainly a ticket out of H-house. I decided to do exactly what I wasn't supposed to do and remained silent.

McCorquodale was dressed now and looked at me for silent approval to move. I nodded in the direction we were to walk and he walked toward the cross gate. The corridor officer walked behind us with the key and McCorquodale stopped far enough from the gate so that the officer could unlock the gate. It was a trip he had made many times before and he knew the drill. I kept my position behind him to observe for any sudden moves. An inmate would have to be desperate to try anything here in the corridor, but it was part of the procedure and it was mental readiness because I could never tell what a desperate man might try if he reached the breaking point.

As he walked out of the gate, I pushed the button to ring the bell signaling to F-house that we were coming. McCorquodale was polite as usual as we walked. He asked me how my day was going and I gave him the standard answer I gave everyone, "Fine." If I had been having the lousiest day of my life I would never tell the inmates. They knew as much and accepted it. On the other hand, I never asked them that because it didn't seem prudent to ask that type of question in this place. Even the best day for an inmate in here could never be a really good day considering what they were facing. I didn't know the spiritual condition of these men and what really lived in their hearts, but I felt the overwhelming presence of hopelessness that lurked here. All these inmates learned of my martial arts training, though I wasn't sure how the word had gotten around. He chose that topic to discuss as we walked. He asked me how long I had trained and if I had ever done any teaching. I told him about the school I used to have. He mentioned that he had some training and had even applied to a school somewhere as an assistant instructor. He never mentioned his rank and I didn't ask. I was taught that it was something you didn't do as a student of Japanese Karate. I was no longer a student of that particular style, but the discipline remained and I chose to follow it.

Halfway up the corridor between F-house and control two, there was a red door with a small observation window. Something caught his eye and he paused to look outside. I could see from behind him there was some sort of maintenance going on close to the fence line. I was never stricter than need be and he was always polite so I allowed him to watch for a few seconds. He stared like a child in a classroom longing to go outside, but knowing he can't. I finally heard a deep breath and a sigh as he looked up and kept walking. Finally he said, "You know, Mr. Allen, I like you." Then he turned his head to look in my eyes and continued, "But, if I had a chance to leave and you were between me and that door, I'd have to kill you." My blood ran cold. It wasn't a direct threat on my life and I didn't take it that way. It was just a factual statement.

Then he very calmly turned his head forward and continued to walk. I knew McCorquodale had nothing against me personally because we had talked many times and even shared a laugh on occasion. But, I also knew that he meant every word he said and I had no doubt in my mind that if that situation ever occurred, he would kill me and would take no pleasure in doing it. He would simply consider it a means to an end. *"There it is,"* I thought to myself. I wondered if that was the element that was needed to take a human life and then file it away in your mind. I wondered if there was something else inside the person I knew as Timothy Wesley McCorquodale that only surfaced in moments like these.

As time went on I discovered that it was the times I escorted them away from H-house that I would get glimpses inside their minds. They seemed more relaxed when they were out from under the intensity of their daily routine on death row. Even if it were only for the few minutes it took to walk to the medical section or to visitation, it was a chance to leave the unit. Even though they were all here awaiting the same fate, some had enemies among each other and could not even be allowed to be together in the Cellhouse. Living under that kind of pressure on a daily basis could make a man snap. Sometimes they did and it was during those moments, that I saw the killer inside come out if only for a moment.

I also understood the importance of having permanently assigned staff in H-house. When those rare moments happened, there would be only a subtle change that an officer who was familiar with these inmates would notice. Often time it was only a slight change in facial expressions. What they each had in common was the look in their eyes. If a change took place, the eyes always looked dead as if they momentarily excused themselves from their conscious. It wasn't physically intimidating, but it was something that struck me down in my soul as if something or *"someone"* peered outside of them. Maybe that was what surfaced in that moment when a life was taken.

Things weren't getting any better at home. Sarah continued to show a side that I did not see before we married and at times seemed vindictive toward the girls and I rarely saw them now. I don't know how I got to a place in my life where I could allow someone to have such control over me, but I did. I was living in Jackson away from my family and my support. I suppose that deep down inside I knew that I had made this bed and now I needed to lie in it. Financial burdens can cause a strain on any marriage or relationship, but it became especially difficult at home between Sarah and me. She at one point confronted me and plainly told me what was on her mind. She said, "You could get out there and find a better paying job than the prison!" Even with my timidity I let her know in no uncertain terms that I loved my job. I also informed her that working in law enforcement had been a dream of mine from childhood and I was not giving it up.

Apparently she sensed the conviction in my words and saw the expression on my face because she dropped it very quickly and never brought it up again. She continued to work her banking job, but finances did continue to come up in our conversations. Finally an unusual twist came up not long after she told me to search for another job. Several new correctional officer positions became available at the prison and I suggested to her that she apply. It would be a state government job with benefits, which she did not have at her current job. We talked about it and she actually had no argument as to why she shouldn't apply. She was in good health and in decent physical condition. She finally agreed that she should pursue it.

After she applied, I remember receiving a phone call at work from Lieutenant Gosse. He knew Sarah and her family. He said that the Assistant Superintendent for security, Ken Parrish, called him to ask his opinion about the possibility of Sarah and me working together. He told him that it would be fine. I was one of his favorite officers and he let me know it on several occasions. That phone call alone told me that she was probably going to get hired. It wasn't long before the letter arrived from the merit system in Atlanta. I knew what that meant because I had received the same one in 1980. Sarah was thrilled at the prospect of having a state job. It was going to take some pressure off of us financially. The only thing we would have to plan for was the different work schedule.

At that time, she was one of only four female officers working at the Diagnostic Center. In those days, there weren't many assignments that a woman could perform in a men's maximum-security facility. The female officers were used to staff the visitation area in the front and at the communications center of control one. She would be the fourth female officer working on rotating schedule between the visitation area and the control room. That would ensure that we never worked the same shift together, which is what the administration wanted. There was one other female officer assigned to a regular shift, but she was always assigned to control one on the midnight shift.

Sarah was going to attend the same school as I in Athens for three weeks. She trained on the day shift until the next school started and fit right in. Sarah had a charming personality and was easy to like on a first impression. It was the same personality that attracted me initially. She had a beautiful smile and was always very friendly. It wasn't until after we married that I began to see the other side and she was very careful not to show it to many people. She had a jealous side and seemed to crave the attention that she received from others, especially men. At the prison, I started to see the attention she received from the other officers and I could tell she liked it.

It was only a short time before a session opened up in Athens. The school always started on a Monday, which meant the registration, was on the Sunday before. The new officers were given a state vehicle to drive to the school. The group gathered at the institution to travel together, but she wanted me to drive her over in our car. The school was Monday through Friday and the students were allowed to come home on the weekends and she had it arranged to ride back to the institution with the group. It had been nearly 2 years since my trip to Athens and it all came back to me very clearly. I had forgotten how beautiful that part of Georgia was. Once I was sure she was settled in, I started the hour and a half trip back to Jackson. On the trip back, I had plenty of time to think. I was almost never alone. With Sarah and work, my mind was almost always occupied. Now that I was alone and listening to music my mind started to wander.

I never lived totally alone. The closest I came to a place of my own was when Charles and I lived together in Forsyth before we joined the army. How strange, I thought, that I should think about Charles at this time. He had been a devoted friend and I had stepped on his heart and crushed it. I was certain that he didn't want to hear from me, but I found that I missed him. Driving through the Georgia countryside made me think of our motorcycle rides through Pine Mountain in 1976. I felt a flutter in my stomach. I missed my friend, though I was certain he didn't miss me. How could he?

I stayed close to home in Jackson during the workweek, but I made the trip to Forsyth on my off days to see my mother and father. I could see the toll the years had taken on my father. He wasn't as spry as he once was. I felt partially responsible for that. Though I had not cost the financial trouble my brothers had, I felt I hurt him inwardly by leaving my family. He didn't see his grandchildren as often as he liked, I'm sure. Looking at him, I thought of an old saying that my mother once told me. She said, "When your children are young, they step on your toes, when they get older they step on your heart." I never grasped the meaning of that saying before. Now, looking in my father's eyes at his tired face, I had a better understanding of what that really meant. I had stepped on both of their hearts.

They were both such wonderful people. They weren't perfect, but then, Who in this is in this fallen world? They were two people who did the best they could with what they were given. Now as I got older, I saw the world from their perspective and I could see that the choices we make do affect other people. I could see it in both of their eyes as I visited with them that my choices especially hurt them. I often thought back to that night the trooper asked my father if I gave him any trouble and the reply that stuck in my heart, "Not *this one.*" No, his trouble with me started later with my poor decisions and tragic consequences. He just didn't seem to smile anymore and it broke my heart to see him that way. I wanted to fix it, but not quite sure how I could.

Sarah and I stayed home when she returned from school on the weekends. Then on Sunday afternoons, she'd pack up and I would drive her back to Athens. We didn't talk much about the school when she was home, but she would bring it up on the drive back to the school. Besides some new instructors, it didn't sound as though any major changes had been made to the curriculum. Everything she described was the same thing I experienced. The routine was the same every week and before we knew it, the school was over and she was coming home.

She returned to the shift on which she previously trained. The big difference was that her hours were from 8 am until 4:30 pm. She did have a rotating off day schedule similar to mine, but our off days were different. At the time, we only had one vehicle so it became a challenge to work around our schedules. When we were both scheduled to work on the same days, she would get ready and go in with me at 6 am. The ladies restroom in the administration area had an outer room with a sofa in it, so she would go in there and sleep until her shift began. It was strange at first, but we became accustomed to it and made it work.

Slowly I started to see some changes in her. We began to argue about small things. My parents didn't like her at first because they blamed her for breaking up Deedee and me. I suppose there was a measure of truth to it, but she was not completely to blame. I ultimately took her up on the advances she was making. It took the two of us to make the decision and live with it. There was something different about her. She didn't want me out of her sight for very long. At one point, it even seemed that she was timing me when I had to drive into town. When I would return, she wanted to know what was taking me so long. I felt trapped. It also seemed as though she looked for reasons to argue with me.

On one trip to my parent's house, we started talking about work. The subject of Roosevelt Green came up in our conversation. Anytime his name was mentioned, I took it personally. We were discussing why he was on death row. I told her all that I knew of the case and about Teresa Carol Allen. How she was working to put herself through school and had been kidnapped, raped repeatedly and finally shot and killed. The very mention of her name angered me because of what happened to her. At some point in the conversation, she started to side with Roosevelt Green. She made a ridiculous point regarding Teresa Carol Allen. She was beginning to raise her voice and asked, "Who was she, some angel?" I almost slammed on breaks to stop the car so I could look at her. I couldn't believe what I was hearing. My wife, a woman, who was a correctional officer and charged with protecting the public just as I, was justifying the rape and murder of an innocent girl.

I was silent until we pulled into the driveway of my parent's home. I tried to take it all in before I spoke. She was suggesting that an innocent college student working a nighttime job in some way deserved her fate. I looked over at her and asked, "Do you believe that she in anyway deserved what they did to her including being murdered?" She was furious now and now I understood why. She was jealous over me defending another woman. I had sided with someone who was no longer alive, had been sexually brutalized and then shot. But, that didn't matter. She was a woman and Sarah couldn't take it. It was a woman that had my attention. She looked over at me with eyes glaring, nostrils flaring and said, "He is going to get out of prison one day and I hope he spits in your face!" It was unadulterated anger at its purist form. I stared at her and thought to myself, *"I've seen this kind of anger before in H-house."* I shook my head and asked as calmly as I could at the moment, "Are you getting out? She turned her head to look out the window and remained silent.

My parents were sitting on their front porch and to my surprise the twins were here. They were so happy to see me, but I knew Sarah was going to be angry about this. My father spoke first, "Where is Sarah?" I looked down shook my head and said, "She's in the car." Mother asked first what was wrong. I tried to explain it all as best I could and when I was done daddy looked down and shook his head as well. I could only imagine what he was thinking, but he never said a word. Daddy took Leighanne to the bathroom as mother and I sat outside and Tracey in my lap. I didn't know what else to say. Mother didn't push it. Finally Daddy returned and sat down with Leighanne following behind him. He said, "Leighanne saw Sarah in the car and went outside to ask her to come in, but Sarah wouldn't even look at her." My heart was broken. Here was this sweet little girl, who had been the object of one of Sarah's overbearing disciplinary actions asking her stepmother to come inside. I wasn't sure what to do. I waited for a while to see if she was going to get out of the car, but she never did. I was trying to spend some quality time with my parents and my children, but worried about Sarah out in the car alone. I stayed for as long as I could, but finally I kissed my children good-bye and told my parents that I would call them and headed out to the car. There she was just as I left her, but now she was looking toward the door as I walked out.

Sometimes we would just let things blow over, but other times there would be an apology followed by a sincere pledge not to let it happen again. It became a way of life for us. The arguments would begin over the smallest thing and more often than not, it was about jealousy. My mother said on occasion that she thought Sarah had a split personality. I wasn't qualified to make that kind of judgment on anyone, but I do know that she could be the sweetest person I knew, but when things didn't go her way, someone I didn't recognize could appear. I wondered if down inside she felt the same measure of shame and guilt that I carried and it was her only way of expressing it. Only she and God knew that for sure because she never mentioned it to me. I believed I carried enough of that for the both of us.

Whatever went on between us at home, we were able to keep it away from work. I counted that as a blessing. We would never be assigned to work together. I was in the rear of the institution and she always worked the front at either visitation or in Control 1 manning the switchboard. The medical section where I would often escort the inmates for an appointment was located just before control one. There was an observation window at the rear of Control 1 facing the medical section. Particularly when thing weren't going well, I would see her peer out from there at me. It was actually more of a feeling I got when I saw her looking at me.

Sarah continued to talk about having a child though I knew we weren't ready for it. We were not stable enough in our marriage to think about bringing a child into our lives. I don't believe she cared about that. She wanted a baby and that became her goal. There were subtle hints and sometimes not so subtle hints about it. I tried to be the voice of reason, but it became apparent that she wasn't going to change her mind. I don't even remember if we made a conscious decision to try, but in July of 1982 we found out that she was pregnant. She was overjoyed so it made me happy. How could I not be happy at the thought of being a father again? Her parents were very happy because Sarah was their only daughter. My parents were happy as well. I vowed to be a better father and I hoped that since Sarah was now going to be a mother, she would not show so much hostility toward Leighanne and Tracey. I missed them so much and I wanted to be in their lives.

I marked my second year with the Department of Corrections in August of 1982. I had just turned 24 years old and I was expecting my third child. It was a joyous event to be sure, but it wasn't exactly the way I had it all planned. As I thought of Charles, I smiled thinking about the plan we made the summer of 1976. But, the smile quickly went away thinking about the fact that I was about to have a baby with my best friend's ex-wife. I couldn't allow myself to get caught up in my shame. I employed an old coping mechanism I learned earlier. I stuffed it away without ever telling anyone how I was feeling.

Sarah and I rented a home not too far from the National Guard armory where Charles and I taught Karate together. Now that we were living this close, Sarah's cousin, Rita and her husband Tony, approached me about teaching again at the armory. He said that he would handle the financial obligation of renting the armory and just pay me to teach. I thought that getting back to teaching would help heal the wounds of the choices I made. I knew it was a selfish thought, but I needed to do something to redeem myself. I looked forward to a prosperous future with the department of corrections. My martial arts training helped to get me noticed by the personnel manager. My hope was that it would continue to help me rise up through the ranks.

I thought back to my humble beginnings as a teenager. I was a Christian and I wanted to help people. It was one of the reasons I wanted to serve in law enforcement. My mother had wanted me to become a preacher. How could I possibly talk to anyone about God when all I felt from him was a heavy hand pressing me down for all the people that I had hurt? In my mind's eye I saw him looking at me and shaking his head with disapproval. I would say a little prayer from time to time, but believing in my mind that it had little chance of being heard. That was the depth of the condemnation I felt.

Because of a rotating schedule Sarah and I had some days off together. But, on the days I was off alone, I would usually go to Forsyth to see my parents. Daddy quit working and was seeking disability based on his back problems. He had back surgery in Atlanta years ago when I was just a toddler. As he got older, it began to give him trouble. Mother was already on disability due to her diabetic condition. It was nice to be able to spend time with them together. When I was growing up I remember that he was so dedicated to work that he was up and out of the house before anyone was awake. I loved seeing them together and most of all happy to be with each other. It carried on over to his retirement as well. He was usually up early in the morning drinking coffee and reading the newspaper.

In September of 1982, I came down for a visit. I never knocked when I came home; I just walked in as if I still lived there because it was still home to me. Mother was sitting in the living room watching TV alone. I sat down on the couch and we said our usual greetings. After a few minutes, I asked her where daddy was. She replied, "He's still in bed, I'll go wake him." As she got up I asked, "In bed?" I looked at my watch and noted the time as 12:00 pm. I knew right away something wasn't right. I could recall daddy being out of work only once when he wasn't feeling well and that was as a child when I was in grammar school many years ago.

I heard mother say, "Bobby's here" and then the sound of them coming down the hall, but the footsteps I heard were not my father's. In fact, there were no footsteps, but rather what sounded like an old man shuffling down the hall. I stood up as they came into the living room. Mother was guiding daddy by his arm and he was still in his robe. He sat down in his recliner and I could hardly believe my eyes. There he was my role model, my hero and he looked ancient. There was no expression on his face as he stared at the TV. I looked at mother and I could see the stress in her face. I asked him how he was feeling and he nodded his head and said, "Alright." I wasn't convinced. I talked with them for a while, but I could see daddy was getting sleepy again. He closed his eyes and slept in his recliner. Mother walked me to the door.

"How long as this been going on?" I asked my mother. "He has good days and bad days," she replied. "Something's not right," I said. She bowed her head and I continued, "I have never known him to sleep this late even on vacations." I could read my mother's expressions and could tell she was worried. "We have got to get him to a doctor soon," I said. She told me that she had already made an appointment with their doctor in Forsyth. I told her to keep me informed and if I could get away from work I would come. Our family wasn't the type to express affection openly, but that day I gave her a hug. I started home, but all I could think about was what I had seen. Now I had something new to worry about.

Mother took daddy to the see the family doctor who had treated my grandfather, daddy's father, and treated him right into the grave. Needless to say I didn't feel good about it. He was also the doctor that had diagnosed mother with diabetes and prescribed insulin doses so high that it scarred her pancreas and now she had acute pancreatitis because of it. That's why she received disability. That was the unofficial report of course. Other doctors would infer that, but none would ever go on record with that. Now here he was again with my father's life in his hands. I was unable to make the appointment with them because of work. I made mother promise to call me and tell me what he said. When the phone rang, I was tensed to say the least. "Daddy's got Parkinson's disease," she said.

She went on to give me the details and said that the doctor had given him some medicine samples from his office. I asked what test he performed to make his diagnosis and she told me there were none. She said that when she described what had been going on, the doctor just took one look at him and said, "He's got Parkinson's disease." I wasn't going to stand for that. I was told he did the same with my grandfather. When they took him to see the doctor, he looked at my grandfather and said, "It's just old age." Then he very nearly killed my mother. I wasn't going to give him a chance to kill my father. Mother and I made a plan to take daddy to Macon to see a doctor on my next scheduled day off. I felt better knowing that he would see another doctor and get the help he needed.

The opportunity never came. It was very early the following Sunday morning when the phone rang. It was mother crying hysterically. I had to calm her down before I could understand anything she was saying. They went to bed as usual on Saturday night, but she didn't sleep much because she was worried. Sometime during the night, daddy sat up in the bed and vomited across the bedroom. That was projectile vomiting and I knew that wasn't good. I assumed she didn't call an ambulance because she was so upset. So she tried to handle daddy herself and drove him to the hospital in Macon. She explained how she tried to get him to the car, but she said he kept walking off from the car over to the tree line at the edge of the yard and was very confused.

She was already at the emergency room at the Medical Center in Macon when she called. Sarah and I got dressed and headed to Macon. The thought of my father in an emergency room was just unfathomable for me. As I raced to the hospital all I could think about was the day I saw him at his home. Suddenly I was under attack. Every scenario of what I "should have done" began to go through my head. When it concerns someone you love, it's all the more painful to think about the things you wish you had done, but knowing in your heart that time has passed.

When I arrived, my brother Rusty and his wife, Darlene were already there. Daddy was in the back and they wouldn't allow anyone to go back there with him. Mother was beside herself with worry and didn't quite know what to do. She cried as she tried to explain everything. She said he was so confused when she tried to get him to the hospital. She would open the car and he would walk away from her. All I could manage to say was, "This is NOT Parkinson's disease!" It was such a long night and no one would tell us anything. Finally early the next morning, they let mother go back to see daddy. She returned shortly in tears to tell us that he had been back there vomiting most of the night. She didn't like the idea of him being alone thorough all of that.

Finally a doctor came out to give the news. After conducting x-rays and tests, they had discovered a mass on the back right portion of his brain. They wanted to admit him for further tests. We were all flabbergasted. It's the kind of news that you always hear of someone else receiving. The reaction is always the same from anyone. "I'm so sorry, that is terrible news." Then you go on about your life. When the news affects you personally, there is nowhere to escape. I remember just being so frightened. We had all been so accustomed to hearing bad health news concerning mother and her diabetes, but never in a million years would I have thought we would be here with my father.

They finally admitted daddy into a room and in a somewhat stable condition. The big issue was that mother and daddy had no insurance and they weren't quite sure what the best course of action was. The morning was busy with doctors and nurses coming in and out of his room and talking with mother about what to do next. Finally a young doctor told mother that he needed to see a neurosurgeon. Therefore, they were going to admit him and allow the neurosurgeon to evaluate him. It was overwhelming because so much had happened in such a short time. We had no time to think about what we should do. Even with that entire morning mother had been through, nothing prepared us for any of us for this.

My brother Don was married and had moved to North Carolina. Our first order of business was to get in touch with him and get him home. Mother took care of that. I stayed while they got daddy situated in his room. Finally we were all allowed to go in to see him. I could tell he was different when I looked in his eyes. There was a far off look on his face.

He was confused and not quite sure where he was. He knew all of us, but had no idea why he was in the hospital. There was a fear inside me that I never felt before. I couldn't quite get an understanding of it. I looked at my father and felt absolutely helpless to do anything.

It was getting late in the evening. I knew that mother would be staying the night, so I went home because I had to work the next day. I told mother to call me if there was any change or if she had news. Otherwise, I would see her the next afternoon when I got off work. I tried to gather my wits on the way home. It was difficult because I was worried about what was going to happen next. I was 23 years old and felt like I'd lived a thousand years. So much had happened in the past year. I didn't have much to say on the way and I think Sarah knew better than to question me or say anything. She allowed me to stay in my thoughts.

I didn't sleep much that night. When I did close my eyes, my mind was flooded of images of my father through the 23 years of my life. He was never forthcoming about his past though he would answer most any question I asked. Most of the information I received about him came from my mother. I thought about how much we needed God at this moment. I knew he was saved, though I never heard him talk about God and the only prayer I ever heard him say was at the dinner table on Sunday's at my Aunt Elberta's house many years before. Mother told me that he used to pray many years before.

My oldest brother, Don, had developed an illness before my brother Rusty and I were born. They were living in Atlanta and he was being treated at Emory Hospital. His symptoms were very close to epilepsy, but that wasn't his diagnosis. In fact, none of the doctors there seemed to be able to identify his illness. I remembered seeing pictures of him as a child and he appeared to be swollen and often wore a football helmet because of the seizures he experienced. He wasn't supposed to live past ten years of age. Mother told me of a time she and my father knelt in front of the TV during a Billy Graham crusade to ask God to heal their son. Mother once said that daddy prayed to God that if He would heal his son, he would never ask for anything else.

A doctor from Emory Hospital gave Don an experimental drug and made the statement, "It will cure him or kill him." Mother and Daddy had to give signed permission for the drug to be used. An intern was sent to stay the night with Don at their home. The next morning, Don awoke and asked for something to eat and never had another episode in his life. The doctor took Don's case files and went to a hospital up north to teach on his case alone. Daddy always said that is why he would never posses more than he had because he prayed that prayer though I knew he was deserving of so much more.

I was in a very light sleep when the alarm went off that morning. I realized that the phone hadn't rung during the night and I took some comfort in that. I dressed and headed to work. I always tried to mentally prepare myself for the day as I was driving to work, but I couldn't get daddy off of my mind this morning. I would just half to wing it. I made my way to the classroom and if anyone spoke I simply nodded. I had become a master at controlling my facial expressions. I sat down in the classroom and waited for the supervisors to come in and start their briefing. I was lost in thought when I heard a voice call, "Allen, you got a phone call at the control room." I felt a sharp pain in my chest. I walked as fast I could to the control room without running. When I got there the phone was passed to me through the small port in the window. Mother was on the phone and I could hear the urgency in her voice, "daddy's had a bad night and you need to get here as quickly as you can." I blurted into the phone, 'I'm on my way." I explained the situation to Lieutenant Gosse and he told me to take off. It wouldn't really have mattered if he had said I had to stay, I would have lost my job that day if I had been told anything other than I could leave. My father needed me and I was going to be there.

I didn't bother to go home to change so I was still in my uniform when I arrived at the hospital and raced to my father's room only to find out that he had been moved. They redirected me to an area of the hospital with which I was not familiar. As I walked off the elevators there were my mother, Rusty and his wife Darlene sitting in the hallway. Mother walked up to me crying and explained to me what happened the night before while I was home. During the night, Daddy had become aggressive toward the staff. This was way out of character for him. She said it had taken three large male assistants to subdue him when he refused to stay in bed. He had been sedated and he was being restrained. Mother said he had already broken one set of restraints and was now in a pair of leather restraints. I couldn't believe what I was hearing.

Rusty and I walked in to see him together. He was in some sort of observation ward with a nurse's desk nearby. The nurse looked up and pointed toward an area with curtains closed. He was partially awake. I eased myself down in a chair by his head and rested my hands on the metal railing of the bed. I didn't know what to say. Rusty sat on the other side. He eventually became fully alert and tried to sit up. The nurse overheard the rustling and walked over and told him, "Mr. Allen, you're going to have to remain calm or we will tie you down." Then she looked to me and said, "The restraints have to stay on." I didn't know what to feel. I'd never seen my father when he wasn't in full control of himself.

He was still for a minute and then started to pull at the restraints and I told him in low voice, "Daddy, you're going to have to be still." He didn't seem to hear me and continued to try to sit up and mumbling to himself. Finally he looked at Rusty then at me while he was struggling and realizing that he could not free himself, he started to cry and said in a pleading voice, "Boys, please don't tie me down!" Rusty couldn't take it and left the room. I sat there bewildered by what I had witnessed and unsure of what to do. Finally I couldn't take it anymore and I loosened one arm so he could turn on one side and he turned toward me. He looked at me with all the love he could show through his tired eyes. He lay still and slowly closed his eyes and began to snore.

I was sitting there in the silence of the room alone. The smell of the hospital environment, the steady beeping of monitor's and the sight of my father, my hero, lying helpless as a child in front of me was overwhelming. I wasn't prepared for this and wasn't sure if I could handle it. I'd always looked to him for strength. Hoping that this was some nightmare, I wanted to find a whole to crawl into and hide until I could awake. This just could not be happening now. I looked around the room and not really sure what I was looking for. I lay my head on my left hand, my right hand on Daddy's shoulder and silently began to cry so that no one could hear me.

Daddy finally calmed down enough so that they returned him to his room. Billie, my oldest sister, had arrived and was waiting. I visited with Billie while Rusty and Darlene took mother out for something to eat, but more importantly, to get her out of the hospital for some fresh air after the night she had. Daddy was sleeping when the Neurosurgeon arrived. He was a very kind, compassionate man named Dr. Boone. He had a very good bedside manner about him and seemed genuinely concerned about our circumstances. He pulled his penlight from his pocket and looked into each of Daddy's eyes. Finally he looked at both Billie and I and asked to see us outside in the hallway. Dr. Boone took the time to tell us that daddy in fact had a brain tumor in the rear right portion of his head. That was what had caused the shaking and why the first doctor had called Parkinson's disease.

He went on to explain the types of tumors that can be present in the brain. One type was actually encased in a type of "sac" they lay on top of the brain and was usually operable. The other type actually grew into the brain and therefore surgery was not an option. He said that daddy had that type and that it had in fact "exploded" in his brain the night before. That was what caused the vomiting and the confusion he was experiencing. It was now in pieces imbedded all throughout his brain. He took a deep breath, looked at Billie and me and said, "I'm sorry, it's not going to be operable and it will prove to be fatal for him." I'll give you two sometime and then I will be back around to talk with all of you this afternoon. He excused himself and all I can remember is standing there looking at Billie. I was daddy's youngest and she his oldest. It somehow seemed poetic that we were the first two to find out that our father would not survive. Billie gave me a little reassuring smile and said, "Let's go inside."

I was still in shock from what I heard. It was almost like a dream. My mind was still trying to comprehend what I heard. I felt immediate denial and thought there has to be some other explanation. As I walked with Billie inside the room I saw daddy lying on the bed now awake. I would find out later that the tumor kept him from sleeping for any length of time. He was very calm and at that moment, he looked as if nothing were wrong. I couldn't make it all the way to the bed. I told Billie I would be back. I got out of the room as fast as I could and then I ran for a stairwell that led to the outside. I needed fresh air. Once I was through the door the air hit me in the face. We were high up and I looked across the city of Macon. My mind was a blur as I tried to focus only to find that I couldn't. I was breathing heavily now and I could no longer contain it. I put my hand over my mouth and began to cry uncontrollably.

I don't remember who told mother. I don't remember a lot after that, just that there were decisions that had to be made and I tried to compose myself so that I could be there for mother and help her make them. When everyone returned, I left the room and went out on my own again. I found a huge window seat looking out over the city. I sat there with no particular thought in my mind as I stared out of the window. I saw a figure walking by me and then noticed he stopped. I looked over to see Dr. Boone standing there. I could tell he was in a hurry, but he took the time to stop and talk with a grieving son who had received the worst possible news. "Doing a little soul searching?" he asked. I looked over and simply nodded my head. He tried to explain in terms I could understand. "There is still a lot about the brain that we don't understand." He stepped a little closer, "It will only take so much and when it becomes overwhelmed, it simply shuts down." He could tell it wasn't much comfort, but I could see he was trying to help. I tried to mange a smile, but it only brought more tears.

He placed his hand on my shoulder, looked out the window and motioned with his head to the city. "You're doing exactly what you should be doing to find peace with it." He knew whom I was seeking at this moment. He continued, "Keep seeking and you'll find it." Knowing that there was nothing more to be said, he smiled and walked away. I looked back out the window and tried to find words to form a prayer only to find that my mind couldn't focus. I was incredibly sad, but also angry. Only one word came to mind as I sat there and I'm sure it is the oldest question in history whenever news like this comes; "Why?"

I returned to the room to sit with my mother. I knew she was going to need a lot of support. As I walked in the room, there was daddy sitting up in his bed eating. My brother had gone to the same Krystal restaurant down the street where daddy and mother had picked me up on leave from the army 6 years before. It was daddy's favorite hamburger and as I watched him eat, I wasn't sure I'd ever be able to go to another Krystal again because I would think of this moment. He didn't seem to be in any pain and had no knowledge of what was happening to him. That would be the next big task. Deciding what we should tell him. I felt a tear roll down my cheek as I looked at him wondering how we could tell my father that he was going to die.

Chapter 7

"Lord, make me know mine end, and the measure of my days, what is:
That I may know how frail I am."
- Psalm 39:4
(King James Version)

Mother decided that my brother Rusty, his wife and I should meet with her to talk to the doctor about the prognosis for my father. Mother didn't want to be alone because we knew ultimately what the outcome would be. What we didn't have were the details. So I took a deep breath and prepared myself for the worst moment of my life to that point. I couldn't imagine a world without my father and all of this was moving entirely too fast for me to process.

We met with Dr. Boone in a small room on daddy's floor. He was very forthcoming of what would happen in the weeks and months to come. He said it would all end with daddy in a coma. The most important thing to him was that we trust the doctors to allow them ways to make daddy comfortable. It was all that could be done. Finally, my mother asked the question that we all avoided; should we tell daddy what was going on? Dr. Boone said it had been his experience that the patient should always be told of their condition. We would, of course, spare him the details, but it was a heartbreaking thought.

My brother Don was on his way down from North Carolina and mother wanted to wait for him so we could all be together when we talked to daddy. I told mother I was going to work as much as possible because I knew a time was coming when she would need me and I wanted to save as much leave time as I could. My sister Rachel was hardly around because she was spending so much time with her husband to save their struggling marriage. It was her business and if that was more important to her than our dying father then that's just the way it was. Before I left I made mother promise to call and let me know when she was going to talk to daddy so I could be there.

I returned to work and because they understood I would be called away, I was posted in general population as a utility officer. According to Sarah, Lieutenant Gosse came to the control room to inform her that whenever my leave expired, I would be placed on contingency leave. That would protect my job, but I wouldn't be getting paid for that period of time. If that were true, I wasn't sure why they never shared that with me. In any event, I didn't care. My father was dying, my mother needed me and even if I lost the job I was going to be there.

Every day after work, I would go home, change and go to the hospital. Not long after we decided to tell daddy about his condition, I got some disturbing news. I arrived at the hospital to find out that my brother Don arrived from North Carolina and my family had the meeting with Dr. Boone and had told daddy his situation. I was very surprised and so I asked her, "Why didn't you call me?" She looked as surprised as I did and said, "We called and left a message at the prison." It didn't take me long to figure out what happened and I became infuriated. I was assigned to B Cellhouse on this day and Sarah had been on the switchboard answering the incoming calls. The message came, but she didn't call me at B house to tell me about it. She was so jealous that she didn't want me leaving her at work to go to the hospital alone. Little did I know it was only the beginning.

My attention was on my family. I didn't want any kind of confrontation with Sarah, but I thought that was an especially low blow. How could anyone be jealous of my dying father? I gave my attention to mother and daddy. I asked mother how daddy responded. As she cried she told the story. He was having a good day as far as recognizing her and where he was. She said that when Dr. Boone told him everything, daddy immediately looked at her and reached for her. He had the presence of mind to tell the doctor about his brother-in-law who had cancer, but was still alive after treatment. Looking back, I think daddy probably said that more for my mother than for himself. I was almost in tears again and finding it difficult to accept all of this.

Sarah and I talked about the trips we were making to Macon and the wear it was having on both of us. Amazingly, she said we should give up our house, move in with mother and daddy to help out and to be closer to the hospital. I talked it over with mother and she readily agreed. I could see the relief on her face. She was both worried and afraid because of the episode of the night she brought him to the hospital. It felt better as well knowing I was closer to them even though I knew there was nothing I could do to change what was happening. Sarah was pregnant and I knew she needed as little stress in her life as possible. With this new tragedy in our lives, we hardly had time to think about our baby coming. I guess in that way, it wasn't fair to Sarah, but it was life and it had thrown curve balls at our plans.

We completed the move in one weekend so we could get settled in as soon as possible and get things prepared for daddy to come home. Since mother and daddy didn't have insurance, we knew they would discharge him as soon as he was medically stable. That was the next week after we moved in. They said mother could bring him home as long as she had help. Since my brother Don arrived from North Carolina with his wife, they would be around as well. We brought daddy home, but then I wasn't sure he ever really came home. The look on his face was never the same. Something was missing. I tried to imagine what was going through his mind, but I couldn't comprehend. He was told that he had an inoperable brain tumor. I couldn't imagine the total loss of control he must be feeling. I was almost in tears every time I was with him. Sometimes he would just stare at the ground and I searched for words to comfort him, but nothing came to mind. I just wanted to be close to him so he would know I was here for him. Most days we just sat in silence. I was heartbroken each time I looked at him.

Most nights I lay in the bed and stared at the ceiling praying for sleep to come. Late one night, just as I closed my eyes, the door opened. I could see a silhouette in the door, but before I could get out of the bed to see who it was I heard a horrible thud and then a grunt of someone in pain. I jumped to my feet and went to the light switch. By the time the light came on, mother was in the room. We saw daddy lying on the floor in pain. He had stumbled on my iron lying on the floor. As we helped him to his feet, mother asked him, "Honey, what were you doing?" Daddy replied, "I was going to the bathroom." My heart sunk. He could no longer remember how to move about the house. There was a half bath no more than 5 steps from his side of the bed. Mother and I got him back to bed and I stayed for a few minutes. Mother lay beside him as he settled down. Just as we thought he was drifting off to sleep, he suddenly looked ahead, snapped his fingers and said, "Ruby, tell her to get down." I assumed he was talking about my sister when she was a child. I was sitting on the opposite side of the bed from her and we looked at each other. She said, "He's hallucinating." "Oh no," was all I could say. It wasn't going to be a quiet night. He didn't even know we were in the room. As the night continued, he got worse.

He was lying on his back and suddenly he reached up and his fingers begin to tinker with some imaginary object. My father smoked for as long as I could remember and at one point he put an imaginary cigarette to his lips and carefully laid it down. I told mother, "He's working on a car." His brain was deceiving him. He was in the past somewhere when he was a mechanic completely unaware of our presence. Mother put her arms around him as she cried and said, "He's never hurt anybody why is this happening to him?" He started to sweat profusely then shake and I sat there with my hand on his. Finally, mercifully and still shaking and sweating, he drifted to sleep though I wasn't convinced he was getting any rest. I cried all the while and finally before I completely lost my composure, I told mother I would be back. I felt numb as I walked toward the door. I glanced over at the half bath and in that moment, I had a flashback.

There was an old wooden stool in their bathroom that his father made many years ago. I was thirteen years old and sitting on the stool as I watched him lather his face and look into his mirror. He was preparing his razor and he saw me watching. He smiled and asked, "You want to watch?" I smiled as I stood up and he led me in front of him as he began to teach his baby boy the finer points of shaving. Just as I'm sure so many loving fathers have done through the ages. He leaned over to ensure that I could see every detail of what he was doing. I heard myself laugh as he mumbled something. My laughter faded from that moment and I was looking at the empty bathroom. My hand was on the doorknob as I looked behind me to see him lying there in his sweat.

When I looked back to the bathroom all I saw was the stool. I opened the door and left quickly. It was only steps away from the room where Sarah and I were sleeping. The light was on and when I opened the door I saw Sarah lying there reading a book. I collapsed on the bed, buried my face in the pillow and lost control. I cried uncontrollably for a few minutes thinking I might get some comfort from my pregnant wife. But, there was none to be found. When I was finally able to control myself, I looked up from my pillow to see Sarah still with her nose in her book. There was no expression on her face. Finally she looked over with contempt on her face and asked, "What are you going to do, sleep with him?" I stared back at her unable to believe what she just said. The man I admired most in life lay next door trapped in an illusion of his past unable to escape as my mother lay helplessly beside him in tears. I immediately stopped crying and looked at her with disgust and simply said, "I just might." I got up and walked out of the room.

In the next few weeks there were countless trips to the hospital only to be released when he was stable enough to come home. I was so thankful that my oldest brother Don was here. He had a van and that was the way daddy was transported back and forth to the hospital. There was no way that mother could afford a ride in an ambulance every trip. Don being here was the only way I was able to work. My father was disappearing. After each visit to the hospital, a little less of him returned home. When he was with us, it was usually only silence.

During one of our visits to the hospital, Daddy's brother, Uncle Robert, came to see him from Alabama. My Aunt Mae, and Cousins Carolyn and Eve came as well. I wasn't there for the visit because of work, but mother told me that they all left the hospital in tears. Uncle Robert was daddy's only brother and it hurt him very deeply to see his brother as he lay dying on a hospital bed. I didn't like seeing daddy like that either, but how could I escape? He was always there through my life and any time I needed him. I would not leave him and mother was going to need help to get through this. Besides, ignoring the truth was not going to make it go away and would not help daddy and mother in any way.

Days ran together and I felt like I was sinking into a hole with no way out. Don stayed as long as he could and then he had to return to North Carolina to work. Reluctantly, he said good-bye to daddy and mother and left with a very heavy heart. Finally, the day came I dreaded, but we all knew was coming. We made a trip to the hospital and the doctors told mother that she couldn't take daddy home anymore because she wouldn't be able to properly care for him. They told us to look for a long-term care facility. With no insurance, that meant a nursing home. My heart sank at the thought of my father in a place like that.

I'd only visited a few nursing homes in my life, but the smell alone never left me.

The facility mother chose was one that daddy had visited many times before because his Aunt Elberta was a resident there. The Forsyth Nursing Home would be daddy's final stop. As we waited for an ambulance to take him, Sarah made a statement that chilled me to my core. She said, "It's sad to realize that he will never go home again." Even with her sometimes selfish, cruel remarks and mannerisms, she showed genuine compassion. The thought that daddy would never see his home again absolutely broke my heart. He had finally found his own spot in the country and now he would never return there. I was amazed how cruel life could be.

I thought back to a comment daddy made just a few days before. He said, "When I get out of the hospital this time, I hope I am out for a while." When he made the comment I realized he wasn't completely lucid. But, how could I tell him any different? I only wanted to protect him, but I felt so helpless knowing there was nothing I could do. Finally the ambulance arrived to move him. Mother didn't want to tell him the truth, so she made up a story that he was being transported to a hospital for is back. I hated she had to lie, but we had no idea how to tell him he was going to a nursing home.

Mother rode in the ambulance with him and Sarah and I followed behind in our car. The trip from Macon to Forsyth only takes about 25 minutes, but it seemed like an eternity. Sarah and I talked some, but my focus was on the ambulance and the precious cargo inside. Every memory of him throughout my childhood came flooding back as I drove. He was a quiet man. I remember he told me once he left home to catch a train to anywhere alone, but soon returned when he saw how fast the train was moving. The gift he gave me was allowing me to pursue my dreams, even though he didn't approve at times.

Later, I would witness him bragging to a coworker about what his son had accomplished. He once told me he did not want me to follow in his footsteps and told me to pursue something else. He allowed me the freedom to choose my own path. There was also no way I could repay him for the way he helped me. Now I could only watch over his wife. My father had a strong, quiet and sometime stern way about him, but he also had a gentle side to him like the night he held Tracey in his arms very tenderly while she suffered with a fever. Also, the time he bent over in tears to kiss me, when I was a child, as he told me he loved me. He was everything I wanted to be as a man and thus far, I felt I was a huge disappointment.

It seemed like an eternity to make the trip because so much flashed through my mind. Then I saw the sign, "Forsyth Nursing Home." My heart was in my throat because this was the final destination and none of us knew when it would be over. I waited at the entrance as they unloaded daddy and wheeled him inside and mother never left him for an instant. They moved him to a rather large semi-private room. His eyes were open from time to time, but I wasn't sure how alert he really was. I could only hope that mercy would prevail and he wouldn't know what was happening to him. The nurses asked us to wait in the hallway while they transferred him to the bed from the gurney.

Sarah stood beside me, but she could tell I was in no mood for talking. We waited in silence. Finally the door opened and we were told we could come in. He was in the bed, covered up and mother on the side. Two nurses moved around the bed. Once they were sure he was as comfortable as could be expected, a nurse asked, "Mr. Allen, do you know where you are?" My eyes widened when I heard his low response, "Forsyth Nursing Home." We weren't fooling him at all and at this moment, he had full awareness of his surroundings. Maybe he was being the man I always knew and didn't want us to worry about him.

Over the next couple of weeks we tried to make him feel more at home by bringing in a few items, like his TV. It seemed to work for the most part. Now that he was settled and had people monitoring him, I could work full time. I was no longer concerned about depleting my leave time and going out on contingency leave. He had excellent medical care and mother was with him all day long. She would not leave him at night until she was sure he was asleep for the night. I worked days, changed clothes and went directly to the nursing home. I wanted to spend as much time with him as I could.

Dr. Robert Fountain and his partner became our family physicians. They stopped in once a day to see daddy. There was no need for a specialist because there would be no treatment other than medications to keep daddy comfortable. Mother liked Dr. Fountain and he comforted her. That was one of the most important issues to me. It was on one of these visits that Dr. Fountain gave us a look into what was to come. He explained that the time would come when daddy would slip into a coma and not return. His vital signs would start to fail and we would have a choice to make. We could send him to the hospital so they could keep him alive on life support or we could decide to just let him slip away.

It's one of those decisions I hoped would never come to me. Mother and I wanted him here, but the compassionate thing to do would be to let him go rather than see tubes sticking out all over him just keeping his body alive. That would be the most selfish, cruel thing to do. After discussing it with Rachel, Rusty and me, she decided that she would let him go when the time came. We just didn't know when that would be and Dr. Fountain could not give us any definitive answer. It was a waiting game. I made a vow to mother I would wait with her every day for as long as it took.

Rachel was still having trouble with her marriage and came when she could. Don was in North Carolina and could not return again because of his job. We begin to see less and less of Rusty. On one of Rachel's trips to see daddy, she and I decided to go to Macon and stopped to visit Rusty at his job. I asked him why he no longer came to see daddy. He said, "I just can't stand to see the old man lying there like that." I felt my face flush. He was daddy's favorite. We knew it as did he. I felt it was the most selfish thing a child could say, particularly coming from him. He often used to say, "My daddy," as though the rest of us had no father. It caused me to recall a situation at home a few months ago.

Daddy could no longer work on his vehicles. He had a 1947 Chevrolet coup and it was the family car all though our childhood. Daddy never got rid of it and now it was considered an antique. One particular Sunday, Rusty was home for a visit. Mother told me that daddy asked Rusty to check the brakes on his car for him. Rusty's reply was, "I don't work on the ground pop!" He did not fix the brakes for daddy. I remember it infuriated me because he thought that he was going to get that car when daddy passed, yet he could not perform a simple task for his ailing father. It was another testament to how selfish my family could be.

Daddy continued to slip away from us. When he was able, I would push him through the nursing home in a wheelchair, anything to get him out of the room and spend time with him. On one of my off days, I was getting ready to go to the nursing home and was surprised to find mother still home. She said she would be along soon. When I arrived, daddy was still asleep. Most nights they had to give him a cocktail of drugs before he could sleep. I waited patiently for mother and when she arrived, she announced to me, "I gave him to God this morning." That's why she remained behind. She wanted time alone to pray. She was coming to terms with what was happening to her husband and did what she knew was best. I could see peace in her face.

I looked at daddy then back to mother as she looked at him. She was combing his hair though he was still asleep. I'm not sure what happened next. Maybe the Holy Spirit moved through my mother to touch my heart, but I knew what I had to do. I told mother that I would soon return. I walked out in the hallway not really sure where I was going. I stood there for a second then saw the sign in the hallway for the men's restroom. I opened the door and locked it behind me. I looked in the mirror and studied myself for a minute and then I got down on my knees. I clasped my hands together and closed my eyes. I took a deep breath and said, "Father I know what I have to do. Please, if there is any way that you will heal him, please bring him back to us. But, if not, please take him home so he won't be in pain anymore." It was the only prayer I could muster.

I walked to daddy's room, stood at the door and looked at my parents. I wanted to believe that God would heal him and give him back to us. I suppose my brain was overriding my heart because I didn't see it happening. Maybe God was just telling me it was time for him to come home. I observed him lying there with his eyes closed as mother talked to him and busied herself around his bed and nightstand. I was glad she found peace. I prayed that she and I could hold on to the peace we felt at the moment.

The good days were less frequent. Some days he was lucid, but most days he wasn't. On my off days I would spend the whole day with mother at the nursing home. This day was

going to be different and haunt me the rest of my life. I walked in to find mother at her usual place; beside his bed and she was reading. Daddy was in and out all day. Finally in the evening, mother told me she was going for some dinner and would return shortly. It left me alone with daddy. He was sweating and shaking slightly. I got up to wipe his face with a washcloth and he whispered, "Bobby." I froze. "I'm here daddy," I replied. I touched his arm slightly to let him know I was there.

There was no response. "What is it daddy?" I asked. I kept my hand on him and leaned in close to his ear and whispered, "I'm here daddy, what is it?" He continued to sweat and shake slightly. I remained close and studied him. I felt my eyes well up with tears as I whispered to him, "I'm so sorry this happened to you, daddy." I brushed his black hair back with my hand. I couldn't resist it any longer. I wanted to be close to him. I moved the rail down from the bed and climbed in the bed and I got close to him. I laid my left arm cross him ever so gently and put my head on his shoulder. I couldn't remember the last time I was this close to him. The Dan Fogelberg song, "Leader of the band" played in my mind as I lay next to my dying father and thought about the stories he used to tell me from his youth. That song described a strong, silent man of inner strength and that was my father.

My life had been a poor pitiful attempt to imitate him, the best man I ever knew. Although I did not want to follow his profession, he was everything I wanted to be as a man and I felt as though I was a disappointment to him. It wasn't fair. I needed more time to make things right. My head was spinning with all the regrets of my life and I was only 23 years old. This was not the plan that Charles and I made 6 years ago. I wanted desperately to hear what he had to tell me. I wanted any sign from him that he knew I was there, but received only silence. I was flooded with emotions. One moment I was angry, the next I was overcome with grief. All I could do was close my eyes and pray it away. I needed someone to know how much I felt cheated and how much I was hurting. He never spoke again after that. The only signs we received that he was there at all was from time to time he would come to and have the awful look of terror on his face as though he saw something that frightened him. Mother always said she believed that he was seeing death come for him. As he continued to spiral down, he was moved to a small private room. I wasn't even sure the medication they gave him was helping. He couldn't tell us anything so all we could do was speculate. I was almost begging God for it to be over.

Rusty came to visit and as we sat in the room, he noticed that daddy's wedding ring was gone from his hand. He asked where it was. I told him that mother gave it to me. I could tell by the look on his face that he was outraged. He sat with his nostrils flaring for a moment, then pointed his finger and blasted at me, "I'm getting that car, do you understand that, buddy?" Immediately daddy jumped in his bed. I looked over at daddy then back to him and replied, "I don't want the damn car!" The doctors had warned us that his hearing would be the last thing to go even if he was in a coma. Today proved that was true. It was a further testament to the selfishness of our family. Here was our father dying a horrible death and all he could think about was an old car.

Daddy was diagnosed in September with brain cancer and we were told he had about six months. Now in December it was very clear he wasn't going to make it three more months. On the morning of December 21st, things got worse. Rachel, mother, Sarah and I were there when Dr. Fountain said it could be most any time. We decided to stay close. Rachel was

to attend a party that night and decided to go. I couldn't believe it. We were just told that daddy might not survive the night. We sat with daddy all day and into the night. Late in the evening the head nurse said that if there was any family we wanted to call, we should do so. Mother called Rusty, so he and his wife, Darlene came as quickly as they could. We had no way to get in touch with Rachel. The staff set up some chairs outside in the hallway for the family and we took turns going in and out of the room.

Daddy struggled to breath, so I went out in the hallway and told mother, "If there is anything you need to say to him, you need to come say it. " She came in and sat on the bed and daddy woke, but he could not speak. All he could do was mumble, but he was talking directly to her. Then he closed his eyes and we took mother out of the room. Rusty sat on one side of the bed and I on the other and each held a hand. Sarah called the preacher from her church and he was in the room with us. We watched him slowly wind down like a clock. He struggled so hard to hold on. Finally he took one last deep breath just after midnight. He didn't move again and Rusty and I lost control. I don't know how long we cried before the preacher came over, put his hands on our shoulders and said, "He's not here, boys." We both went out into the hallway with mother who was now crying. Everyone went to the lobby so the nurses could clean daddy's body for the funeral home. In desperation, we called Rachel's ex-mother-in-law to contact the police in Warner Robins to see if they could locate Rachel at the party.

I went back down to the room we just left. I felt compelled to see him again. I opened the door and looked in to see the top of my father's head. But then, the preacher said that he wasn't here anymore. I didn't know how to cope with that. Daddy was always in my life. Whenever things went wrong, I could go to him and ask him anything. Sometimes just being in his presence was enough to reassure me. I felt lost, but now I knew we had to take care of mother. She was his wife for 35 years. I slowly pulled the door as I backed away from the room watching him until the door was fully closed.

My father died on December 22nd 1982. He knew there was a grandchild on the way, but would never see it. He saw the twins only once in the nursing home, but could barley move as they jumped on his bed. Now we had the painful task of contacting the family and having them come say their goodbyes. I attended a funeral before, but death never hit this close to home. Mother, Sarah and I went to the funeral home to pick out the casket and his suit. When we left there, mother and I lost our composure and cried all the way home. I was stuck in a nightmare from which I could not wake. I wanted to wake up as though none of this had happened.

The local funeral director was a family friend and had buried both of daddy's parents. Whether he believed it or not, he had a way of convincing me that daddy was being taken care of and now it was our job to look after mother. I intended to do just that. The next 2 days were a blur. I wanted it to be over, but on the other hand I knew that once he was buried he would be gone from my sight and life would become very lonely for me. There were arrangements to be made. Don was coming from North Carolina and daddy's brother and sisters had to come from out of state. We needed some time. When I told the funeral director, I could tell it didn't sit well with him. But then it hit me; Christmas was just around the corner. Daddy was going to be buried on Christmas Eve and Christmas would never be the same.

I sat with mother during the viewing. I was amazed how many people daddy touched in his lifetime. I watched people come and go and stop by to pay their respects. None caught my attention more than a girl named Betty. She was a friend of my brother Don and was a close family friend. Betty had tragedy of her own, though. She married and had a baby, but the baby died. I could tell that it changed her. She was once very loud and talkative, but now she was humbled. She looked at daddy and then stopped by to see mother. As she sat there, mother said, "I have something for you, Betty." Mother reached into her purse and retrieved an old change purse. Then said; "Bill wanted you to have these back someday, but he never got to give them to you." Betty opened her hand and mother placed 5 Eisenhower silver dollars in her hand and her mouth dropped open.

During a bad time in Betty's life, she stopped by daddy's gas station and needed gas. All she had were 5 silver dollars that she had taken from her child's piggy bank. She wouldn't take no for an answer when daddy protested and offered to pay for her gas. So he pumped her gas and left. Daddy took 5 dollars out of his wallet, paid for the gas and put the silver dollars in his pocket. Later that night at home, he gave them to mother and said, "I want to give these back to Betty next time we see her." The next time never came in his lifetime. Mother put them in her change purse committed to carrying out his wish. Mother smiled at Betty and she closed her fingers around the silver dollars and Betty said, "I remember." She held her hand close to her mouth as she began to sob silently. It was just another testament of the life of Bill Allen and the way he helped people. I watched Betty for a minute and then walked over to see my father. I looked down at him and it was as though he were sleeping peacefully. A tear roll down my cheek and landed on his suit and I thought about how I would never be able to fill his shoes no matter how hard I tried. I leaned down, kissed his cheek and lay my head on his chest one more time.

I asked friends of mine from the prison to serve as pallbearers. Mother liked the idea and the prison graciously allowed the men to come down with a state vehicle to join the funeral precession. It was going to be a long one because mother wanted daddy to lie in state at his home church in the little community of Russellville where his family lived. When I arrived with my friends at the church, we all walked in together. As I made my way down the aisle my eyes were on daddy in his casket. I could feel the tears already, though I was trying to fight them back. He was dressed in a blue suit, powder blue shirt and a red tie. He looked as though he had not been sick a day in his life.

After the service we made our way to the cemetery we chose in Forsyth 10 miles away. There was a limousine for the family, but Sarah chose to ride with what she called "her family" in the state van. I wasn't in the mood for her mind games so I didn't say anything. The cemetery was on a hill on the outskirts of Forsyth. It overlooked a serene cow pasture and beautiful trees. There was a huge cross in the center of the cemetery and daddy was laid to rest near the foot of the cross on Christmas Eve, 1982. It was appropriate for the life he lived. After the graveside service was over I looked at the casket sitting on the stand. My life with him flashed though my mind. Twenty-three years was all I had with him, but I knew it was a blessing because some don't even have that and I felt blessed to have known him at all. I walked over and touched the casket just to be close to him one last time. My role model for manhood, my hero, was gone.

I took the week off to be with mother. The large whole in my life was nothing compared to what she felt. We tried to celebrate Christmas, but the feeling wasn't there. Sarah and I attended her parent's home on Christmas day, but I found myself wandering in their back yard trying to come to terms with this new place in my life. I never felt so lost. I knew I had to find a way back to some since of normalcy. I just wasn't sure how that was going to happen. Sarah was due to have our baby in 4 months and I had to get my head around becoming a father again. Our baby deserved to have a father. I had not been there for Leighanne and Tracey and I wanted to rectify that. It was the best way I knew to honor my father.

I returned to work in January 1983 determined to make something honorable of myself and it was hard. On my first day back I remember sitting in the classroom before the briefing began and starring straight-ahead thinking about my life. I heard a voice say, "Mr. Allen are you alright?" I was lost in thought and I shook my head to bring my focus back to the present. It was one of the new officers hired in the last couple of weeks. He was older with white hair and looked like a kindly grandfather. I mustered the best fake smile I could manage and replied, "Yes, I'm fine."

He knew it was a lie. He said, "I'm sorry to hear about your father." I nodded because I was afraid that if I opened my mouth to speak, I would begin to cry. He continued, "Yeah, it's hard to lose those guys because they cannot be replaced." I looked up at him and realized he was trying to comfort me and I simply said, "Thank you, I appreciate it."

I was grateful when the supervisors walked through the door because I didn't want to continue the conversation. When the lieutenant called the roster, he called my name for H-house. I was grateful because I wanted to get my assignment back and focus on my future. The funeral director had told me that he was convinced that "they" meaning the dead, could see what we do here. I wanted to believe that and if indeed daddy could see me, I wanted to do something honorable with my life to honor him.

There was a change in management a few months before I was reassigned to the general population. Lieutenant Jackson was now the unit manager, retired military and had tightened security in H-house. Some said that he was hard to work for, but in reality, he was just all about doing the job correctly. I found him very easy to work for because he was always the same and I knew what to expect. While I was gone my friend Dave Harris had been promoted to the unit clerk and that created an opening on the split shift. There were three positions on the split shift. They were support officers who conducted cell searches, escorts and any other duty deemed necessary. A sergeant assigned the same hours supervised them.

Dave recommended me to fill the position he vacated and the Lieutenant agreed. It wasn't really a promotion, but it would put me in a position for the administration to take notice of me. It also meant that I would no longer report for shift briefing with the general population officers in the classroom. I reported to the sergeant in H-house daily. I took it as a vote of confidence from the Lieutenant. If he noticed me, it meant that I was doing something right. I needed this after what I had been through. Because I would be on the split shift it also meant that Sarah and I would have the same hours. She didn't have weekends off as I did, but it made our commute to work a lot easier. I felt a new surge of energy and I wanted to ride it as long as I could. I wanted to see just how far I could rise with the department. I also experienced the jealousy from some of the older officers on the unit. I was

a new comer and some of them had been there for years. The Lieutenant was very professional and I believe he was building a team around him with young, highly motivated men.

We were the elite of the unit and all of us were specially selected. There was no applying for the positions, one had to be appointed. That made me feel all the more special. Being on the split shift meant I was no longer assigned to the individual units. The general population supervisors assigned those positions. Since Dave was promoted to unit clerk, he would no longer be involved in the daily operations with the inmates directly, he was administrative support for the unit manager and he would be typing, filing and maintaining files for staff officers as well as the inmates. We all reported at 8 am in the Lieutenant's office for briefing. Our first duty of the day was always cell searches. The split sift sergeant maintained a chart of cells searched and always shuffled the order around so that the inmates would not identify a pattern of how we searched. We searched 5 cells a day.

The rest of our day would be in support of the unit. We helped with feeding duties when the food carts came, helped process yard call activities and of course helped escort inmates for appointments away from the unit. I liked my new duty and was really excited about the possibilities. Soon after my posting on the split shift, a new unit manager was assigned and we were speculating who might come next. A Lieutenant could not change any policy or procedure on his own, but he could certainly influence it. The unit managers were selected very carefully just as the officers. The decision was in the warden's hands because of the sensitive nature of the duty. In a sense, you could say we were holding our breath until the announcement was made. The following Monday morning we got our answer.

The split shift had assembled in the lieutenant's office at 7:30 am to wait. At about 7:45 am we saw the new unit manager walk through the H-house gate; Lieutenant Bill Treadwell. He had been one of the second shift supervisors. He recently transferred to the diagnostic center from the Central Correctional Institution in Macon, Georgia. He started his career at the diagnostic center as a correctional officer, but transferred to Macon to be closer to home. He also was from Forsyth and had been promoted while stationed at Central. But, his training went much deeper than that. He was a World War 2 veteran army officer. He was related to one of the more prominent families in The Forsyth area. Lieutenant Treadwell had an outgoing personality and never met stranger. When he walked through the door he took charge immediately and introduced himself, though he needed no introduction. He was almost 60 and in very good shape for his age. He had salt and pepper hair. In a strange way, he reminded me of my father.

There were mixed emotions about Lieutenant Treadwell taking over, but I liked him right away. We never did more than speak in passing, but he was known as a talker. He would much more readily talk to an inmate rather than use force. We were all interested to see how well his philosophy would work in H-house. Some of these men had no interest in talking to anyone and those were going to be his greatest challenge. It was a challenging assignment for any officer and I could only imagine what it must be like for the unit manager. He had the responsibility of keeping order here not only of the inmates, but the staff as well. I decided I wasn't going to pass judgment, but wait to see what this new lieutenant would do.

Lieutenant Treadwell was quiet during his first week. I sensed he was observing the current operations. That didn't last long, though. Two of our most notorious inmates, Billy Mitchell and Roosevelt Green presented his first challenge. These two were in unit H-2 where the "worst of the worst" were housed and they became friends. They were so difficult

to manage that they refused to pull food trays off of the food carts. Therefore, the officers had to enter the unit with inmate workers from the kitchen to pass out food trays.

When Lieutenant Treadwell assumed command, Mitchell and Green were in the isolation unit for some infraction and decided they were never leaving the isolation cells. They sent letters stating they had fashioned weapons and would use them if anyone entered their cell. All eyes were on Lieutenant Treadwell. This wasn't a situation where talking would work. These were very dangerous men and they meant every word they wrote. We stood in the corridor of H-house talking about what was to be done. They could not be allowed to issue written threats and the other inmates knew what was happening. I don't know if it was purposely sent out as a test for the new lieutenant or if this was just an incredible stroke of irony. Either way, the test arrived and we all waited for the response.

We could see Lieutenant Treadwell in his office talking with the sergeants and the senior counselor. Finally they sent for the three of us and Dave came out from the clerk's office. Lieutenant Treadwell said, "We cannot allow these men to dictate their own terms and we are not going to allow them to threaten us with weapons; real or not." It was a bold move on his part and he was setting the standard for the way we would respond under his leadership. He continued, "Sergeant Smith will take you through our response." Sergeant Smith was the newest of the H-house supervisors. He had just recently been promoted to sergeant and given command of the split shift. The only defensive weapons we possessed were batons that we kept on us at all times. However, there were two "Stun guns" locked in the Lieutenant's office. One was long, cylindrical and one end resembled the grip of a baseball bat. The business end of the tube shot out a small beanbag that was capable of disabling an inmate temporarily.

The second was small hand held metal tube approxiamtely12 inches long. It held one round that looked like a shotgun shell. When the slide was released, it discharged small plastic pellets that did not penetrate the skin, but caused excruciating pain on impact. Sergeant Smith unlocked the box. We made our plan. At each cell, the inmate would be given a direct order to back up to the cell door so we could handcuff them and bring them out. If he refused, the signal would be given to open the door. One final order would be given to place his hands behind his back. If he did not comply, Officer Charles Kindle would point the large stun gun at him and fire the beanbag. Then Dave and I would be the point men through the door and depending on his condition, would cuff him and bring him out of the cell. Once he was out and secure, we would repeat the scenario in the next cell.

It all sounded like a reasonable response. The problem was, none of us had ever used the stun gun before and we had no idea what to expect. We got our equipment ready and proceeded to H-2. We were joined at the gate by Officer Steve Sanders; one of the newest officers on the first shift. There were now five officers, Sergeant Smith and Lieutenant Treadwell. At the red door of H-2 Sergeant Smith gave the order, "Lock'em down!" We heard the officer make the announcement on the P.A. system and the sound of cell doors slamming. The H-2 officer yelled back, "All clear!" The corridor officer opened the red door and we were now inside the "sally port" where I had been 3 years before on my first trip to H-house. Sergeant Smith yelled up at the officer in the observation deck, "Go back to H-I-1 and 2, look down inside and tell me if you see anything that resembles any kind of weapon." The officer yelled back, "Stand by."

Behind the cells in H-1 and H-2 was a long catwalk with observation windows in the rear of the inmates' cells so the officer could look down in each cell. It was standard procedure for the officer to walk the catwalk before anyone entered the unit. Sergeant Smith was simply covering himself by telling the officer to check. This was done so that he could include that in his report later. It only took a couple of minutes and the officer returned. "They're both lying in their beds covered up with blankets, Sergeant." Sergeant Smith looked around at us, "Everybody ready?" We all nodded our heads. Sergeant Smith said, "Hit it," and the door popped open. Dave and I were the first officers through. All the inmates locked in their cells were watching us very carefully as we walked to the isolation cells. They knew something was about to happen. When Dave and I reached the isolation section, we stopped and waited for the Sergeant, who had the key for the gate. Mitchell was the larger of the two and the one we perceived as the leader. We passed by H-I-1 and went to H-I-2 where Mitchell was housed. The plan was that if Mitchell complied, then maybe Green would submit. We waited at the solid red door that kept him isolated from the outside.

Mitchell was particularly nasty. He went his own way and tested the boundaries of our authority every chance he got. He saw himself different from the other men, almost as if he were more notorious than the rest. In reality, he was only a cowardly thug with a gun. In August 1974, Mrs. James Carr and her 14-year-old son, Christopher Carr, were opening a convenience grocery mart for business in Worth County, Georgia. Fifteen minutes later, Mitchell entered the store. After walking by the drink box, he returned to the front counter where Mrs. Carr and her son were. He pulled a pistol and demanded money from Mrs. Carr. She handed him $150 from the register. He also demanded money from her so she handed him $15 from her purse. He got money from Christopher and ordered them to the rear of the store. Mrs. Carr and her son walked to the rear of the store with Mitchell's gun pointed at them. They ended up at the cooler door. Mitchell opened the cooler door and carried Christopher inside and then stepped back out and told Mrs. Carr, "I've never had me a white bitch before," shoving her towards the bathroom. She protested, "Oh my God no!" Instead, Mitchell said, 'into the cooler," and shoved her in with her son. At Mitchell's order, they both got down on the floor, Christopher sitting and his mother squatting. Mitchell then shot Christopher in the left side of his chest and Mrs. Carr in the back of the head and left the cooler temporarily. Moments later he returned and shot Christopher again, but this time in the back of the head. He shot Mrs. Carr three more times before returning to the main part of the store.

Two young boys had entered the store and Mitchell pointed his gun at one of them and snapped it several times, but it did not fire. He took money from one of the boys and then marched them to the cooler and again snapped is gun several times, but it did not fire. He closed the cooler and left the store. Christopher Carr died from the gunshots, but Mrs. Carr survived her injuries to testify against Mitchell. Now he sat here in a cell on Georgia's death row as though he were some type of gangster when in reality he was just a child murderer. Today his metal would be put to the test.

Sergeant Smith waited for everyone to get into position. Officer Kindle was up front with the stun gun. We all flanked Kindle. Lieutenant Treadwell was in the rear observing everything we did. Dave now had the key to the solid door and on orders from Sergeant Smith he opened the door and fond Mitchell already standing. To our surprise, Lieutenant Treadwell now stepped up to the front and said, "Mitchell, I want you to back up to the cell door and put your hands behind you so these officers can cuff you and the we are going to search the cell." Mitchell just looked at us with defiance. He wasn't going to budge. "This is your last chance, Mitchell," the lieutenant warned. Mitchell looked down at the stun gun Kindle was holding and then back to Lieutenant Treadwell and placed his hands on his hips.

All the inmates had seen the stun gun, but it had never been used. The lieutenant stepped back and simply said, "Sergeant Smith." The sergeant looked toward the control room and yelled, "Open two." The buzz came and the door popped open. I was closer; so I pushed the door all the way open. Mitchell still had not moved. Kindle sniffed and then raised the barrel. He hit the release and there was a loud, "Bang." The bag made contact in the upper abdomen exactly where it was designed to hit. All we heard was a moan because air left his body quickly. He grabbed his chest and fell to the side on his bunk that was attached to the wall. Dave and I were first through the door and we each grabbed an arm and pulled them behind his back and I cuffed him. He was almost lifeless. We pulled him out of the cell and laid him on the floor. He recovered very quickly and got to his feet. He had a reputation to protect and he didn't want any of these inmates to see him being dragged through the unit.

While we were walking by the row of cells toward the door, one very small inmate named Johnny Gates, yelled out at us, "Y'all through." It was an idle threat because Gates was no threat at all. It was more of an attempt to gain favor from the larger Mitchell, who was now in handcuffs. If Gates were ever out of the unit and alone, he was very timid. He stood approximately 5'7 and maybe weighed 110 lbs. Mitchell walked in silence probably reflecting about what had just happened.

Once out in the corridor, there were officers waiting to take Mitchell to the medical section. It was departmental policy that if any type of physical force were used, the inmate must be checked and cleared by medical staff. Once he was secure, it was time to give Green an opportunity to voluntarily come out of his cell. We walked back in to H-2 and once again, all eyes were upon us. Having been through the routine with Mitchell, we knew our positions and what to do. The solid red door was opened and there was Green already on his feet. He heard everything that transpired next door.

Once again, Lieutenant Treadwell stepped up and said, "Green, you know why we're here. I need you to turn around and back up to the cell door so these officers can cuff you." He didn't move and instead stood there and looked at us. The lieutenant stepped back and said, "Sergeant Smith." Smith was ready, "Open one!" the buzz and then the door popped open. Once again I pulled the door all the way open. Kindle stepped up and Green assumed a defensive stance. He turned to the side and put his hands up in some sort of martial arts stance. I thought to myself, *"You've seen too many movies."* Kelly released the slide and then we heard a muffled, "bang." Something had gone wrong. Almost like a misfired weapon on the firing range. We all could almost see the beanbag leave the barrel and hit Green on his hip. It had no affect on him. His hands went up higher and Sergeant Smith perceived that as threat and yelled, "Get him!"

Dave and I both carried smaller batons, approximately 18 inches long, which was ideal for close quarters encounters such as this. I was closest to the cell door, so I went through first with Dave right behind me. Green's hands rose up higher to his face, so I swung with my right hand to strike him at the base of his neck to stun him and hopefully incapacitate him. My martial arts training ensured that if I hit my target, he would go down and it would be over. But, he wasn't going that easy. Instead he flinched and my baton landed at the base of his left ear. It had the desired effect, however. His knees buckled and He slumped slightly. The baton was of no more use, so I dropped it and grabbed him with both hands around his shoulders, trapping his arms at his side. Dave went low and we had him down on the bed on his stomach. All of a sudden, the new officer, Sanders, came through the cell swinging his full length baton over his head like an axe striking Green across his lower back. One strike even hit me on the forearm. He was flailing the baton like a madman and was totally unnecessary.

Dave finally grabbed him and threw him out of the cell toward Sergeant Smith and Officer Kindle who then pushed him to the side. Smith and Kindle then came inside and helped us handcuff Green with his hands behind his back. He was able to stand and walk to the front of H-2 without assistance. We walked directly to the medical section escorted by Sergeant Smith, Kindle, Dave and me. He didn't speak on the trip up the corridor. Once in the medical section, Sergeant Smith cleared the hallway outside the clinic of all diagnostic inmates. All U.D.S. inmates took priority over any other situation.

Not that they were any more important, but the idea was to get them checked and then back to the more secure area of H-house. Green sat down on a stool. The doctor questioned him and asked if he was all right. Green responded, "Yeah, I'm fine." The doctor continued, "What's that on your ear?" There was a small mark under his ear where my baton had landed. He nodded in my direction and responded very calmly, "That's where that cracker right there hit me." The doctor nodded and examined him. Then he said, "He's cleared to go" We returned to H-house in silence. Mitchell was talking with Lieutenant Treadwell in his office along with the senior counselor and the other staff counselors. Normally there would be only one inmate at a time out in the corridor, but there was plenty of security and these were extenuating circumstances.

We took Green back to his isolation cell and returned to wait in the corridor. All of the administrative offices in H-house had large unbreakable glass so we could see what was happening in the office. Mitchell was talking alright, but I could tell that he wasn't too happy. It was amazing to me though that Lieutenant Treadwell had him in his office at all after what had just happened. Lieutenant Treadwell definitely had a different way about him. After a few minutes, Mitchell returned to the cross gate accompanied by Lieutenant Treadwell and he said to Sergeant Smith, "Take him back to H-2 and bring Green out here." We did as instructed and this time Green complied and allowed us to cuff him.

We took Green to the office and once again the counseling session began with Lieutenant Treadwell and the counselor. After a few minutes, Lieutenant Treadwell returned with Green to the cross gate and told Sergeant Smith, "Return both Green and Mitchell to their regular cells in H-2." Then he turned around and went back to his office. We returned them to their cells with no altercation. Then we returned to the corridor. We all stood there dumfounded. The morning had started with us hitting Mitchell with a stun gun, using a baton on Green and after spending time with Lieutenant Treadwell they were out of isolation and back in their regular cells and apparently calm.

Lieutenant Treadwell's management style appeared to work. I could tell it was going to be interesting working for this new lieutenant. He definitely had charisma. As time went by, I found out that one either liked him or hated him. There was no in between where he was concerned. The older veterans seemed to dislike him the most and the younger officers seemed more willing to accept his new approach, including me. I never believed it was all about beating the inmates down and then banishing them to a cell forever. I had no problem using force when it was necessary, but I liked the idea of talking to them to accomplish the same goal.

In time, H-2 no longer had to be fed by diagnostic inmates with us supervising. They all agreed to accept the food cart in and pass out food trays as every other unit did. In the months to come I watched as Lieutenant Treadwell and his team called out inmates from every unit and counseled them. I noticed that they called out the stronger more influential inmates from the units. They were the ones that controlled the mood of the units and Lieutenant Treadwell seemed to be controlling them. The air about H-house seemed to be relaxing. Whether they liked him or not, the officers had to acknowledge that his way worked. We all settled into a new regime in H-house and even though he did not manage with an iron hand, we all knew who was in charge.

Sarah and I continued to stay with mother to help her out and mostly so she wouldn't be lonely. I wanted to be close to her, but she and Sarah butted heads until the day came that tempers flared. Mother and Sarah could no longer stay in the same house together. We moved in with her parents until we could find our own place. My father had just died a few months before and mother and I both were still traumatized from the sudden way we lost him. Sarah was my wife and pregnant with my child. I felt so torn with my loyalties. The only place I found any peace was at work.

The first part of April 1983, Sarah and I moved to Barnesville, Georgia. A friend of mine who once worked at the prison was now the manager of an apartment complex there and he set us up in a 2-bedroom apartment. Barnesville was another small town like Forsyth and Jackson and I was somewhat familiar with it. It was one of the towns Charles and I had to pass through on our motorcycle trips through the mountains. I was now alienated from my mother who I knew needed me more than ever, but we were expecting a child and after what I had done to Deedee and the girls, I felt I had to make this work. It made my heart ache to think about mother alone in Forsyth, but I felt trapped in this life I had created for myself and with no way to escape.

Late on the night of April 27th 1983, Sarah began to have contractions. As my luck would have it, our car was giving us trouble. I went down to my friend's apartment to see if he could help. He had a friend in the complex that drove an ambulance for a private company and he was more than happy to help. He brought his ambulance around and got Sarah comfortable inside. The hospital we chose to use was Henry General in Stockbridge, Georgia. It was approximately 40 miles north of Barnesville just outside of Atlanta. We started on the trip and the driver said, "The only reason I wouldn't be able to take you is if a call comes over the radio for a heart attack victim." He no sooner had it out of his mouth when the call for a heart attack went out over the radio. We weren't sure whether to laugh or cry because Sarah was in labor. The driver quickly turned around and headed back for the apartments and said, "You can take my car and go to the hospital."

It was a blessing to be sure, but I wasn't sure what I was going to do if Sarah started to have the baby on the way to the hospital. I said a prayer and started the trip. As soon as we made it to the hospital, I called Sarah's mother and told her where we were. I waited nervously with Sarah. We already knew it was going to be a cesarean section birth from the doctor's visits. It didn't take her mother long to arrive and she waited patiently with me. This wasn't her first grandchild, but Sarah was her only daughter so it was special in that sense. It wasn't long before the doctor came in and said it was time. They took Sarah to the operating room and showed my mother-in-law and me to the waiting room.

I was surprised at how little time we had to wait. In no time, the nurse was out and told us that we had a brand new baby girl and that we could see her in the nursery upstairs on the next floor. When we got to the elevator, the nurse was there with our new baby in an incubator waiting to go upstairs. All we could see was a pink cap on her head. When we got to the nursery, we had to wait a few minutes before they brought her out. We looked at each other and smiled as we waited in anticipation. Finally, the curtain opened and there was our baby. We looked at her and then looked at each other. She was so wrinkled and she had such a long nose. My mother-in-law said "Maybe that's not out baby." We looked at the window and both of us burst into laughter.

It wasn't long before they brought Sarah to her room. Once they got her settled, they brought the baby in. She had changed in the few minutes since we saw her. She was growing more beautiful by the minute. When the nurse put her in Sarah's arms and I saw her with the baby for the first time, I saw her in a different light. She was going to be an excellent mother. I could tell just by the way she was holding her. She looked at me and asked, "Are we going to use the name we decided on?" I smiled and nodded. We had picked out names before hand, but did not know the sex of the baby. In the early morning hours of April 28th 1983, Leighanne and Tracey had a new sister named Kimberly. We were blessed again.

I returned home that morning and just had to call mother to tell her about her new granddaughter. She was excited about the news and happy that I called. I knew my mother well enough to know that she was very happy to hear her son's voice. She told us early on that Sarah was pregnant with a girl and could tell by the way she was carrying the baby. I was so very glad to hear her voice and it just made me hate it all the more the way things were between us. I was alone for the next few days and it made me realize in my solitude how much I missed my father. I visited his grave in Forsyth to let him know that he had a new granddaughter. He had known that Sarah was pregnant, but as time went by we all realized that he would never live to see the baby. Even 4 months later, I still cried every time I stood over his grave.

I guess mother decided that enough had gone on between us and she stopped by for a surprise visit. I was off that day and she wanted to take me to lunch. When I went outside I saw that she bought a new car. She was now receiving daddy's disability. It was bittersweet because daddy applied for disability after he retired, but was denied. After the cancer was discovered, mother once again applied for him and we thought there was no way they could turn him down with his condition. He lived to receive one check before his death. The only consolation was that mother could now collect a portion of it and it helped her to make ends meet. With all that happened with daddy, there was no room in our lives for un-forgiveness. Daddy's illness and death had shown me that life is much too precious to allow time to slip by. I was glad that mother was bold enough to make the first move. I didn't want to waste any more time away from her. She had a new granddaughter and I wanted her to be a part of Kimberly's life. Sarah and Kimberly came home in just a few days and I took some time off to help Sarah get situated. She decided she wanted to breast feed Kimberly. Sarah wasn't much endowed in that area and I was concerned. However, I don't remember the doctors being concerned about it and so I didn't let it worry me. She fed Kimberly on a regular schedule, but she never seemed satisfied. She cried a lot and didn't sleep very long and we were worried that she might have something more serious wrong. Although Sarah was a good mother, she wasn't experienced. We were just about ready to make a doctor's appointment for her when mother stopped by to meet her new granddaughter.

There is something very special about a mother who has become a grandmother. They bring with them a wealth of knowledge that one cannot find in any textbook. Mother could tell that Sarah was worried. She kept telling mother, "She just won't stop crying." Sarah was just about in tears herself. Mother took her form Sarah's arms and held Kimberly for a few minutes. I don't know if it was instinct or she saw something we didn't. She immediately asked if we had any baby bottles. I replied with a smile, "Yes we most certainly do." It made me smile because as any new mother would do, Sarah had spent her last few months collecting everything she would need. We definitely had bottles.

Sarah got one from the kitchen. Mother gave Kimberly to me and filled the bottle with water and put some sugar in it. Then she came back, took Kimberly from me and sat down in the living room. She cradled Kimberly in her arms and barely put bottle to her mouth and Kimberly's lips went to work. She downed the bottle of sugar water in no time. Mother smiled and looked up at us and said very compassionately, "She's just hungry." Apparently Sarah's breast was not producing enough milk to satisfy Kimberly and I could see relief written all over her face. I too, let out a big sigh of relief. Mother said, "Go to the store and buy some baby formula and let's see how she does with that." I hurried as fast as I could and returned with what she had written down for me to buy. Once the bottle was filled, Kimberly finished that in short order. Kimberly had helped repair a wounded relationship between mother and Sarah. Though they would never be really close, they remained friends through the years. I smiled as I saw Sarah and mother talking and smiling together.

Even with Kimberly's birth, Sarah and I continued to drift apart. There were always bouts of jealousy between us. She wanted me to stay at home even when she had to work and I was off. As a new father, I know it was my place to stay home and keep our daughter but, when I was off, I didn't want to be trapped at home. My off days always started with a stop at the cemetery where I found myself standing at the foot of daddy's grave talking to him. As a Christian, I knew he wasn't there, but that was where we had left what was left of his life here on earth and I needed to be close to him. There were so many things I didn't get to say to him. So many questions I didn't ask him and now I wondered where I would turn when I needed a voice to guide me. My trips to Forsyth started at the cemetery, but always ended at mother's house. Some days we sat in silence just needing to be in each other's company.

As the summer of 1983 approached, Sarah and I began to argue more and more. So much in fact that we finally separated and I went to stay with mother. I missed Kimberly, but it felt good not to come home to an argument every day. I started to hang out with a friend of mine from high school, Hugh Tillman. He had been another of my friends who studied martial arts with me. My father had recently died a horrific death, my second marriage was in trouble, I had three daughters and I wasn't home with any of them. All Hugh and I did on my days off was ride around and drink beer like teenagers. I tried to keep my personal life away from work and I was very good at masking my true emotions. I was becoming a master of stuffing my true feelings and never let anyone know how much I was hurting on the inside.

I began an affair with a woman 10 years older than me and what was worse, she was a prison employee. I did not want to jeopardize my career because it was the only identity I had that made me feel life was worth living. I wanted to express to someone how much I was hurting, but I just didn't know how. Alcohol seemed like the solution. I would pick up Hugh and after a few beers, I could convince myself that I could work my life out any way I wanted to. Eventually the morning would come and I found myself right back in the life I had created. It wasn't just my life that my actions were affecting. Leighanne and Tracey were now 4 years old and still without their father. Kimberly was just a baby and did not deserve the life I was carving out for her at such a young age. The affair I had begun was with a woman with 4 children of her own and I could tell that she wanted more than I was going to be able to give her. She wanted a husband and a father for her children and how could I possibly fill that role when I wasn't even doing it for my own children? Everywhere I turned, I felt my father's eyes upon me and I knew I had to be a terrible disappointment to him. I dared not pray to God for anything lest I be struck down. That was my feeling. There was no way under his creation that I could see a scenario where he wanted to hear anything from me. Once again, if I took a drink, it all disappeared for an evening.

Sometimes I would ride alone and not drag Hugh into the selfish world I created. When those times came, I found myself driving very slowly through the countryside looking at the sky at how peaceful the clouds looked as I attempted to drink the demons screaming at me out of my head. I was a haunted man and I felt that no one was remotely interested in what I was feeling. Usually, my drinking moments led me to the cemetery where I would try to talk to daddy only to find that I could only say, "I hope that you have peace," I almost always hung my head in shame as I cried trying to figure out how I had become such a disappointment to the ones I loved the most. I had such an honorable plan for my life at 17 and now only 7 years later, it was a disaster.

I have no idea how I was keeping it together at the diagnostic center. Sarah worked there, the woman I was involved with worked there and I became paranoid thinking that everyone around me knew every sickening detail of my wretched life. I hated myself and had no idea what to do about it and I didn't know how I was ever going to recover. I found myself thinking only of getting off duty, changing clothes and drowning my hatred for myself in the first alcoholic drink I could find. I thought about death, but I knew I did not have the courage to act on it and I certainly wasn't going to tell anyone how I was feeling.

As the summer came to an end, Sarah and I decided to reconcile. I don't know if it was because it was what I really wanted or just simply out of a sense of duty. I knew that Kimberly needed her father and I wanted to be a father to the twins. Sarah had even softened her demeanor toward the twins. Deedee in no way wanted to acknowledge Kimberly as Leighanne and Tracey's sister. I did, however, break the heart of the woman I was cheating with and that gave me another reason to hate myself. Everywhere I turned, I was hurting people. Sarah moved back to Jackson during the summer while we were separated. With help from her parents, she moved into an apartment and bought a car. They were doing more for my family than I was. I had to make this all right in some way. I was my father's son and his memory did not deserve what I was doing to his family name. I was named after his father and his brother and I had to restore honor to that name.

Once Sarah and I were back together, we moved into a singlewide trailer in a small mobile home park in Jackson. We renewed our friendship with her cousin and her husband. I once again started to teach martial arts at the National Guard armory. It was a way back to some sense of normalcy for me even if my heart wasn't in it. I continued to teach until I felt as though people weren't watching me anymore. I don't know that they were from the beginning, but my shame and guilt ruled my life at that time. I needed to feel like I was being productive again. Being a soldier, teaching martial arts and becoming a becoming a police officer was supposed to be about helping others and all I had succeeded in doing was serving myself. In time, I began to feel like a husband and a father again. Sarah and I still argued at times, but we managed to stay together. I turned my attention to work again. It was the one area where I still hadn't done any damage. I wanted to maintain my honor in one arena of my life. Lieutenant Treadwell liked me. I seemed to have that affect on people. Deep inside I knew there was a good man trying to get out. My life had been marked with tragedy very early and it affected me very deeply. I tried desperately to put my faith in God, but I was angry because my father was taken away. I never said it openly and maybe that was part of the problem. I needed to say it, but had no idea at that time that God doesn't mind me being angry with him.

As fall gave way to winter 1983, I began to discover things about Sarah and through our own admissions; we made an attempt to get honest with each other. I discovered that I wasn't the only one who had been unfaithful in our marriage. She named people she had been unfaithful with and some of these men were people with whom we both worked. Some of them even considered themselves to be my friends. It was a devastating blow, but how could I be angry? We vowed to put it aside and move forward for Kimberly's sake if not for our own. I just wanted to concentrate on my career before that too was gone.

One cold morning in December, Lieutenant Treadwell told Sergeant Smith to bring the split shift crew into his office for a meeting. Lieutenant Treadwell was known for his meetings, but this was different and we could all sense it when we walked in. He wasted no time getting to the point. "Men, we have an execution order." Dave spoke first, "We get those sometimes, Lieutenant." It wasn't unusual to get an execution order. It happened from time to time and when they came, the inmate was required to be notified. That usually signaled another step in the appeal process.

Lieutenant Treadwell said, "No, this is different." The room got silent. He started again, "John Eldon Smith has exhausted all of his appeals and it looks like we are going to go." No one could believe it. We had seen inmates come to the counselor's office and be notified of a death warrant, but then sent back to his unit. This time, we were notified first and no one was prepared for it. We had never proceeded to a point beyond receiving an execution order. Now it appeared there was a very real possibility that we might actually execute someone. It was a surreal moment for me. I thought back to the first time I heard about Teresa Carol Allen and saw Roosevelt Green's picture in the paper. I remembered the anger I felt when I saw him smiling in the picture. Now, 6 years later, I was working on death row and was going to participate in an execution. It would be the first scheduled execution by the state of Georgia since it was reinstated in 1976.

Chapter 8

"But if a man willfully attacks another to kill him by cunning,
You shall take him from my altar that he may die.

- Exodus 21:14
(English Standard Version)

John Eldon Smith was a small man, balding and wore thick black glasses. He looked more like a high school science teacher than a convicted murderer. His demeanor was very meek and he was always respectful. In fact, except for the occasional medical appointment or pastoral visiting chaplains, I would have forgotten he was even in H-house. He didn't appear to be a threat of any kind to anyone. But, the facts of what led him to H-house told a different tale.

In August 1974 Smith, who also went by the alias Anthony Machetti, was married to a woman named Rebecca Adkins Smith Machetti. She was divorced from Joseph Ronald Akins and had three daughters by him. Ronald was recently remarried to Juanita Knight Adkins. They had only been married for twenty days. Smith and Rebecca Machetti devised a plan to murder Ronald in an attempt to collect his life insurance money of which Rebecca and her daughters were the beneficiaries. At the time, they lived in North Miami Beach, Florida. Smith and his accomplice, John Maree, traveled to Bibb County, Georgia and lured Ronald Adkins and his wife to a new housing development on the pretense of installing a TV antenna. When Adkins and his wife arrived at the appointed time, Smith killed them with a shotgun after which he and Maree returned to North Miami Beach. One report stated that Smith had hoped to land a job as a mafia hit man, but instead, it landed him on Georgia's Death Row and now facing execution in the electric chair.

It amazes me what human beings are capable of doing for money. Maree, Smith's accomplice, was to be paid only $1,000 for his role in the killing of two people. Smith in no way looked like a mafia hit man and I was doubtful that if confronted, he could even defend himself. Once again, a gun made all the difference in the world. He pulled a trigger, got in a car and drove home like he had completed a typical day's work. Its appalling how little human life means to some people and how one could stand before the creator of the universe and attempt to justify that. For her role in planning the death of her ex-husband, Rebecca

Machetti was also sentenced to death in the electric chair. I wondered how her daughters felt about their mother planning the death of their father for money.

Days went by and we waited for word of a stay of execution to come from the 5th circuit court of appeals; at that time, the court that had jurisdiction in Georgia. But, no stay was granted. Finally, we received word that there would be no stay and even the U.S. Supreme Court had denied Smith's appeal. There was nothing to stop the order of the court. The institution came alive with the administration staff busying themselves organizing the procedures by which Smith would die. Only once before had the institution come this close to an execution. In 1980, just before I was hired, one inmate dropped his appeals and decided he wanted to die. I was told that there was a scramble to build the H-5 execution chamber to house the electric chair that had been transported from the state prison at Reidsville. But, it turned out to be a ploy by the inmate for attention and he soon picked up the appeal process again.

I saw the original large white chair in which so many had died over the years. It was a relic. But, that chair was sent back to Reidsville to be put on display and Smith would now be executed in a brand new, more modern chair. Once the administration was convinced the appeal process was exhausted, preparations were under way. When that day came, Lieutenant Treadwell had been in meetings the entire day. When he finally returned, Mr. Willis Marable, the warden's administrative assistant came with him. He held the key to H-5, the execution chamber. It was to be cleaned and prepared.

The H-5 execution chamber could be reached two ways. There was a door past the isolation cells in H-2 that led directly to the holding cell. The other entrance was an outside door, which could be reached by exiting a corridor door between F-house and H-house corridors and was located just past Lieutenant Treadwell's office. It was decided that Smith would be taken through the outside door. To enter through H-2 meant walking Smith past the row of cells of inmates. Besides being insensitive, we weren't sure what kind of reaction we might get. I know most movies I'd seen suggested that the condemned man walked past every man on death row on his way to the chair, but that wasn't going to be the case.

I took a crew of diagnostic inmates from F-house to clean H-5. I'd been inside H-5 several times and each time I approached the door it was like entering a forbidden city that time had forgotten. I placed the key in and turned the lock. It resisted because this place was rarely visited and when the door opened, a musty smell escaped. When I flipped the switch, the florescent lights flickered. The outside entrance opened into the witness room. There were several rows of benches that resembled church pews. To the right of the witness room a door opened into the autopsy room. It was an eerie sight to see the long metal table with a small drain hole where the head would lie. Under the table was a bucket to catch any fluids that escaped from the body. Georgia Law requires that the body be examined after a death sentence is carried out. Immediately after the execution, the inmate's body would be brought to this location so the G.B.I. crime lab could inspect the body. Directly in front of the pews was a large viewing window that contained bulletproof glass. Even from the outside doorway I could see the very thick wooded electric chair. It was stained a medium color brown and covered with varnish so that it glistened in the light. It was a remarkable, yet chilling sight to behold. It was an instrument of death just waiting for its first victim. No matter what ones position on the death penalty, it stirred emotions.

It sat in the middle of an all white room. The lights made it all the more brighter. Curtains hung on the inside of the window and would be closed as soon as the condemned man was pronounced dead, like a closing act on some macabre play. The chair was centered in the room as if it were a throne. Directly behind the chair was a two-way mirror that hid the control room. To the right of the chair was another door where the condemned man would appear as he was escorted into the execution chamber. Just before the doorway, there was a very small window in the ceiling to afford the condemned man a chance to see daylight. Through that doorway was the holding cell to house the inmate for the 72-hour mandatory deathwatch. It was just steps away from the electric chair. We were told that particular procedure was going to be altered. The reason was that during those 72 hours Smith would receive pastoral and legal visits with attorneys and possibly personal visits. There was a catholic mass on Wednesdays in H-house and Smith was a regular attendee. He also received visits from a spiritual group based out of Atlanta that met with any death row inmate that would talk with them. But I don't recall Smith ever received a personal visit from anyone. It was quite a lonely thought. But, it was a world he created for himself.

There certainly wouldn't be a visit from his wife. She was on death row at the women's facility in Milledgeville, Georgia. At that time, she was the only woman on death row. Some said she manipulated him into killing her ex-husband. I'd never seen her in person, but I knew that Smith looked very gullible. When I looked through my Christian eyes at him, I almost felt sorry for him. Yes, he had taken two lives away, but I wondered what was really going on in his mind at that time. There had to be something very wrong to lead a person to commit murder at the behest of another. A conflict began in me. My flesh cried out for vengeance on these men who killed, but my soul, the part of me that belonged to God, said that there was more going on here than I could comprehend. Again, I employed my technique of stuffing it inside because I had a job to do.

I looked around for the detail of inmates that came with me, but they had stopped at the door. They were standing there as if they saw a ghost. There were no ghosts here, not yet at least. None of this had been used before. Finally I told them, "Let's just get the outer room and then we can go guys." They looked somewhat relieved and went about their duties without saying a word. I could tell by their actions that they wanted no part of this. It was an awesome sight to behold especially for the first time. All of this was designed to take the life of a man. Thinking about that sent a chill down in my soul. After they finished, they exited as quickly as they could. I stood at the door and looked at the chair as though it were a living thing. I turned the light off and left it in its solitude.

Finally we received the order to remove Smith from H-house. The 72-house deathwatch was about to begin. The split shift got the duty. Sergeant Smith, Officers Kindle, Carter, Harris and I walked to H-4 where Smith was housed. We brought with us a small laundry cart that we used whenever an inmate was to be moved from one area to the other. It was a canvass cart with wheels that resembled something you might see in a coin-operated laundry. Once everyone was in their cell, we rolled the cart into the unit. They all suspected something because all eyes were on us. As we pushed the cart down the range it made an eerie squeaking noise. The noise halted as we arrived at our destination.

Sergeant Smith looked in at Smith and said, "We're going to be moving you at this time, Smith." He didn't appear surprised at all. More than likely, his attorneys had advised him that we would be moving him. I spoke next, "Smith, I need you to pass out your clothing." Before he left his cell, we had to strip search him. He complied and then waited for me to return his clothing. Once completed, the signal was given to open the cell. The cart was too wide to fit though the cell door so we pushed it up close to the bars. He went about the business of emptying his personal belongings into the cart. The last item on the cart was his mattress. Normally, the inmate pushed the cart himself, but under these circumstances, I pushed it out for him.

Once outside in the H-corridor, Dave Harris took over. As the clerk, he was responsible for carefully inventorying and itemizing every piece of personal property Smith possessed. When the inventory sheet was filled, Smith was asked to verify its contents and sign the form, which was also signed, by Harris and one witness. Then the box containing his personal items was sealed in his presence. The process was repeated until all of his personal effects were sealed. We finally had three large boxes filled. Lieutenant Treadwell was overseeing the inventory and said, "Smith, these items will be placed in our control room and if you receive a stay of execution, we will return theses items to you." Smith nodded and the lieutenant continued, "If not, they will be released to whomever you choose." Unsure of what to say, Smith simply looked at the lieutenant.

We were informed earlier that the deathwatch procedure was changed, so we did not go directly to the holding cell beside the electric chair. Instead we were instructed to escort Smith to a holding cell in the medical section. It was decided it was the best location to begin the deathwatch because it was closer to the visitation area. There was an entourage of us following Smith to the medical section. Two officers walked in front to clear the path of any inmates walking down the corridor. Harris, Sergeant Smith, Lieutenant Treadwell and I walked in formation beside and behind Smith. When we reached the medical section, we waited just outside while the medical corridor was cleared. Once that was done, we proceeded past the small infirmary and finally to the holding cell where two officers waited with a logbook. Then we relinquished custody of John Eldon Smith and our job ended.

It was decided by departmental officials that those of us assigned to H-house should not participate in the final phase of the execution process. It was believed that if the inmates living on death row discovered that we were actively participating in their deaths, it would jeopardize out effectiveness in supervising them. I personally thought it was false sentiment on the part of the department. We worked with these men daily to be sure, but now we were going to be the ones removing them from the cell house to be executed. These other inmates had no idea that we would surrender custody to someone else. All they would see is that we removed someone and find out later that they were executed. From this point on, Smith would never be left alone. He would be with two officers from each shift until he either received a stay of execution or was executed. The logbook that the officers kept was to document everything Smith said and every move he made. No matter how trivial it might seem, everything was documented. Because the death penalty was so highly debated and protests were sure to happen, nothing was left to chance and every conceivable legal detail was anticipated.

The last execution to take place in Georgia was October 16, 1964, 19 years before. There were so many changes since that time; a new commissioner, new warden, new staff and a new location from the last execution. Along with all the other changes, came new procedures for putting a man to death even though the method had not changed. The awareness of capital punishment demanded that every step we made be as professional as possible. I don't know if the rumor was true, but it was said there was no one in the department at that time who could remember the former procedures. The new procedure was explained to Lieutenant Treadwell and he informed the staff in H-house of the new procedure that would end the life of John Eldon Smith. We already knew that the 72 hour deathwatch would not take place in H-5, the execution chamber, as was initially laid out. If no stay of execution were granted eighth hours before the scheduled execution, Smith would be moved to the holding cell in H-5. There was no designated hour for the execution to take place. Once the issuing judge from the county where the inmate was convicted signs the execution order, the execution can take place anytime during a seven-day window. It is carried out at the discretion of the commissioner of the department of corrections. There would be no last minute call from the governor as the movies always portrayed. The Georgia constitution was rewritten removing the governor from the process altogether. After the courts ruled, the only body to stop the execution is the Georgia state board of pardons and paroles. At the last hour, it has the authority to grant clemency.

If Smith were transferred to H5, it meant that the execution was imminent. There, he would receive his last meal that consists of anything he wants within reason. One officer said, "If it were me, I'd ask for humming bird tongues." That statement was made on the assumption that the execution could not take place if the last meal could not be granted. Again, it was another myth from the movies. Just hours prior to the execution, his head and a portion of his left leg below the knee would be shaved. This was to allow for the headpiece and the leg band to be attached. The chair itself is not wired with electricity. Electrodes are attached to the headpiece and the leg band and the condemned man's body completes the circuit. The chair is simply to hold him in place.

In the last hour, witnesses are assembled at the front gate. The state chooses five witnesses; the news media is allowed five and the condemned man himself can have five. All would be transported, by van, to the rear of the institution. There they are directed to their seats in the witness room to wait. Finally the condemned is escorted into the execution chamber by the execution team. The primary objective of which is to make sure the condemned walks to the chair, by force if necessary. Then each has a specific task to perform. There are straps for the arms, the chest, and legs. Finally the headpiece and leg strap are attached. A new feature for the redesigned chair is an adjustable backboard so that the condemned will be secured to the chair. The warden then affords the condemned the opportunity to make a last statement, which is recorded. Once completed, a prayer is offered if the condemned so chooses.

Following the prayer, the warden reads the execution order to the condemned and to the witnesses. The microphone is necessary because of the very thick glass. During that process, the condemned is strapped in the chair looking directly at the witnesses. After the execution order is read, the execution team reenters the execution chamber to attach the headpiece and the leg band. Following that, the electrician enters and attaches the electrical wires to the headpiece and the leg band. The department of corrections had to provide a large industrial generator for use only in executions. The Power Company would not supply electricity for an execution for fear of being sued at some point for causing a death. The electrician was an institutional maintenance employee. After the wires were in place, the condemned's forehead is wiped for perspiration and a black vinyl hood placed over his face. One final check of every strap is conducted, the microphone is switched off and everyone leaves the execution chamber. My thought was that it must feel like the loneliest place in the world and I could only imagine that it seemed like an eternity in those few minutes.

The warden enters the control room located behind the execution chamber to view the executions through a two-way mirror. The commissioner of the department of corrections maintains telephone communication from his office in Atlanta where he waits with the attorney general of the state of Georgia. The warden asks the commissioner if there is any final word to stop the execution. If no order to halt is given, the warden gives the order to proceed. There wouldn't be any hooded man waiting in the shadows to pull a single large switch. Instead, it would be a two-minute automatic system.

The new system used three small buttons that uniformed officers pushed when the warden gives the order. Only one button is live and none of the three officers knows which button it is. The engineer who set up the system would not be in the control room, so he could not tell who pushed the live button. It would all be anonymous. Once the buttons are pushed, the officers lay the controls down. It is a two-minute cycle with three phases. Phase one sends 2,000 volts of electricity through the wire. Phase two drops down to approximately 1,500 volts and phase three is the "trickle down" phase at approximately 200 volts. Though not very high voltage, it is enough to cause death and actually bring the bodily fluids to a boil. Therefore, a "lapse time" was created to allow the body to cool before physicians can check the body. Two physicians are required to check the body to ensure that the "order of the court" is carried out. It is a myth that anyone who survives the execution can go free. If, in fact the condemned man does not die, the process is repeated. Though most agreed that after electricity has been applied to a person for two minutes, he would be brain dead even if the body survived. After the physicians check, if the condemned has died, the warden returns to the microphone and advises the witnesses that the court ordered execution has been carried out and gives the time. The curtains are closed and the witnesses are removed.

John Eldon Smith was scheduled to die Thursday, December 15, 1983 at 8:00 am. After a final attorney's visit, Smith was escorted to the holding cell in H-5 on Wednesday evening, the 14th of December. By all appearances, it appeared it was going to happen. It was like a cloud descended over the diagnostic center. There was an air of anticipation throughout the institution. There were all sorts of opinions. Many believed that it wouldn't really happen and that the U.S. Supreme Court would stop it. It was a fair assumption because it had happened so many times before. But then things had never gone this far before. Then there were those who waited with enthusiasm.

I remember the Wednesday evening Smith was being moved. I had to go into the H 1&2 sally port to retrieve a report. The officer's platform was above me and as I reached up for the report, one of the newer officers began to sing the song "tomorrow" from the Annie movie, but with his own version of the lyrics. In a high pitched voice he sung, "Tomorrow, tomorrow we're gonna burn John Smith tomorrow." It took me by surprise. I wasn't sure how to respond. I smiled at him for his imagination and turned to walk away.

After I got back to the corridor my smile left me immediately. It was a heinous crime. Smith had killed at the behest of his wife for money. He killed a newlywed couple and drove away as if it were nothing. It was particularly cold blooded. But, then I thought about what was going to happen tomorrow and what I had been told about the procedure. A man was going to die sitting in a chair while people watched.

Emotions stirred inside me. My Christian beliefs came to mind and I remembered hearing a preacher quote from the bible, God's own words, that vengeance was for him and for him alone. Many officers were fond of quoting scripture in an attempt to justify what was about to happen. Mostly I heard, "The bible says an eye for an eye." I couldn't pretend to know the mind of God and I hadn't been in church in a while. Mostly because I was ashamed to face God after the things I had done in the past couple of years. I had no right to have an opinion. But, deep down inside I wondered if what we were doing was what God really wanted from his people. I did as always and kept my doubts to myself and dare not let any of these men I worked with know the struggle inside of me. Again, I employed my defense mechanism of stuffing my feelings as far down inside as I could get them. I began to wonder just how much I could keep inside.

Though none of us in H-house would be directly involved in the execution, we were ordered to report early on Thursday the 15th because no one knew just how the inmates in H-house were going to respond. Sarah and I arrived at 7 am and I could hardly believe my eyes. There were so many people around the front gate. There were a lot of law enforcement personnel at the gate as well. It looked as though every news station from Atlanta was here. I saw many people holding signs of protest. One of our outside detail officers was in charge of security.

He was on hand to identify prison staff that entered at this time every morning. The other law enforcement personnel were there for security purposes. No one had any idea what someone might do to prevent the execution from taking place so every precaution was taken. It was a beautiful day. It was cool, but the sun was out. Not that any of that would mean anything to Smith. Even if he were remotely interested, his only view would be a small porthole in the ceiling. He would only be able to see the blue sky. The last time I saw Smith, he appeared to be ready to go. No one can truly know what is happening in a person's mind, but by all outward appearances, he was relatively calm. Smith was never disrespectful and was by no means a troublemaker. He was too small to have caused any type of physical harm to anyone. He kept mostly to himself. However, today, he was the center of attention and on everyone's mind.

It was business as usual through the rest of the institution. I headed to H-house to find Lieutenant Treadwell already in his office with the counselors. There were now three full time counselors on duty in H-house. A psychologist came to H-house once a week, to talk with inmates and he was here today as well. We all waited around Lieutenant Treadwell's office for 8 am and on standby in case there was trouble anywhere. I peered out of an observation window on the door beside Lieutenant Treadwell's office. This was Smith's last exit the night before on the way to H-5. Beside me stood the new counselor and we shared the window. I could see the generator just outside of H-5 and the van waiting to take the visitors back to the front gate.

I heard a noise coming down the corridor from H-house. Some of the inmates were apparently banging on their cells in some sort of a tribute to Smith. I stepped away to look down the corridor and then came back to the window. The counselor had moved closer to the window so that I now had to look over his shoulder. In a low voice he said, "Yeah, those

guys got a right to protest about what might happen to them." I looked at the back of his head in amazement and that's when I noticed that he was visibly shaking as though he had a chill. He was emotionally upset. I was still torn with my emotions about how to feel about all of this, but what I was sure of is that the victims of these men could not be forgotten. In my short time on death row I had witnessed the way these men were treated by outsiders like the visiting pastors and their attorneys. They all acted as if these men were victims of the system and unjustly accused and sentenced. I recalled that shortly before we received Smith's execution order, he was visiting with a pastor from Atlanta. She wanted to give Smith a pack of Cigarettes. Inmates could not take or receive anything from visitation. Her remark was, "Why don't you let this poor man have these cigarettes?" I simply shook my head, but in my mind I was thinking, *"What about the poor man and woman he killed to get here?"* I wasn't without compassion, but I didn't think any of these men were victims. They had killed people and as with most cases, in a very heinous way. These were convicted murderers and I knew that they should not just be set free so that they could kill again.

Now a correctional counselor stood in front of me, visibly shaking and saying these men have a "right" to protest what might happen to them. I felt nauseated. I wasn't sure about executing them, but I sure wasn't in favor of freeing them so they could kill again. Somewhere in this crazy, mixed up world, they had to take responsibility for what they had done. Most never mentioned their victims and I never heard one man cry out that he was innocent.

While my mind was racing with thoughts, it had happened. I saw white smoke from the exhaust of the white state van and passengers being loaded inside. Then the van sped away. John Eldon Smith had died in Georgia's electric chair becoming the first person to be executed in 19 years. History was being made and I was in the middle of it all. The new concern was how the other inmates were going to react to it. Lieutenant Treadwell decided the best course of action was to continue our duties as if it were any other day. As the day went on, we saw that the other inmates didn't seem to react out of the ordinary.

Reports began to make their way back to us of Smith's last few minutes. He had walked unassisted to the chair and by all accounts, jumped right in as if sitting down in a barber chair. We all believed that at that point in time that he resigned to the fact that it was over and that he was going to sit in the chair one way or another. If he didn't have anything else, at least he had his dignity as a human being and he left with that. He refused to pick any personal witnesses and the priest who held mass every Wednesday afternoon made his final statement. It was a verse from the bible. It was also reported that at one point Smith said, "Well, the Lord is going to get another one."

It made me wonder why we, as human beings, have to wait until the worst possible moments of our lives to reach out to the God who created us when he waits with open arms for us to come to him. In this case, two people, newlyweds, looked forward to a long life together had to die in order for Smith to find God. The mysteries of this life escaped me. When Cain killed his brother Able, he initiated a horrible legacy for mankind that lasted all the way down to John Eldon Smith and this was not the end of it. There were 119 more men just down the corridor that were waiting for the final judgment of their fate. When the execution team members began to strap Smith into the chair, his last words were, "Hey, there ain't no point in pulling it so tight." The fact was that no one knew for sure what the

reaction would be when 2,000 volts of electricity entered his body. The one who knew least of all was Smith himself. I thought to myself, *"Guess that doesn't matter now, because he isn't here to tell us."* I remembered for so long that most officers, including me, thought that we would never see an execution take place.

Now we lived in a world where men were going to die in the electric chair and I wondered what effect, if any, it would have on the future criminals of Georgia. One protester of the death penalty had made that assertion earlier in the day when he said, "The death penalty is not a deterrent to crime." It had been 19 years since the last execution so it remained to be seen. John Smith's attorneys arrived to pick up his personal belongings and I was given the duty of retrieving them. The items were stored in Control one. As I walked to the front of the institution I pondered the day's events. I'm sure it was my perception that changed, but the institution seemed different. The Georgia electric chair came alive and I could only imagine what was going through the minds of the inmates.

I wondered if they all were thinking the same thought; *"Will I be next?"* There were some sentenced to death before Smith so it didn't appear that executions were happening in relation to sentencing dates. I imagined that made a lot of them nervous.

Once inside the control room, I looked at Smith's three boxes of personal belongings. I was present only two days before when these boxes were inventoried and sealed. It was mostly legal papers, a few personal magazines and some candy he bought from the inmate store, but didn't have time to eat. There were no clothing items. All clothing was state issued. Carl Isaacs, Timothy McCorquodale, David Jarrell, Johnny Johnson and Troy Gregg had seen to that with their escape attempt in 1980 from Georgia State Prison. As I looked it seemed quite sad that all that was left of a man's life after 52 years of living could be placed in three cardboard boxes. I used a dolly to take the boxes to the front and drop them off at the visitation desk. For our part in H-house, that was the end of John Eldon Smith and he slipped into obscurity.

Life with Sarah continued on a rocky path. My only solace during that time was my children. Leighanne and Tracey readily accepted Kimberly as their sister, but Deedee and her new boyfriend weren't so accepting. It got back to me through my sister that when the girls were asked how they liked their new sister, Deedee was very adamant that they had no sister. I know that I hurt Deedee and the girls, but Kimberly was an innocent child and had nothing to do with that. I thought that it was very unfair for all three of my girls.

During 1984 Sarah and I separated about as much as we stayed together. We both continued to cheat on each other. It was as if we were involved in something unholy and God refused to bless it and caught in the middle was a beautiful, precious little girl. When we were apart, my mind continued to race with the thoughts of what I had with all my children and what I gave away for lust. When I was away from them, days seemed meaningless and so, I drank to cover up those feelings. During those moments forgotten faces returned to my mind; like Teresa Carol Allen, Ronald and Juanita Akins, Donna Dixon accompanied by the faces of the men who killed them. One by one they would flash through my mind. There was a time in my life when I would have called on the name of Jesus Christ to help me in my distress. Now, I seemed so far away from him and usually felt too ashamed to call on him after the pain I caused others. Now, when the faces of the dead and their killers called in a ghostly way, I required alcohol to make them disappear.

All the maximum institutions in the state had tactical squads that could be mobilized anytime there was a riot or disturbance anywhere in the state. They were 18-men units trained to retake a prison when negotiations failed. In 1984, during a training exercise, 16 members of the tactical squad resigned over an issue of physical fitness. Though all the men on the squad were big men, most were overweight and unable or unwilling to perform the physical training. All tactical officers were also correctional officers in the institution. Resigning their positions on the squad did not affect their employment. The only two officers left on the squad were assigned as squad leader and assistant leader. A letter was posted on the officer's bulletin board announcing a selection process for the remaining positions on the squad. Since tactical officers were now expected to be physically fit; try-outs would include a physical training test. I intended to be one of those selected no matter what test I had to pass to achieve that. Those of us that applied were also informed that a new obstacle course was built just for the squad and that would be part of our test.

The tactical squad met once a month to drill. That consisted of physical training, firearms training, use of chemical weapons and drill in tactical formations for controlling a crowd. Since most riots usually had a fire at some point, special training in fire control was mandated for all squads. The first step in the selection process was the physical fitness test. We were required to run approximately 1 mile from the front entrance to the obstacle course. There were several applicants so we all ran in a group. One by one they started to fall away from the group until only two of us remained. I looked over and it was Mike Simms, the officer with whom I attended the academy. I couldn't waste energy on a smile, so I nodded. I was slightly in front, but he kept pace with me. We left the paved road and moved onto the dirt road that led to the obstacle course. The change in the running surface interrupted my stride a bit, but I was in front and I was determined to stay there. Mike stayed there with me. I looked up to see that we were approaching the obstacle course, so I picked up the pace. I knew it was the end so I wanted to burn myself out to maintain my lead. Mike wasn't going anywhere. He stayed only a couple of paces behind me.

When we reached the end we both shouted out in pain and then started to laugh. As I walked around to regain my breath, I saw the only two remaining members of the prior squad; Donnie Moore and Tommy Henson. They were now the Squad leader and assistant squad leaders, respectively. I knew Tommy from high school and we had also studied at the same karate school together and he later became one of my students at my failed martial arts school. He looked over at me, winked and gave me a thumb up. I knew Donnie and his family from Forsyth and he was busy writing down our qualifying times. They were both dressed in their Tactical uniforms; navy blue with a Tactical squad patch over the left pocket. It resembled an inverted triangle with the words "Tactical Squad" written in silver and a lightning bolt passing through the words. There was no nametag worn on this uniform. The trousers were bloused over the top of the boots and that gave it a military appearance.

It was impressive and I could see that 18 men dressed in this uniform wearing full tactical gear would be intimidating. When our breathing returned to normal, Mike looked over at me and said, "I knew you were going to kick it at the end so I told myself that if you did, I was going with you." We both laughed as we walked over to get our qualifying times. My time was 7:00 minutes and Mike's was 7:03. We waited and encouraged all those finishing. After all the qualifying times were given out, we began the next phase of our test. The obstacle course was new and this was the first time I'd seen it. There were hurdles to jump, a balance beam to negotiate, two walls to climb, and at the very end was a sixteen foot, knotted vertical rope to climb. If we did not complete any portion of the course, we would be disqualified.

We were lined up in the order we finished the run so Mike and I were first. At twenty-four years old, I was in good shape. All the years of martial arts training benefited me greatly. Neither Mike nor I had any problems completing the course. there were some who were a little overweight and it told on them. Some made it through the run, but the extra weight became an issue on the obstacle course. The next step would be the firing range. Every officer had to qualify annually with a minimum score of 70 to maintain certification. Tactical Officers had to qualify with a score of 80 to maintain their positions on the squad. It was the same with First aid and CPR. An 80 percent score would be required. The following week, the firing range was opened for us. Everyone qualified with at least a minimum score. Then we were told that the final selection would be made by the Assistant Superintendent of security. All members of the tactical squad received hazardous duty pay of $100.00 per month. But, that wasn't my reason for wanting to join. It was a chance to get noticed by the senior members of the department and to have access to advanced training. Having the certificates for training in the personnel file went a long way at promotion time. I also wanted to be a part of something special. I was already permanent staff in H-house, but I wanted as much exposure as I could get. I made some terrible decisions in my personal life and I wanted to make sure that my professional life took a different turn.

It only took a week for the selection to be completed. The letter was posted on the officer's bulletin board in the classroom. The names were posted alphabetically so I looked at the top of the list as I had always done in school. There was my name and I smiled. It was one more step up the ladder and a chance to be noticed. The Assistant Superintendant was pleased as well because we heard the rumor that he said, "This new squad is physically fit and they got some size to them." The last squad members were big men to be sure, but not all that physically fit. That is, with the exception of Tommy Henson and Donnie Moore.

Sarah and I continued our yo-yo relationship. Neither of us seemed to be able to find a way to say good-bye. It seemed we were staying together just for Kimberly. I taught martial arts on occasion. Other than Kimberly, it was my only comfort while I lived at home with Sarah. There was no trust in our relationship because of the way we lived. We did insane things to each other. On one occasion, she drove to the armory in her nightgown and housecoat on the pretense that we needed milk. What she was actually doing was checking up on me. I was standing outside with some students when she drove up to the door, rolled the window down and handed me a $10 bill for milk. When I asked where Kimberly was, she replied, "At home asleep." Kimberly was only 1 years old and I was flabbergasted. "Alone?" I asked. She saw my anger and said, "She's fine" and drove away without waiting for a response. That had become the norm for our marriage. She would do something ridiculous and me countering with something equally ridiculous. It was no life for two adults to be living and it was no example for Kimberly. We attended church at times, but most times it was because of her parents attending and we went to be seen. Neither of us was living anything close to a Christian life. We never prayed together and we never opened a bible unless we were at church.

On my off days I felt drawn to my father's grave. I would spend time at the foot of his grave just staring at the nameplate in the ground. I said how much I missed him and needed him to be here so I could talk to him. I would stare out at the peaceful pastures off in the distance and realize how selfish my wish was. He was in pain here and I watched him suffer. I didn't want that for him. He was beyond this world of pain and I prayed that he found peace. He was such a good man and I felt as though I had dishonored him with the sinful choices I made. I would attempt to talk to him and as I said, "Daddy," it always left me in tears and often drove me to my knees. There were times when I would lay down next to his grave and run my fingers along the raised letters of his name on the nameplate. I knew he wasn't here, but this form beneath the soil was how I knew him. After a visit to the cemetery I always ended my day with my mother. Very often, we just sat on the porch staring out in the yard in silence. I'd return home feeling empty and praying for my off days to end quickly so I could get back to work. It was the only thing at that time that had any meaning for me.

When the execution of John Eldon Smith occurred we assumed it was a fluke or that someone dropped the ball in some way. The truth was his appeals were exhausted and there was no other recourse for his attorneys to pursue. Even with that being said, we also thought there would be no other executions in sight and we would put the electric chair back to sleep, in a manner of speaking. Then shortly after my birthday in July 1984, we received word that another appeal process had been exhausted for an inmate. His name was Ivon Ray Stanley. Prior to Smith, 19 years passed since an execution was carried out in Georgia. Now seven months later, we were facing the possibility of another execution. The thought that appeals may be running out for everyone cast a new light on anyone sitting on death row. A few inmates had their sentences commuted to life and placed in regular prison population. Prior to Smith's execution, it seemed Death row was little more than a holding area until that happened to all of them. Not anymore. Now a death sentence seemed more likely to be carried out and it made the inmates nervous and the staff more cautious.

Ivon Ray Stanley was just 20 years old when he committed capital murder. It was a particularly harsh murder. It wasn't out of anger or jealousy as some murders. It was to obtain something that he wanted and someone else possessed; money. His accomplice, Joseph Thomas, also shared his fate on death row. However, in July 1984, it was Stanley who would answer first for their horrific crime.

On April 12, 1976 Clifford Floyd was making his regular rounds through Bainbridge, Georgia collecting weekly insurance premiums and was being watched. A month earlier, Joseph Thomas and Ivon Ray Stanley were overheard talking about robbing the insurance man. The two agreed that after the robbery they would have to, "get rid of him because he will tell who we are," After Thomas was arrested he described what happened in detail.

Floyd came by Thomas' house to collect an insurance payment. After he left, Thomas sent a friend over to Stanley's house to tell him to come to Thomas' house. Stanley came over and Thomas told him, "You can get the insurance man if you want him." Stanley ran from Thomas' house and caught up with Floyd. On a pretext he persuaded Floyd to return to Thomas' house. Stanley was armed with a .22 caliber pistol, which Thomas had given him. When Thomas came out of the house, Stanley had already pulled the gun on Floyd, emptied his pockets and told him not to move or say anything. Stanley, armed with a pistol and Thomas carrying a hammer, forced Floyd to go to the woods with them near Thomas' house. As they were walking, Floyd and Thomas exchanged some words.

Angered, Thomas struck Floyd on the forehead with the hammer. Thomas walked back up to the hog pens near his house, obtained a length of rope, and returned the woods where the other two were. Again leaving Stanley and Floyd alone, Thomas went back to where Floyd parked his car and drove it away in search of a hiding place. After searching the car, Thomas found a .22 caliber pistol in the glove box. Leaving the car he walked back to where he left the other two men and found Floyd now tied to a tree. Stanley said, "You know we gonna have to get rid of him." Thomas responded, "Yeah" and then went back to his mother's house and came back with a shovel. Thomas began digging a shallow grave approximately 11 inches deep. He then handed the shovel to Stanley to finish digging the grave.

Once they finished, Stanley went over and untied Floyd from the tree, but left his hands bound. Blood was flowing from Floyd's head. Thomas ripped part of the man's shirt and stuffed it into his mouth to silence him. As they approached the grave, Stanley handed the gun to Thomas and told him, "You gonna do the rest." Taking the gun, Thomas turned his head away and fired five times at Floyd's head. Stanley then took the shovel that had been used to dig the grave and hit Floyd twice. He handed the shovel to Thomas who continued to beat Floyd. He hit him once in the stomach, twice in the head and once in the chest. However, Floyd was still alive. Floyd was now lying in the grave and Stanley began to cover his lower body with dirt. When he had partially buried him, he handed the shovel to Thomas who began to throw dirt over Floyd's face. Through all of this, Floyd was not only struggling for breath but, as dirt began to cover his head, he attempted to say something. Twice, according to Thomas, the insurance man pleaded for his life. When Floyd, still breathing, was completely covered in his shallow grave, the two men left.

Later they moved the car to an old logging road, but it bogged down in the mud. It was reported that at the time of Floyd's last known collection, he would only have collected $234. The next day, four anonymous phone calls were made to the police telling them where they could find the car and giving misleading information about the victim. Through phone taps, one of these calls was traced to Thomas' home. When police arrived, he was the only one at home. He subsequently admitted to making the call. An autopsy performed later on the victim disclosed a gunshot through his upper lip; Numerous lacerations on the scalp, head and body apparently made by the edge of the shovel. A depressed skull fracture pushed into the brain consistent with a blow from a hammer; brain hemorrhage, a broken sternum, and according to the medical examiner, "a rather striking accumulation of both blood and dirt found in the bronchi of both lungs, scattered up and down the trachea and in the larynx and also in the upper most part of the stomach. Based on the autopsy, death was caused by a mixture of blood and dirt, vomiting it up and then inhaling the mixture into the lungs. In short, Clifford Floyd either strangled or suffocated on his own blood while he lay in his shallow grave. According to the medical examiner, it took approximately thirty minutes. It was probably an eternity for Mr. Floyd.

Thomas was arrested two days after the murder and confessed in detail. His confession was tape recorded and played at his trial. He testified that he had no memory of the incident after taking two pills that he purchased from someone. I suspect that his recall of the events that led to his new address on death row changed when he acquired an attorney.

It's one of the reasons I possess such a low opinion of those on that side of the law. In my experience it's all a play on words and not actually finding the truth. I never heard any inmate on death row stand up and proclaim his innocence. Not even one. There were always excuses and a lot of finger pointing and of course there was my personal favorite, "I made a mistake." I could never fathom how causing the mental, emotional, physical torment and death of another human being was a "mistake."

The execution date for Ivon Ray Stanley approached with no stay of execution in sight. The daytime execution of John Eldon Smith had been a mistake. Because it was at 8:00 am, it seemed as though it encouraged people to come to the institution to support, protest or watch out of curiosity. Since there was a seven-day window with no set time, the revamped procedure called for a nighttime execution. The thought was that hopefully, it would deter people from coming out. Once we were down to the 72-hour deathwatch, Sergeant Smith, Officers Kindle, Carter and I went in to pack up Stanley and move him to the holding cell in the medical section. Stanley was always very quiet and timid. He knew why we had come and went right to work packing his personal effects. Stanley never received any visitors or mail so all his property was state issued. Once completed, we conducted the strip search and then we departed for the medical section and we turned Stanley over to the two offices conducting the deathwatch. Even after the execution of John Eldon Smith, none of us were really convinced that Stanley would be executed. It was as if everyone was holding their breath to see which court would act first in granting a stay of execution. After three days, none came and it appeared as though Stanley was going to become the second person to die in this new age of the death penalty. Lieutenant Treadwell advised us that the execution would take place sometime around midnight. Because it was still so new, he decided that we should be present in H-house when the execution took place. In the early evening of July 11th, Stanley was moved to the H-5 holding cell.

I arrived that evening at around 10 pm and the front gate was already buzzing with activity from the protesters. When I walked through the cross gate at F-house, I saw Lieutenant Treadwell already in his office. We sat in his office and waited for a sign of anything unusual from the inmates, but none came. H-house was silent tonight. Dave Harris arrived next. Lieutenant Treadwell was a dedicated coffee drinker so we joined him for a cup. Later in the evening, we were joined by a priest who was also one of the chaplains for the institution. We sat in a group in the corridor outside Lieutenant Treadwell's office talking about the day's events and about this new era of executions. Lieutenant Treadwell had a way of always keeping the mood light and humors in any situation. Whenever he saw us going down a dark path, he would change the tone by telling us one of his war stories from World War II. I liked him and he began to teach me how to deal with people. As the hour approached, we kept watch out the observation window on the outside corridor door. This door became the gateway to the H-5 execution chamber. Smith and Stanley both exited this door on the way to their rendezvous with the electric chair. Now it became our visual aide to what was happening in H-5. Just as with Smith's execution, we saw the white van transporting witnesses' already parked outside. It was after midnight and there was nothing left to do but wait. In contrast to Smith's execution that took place in the early morning hours as the institution was coming to life, it was now after midnight and deathly quiet in the corridors of H-house. It was eerie and as if the walls of the prison itself sensed the angel of death had arrived and was waiting.

As the clocked ticked, even Lieutenant Treadwell ran out of conversation as if in reverence to the time that was approaching. It was all still very new to us and sense there had only been 7 months in between executions, it made it just that much more real for us. I watched through the window with Dave looking over my shoulder. Finally at approximately 12:27 am, the white van came to life. The lights turned on and it made its hasty getaway to the front entrance. Ivon Ray Stanley was dead. Unlike The execution of John Eldon Smith, Lieutenant Treadwell started receiving reports of Stanley's execution right away. Like Smith before him, Stanley walked unassisted and seated himself in the chair. He was given the opportunity to make a last statement and asked if he wanted a prayer, but unlike Smith he refused both. Smith had allowed one of the Institutional chaplains to quote scripture as his last statement and also say a last prayer. Stanley, true to his walk in H-house, had remained quiet. I never expressed it to anyone, but it touched a nerve deep inside of me when I heard the report that he asked for no prayer. At his last moment of life, there was no one to pray for his soul, though he was about to meet the creator of the universe. I wondered if anyone had ever witnessed a word of what Jesus Christ had done for him nearly two thousand years before. It did not sit well with me.

Then I thought about Mr. Clifford Floyd and the hell he went through in the last thirty minutes of his life and if he had the wits about him to cry out for the loving peace of Jesus Christ in his last moments. I also thought about the good people of the world, like my father, who just simply ran out of time. I was torn in so many directions and it was making my head swim. My mind cried out that justice had been served for Mr. Floyd and my heart ached for my father and somewhere in between was the thought for Ivon Ray Stanley's soul. There was no way I could ever tell my fellow officers what I was feeling here tonight. I would be branded as a bleeding heart and most assuredly ran out of H-house.

Lieutenant Treadwell released us for the night and I purposely waited for the others to leave before I walked out. I made my way down the long dark tunnel with my thoughts. I wore a blue uniform and that made me part of a team of professionals who weren't having the thoughts I had. I wanted justice for these men and women that had been savagely killed, but I was also a Christian who had been taught that sin is sin in the eyes of almighty God and I had certainly sinned against God. I pushed the big Iron Gate as I welcomed the night air in my lungs. I looked up at the night sky and wondered if Ivon Ray Stanley was now looking at us from a different vantage point. Lieutenant Treadwell told me the last words of our warden to the commissioner of the department of corrections when the execution was completed and it burned deep inside of me that all of this was just a beginning. He said, "Send us another one."

Orange belt 1974

Executing Flying sidekick in 1975

Performing jump kick at 17 years old. The student on the receiving end is Hugh Tillman who was with me during my motorcycle wreck in 1985

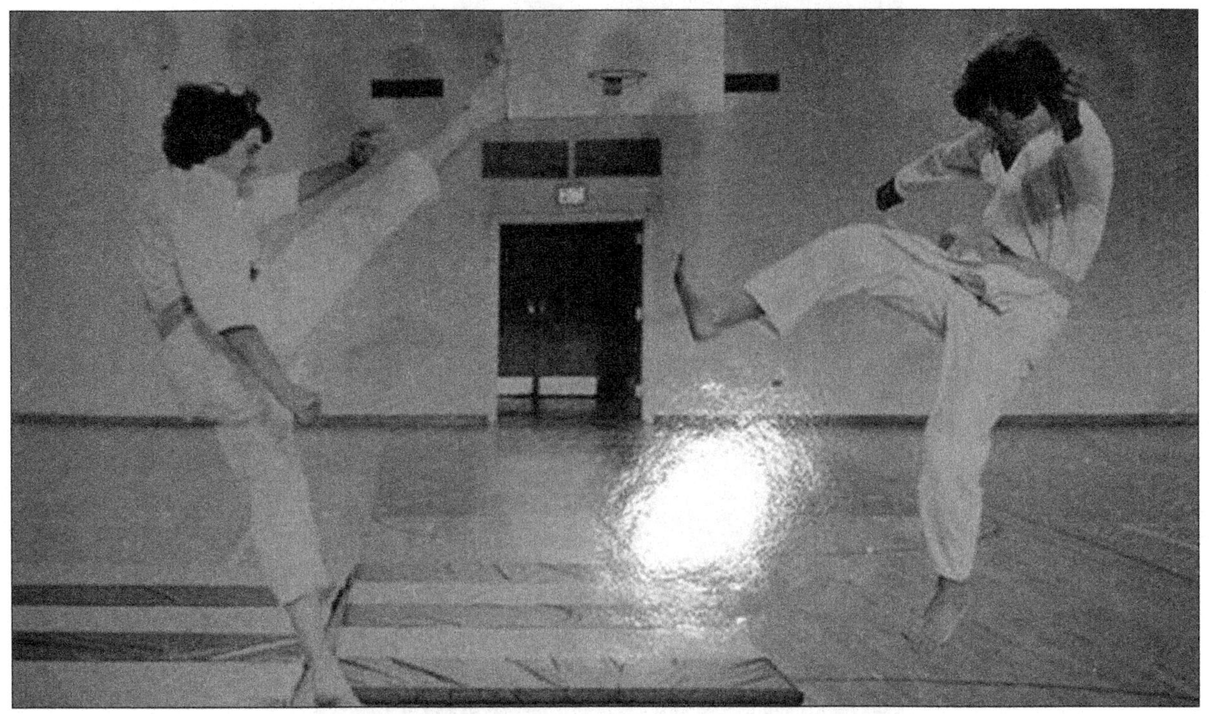

Me and childhood friend Buck Wilder at Tift college in 1974. Buck is now a Chief Magistrate Judge in Monroe County Georgia

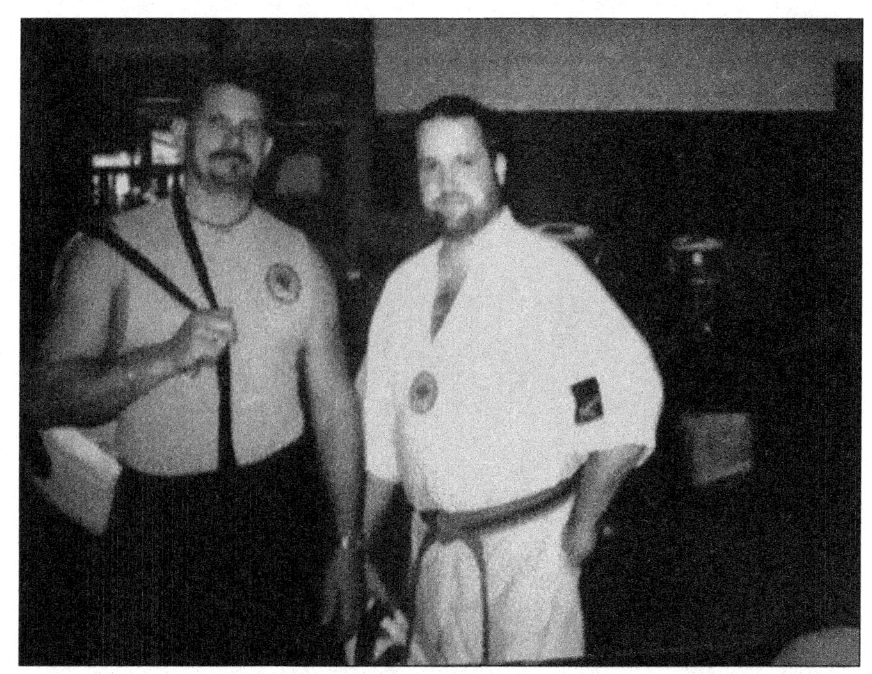

Me and fellow student Chris Shore at Taekwondo tournament 1999

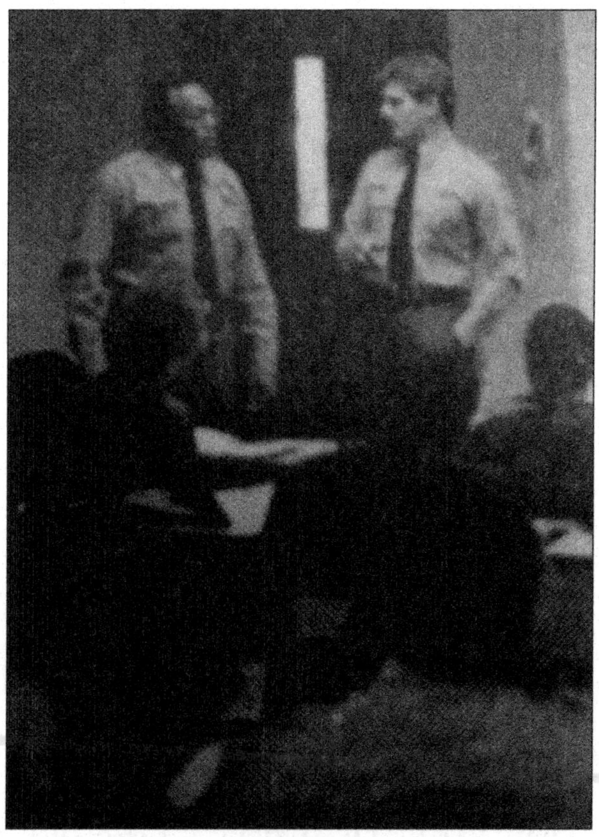

Classroom instruction on Intake day

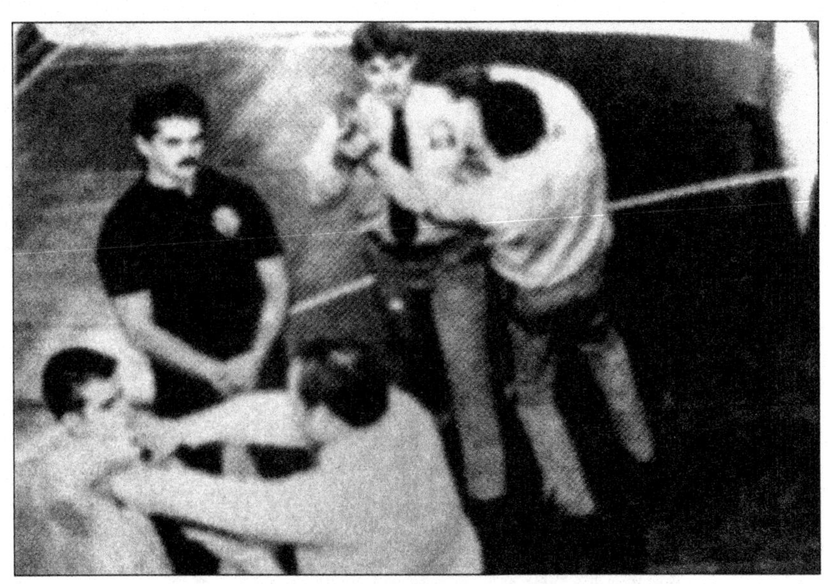

Teaching defensive tactics at GPSTC 1987

1986 Officer of the Year for the state of Georgia

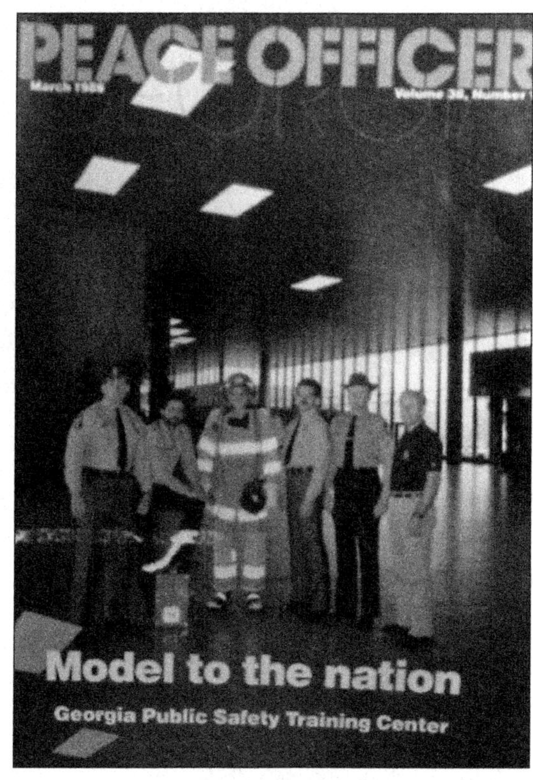

Cover of the Georgia Peace Officer Magazine 1987

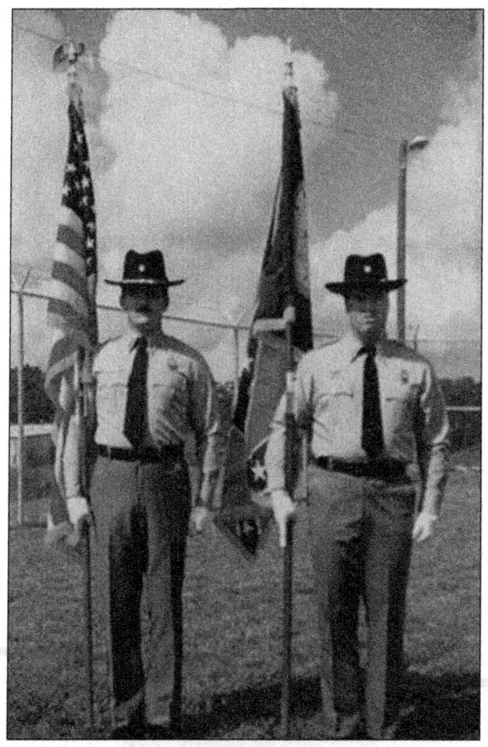

Me at left and one of my best friends Terry Duffey as color guard

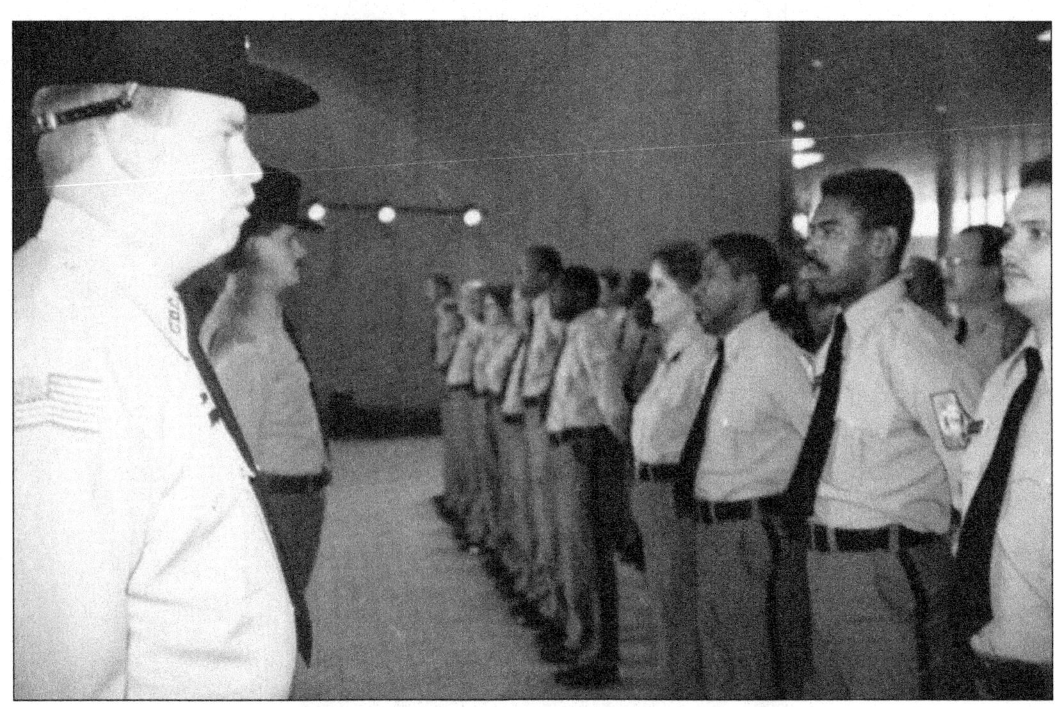

Terry Duffey and I inspecting a graduating class 1987

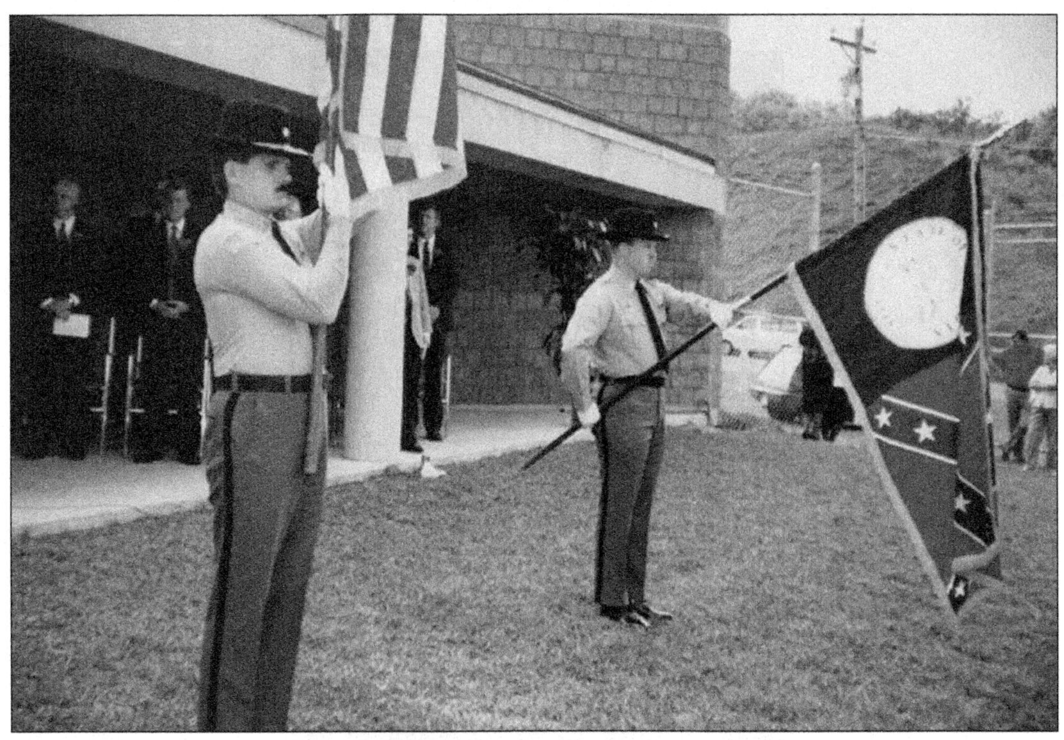

Terry Duffey and I as color guard 1988

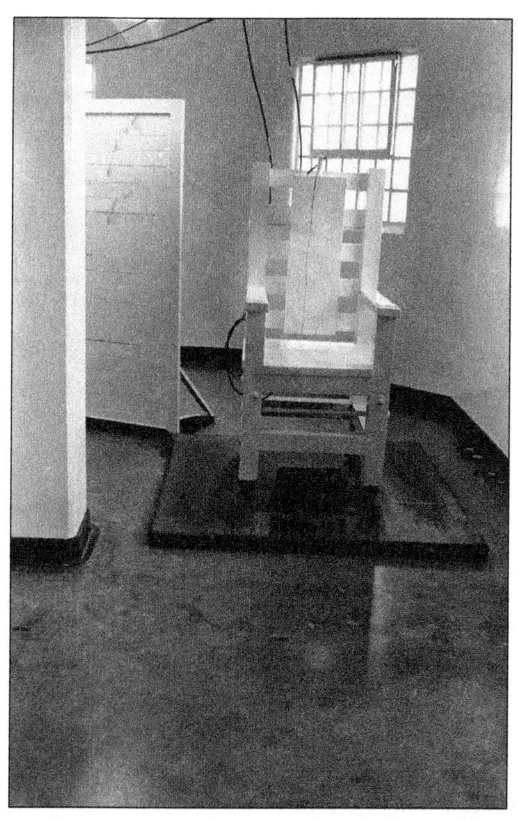

Georgia's first electric chair on display at Georgia State Prison

Georgia's redesigned electric chair at the Georgia Diagnostic Center 1983

View of the electric chair and execution chamber from the witness room at the Georgia Diagnostic Center

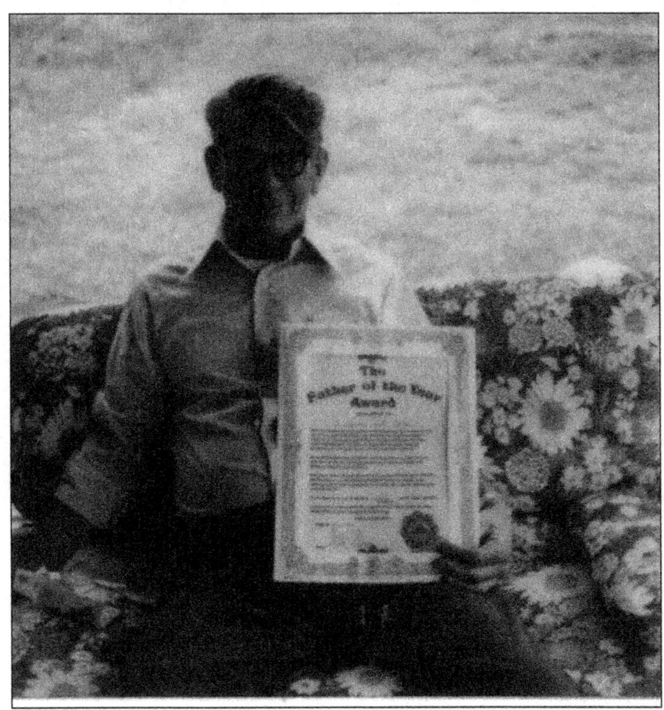

My father, Bill Allen

My mother, Ruby Allen

Majik Market store where Teresa Carol Allen was abducted in 1976, now a hair salon

Final resting place of Teresa Carol Allen in Cochran, Georgia

Chapter 9

"For the living know that they will die, but the dead know nothing, and they have no more reward, for the memory of them is forgotten"

- Ecclesiastes 9:5
(English Standard Version)

There seemed to be a cloud hanging over H-house in the weeks that followed Stanley's execution almost like an air of uncertainty. None of the inmates dared verbalize what was happening. To talk about it made it all the more real, but the staff had no problem talking about it. I still found myself torn. On the one hand, these men were convicted of some very horrific crimes. On the other hand were my Christian values and grace and mercy were a part of those beliefs. I didn't for one second think we should open the doors and allow these men to go free and I believed everyone should be held accountable for the choices they make. Every time I learned the details of an inmate's crime it became more apparent to me these men could never be allowed to live among the law-abiding people of society, which included my family and me. Whenever I thought about the crimes as a parent, I became angry and wanted to take revenge myself, such as the case with Timothy McCorquodale and the rape/murder of Donna Dixon. It was easy to be disgusted by them when my focus was on their crimes. But, inevitably I would become involved in a conversation with them and realize they were human beings. Then I would be reminded of what I'd heard from more than one of the inmates in H-house; "I just don't remember." It can be argued that the things they did were so traumatic their minds blocked it all out. I know the brain has the capability to protect itself in that way. But, there was also the possibility that something evil was involved and I felt it the first time I walked into H-house.

Every now and then the phrase I heard from our Training Officer, Larry Branch, flashed through my mind; "Inmates are in prison as punishment, not for punishment." I believed that statement and why should it not apply to these men with death sentences? I believe it was the nature of the crimes that encouraged officers to demand a measure of their own justice. They weren't alone because I felt it as well. That was the constant struggle. Some of these men served in the U.S. military in the service of our country. It was easy to spot the instilled discipline in those who served. However somewhere in their lives, that discipline failed them in a major way and they ended up here.

One of those men was Harold Glenn Williams. He was a new inmate that arrived in H-house and was a U.S. Marine. He claimed that he was on the security detail for President Carter at Camp David and the White House. His physical demeanor was not very intimidating, though he thought it was. He was short and did have muscular legs, but other than that, he didn't look to be in superior physical condition. He had received a death sentence for killing his own grandfather over insurance money from his grandmother's death and then set the house on fire.

I was never certain of his defensive tactics training from the military, but once he found out about my martial arts background, he would brag to other inmates and officers that I was the only one in H-house who could do anything with him. Strangely enough, he seemed to develop an admiration for my skill. On escort duty away from H-house we developed a rapport. Anytime these men showed respect, I returned the respect as well. It didn't mean that I thought they were less dangerous; it was just a way of developing a working relationship with them. Williams actually seemed to like me. When I escorted him away from H-house, he was jovial and usually initiated conversation. I don't believe any of it was an act because the staff had no effect on any of their cases one way or the other and there was no reason to attempt to impress any of us. I believed it was their true personality that I was seeing, though usually a day would come when I would see the dark side of their personality. I believed that side was capable of the rage associated with the heinous things they did when the murders were committed. I was also surprised how lightly the trigger could be set off to throw them into a rage. It didn't take long for Williams to display his uncontrollable side.

I remember it was a hot afternoon and Williams was due for an appointment. The first shift Sergeant, Sergeant McCann was on duty along with Officer Kindle and me. As the cross gate opened, Sergeant McCann came yelling through the entrance to get Williams out for an appointment. Sergeant McCann, Kindle and I stood at the entrance to H-3 and waited. The unit officer handed out Williams clothes for us to search while he was opening the inside gate that would allow Williams access to the red door. By now, it was a procedure that Williams went through many times. We saw Williams through the observation port in the door. The unit officer passed the key through the door and Sergeant McCann took the iron bar off the door then unlocked the door to let Williams out.

Suddenly, Sergeant Smith yelled down the corridor to put Williams back in H-3 because there was a mistake in the callout schedule and another inmate would come first. It wasn't a big deal because we prioritized all appointments and some took precedence over others. Williams would just have to wait. Sergeant McCann opened the door to H-3 again to allow Williams (who was now fully dressed) back into H-3 to wait until later. I could see the look on Williams face and he wasn't pleased. His face was flushed. Kindle and I looked at each other then back to Williams. He turned to walk back to the door and then stopped. Sergeant McCann saw it as well and said, "Williams, go back inside and don't start anything." He looked at Kindle, Sergeant McCann and me for a second, turned to the door, but I already saw what was on his mind.

I was standing with my arms crossed over my chest, but I slowly moved them down in front of my midsection to rest my left hand over my right as I slid my right leg back slightly, my right heel off the floor with my weight now on the ball of my right foot so that I was standing at an angle to him. I was poised ready to spring off of my right foot. Sergeant

McCann was holding the door. Kindle was to my right and standing head on like a bull with his head slightly down. Williams took about two steps inside the door and as the sergeant tried to shut the door, he decided he wasn't going to wait and turned around. His left hand went up to force the door open and pushed McCann back into the wall. His right hand was about to slide out toward Kindle and me, but we were faster and I was there first. I sprang off of my right foot and slid my entire body forward toward Williams. My left hand moved to block his right arm and my right hand moved to my center chest to block any move he might make to my face. My left arm continued over around his neck and I pulled his head close to me. I allowed his forward motion to continue as I brought him over my left hip, threw him to the floor and I allowed my body to fall on his so that I now was on top of him. I had him secured under me in a headlock. I executed a perfect left hip throw just the way I trained for many years. Kindle was on top of me to make sure that William didn't move.

Kindle and I rolled him on his stomach as I pulled his right arm behind him and then ordered him to bring his left arm to his back and Kindle cuffed him. It all happened so quickly that I never had time to think about it, I just reacted. All my years of training paid off. Williams lay on his stomach protesting loudly as Kindle and I made it to our feet. Sergeant McCann spoke first, "There's blood on the floor." Kindle and I both looked at ourselves and said simultaneously, "It's not me." Then we helped Williams to his feet and that's when we noticed the small cut under his left eye. I looked down at my shirt and noticed my pocket was torn where my ink pen sat. Apparently when I pulled Williams close to my body, he had cut his upper cheek on my pen and tore the pocket in the process.

Sergeant McCann ordered Kelly and me to escort Williams to the medical section to be checked out. We kept him handcuffed because we weren't sure if there was still a fight in him. On the way, he began to joke with Kindle and I about what had happened. His temper went away as quickly as it came. I wondered if for that brief moment in time, the killer inside him that murdered his grandfather had shown his face and then quickly retreated deep inside Glenn Williams again. I even wondered if he knew what happened. I didn't question him about it, but I filed that away in my mind because something told me this wouldn't be the last time I would witness something like this. I didn't know if Williams brought a bad spirit in with him or if a cloud had in fact descended on H-house because of the executions, but we began to see changes in behavior through all the units. Even though it wasn't unusual to have an execution order come in, with two executions behind us, anyone receiving an execution order became unnerved.

55-year-old Son Fleming received an execution order during that time. Fleming was never a problem and was always laughing and even joking with officers during his escorts. He was sent to death row for the murder of small town Police Chief Ed Giddens. Fleming and his accomplices had robbed a grocery store and were speeding through town where Chief Giddens was on his last shift before moving to Florida. He pulled the car over and was searching it when he was overpowered and abducted. He was shot with a .22 caliber and his own gun, a .357 magnum and his body abandoned in a rural lake.

Now the angel of death was calling for Son Fleming to answer for his part in the policeman's murder and he wasn't emotionally able to handle it. His execution order was read to him and he was isolated in the medical section for deathwatch. As the hour moved closer to his appointment with the electric chair, he collapsed in the holding cell. Lieutenant Treadwell

was called to the medical section and asked me to come along with him. When we arrived in the medical section, Fleming was lying on a medical gurney. He seemed to be lifeless, but as we moved closer to the gurney we could see that he was mumbling incoherently, his head rocking slowly back and forth. Finally he recognized Lieutenant Treadwell and I and reached his hands out. I was closer so he grabbed me first. He tightly gripped my hand and that's when I noticed the strong ammonia smell. I looked down and saw that he was lying in a pool of his own urine. He was terrified.

He gripped my hand with both of his hands and pulled it close to him. He was trying to speak, but I couldn't understand him. I quickly surmised that he was pleading for his life. Lieutenant Treadwell sensed it as well and said, "Officer Allen's going to take care of you." I snapped my head to look at the Lieutenant because I knew there was nothing I could do. Then I realized that it was the Lieutenant's way of consoling a man who had no hope. Now he looked to me as if I were the only one who could save him from a certain death. He continued to cry large tears, mumble and rock his head from side to side.

Having the knowledge of what these men did to get here hardened my heart and I could only focus on the victims and what they went through. It was easy to say from a distance that they were getting exactly what they deserved. Thinking about Chief Giddens, a fellow peace officer, lying in a lake shot with his own gun was enough to make anyone's blood boil with anger. But, as I looked at Fleming lying in fear begging for his life, I felt a glimmer of compassion welling up in the pit of my stomach. I looked up and my eyes darted around me afraid that they all could see through me and know what I was feeling. No one was watching so that told me it was my own personal and professional convictions that were at war with each other. Fleming continued to mumble as he gripped my hand. I finally did the only thing I could do and slightly patted his hand as I tried to free my hand from his. I could tell that he didn't want to let go, but finally relented and released me. As Lieutenant Treadwell and I walked away, I glanced over my shoulder at Fleming and had an uneasy feeling that I hadn't done all I could for him and I wasn't sure from where the feeling came. Inside I was proud of the professional I had become in dealing with these men, but deep inside I wondered if I was here for another reason and wasn't quite sure what it was or what to do with it.

The next day, Fleming received a stay of execution and was returned to our custody in H-house and it gave his attorneys a new course of appeals. When he came walking through the gates I could see the relief all over his face and he was even joking with the officer who escorted him. I wasn't sure how to feel about that. He was given another chance, but Chief Giddens was still in his grave. The scales of my compassion had now tipped in the other direction and my anger returned. While these inmates received too many appeals for me to keep track of, their victims were given no second chances. Confusion clouded my mind again about how justice would be served. I wondered how my emotions could bounce from one extreme to the other so quickly. I shook my head as if to snap myself out of it and relied once again on the method of "stuffing" it down inside so I wouldn't have to deal with it today.

In the weeks that followed the cloud that seemed to descend on H-house grew thicker. For the most part it was just attitude. Those who were normally talkative seemed to be withdrawn while other inmates seemed not affected at all. They continued through their daily activities as though nothing changed. Of the 118 inmates on death row, only a very small group ever attended any spiritual services that were offered. I don't know if any of the inmates were searching for a spiritual connection with God individually, but nothing changed in the spiritual services that were offered. I'd often heard the term "Jail house religion" to refer to those that come to jail or prison and get religion hoping that it will save them from current circumstances. I didn't witness any of that.

Then one afternoon the attitude spilled over to a physical confrontation. I was returning from the administration area at the front of the institution and as I approached Lieutenant Treadwell's office, I saw several officers dragging a handcuffed inmate through the cross gate at H-corridor toward the administration area. I took one look at the top of his head and recognized him immediately. It was Roosevelt Green. He was one of the killers of Teresa Carol Allen, the young college student who had been murdered less than a mile from my home. Green was no stranger to physical force. Along with the episode with the stun gun when Lieutenant Treadwell first took over H-house there were his own encounters with other inmates. One such rival was Ronald Keith Spivey who had thrown hot, boiling water and baby oil on Green when he first came to death row and had left him scarred.

One of his defiant stands had required officers to go into H-2 and remove him by force. During the struggle, he had bitten an officer on the hand and left a bloody mark. Now he lay on his back outside Lieutenant Treadwell's office with his hands cuffed in front of him. It was Green, but he looked different to me. He had an unholy gleam in his eyes and a sinister smile on his face that seemed to go from one ear to the other as he rocked back and forth on the floor and mumbled in a rhythm. It was almost as if he were chanting. Finally the words came clear to me. With his hands in fists and rubbing his knuckles back and forth together he was saying in a voice that didn't seem to be his, *"I love it, I love it."*

The longer I worked around these men, the more I began to see other personalities appear. I had no training or education in such matters, but I know what I witnessed. Just the look on the faces I'd seen and now I was hearing a different voice associated with the almost distorted face of Roosevelt Green. As I walked past Green and down to the cross gate to enter H-corridor, I couldn't get the face or the voice out of my mind. Every time I saw something change in these men, it took me back to the first day I walked back to H-house and the look on Carl Isaacs face. There was the same grin on his face that I'd seen on Green's as though something evil were looking back at me. It sent a chill through my soul. With no other execution orders being handed down through the summer and fall of 1984 the atmosphere in H-house seem to lighten a bit as though all of the inmates were breathing a sigh of relief.

But, I still held in my mind the image of Green and also the strange behavior I witnessed in Glenn Williams. It was a reminder to me that there was nothing normal here. Each day brought its own set of circumstances and I found it necessary to report early each day to get a feel for what was going to happen that day. Sometimes even that wasn't enough because the environment could be so volatile.

Then with no warning, the calm was broken when an execution order arrived for Alpha Otis Stephens. Our roster and files had Stephens listed as James Daniels. Apparently, "James Daniels" was an alias he used at some point and stayed with him through the legal system. But the "Stephens" name evidently was his real name because it was used on court documents. Whatever the case, he had an unusual set of circumstances. He had been on death row before I was posted in H-house and had his sentence overturned. Apparently the state of Georgia decided to pursue the original conviction and continued to fight through an appeal.

They were successful and the death sentence of Alpha Otis Stephens was reinstated and he was returned to H-house. Whether by exhaust of appeal or his death sentence being reinstated, his time ran out and we were facing an active execution date and we were instructed to prepare Stephens for the deathwatch in the medical section.

We followed the procedure and removed him from the death row population and turned him over to deathwatch officers in the medical section. When we left Stephens in the medical section, the look on his face was one of a defeated man. He seemed to know that his time had run out and there was nothing to be done about it. He continued to receive visits from his attorneys who would work up to the last minute to save his life, but his facial expressions told the real story. It was a mixture of fear and uncertainty. None of them ever knew what to expect passed this point when they were removed from the familiarity of H-house. Though it was a prison unit, it became the only home they knew for many years. Then suddenly pulled from familiar surroundings and thrust into a nightmare. I thought in some way that it was a reflection of the nightmare that they had created with the innocent victims and their families. The nightmare Stephens caused for himself and his victim began in August 1974.

Alpha Otis Stephens escaped from the jail in Houston County Georgia. On August 21, he ended up approximately 34 miles away at the home of Charles Asbell in Twiggs County allegedly accompanied by another man. Charles Asbell was not at home at the time and Stephens broke into the house wherein he located a .357 magnum pistol, loaded it and a number of other weapons, which he placed in a 1972 dodge. While the burglary was in progress, Roy Asbell, Charles Asbell's father, drove up in his ford Ranchero. Stephens's later statement to officers was that Asbell said, "What are you doing in my house?" Seeing rifles in Stephens's car, Asbell pulled his gun. Stephens ran to Asbell's car jerked Asbell out of the car and hit him in the face several times. Asbell begged not to be hit anymore. Stephens is 6 feet, 2 inches tall while Asbell is 5 feet, 6 inches and at the time Asbell was crippled from a tractor accident. Asbell usually carried several hundred dollars on him and when he offered Stephens money in exchange for his life, Stephens took the money and kicked Asbell again. Stephens hit Asbell with the pistol, knocking him back into the Ranchero and told his alleged partner to kill him if he moved.

They drove approximately three miles to a pasture, where they stopped and Asbell got out of the car and tried to escape. He hobbled to an abandoned building being used as a barn, but Stephens took the .357 magnum and ran after him. He took more money from Mr. Asbell and then placed the pistol in his ear and fired twice. Both bullets passed through Asbell's skull and exited at his right temple, causing his death. An autopsy showed that he sustained a broken jaw and several skull fractures. A trail of evidence connected Stephens to the crime. In pre-trial statements to the police, he confessed his crime fully, as well s a string of other serious crimes, which he committed after his escape and before the Asbell murder. He presented no defense at his trial. However, during the hearing on sentence, he testified that his partner fired the fatal shots.

All the comments I'd heard or read of the murderer's accounts of what happened were stored in my mind. "I don' remember," 'I don't believe I could do them things," and now either a real or fictional partner that pulled the trigger. It's easy to suggest that it's a guilty man's attempt to lay blame on someone other than himself and it may well have been only that. But, with the evil I saw and heard in this place it was also the possibility that evil was embedded here or had visited these men at a particular moment in their lives. In any case, Alpha Otis Stephens had been convicted of capital murder and was sentenced to pay the ultimate price for whatever his part and as his hour moved closer, it looked as if there would be no legal maneuver to save his life.

In an earlier U.S. Supreme Court Ruling the air of discontent for convicted killers who sought out last minute pleas and legal tricks could be heard in a decision that was handed down in the case of Alpha Otis Stephens. One Justice wrote, *"That Stephens is innocent of the brutal, execution style murder, after kidnapping and robbing his victim, is not seriously argued. This is a contest over the application of capital punishment. A punishment repeatedly declared to be constitutional by this court. In the nearly nine years of repetitive litigation by the state and federal courts there has been no suggestion that the death sentence would not be appropriate in this case. Indeed, if on the facts here it was not appropriate, it is not easy to think of a case in which it would not be so viewed. Once again, as I indicated at the outset, and even the typically "last minute" flurry of activity is resulting in additional delay of the imposition of a sentence imposed almost a decade ago. This sort of procedure undermines public confidence in the courts and the laws we are required to follow....accordingly; I would deny the application for a stay."*

Even the Supreme Court of the United States was becoming irritated at the last minute legal tricks the attorneys attempted. It always seemed to be the same. There was never a question of innocence or guilt; it was just a play on the application of the death sentence. It sickened me that the attorneys attempted to play the race card in these cases when each individual case was uniquely cruel and monstrous in its own way, no matter a killer or victim's skin color. In most cases the murders were so savage that they even negatively touched harden police veterans. Now it was echoed in the words of the justices of the highest court in the land.

Finally the day came when there were no more arguments to be made and no *"last minute flurries of activities"* present. It was simply over and we were given the order to move Stephens from the medical section to the H-5 holding cell beside the electric chair. When we arrived, Stephens was sitting on his bunk with his elbows on his knees, hands clasped together and his head dropped low and staring at the floor. There was no way to imagine how he was feeling. When he heard us walking up to his cell door he looked up for a second and then back to the floor. There were two deathwatch officers outside the cell with the logbook recording everything that was said and done. One officer stood to his feet and produced the key to the cell door. Lieutenant Treadwell, Officers Kindle, Harris, Carter and I were to take Stephens on his last mile. Lieutenant Treadwell looked through the cell bars and said, "Stephens, we're going to move you to the back now." He knew what that meant and I could imagine his gut fluttering with fear.

He looked up at Lieutenant Treadwell and walked up to the door. Dave Harris told him, "We need your clothes Stephens." He was totally oblivious to his surroundings and just simply forgot to submit to a strip search; a procedure he had gone through countless times in the past. He slightly shook his head as if it all just came rushing back to him and began to remove his clothes. Kindle and Carter handled the search of the clothing. Finally when he

was completely nude, Carter ordered him to turn around and spread his buttocks to make sure he wasn't hiding anything. As he began to dress, the officer with the key unlocked the door and we all stepped inside. Once Stephens was dressed, Harris walked behind him, knelt down and put the leg shackles on as I was placing him in handcuffs. Once he was secure, we stood to the side and pointed him toward the door. Since he was securely restrained, Lieutenant Treadwell led the way so he could clear any traffic from the corridor. It was a slow walk because Stephens could only make short steps with the leg shackles attached. He kept his gaze down to the floor as we walked and those inmates who were walking in the corridor seemed to know who he was and where he was heading because we met most with a stare and they quickly moved to the opposite side of the corridor without being instructed to do so. A popular term came to mind; *"Dead man walking."* As far as I knew, it had never been used to describe any inmate that we walked to the execution chamber, but today it seemed to fit the circumstance.

We turned the corner at control 2 and started down the corridor toward H-house and into familiar territory for Stephens. He walked this same corridor many times en route to the medical section or the visitation area. He did look up briefly toward F-house as he walked his slow march, but then turned his face again toward the floor. He knew that his walk wouldn't end in H-house and what had become his home. The officer in F-house saw us approaching and instinctively moved the inmates in his charge from the path we were taking. When we arrived at the gate, he was standing ready with the key and slid it open so that our rhythm was uninterrupted. Once through, he quickly slammed the gate with a force that made it seem melodramatic as though we were in a scene from a movie for which there would be no happy ending for Alpha Otis Stephens. Once through the gate, we were just steps away from the corridor door that would lead to our destination. It was the same door where I stood as the life of John Eldon Smith came to an end in the early morning hours of December 15, 1983. Now we were here almost one year later to send Stephens to his destiny. Smith was the only daytime execution. When we got to the door Stephens looked up to see the sunlight shining through the observation window and I wondered what was going through his mind knowing this was the last daylight he would ever see.

Sergeant Smith was waiting at the door with the key and I could hear the seldom-used lock screech in protest as he turned the key. Sergeant Smith stepped though the door and out of the way to reveal a clear blue sky with the cool air of the Georgia December afternoon. Before we stepped through, Lieutenant Treadwell handed the H-5 key to Officer Kindle and then excused himself to his office. I pointed and said softly to Stephens, *"Let's go."* He looked up to the blue sky and without saying a word, stepped out on the concrete walkway as he started his last mile. It seemed fitting that a man should have his last look at the sky on such a beautiful day. We were still at the same slow pace, but no one involved was in a hurry. Whether out of respect or just simple understanding, no one said anything as if in reverence for the moment. At that time I felt no remorse for what I was participating in and I know that the other officers felt the same. It was the choices that Stephens made and the actions he took that brought him here today. If there was any satisfaction at all it was in knowing that I walked here today as a representative for those who could not speak here; Roy Asbell and his family.

We finally reached the outer door to H-5 and since Stephens had no idea where we were going, I instructed him to stop. Kindle stepped forward with the key as the two deathwatch officers waited just behind Stephens. Again, the lock resisted, but with a slight tug, the door came open. As Kindle reached inside for the light switch I detected that same musty smell as before. The lights revealed the church like seats all in a row. Kindle stepped through followed by Stephens, then Harris, Carter and me followed by the deathwatch officers. Straight ahead was the door that led to the execution chamber that housed the electric chair. It was the only route to the holding cell in the adjacent room. As we entered the chamber, Stephens looked up at the object of his demise. The chair was covered with new white sheets as though that would somehow conceal its identity, but there was no mistaking its ominous shape. Every time I saw the chair the hairs on the back of my neck raised, but I could not fathom what was going through Stephens's mind knowing that in a few hours he would die there. I was watching Stephens for any reactions when I saw him slightly raise his head to look at the chair and spoke words that pierced the air; *'Why don't y'all go ahead and burn me now."* My blood ran cold at the thought and no one acknowledged that he had said anything. I could think of no response to that. We all chose to just let the moment pass. Just a few short steps way was the holding cell. Once inside, we removed the leg shackles and the handcuffs.

As we walked away, I looked over my shoulder at Alpha Otis Stephens one last time. I wondered if anyone knowing the hour of their own death could truly grasp the inevitability of what was about to happen. It was a face without expression. Was it possible to be so frightened that nothing registers? I've heard people say that modern day prisons are not really punishment at all. That even death in the electric chair was too humane for those who had taken lives in the manner that brought them to us. Those who made statements like that never had to look into the face of fear like I saw here today. The psychological stress from the process of preparing one to die was in itself punishment; knowing that your death is imminent and that you have no control over any part of it and no way to escape it. It was a nightmare from which Alpha Otis Stephens could not awake. As I walked away he was still staring at the floor. No, there was punishment and perhaps the most severe punishment of all was the psychological torture in those last few hours of what his life could have been if different choices had been made.

I shuddered as I walked out of H-5 and tried to imagine myself sitting in that cell thinking about the events that were unfolding. Just that thought alone was too terrifying to contemplate. Then the other side of the argument began to run through my mind. Charles Asbell no longer had a father and I wondered if he would gain any satisfaction here today watching Alpha Otis Stephens in obvious mental anguish. I wondered if the "eye for an eye" argument was in the forefront of Charles Asbell's mind. After the way his father was killed he certainly had every right to feel that way and expect justice to be carried out. There was a struggle in my mind because I had the ability to see both sides of the story; the victim and the killer. I couldn't allow that to show here nor could I discuss it with anyone. It was more information to stuff inside.

I never took my feelings home with me either. Sarah and I were growing apart and we were separated almost as much as we were together. But, it was a subject I could never bring to her anyway. After the verbal abuse I received from her concerning Teresa Carol Allen and Roosevelt Green I had decided never to allow my feelings to show with her and definitely not share my thoughts. Every thought stayed within the confines of my mind and every feeling secured deep inside of me. I had no idea I was creating a dungeon deep inside where I hid parts of myself that were never to be discussed with anyone. If anything ever felt uncomfortable, it got pushed down.

It was to be another midnight execution. When we returned to H-house I checked my watch. It was 4 pm. It was approximately 8 hours until Stephens's execution. Lieutenant Treadwell dismissed everyone. As with Stanley, Dave Harris and I would return with Lieutenant Treadwell to H-house at 7pm to wait out the execution and see if there was any reaction from the other inmates on death row.

Sarah told me about the day's events in visitation on the ride home. When an execution was imminent, visitation was always very hectic. Attorneys for the condemned man spent a lot of time with him and if there was any family or friends, an extended visitation was given because that may very well be the last time the person would be seen alive. She said it was the usual busy day before an execution. I heard her talking and I nodded now and then, but I wasn't really in the conversation. I had stopped taking the chance to share my feelings with her concerning H-house and certainly not about a pending execution. I don't know if she sensed it, but she didn't press me for any information or even ask questions. I took my uniform off at home because otherwise I couldn't relax. It was as if the uniform put me in character for my job. When I wore it, I had a level of professionalism to maintain so as to reflect honor on the colors that I wore. I needed to be able to relax before I returned to the institution if even for a few hours. The longer I worked in H-house and participated in the execution process, the harder it became to let go of it at the end of the day. It wasn't a job that one could leave at the gate when I clocked out and went home. My thoughts came with me of the events I witnessed. After dinner, I tried to relax in front of the TV to take my mind off of it. I stared at the TV, but nothing seemed to register because my thoughts were somewhere else. Finally, Sarah had to remind me that I needed to get dressed to report for duty. As I was dressing, my mind was already there in H-5 where I left Stephens. I kissed Kimberly and Sarah and headed off for the institution, which was just 13 minutes away.

When I pulled up to the front gate, the protesters were already beginning to arrive to start the show. They had their signs out ready for the news media to arrive on the scene. Driving down the driveway in the evenings was a pleasant experience. With an execution scheduled, no one was allowed on the property and I drove slowly to take in the scene. I was still amazed of the beauty of the property even after 4 years of employment. The lake to my right looked like a sheet of glass and there was no breeze to move the pine trees around the lake and in the mobile home park at the edge of the lake. It was a peaceful scene as I drove. Then I turned my attention to the end of the road and saw the gun tower; it broke the peace and serenity of the evening. Alpha Otis Stephens waited inside for the last few hours of his life. By now his head and left leg were shaved in preparation for the headset and leg band. I threw my hand up at the tower officer as I walked toward the tunnel. It was only our third execution, but they were becoming familiar with the staff that participated. I was part of the support staff, but there were members of the actual execution team that participated in the final phase of the execution. I knew one of my friends would push one of the three buttons, but had no idea what duties the others had. That's how the administration wanted it.

I was sure they were already inside waiting for their orders. They trained for it as with any other duty. I had no idea how they felt about it personally, whether they took pleasure in what they did or if they thought of it as a function of the job. I thought of every angle as I made my way up the tunnel toward the administration area. There were lights on down the hallway toward the superintendent's office. That was where the representative from the attorney general's office would wait for a word from any court for a last minute stay of Execution. Stephens's attorneys would work until the last minute even if they were grasping at straws.

When I arrived in H-house I saw Lieutenant Treadwell through the glass in his office. When he looked up and saw me he smiled his broad smile at me. He was doing his favorite thing and that was talking. I saw the back of someone's head through the glass and when he saw Lieutenant Treadwell smile, Dave Harris turned to look at me. I stopped at the door we had taken Stephens through just three hours before to look through the observation glass. I saw the big green generator sitting at the corner of the building. It sat there like a monstrous partner of the electric chair, quietly waiting for its turn to roar. By all appearances, it would have its turn in the process.

I walked down to the cross gate to speak to the corridor officer. He met me at the gate and I asked, "How has it been?" He nodded slightly and said, "Quiet." If the last two executions were any indication, it would stay that way. I'm not sure if the other inmates did it out of respect for the condemned man or if they were lost in thought thinking about their own mortality. It was quiet at the moment. All members of the Tactical Squad were always placed on standby, which included Officers Carter, Kindle, Harris and me. Then there was an accompaniment of law enforcement personnel at the front gate. But, just as before, the entire institution was quiet. At Approximately 11:30 pm, Dave and I walked over to the observation window on the door and observed the white van parked outside. Things were moving along on schedule. All that was left to do was waiting for the van to pull away and at that point we would know that Stephens was dead. We sat down again because we were familiar with the execution procedure in H-5 and how much time was involved. We continued our conversation and then at approximately 12:30 am, Dave and I got up from our chairs and looked out the window. We expected to see witnesses filing into the van at any moment. At 12:35 am there was still no movement at the van and we looked at each other because every step of the execution was carefully planned and we knew something was wrong. We both stood at the door and waited and at approximately 12:40 am, we saw the witnesses climbing into the van. Lieutenant Treadwell wanted to wait until he received word of what happened and we waited with him.

At 1 am we received word of what had taken place in H-5. Stephens had walked to the chair unassisted just as the two condemned men before him. Everything was proceeding according to schedule and at approximately 12:17 am, the order was given to start the 2-minute automatic system. With the two prior executions the only movement detected was clenched fists. With Stephens's execution the unthinkable had happened. While the final phase was shutting down, it appeared as though he was still alive. There was a mandatory 5 minute lapsed count time to allow the body to cool down before the doctors could examine him to make sure that death occurred and the execution was successful. At 12:22 am, as the lapsed count commenced, it was reported that his head began to move slightly.

The staff was given orders not to vary from the procedure and to continue the lapsed count time. At approximately 12:25 am it was reported that Stephens head begin to move and "bob up and down." At four minutes of lapsed time, the observer detected that Stephens was still breathing. The doctors observing agreed. The observer asked the commissioner if they should proceed with the process again or check him first. They were ordered to check him first and not to vary from the checklist. At 12:26 am the doctors verified that Stephens was indeed still alive. There are those that say as soon as the electricity enters that brain that the condemned man is brain dead. I don't know and have never investigated if that is true. But, if death did not occur at that moment, the 5 minutes of lapsed time would have been an eternity for the condemned man. Some hold to the fact that if he indeed were alive and was waiting in pain, then he got what he deserved after the pain and suffering he caused his victim and his family. As a member of the law enforcement community, I might have agreed with that. But, that wasn't my only perspective. I also had a Christian heart that allowed me to see things in a different light. I was at conflict with my inner self.

Once the doctors reported that he was alive, the commissioner said flatly, *"Repeat the execution."* The commissioner ordered that the connections to the condemned man's body be checked again. Before the order was given the commissioner asked if the witnesses were told that the procedure would be repeated and the superintendent said no. The commissioner instructed the superintendent to inform the witnesses, but not to give any details. Then the order was given to proceed with the entire process all over again. Once again, in the third phase of the execution process, his head continued to move and he continued to breathe. It was unbelievable. At 12:32 am, two minutes into the lapsed count time, the observer reported that he had stopped moving and did not appear to be breathing.

With the lapsed time completed the superintendent entered the execution chamber with both of the physicians. After both completed their examinations, Alpha Otis Stephens was pronounced dead at 12:37 am. It had taken approximately 20 minutes for him to die. No one knew what Stephens had endured in those 20 minutes. No one knew if there was physical pain and suffering. The most intriguing piece of information would not come out for many years. It was reported that during the first lapsed time count, the curtains in front of the viewing window in the execution chamber begin to move as though something or *someone* had brushed against them. There were no open doors and no windows inside of H-5. It sent chills through those who witnessed it. It shed new light on the possibilities of what happens as we pass from this life to the next plain of existence.

As a Christian I wondered what was happening to his spirit in the 20 minutes it took for his body to die. Scripture says, *"therefore we are always confident, knowing that, whilst we are home in the body, we are absent from the Lord: (for we walk by faith not by sight) we are confident, I say, and willing rather to be absent from the body, and to be present with the Lord."* There is so much guessing concerning the state of man's spirit and body when the brain is considered "dead," but the body remains alive. As I walked out of the institution I was contemplating what happened in those 20 minutes in H-5 before Alpha Otis Stephens took his last breath and thinking about Ronald and Juanita Akins newlyweds dying by a shotgun blast, Clifford Floyd lying in his shallow grave choking on his own blood and Roy Asbell trying to escape by limping away only to be executed by a gunshot in the ear. The angel of death claimed their lives and now was here to claim Alpha Otis Stephens. I wondered if

the curtain moving in the execution chamber was Stephens or a brush of wings that was waiting for him to die.

My mind swirled in confusion as the officer and the Christian battled within my mind and soul. I wondered about my role here in H-house and if in any way I was doing God's work. My heart burned with compassion for the families of these victims each time I drove through the gates and saw these people with their signs condemning the state for capital punishment, yet having compassion for someone like Alpha Otis Stephens as he walked past the electric chair and seeing the look on his face as he waited for his turn. I still remembered the expressionless look on his face as we passed by. I closed my eyes as I recalled the day's events and its ultimate ending. Then I looked up at the beautiful night sky full of stars and asked the question that would plague me for many nights to come in the future; *"God, what am I here to do?"*

Chapter 10

"Whoso sheddeth man's blood, by man shall his blood be shed: for in the image of God made he man."

- Genesis 9:6
(King James Version)

I still remember the first day I saw Roosevelt Green. It was like a personal mission was fulfilled. From the time I knew I was being hired at the Diagnostic Center, I wanted to look into the face of a man I considered to be a monster. After being assigned to H-house I had escorted him many times and there were times of conflict between us such as the incident in his cell when Lieutenant Treadwell first came to H-house. At first, I avoided eye contact with him on the escorts. But eventually my curiosity got the best of me and we exchanged a look in each other's eyes as I performed a strip search on him prior to an escort. It was the same cold look; something seemed to be missing. Some officers took pleasure in seeing who could stare each other down first, but I didn't get caught up in that game. I treated them with as much courtesy as they would allow. If they wanted none, then I was just silent as we walked through the institution but I found that most of them were cordial.

Green demonstrated on several occasions that he was a dangerous man. The first shift sergeant and a new officer made the mistake of underestimating Green as they led him from one of the isolation cells to the shower. He produced a metal shank that he'd fashioned from a typewriter rod from the inmate law library. He stabbed the sergeant in the arm several times and the other officer on one cheek narrowly missing his eye. Those incidents happened before Lieutenant Treadwell came to H-house and helped to change his behavior. But until that time, anytime he left his cell, he was escorted by at least three officers with batons. It was during one of those trips, that I became the focus of his rage. I was one of three escort officers walking Green back from an attorney's visit. His hands were cuffed behind his back and I walked directly behind him, a sergeant was to his right side and a third officer was slightly to my right side. I accidentally stepped on one of his heels and he thought that I had done it intentionally. He stopped in the middle of the hallway and turned to within an inch of my nose and said, "Man, I'll kick you in your nuts." I stood defiantly, but this time, I participated in the staring game. I looked deep in his cold eyes as he glared into mine. After a few seconds I motioned ahead with my right hand and calmly said, "Let's move."

Men like Roosevelt Green are all too familiar with violence. Maybe it was a product of his upbringing and it was the only way he knew how to respond to any emotion. No matter if he felt fear or anger, he responded the same; with defiance. I think my reaction took him quite by surprise because he was used to butting heads with everyone. He stood there for a few more seconds and I stood with him. The Sergeant and officer stood frozen in their tracks. They were ready to respond, but unsure of what to do. In terms of use of force, there was nothing we could do because Green was already restrained. Neither of us dared blink. Then finally he turned and started down the corridor again. It was the first test of our individual wills. But from that, we reached a mutual understanding of each other. He proved he wasn't going to back down and I proved to him that I was not afraid of him or to escalate to the next level. I suppose it could be called a mutual respect as enemies in a war zone may have for one another.

Officer Dave Harris had been the unit clerk for some time now. Lieutenant Treadwell wanted him to have a back up for days when he was on leave for vacation and I was selected. Mostly the job involved filing, typing reports for Lieutenant Treadwell, general administrative support and handling incoming and outgoing mail for the inmates. They were duties to which I easily learned and adapted. I'd taken a typing class in school and wondered how it might benefit me and now I had my answer. Dave was about to go on vacation and I worked in his office for a week to familiarize myself with the details. Once he was on vacation, I found that I had a natural talent for administrative work and I enjoyed it. It was a welcome break from the daily cell searches and escorts that we had to perform.

I read of the horrific crime that Roosevelt Green committed in the newspapers and the most striking thing to me was the name of his young victim; Teresa Carol Allen. But, there had been no details of the crime. On this day, my time working on Georgia's death row was going to change forever. I don't know why I was chosen to discover what I saw. But as time goes on, God reveals what his plans are for us. It's not given to us to know the plan for our lives, but rather what to do with the plan that is given to us. The brutality of what man is capable of was made very clear to me that day. It would be a portrait imprinted on my mind of the evil around us every day. I received a box from H-2 that was to be mailed out. My job was to inspect it and prepare it to be mailed. The sender was Roosevelt Green. Inside the box was a huge stack of Xeroxed papers. It was a copy of his trial transcript from 1977. I started flipping through the pages to look for contraband and inside I found the whole nightmarish story of the last night of a young woman's life.

At approximately 3 pm on December 12, 1976, 18-year-old Teresa Carol Allen arrived at the Majik Market in Cochran, Georgia. Shortly before 7 pm, the store was found to be empty. The cash register and safe were open and empty and Miss Allen's automobile, a late model Grand Prix, was missing. The Majik Market area supervisor determined that $466 was missing from the store. On December 14, 1976, Miss Allen's body was discovered lying in a wooded grassy area jut off of a dirt road near highway 41 in Monroe County. Footprints, two 30.06 shells, a 30.06 metal jacket of a bullet, parts of her flesh, teeth and bone, tire tracks and a nylon stocking were found near the body. The cause of her death was determined to be a loss of blood from bullet wounds.

Examination of the body disclosed bruising on the inside of one thigh, lacerations of the vagina, and blood and mucous like matter in the vaginal canal. A pathologist later testified

that the wounds in the abdomen, arms and face were caused by a high-powered bullet and that the location and nature of the wounds were consistent with the theory that Miss Allen had her arms crossed across her stomach when shot and the bullet passed through both arms and her abdomen. There was another shot that entered the left side of her neck, penetrating the lower face and exiting the right side of the head. In the early evening hours on the day of the robbery, Carzell Moore and Roosevelt Green were let out at Moore's house. Moore's house was 4 blocks from the Majik Market. Green was wearing high-heeled shoes. In early January 1977, Thomas Pasby accompanied Moore to check out a car that Moore intended to buy. At that time, Moore asked Pasby how he felt about killing when Pasby was in Vietnam. During their discussion, Moore told Pasby, "Well, I killed somebody, too," and then told Pasby the following story:

Moore said that he and Green went to the Majik Market in Cochran. Moore told Green to go in and take Miss Allen to the meat counter in order to attract her attention so that Moore could come in the front of the store with a rifle. With that done Green and Moore robbed the Majik Market. When they left the store, they took Miss Allen with them forcibly. They left in her car with Moore driving. Shortly after leaving the store Green turned to Miss Allen and said, "Bitch take off your clothes." She told Green that she was a virgin and pleaded with Green not to rape her. Green raped her anyway. Green then changed places with Moore and Green drove while Moore raped Miss Allen. After driving further, Moore told Green to stop the car. Moore told Miss Allen to get out and told Green to drive to a gas station to gas the car. After Green left, Miss Allen begged Moore not to kill her.

She crossed her arms over her stomach to protect herself as Moore shot her in the abdomen with the rifle. Then he shot her in the face in an attempt to disfigure her so it would be harder to identify her. When Green returned, the two of them picked her up and threw her into the bushes. Moore told Pasby that one of her hands was so mangled by the rifle blast that he thought it was going to fall off. One of her hands was indeed almost severed from her body. The attendant at a nearby gas station recalled selling gas for an automobile like that of the victim with a Georgia tag that showed only the letters RENS as from Laurens. The tag on the victim's car was in similar condition. Green later arrived in South Carolina in possession of the car with a large amount of change and a roll of bills. Green asked a friend to burn the car (which the friend refused) and traded the 30.06 rifle for a .25 caliber automatic.

A Cochran florist testified the rifle was stolen from him about the time and in the vicinity that Moore was seen with it. When Moore was informed while in jail that Green had been arrested with the Allen car in South Carolina he stated; "Damn, I told Green to get rid of that car and rifle." Later, Moore stated to Pasby again, "You know, Green was supposed to have gotten rid of that car and rifle." A plaster cast of a footprint found near Miss Allen's body was of a similar size and impression as a Hushpuppy shoe taken from Moore's room. Tire tracks found near her body were in size and tread design to the tires found on Miss Allen's car. There was other forensic evidence that circumstantially connected Moore to the crime. Moore testified in his own behalf that he met Green in an Alabama prison in 1975. On December 11, 1976 he saw Green in Cochran looking for him. Green, out on escape, was using the name Jerome Miller. Moore loaned Green some of his clothes and shoes. They went to various places on December 11 and on the day of the robbery; they went to Rosa

Crawford's house to watch a football game. Rosa's parents drove Green and Moore to Moore's house, where Green borrowed the pair of Hushpuppy shoes from Moore. Green left and Moore began drinking, watched TV and became nauseated and passed out. He awoke later that night and went outside.

The local café was closed so he sat under a tree and smoked. A friend came along and they smoked together. Then he went home and went to sleep. He denied making the statement to Pasby about robbing the Majik Market, raping Teresa Allen and killing her. He denied getting the 30.06 rifle. He denied a witness's testimony about Moore asking about a place to rob. He denied statements he made about the rifle. He denied that he made the statements to Pasby while in jail. Moore explained the forensic evidence by stating that he had skinned himself by having intercourse with his girlfriend. He also testified that Green exchanged his high-heeled platform shoes for Moore's hushpuppy shoes prior to the evening of the robbery. In rebuttal, the state presented testimony that when Green visited in South Carolina the morning following the robbery he was wearing high-heeled platform shoes and not hushpuppies. Moore tried to pin the murder on Green.

I'd heard the stories that circulated in Forsyth after her murder and everyone's speculation of what had happened, but now I was reading the terror of what she endured from the account of one of the killers. As so often happened to me here on this unit I felt a chill run down my back. As I looked up from the pages and out of the window into the corridor, I had a strange feeling that someone was there. Even in daylight and the voices carrying down the corridor from F-house, H-house still had a haunting affect on me. It often caused me to look up, as though my name were being whispered in a tone that only I could hear. That just made it all the more unnerving. But, no one was there. I turned my attention back to the large stack of documents in my lap. I started thumbing through pages and I saw a picture flash by. I felt as though I'd seen a ghost. I sat there contemplating my next move. Everything I'd heard in the last eight years streamed through my mind and all the theories of those who speculated about what they did to her and the real truth lay in my hands. After all of my own speculation, I sat nervously as the faces of Leighanne, Tracey and Kimberly appeared in my mind. My hands started to shake and I felt nauseous. I closed my eyes and sat in silence for a moment and finally, I took a deep breath, opened my eyes and flipped back through the pages and stopped at the picture.

It was a bad copy, but there was the face of Teresa Carol Allen. It was difficult to make out at first, but she appeared to be lying on an autopsy table. She was no longer just a name in the newspaper. She was here. At first, I wondered if she had died with her mouth open, but as I studied the picture I realized that it wasn't her mouth, but a huge hole where she had been shot. That was what Moore described as his attempt to disfigure her. She died less than two weeks from her nineteenth birthday, December 25th. I recalled the bruise that was discovered on her inner thigh. She said she was a virgin. Her only sexual experience in life was a savage rape by two men who only wanted to satisfy their own selfish lust. One of God's greatest gifts to mankind, the ultimate expression of love, was perverted in a very evil way. Apparently she made the choice to wait for that perfect moment that comes between two people when they fall in love. It was the simplest wish of any young woman; to have a husband, children, grandchildren and a family, but would remain forever an unrealized dream. My mind contemplated, for her, those two terrible words that haunt mankind; "What if?"

My stomach was aching and I felt flush as I looked at her face and imagined my girls lying on that table. I had no concept of what her parents felt or were still feeling over her death. I felt dizzy. I closed the file and put it back on the desk. I felt my eyes watering and I knew I had to get out of the office. I started down the corridor toward the cross gate in H-house where the officer's restroom was located. I stood at the cross gate waiting for the corridor officer to come with the key. The picture rolled over and over in my mind. I stared straight ahead and didn't even realize the officer was opening the gate. "Allen, are you alright," he asked. I managed a fake smile and said, "Yes, I'm fine just need to go the restroom." I walked hurriedly to the back of the corridor and I was already reaching for the doorknob and prayed that no one was in there. I yanked the door open and quickly closed and locked it. I closed my eyes and took a deep breath and sat down on the toilet. I pulled my wallet out and turned to pictures of my girls. I thought about what I saw and I could feel tears forming at the corner of my eyes. I put my hand to my mouth and then up to my eyes to wipe the tears away. Then I lost control and moved my right hand back to my mouth and sobbed quietly as I rocked back and forth on the toilet trying to be as quiet as I could.

I wouldn't survive it if that were any one of them lying on that autopsy table. I was flooded with emotions. Anger for what that young woman had endured in the last few hours of her life. Fear at the loss of control I was feeling knowing that I couldn't protect my girls every minute of every day. My heart broke thinking about her parents having to find some way to cope with her being ripped from their lives. As I looked in the mirror I recalled the day that Sarah lashed out at me asking that ridiculous question about Teresa Carol Allen; "Who was she, some angel?" I felt sick all over again that my wife and the mother of my youngest child could ever let a question like that slip past her lips. I wanted to take that transcript to her and make her read it while she was holding Kimberly in her arms.

I finally shook my head and forced myself back to the present. I had to get back to the office so I splashed some water on my face and dried it with a paper towel. I closed my eyes again to say a prayer for strength and then opened the door. As I walked up the corridor toward the cross gate I looked over at H-2. Green was back there behind that door. I recalled a statement he had made to one of the other inmates in an attempt to lessen his involvement in the nightmare. "All I did was rape her." "ALL" he did was rape her, as if that in some way excused him from being where he was. He tormented her, brutalized her and finally picked her up like something he found beside the road and threw her into the brush. The more I learned the harder it was to maintain my professionalism and I had to keep that in order to work here. It was easy for some of the officers because they just simply allowed their disgust to show through and that made it easy to hate the inmates and in turn made the inmates hate them. I remembered a point being made in a morning meeting in Lieutenant Treadwell's office. A letter had come from one of the inmates complaining about Officers Carter and Kindle.

Carter and Kindle prided themselves on being hard. I was all about going by the book, but that was as far as it went. I believe most of the officer's thought they had to be hard to be effective. It just wasn't my style or personality. In fact, during our meeting, Lieutenant Treadwell made a point to say, "I doubt if they hate Allen." The other officers may have seen it as weakness, but I took it as a compliment because I modeled my behavior after Lieutenant Treadwell. Now it was becoming difficult to maintain that state of mind after what I just read and seen. I finally made it back to the office and sat down in the chair and looked at the huge stack of documents on the desk. I lay my hand on top of the stack and immediately had a flashback of the picture. It was burned into my mind. I quickly boxed up the stack and sealed it with tape in preparation for its trip to the mailroom.

Even though I was temporarily assigned to the clerk's office, I still had to assist with my regular duties like escorts and cell searches. The day after I made the grisly discovery in the trial transcript, H-2 was due for a cell search. It was Green's unit. With the picture now engraved in my memory forever, I was going to see him for the first time after I read the account of the rape and murder. I wasn't sure how I was going to react. After we got the signal that H-2 was locked down, the door was opened and the four of us entered Sergeant Smith, Carter, Kindle and I. We had a list of five cells that were pre-selected by Sergeant Smith before we entered the unit. We carried a tan canvass bag that contained tools we needed for the "shakedown." There was a flashlight, rubber gloves, some devices for probing corners and tiny cracks in the walls and a rubber mallet to carefully check each bar of the cell itself to ensure that they had not been cut.

After the inmate was stripped searched, we took the mallet and went to work hitting the bars. The inmate is taken out of his cell and two officers go inside while one officer and Sergeant Smith wait outside with the inmate. The two officers inside the cell conduct a very thorough, systematic search of every item in the cell. The first cell I checked the bars and stood with the inmate outside the cell. With so much personal property, it could take some time. I crossed my arms over my chest and waited, but being very observant. The television was playing out loud today and apparently they were all listening to music videos. I heard the song, "you are," by Lionel Richie. I could see movement in a cell down the row from our location. I walked a few steps to get a better view and I could see Roosevelt Green. He was dancing in his cell to the music. He acted as if he didn't have a care in the world and maybe in that one moment in time, he didn't.

In that moment I saw him as a human being and not just a rapist and a murderer. I didn't know anything about Roosevelt Green prior to his involvement in the murder of Teresa Carol Allen. But, as I watched him moving to the music, I realized that he had a past that must have included hopes and dreams just as any other man did. I didn't know what set him on his path of death and destruction that ended up on Georgia's death row. As I watched him I wondered if he had ever loved anyone or been loved by anyone. He had a mother somewhere that gave birth to him and I assumed loved him at some point in his life or was he the product of a broken home that caused the anger in him. Whatever it was, it had destroyed the life of Teresa Carol Allen, her family and finally his own. He sat on death row waiting to die.

On the morning of December 7, 1985, Lieutenant Treadwell called Officers Carter, Kindle, Harris, Sergeant Smith and me to his office. We usually knew what it meant when he assembled us in his office like this, but it had been less than a month since the execution of Alpha Otis Stephens so we weren't really sure if this was about an execution. As it turned out, we were indeed here for that purpose. Once we were all assembled and the door was closed, he made his announcement. "Men, we have an execution order for Roosevelt Green." No one showed any emotion, but I felt my heart jump. I had viewed his trial transcript just a few days before. Something told me that Green knew what was coming and that's why he

mailed out his transcript. Perhaps his attorney knew before anyone in the state system did. In any case, the images of his victim were very clear in my mind.

For me, it was like none of the other three executions we had performed. Because of the circumstances of the case; her name, being found so close to my home, his escape from the Monroe county jail and that smirk on his face. Finally, the look on his face as he lay in the floor and rocking his head back and forth with that sinister grin on his face as he said, "I love it, I love it." Yes, it was personal for me. Seeing him face to face had been the initial goal of me wanting to work on death row. Now it was all very real and coming to a close. She had been in my mind ever since I first saw her picture in the newspaper. The culmination of it all was when I saw the picture of her in his trial transcript. Now he was about to answer for it with his life. Lieutenant Treadwell continued. "There will be some changes the night of the execution. After we escort Green to the holding cell the warden wants Allen in charge of security at the front gate the night of the execution." He smiled slightly at me as he made the announcement. The administration was starting to take notice of me and that was all due to Lieutenant Treadwell. I felt a surge of pride and I owed it all to him. He continued, "We will start the deathwatch procedure this afternoon at 4 pm. That's all I have gentleman, when you leave here, get Green out for the counselor's office and I want someone standing in the corridor outside the office."

We left and went directly to H-2 and notified the officer that Green was needed outside. We stood at the door until he was out in the small corridor inside of H-1 & 2. When we got clearance that he was ready, Kindle went inside to search him and afterwards the corridor officer opened the door. We tried not to seem too conspicuous, but Carter and I stood close by. Once the H-2 door was closed and locked, the corridor officer opened the cross gate that led out to the administration area. The counselor was expecting him and motioned for him to come in. Once he was in the office, Carter and I both stood outside the office. We could see their lips moving, but couldn't hear what was being said. I saw the pages of the document on the counselor's desk as he read them. Green wasn't moving at all, but stared at the wall in front of him. After a few minutes, Green nodded his head. It was the execution order and the counselor read it to him officially notifying him that his execution was imminent.

I stood there and watched Green's face. I didn't detect any change. Then I tried to imagine the impossible. How would I react if I knew that my death was going to take place in the next two days? No way could I begin to fathom that without sitting in that chair and hearing those words knowing it was about to happen to me. Those who claim that there is not enough punishment involved in the process would never understand the gravity of this moment. For the next two days Green would have to contemplate what was about to happen to him in the confines of his cell, alone. Maybe that was the true punishment that lay in the process. The inevitability of what was to come once the chain reaction was set in motion after seeing the words on the paper, "Death Warrant." Once the meeting was over, Green got up and walked out and for the first time in a long time an exchange took place between he and I. As he exited the door we made brief eye contact and he quickly looked away. I didn't see the arrogance that was there before. I didn't detect any anger. There was no defiance in his mannerism. He wasn't Roosevelt Green the convicted rapist and murderer. For the first time I saw the human frailty that lies in us all. For a fleeting moment, I saw fear in his eyes.

At 4 pm Lieutenant Treadwell appeared at the cross gate with Sergeant Smith and Harris right behind him. Cater, Kindle and I knew what that meant. He motioned to the

corridor officer, to unlock the gate as he walked through and asked, "Everyone Ready?" We nodded. Sergeant Smith handed me a set of Leg irons. Kindle was already reaching for his handcuffs. Dave Harris went to the corner and pushed a laundry buggy to the door at H-2. He was going to push Green's personal belongings to the administration corridor to be inventoried. They were duties that were becoming second nature to us because we had done them three times before. Sergeant Smith yelled into the observation window, "Lock down H-2!" We waited for only few minutes and finally got word from the H-2 Officer and entered the H-1 & H-2 corridor. Once inside, we opened the cover to the H-2 observation window and looked inside.

The H-2 officer said, "All clear." I thought back to the first time I stood here when I was a rookie officer helping to shower Isolation.

I remembered looking around and having the feeling that I was in a dungeon. It wasn't as intimidating as it was 5 years before, but, at times, I could still feel the presence of evil here.

Sergeant Smith yelled, "Pop it" and we pulled the door open. Everyone was quiet when we came to get someone for deathwatch. They just watched as we walked down the range to the cell we were looking for. Green was cell number '36" the next to the last cell. In number "37" was his friend, Billy Mitchell. Green was ready. Everything was packed and he sat on his bed. When we stopped at his cell, he was looking down at the floor. He looked up and without us having to say anything, he began to undress and pass his clothes through the bars. Carter took him though the strip search. Once he was dressed again, we motioned to the officer to open "36." The familiar buzz and the door opened. He stepped out and Harris loaded his personal property in the buggy. Kindle handcuffed his hands behind his back. Then it was my turn. The procedure was to apply the leg irons from behind the inmate with him on his knees. But, because of the circumstances and the fact that he was outnumbered 6 to one, I knelt down in front of him. I clicked the cuffs to each ankle. Before I stood up, I looked up to see him staring down at me.

I stood up, looked over at him and he was looking back at me. For a moment, I recalled him dancing a few days before to the Lionel Richie song, "you are" and the jovial mood he was in at the time. Things were quite different now. He closed his eyes and took a deep breath and then reopened them and looked straight ahead. No matter what he had done, he was a child of God, Too. The scripture John 3:16 came to my mind, "For God so loved the world that he gave his one and only son, that whosoever believes in him shall not perish but have eternal life." The Christian buried deep within me remembered that "whoever" included men like Roosevelt Green if he repented and asked for forgiveness. I felt a moment of compassion for him.

I took a deep breath as well and looked ahead. I was standing on his right side and with my left hand I reached for his elbow and tugged slightly ahead until he began to walk and I walking with him. Kindle walked on his left side and the others behind us with Harris pushing the cart. I felt really strange and it seemed in my mind as though we were all walking in slow motion as if in some macabre movie. I started to think about the times of my life and the things I had done. Abandoning Deedee and our girls at such a young age was a very selfish thing to do. While I had not killed anyone, I remembered that God does not measure sin as lesser or greater. Sin is sin in His eyes and I felt convicted walking

beside Roosevelt Green. The words to the song, "Behind Blue eyes" by the group, the Who, appeared in my mind. I looked over at Green and he looked back at me as if he somehow knew what I was thinking, but I saw no condemnation in his eyes and then he looked forward again and so did I. The songs speaks of innocent blue eyes, but deep inside there is a self hatred for what he feels about himself and what he has done.

He would look at me and then me to him. It was as if we were tuned to each other. The door was already opened and we walked into the H-2 corridor. We paused as the others caught up and then we were all packed tightly together in the corridor. Finally the red door closed behind us and that signaled to the officer to open the outer door to the main corridor of H-house. It was a short walk to the H-house cross gate with Green saying nothing. But then I thought to myself, what was there to say at a moment like this? Silence seemed to be appropriate. After the inventory of his personal belongings, we made our way slowly up the corridor to the medical section where two officers were already waiting with the logbook in which the last moments of Roosevelt Green's life would be recorded. Inside the cell was a fresh prison uniform that he would wear until we moved him to the deathwatch cell in the execution chamber.

Green spent most of the following day in visitation with his attorneys. But on one of my trips to the administration area, I looked over and saw a woman sitting in the visitation area with him. They both looked up and there was no denying who she was. He had the exact same facial features as she. She was definitely his mother, but there seemed to be a distance between them. She stood and seemed to be praying, but he was sitting in his chair with his eyes open and didn't seem receptive at all. I couldn't recall her ever visiting him in the four years that I worked on death row. Maybe time had taken its toll on the relationship. But, at least she was here now and the only thing that remained to be seen was if she would attend his execution should it go forward tonight.

At 4pm on January 8, 1985, we were informed there would be no stay of execution for Green and we were ordered to remove him from the medical section and escort him to H-5. Carter, Harris, Kindle, Lieutenant Treadwell and I departed H- house en-route for the medical section. We carried with us a new inmate uniform and a new pair of shower shoes. We also brought along our leg irons and handcuffs. When the deathwatch officers saw us walking down the medical corridor, they closed their logbook and stood up because they knew why we were here. One officer reached in his waistband for the key and unlocked the door just as we arrived and Green looked up to see all of us. There was no expression on his face as he stood up. There was a final medical examination to be conducted before we would take him to H-5. We escorted him without restraints through the corridor to the main examination room. We paused at the officer's station so that the medical officer could clear the hallway of inmates. Then we escorted Green inside the exam room where a doctor and his staff were waiting for us. There was only one door for the room, so the two deathwatch officers stood in the corridor to stop anyone from entering. Using his interpersonal communication skills, Lieutenant Treadwell instructed Green on what was about to happen to him. "Roosevelt, we need you to strip down and then we have a couple of medical procedures that we need to complete before we take you to the back."

Green knew what, "the back" meant because his eyes quickly looked up at Lieutenant Treadwell. There was no argument from him and he started to undress. Finally he stood naked in front of us all. The doctor began his examination. He examined his hair, looked up his nostrils, in his mouth and both ears. Finally the doctor looked at us, then to the floor nervously and I could see that he didn't really want to give the next command. We looked around at each other and Lieutenant Treadwell sensed it also and came to the doctor's rescue. "Roosevelt, I need you to bend over on that gurney so the doctor can give you the final examination." It was the hardest thing that one could ask a man to do especially in the presence of eight men and a woman while a man is at his most vulnerable. Green knew there was no getting out of it so he simply complied. The doctor had on a fresh pair of latex gloves and reached in for his target. I heard Green grunt slightly and for the first time felt empathy for him as a man. When the doctor was finished he immediately started to take off his gloves and said, "There's nothing up there but feces."

Green was given a washcloth to clean himself and then handed the new uniform which included boxers and a tee shirt. There was no belt or boots with shoestrings. Instead he was given a new pair of plastic shower shoes. Once he was dressed we went to work with the restraints. Kindle had the leg irons and applied them first. Then I applied a waist chain through his empty belt loops. I cuffed his hands in front of him, but then attached a device known as a "black box" that joined the handcuffs to the waist chain. It effectively restrained his hands at his waist so that he could not move them. Now he was completely shackled so that all he could do was "shuffle" his feet as he walked which made running impossible.

Once we were all in position, Lieutenant Treadwell gave a nod in the direction of the door. I was standing on Green's right side so I gave his left elbow a light tap. Roosevelt Green took the first step of his last mile. The eight of us walked slowly as if we were in a funeral procession and in a sense, I suppose we were. There were no words spoken and certainly no sentiment to be shared. I couldn't detect any emotion on Green's face and I wondered in the past three executions what might be going through a man's mind at this time. Looking at their faces gave no hidden answers. I remained on Green's right side, Kindle on his left side and Carter walking behind. Lieutenant Treadwell and Harris walked out front to move any inmate traffic out of the way. But any inmate that approached from the opposite direction could see the contingent around Green and instinctively moved to the other side of the corridor.

We made it through control 2 and were now coming down the home stretch to familiar territory for us all and what had been Green's home for five years. I looked ahead to F-house to see inmates pointing at us. Lieutenant Treadwell and Harris saw what was happening and hurried ahead to have the officer contain his inmates to one side of the Cellhouse. I felt almost prideful to be part of this process. It was like I was in some eerie parade that everyone wanted to see. When that thought hit me, I wasn't sure how to handle it. I was a young Christian man walking another human being to his death and I felt guilty by a surge of pride. Then on the other side of the coin was the dead face of Teresa Carol Allen staring at me from the pages of Roosevelt Green's trial transcript. It was a battle in my mind. I felt anger from seeing her face on those pages yet also felt compassion for a convicted murderer walking to a carefully planned out death.

I was a professional and very good at my job. The outward appearance was easily maintained. Press the uniform, shine the shoes, polish the badge and I was the shining example of the future of this department. But, they never once mentioned to me how I should deal with the inner battle in my mind. I never received any instruction on how to process the feelings that came with my chosen profession. I was never told what to do with a face that I buried deep inside, but would come to revisit me at night when the safety and security of daylight retreated into the shadows. They never mentioned how to explain to my family the evenings when I stared at the walls or the weekends I couldn't stay sober because of the fear that if I did, my mind would be invaded with nightmares or flashbacks of murdered faces lying on their slabs.

One look at Roosevelt Green and my perspective changed entirely. In a few hours his earthly thoughts and problems would be over, but mine would continue. I wondered if his mind were racing as well. Rolling through the thoughts of what could have been. I often wondered if he ever thought of the life that he helped to extinguish. If he ever for one moment considered the family that he changed for the sake of one selfish lustful moment. I searched my mind in an attempt to remember any time he ever seemed remorseful for what he had done, but found none in my memory. There always seemed to be so much anger in him. I looked for any reason in my memory that would allow me to forgive him for what I saw in the pages of his trial transcript. All I found was my Christian belief that if I wanted to be forgiven then I had to forgive. It would have to be enough. We finally arrived at the red door. Kindle produced the key and opened the door that allowed fresh, cool air to brush past our faces. Lieutenant Treadwell stepped through the door and Green followed. He looked up at the January sky with the sun beaming down. The walk from here to H-5 would be his last chance to see an earthly sky. There was no way I could imagine what he was thinking or feeling. It was the last smell of unprocessed air in his life.

We finally stood at the back door of the execution chamber. Kindle inserted the key in the lock and with a turn, the door was open. Once inside Green walked past the chair covered in white sheets. It only required one glance and he knew what was waiting for him, but there were no words. He looked ahead to the end of his last mile. The holding cell was cold and bare. There was only a bunk and a combination sink and toilet. There was no need for the standard wall locker as in all other cells because he would only be here a few hours. At the door to the holding cell, we removed the restraint devices. His bedding was lying on the foot of the bed and once inside, he went right to work. The deathwatch officers were getting their chairs and table situated so they could see directly inside the cell for any movement. Kindle closed the cell door and handed the key to the officers at the table.

Carter, Kindle and Harris walked out and that left Lieutenant Treadwell and me at the cell. Lieutenant Treadwell said, "Let the officers know if you need anything, Roosevelt." Green had his back turned and when he heard the Lieutenant he walked to the front of the cell and surprisingly stuck his hand though bars. He shook Lieutenant Treadwell's hand first and looked deep in his eyes. Then he reached for mine and said to us both, "I just want you both to know that I always tried to be the best man I knew how to be." He was now looking in my eyes. As he grasped my hand I studied him. There was no malice in his voice and at this stage of the process; there could be no hidden agenda. I thought about all the conflicts that we had through the years even to the point where he had threatened to kill me. But now, it appeared to me that he was trying to make peace in the only way he knew how.

I said, "I know," as he looked deep in my eyes I released my grip and walked away knowing that was the last time I would see Roosevelt Green. One of the death watch officers followed behind us and we paused at the entrance to the execution chamber so he could unlock the door and let us out. As we were walking toward the corridor door that would give us access to H-house, Lieutenant Treadwell asked, "Did you feel it too?" I replied, "Yes sir, I did." Just before we reached the corridor door he stopped and looked at me and said, "After Green was done shaking my hand, I tried to let go and he grasped my hand a little more firmly causing me to look in his eyes." My eyes met his and he knew I was puzzled so he continued, "It was a condemned man's last show of respect and once he was sure I understood, he let go." I replied, "Yes, sir, I felt it as well."

I thought about what the lieutenant said. I tried to replay that last moment with Green and I did remember the grip and I did recall that he looked deep into my eyes in a way that he never had before. Maybe that was as sincere as he could be at that last moment. I always tried very hard to believe that there is some good in everyone because we are all created by God. Sometimes it was difficult to believe that God was here and working in this place witnessing the daily lives of murderers and reading of the carnage that some of them did. I thought of Teresa Carol Allen and wondered if she could forgive Roosevelt Green for his part in her death. Whatever the case, Green would find out in just a few hours because barring a last minute stay of execution, he was going to join her on the other side.

As soon as we were inside the door, Sergeant Smith told Lieutenant Treadwell that he was to call the Assistant Superintendent of security. I walked down to the cross gate at H-corridor just to kill time because my shift was about to end. While I stood there chatting with the corridor officer, Sergeant Smith called me back to the Lieutenant's office. Once inside the door Lieutenant Treadwell told me to take a seat. He explained my duties at the front gate for the night and gave me a wink. I smiled and said, "I won't let you down." He said, "That thought never crossed my mind."My new duty meant there would be no going home. I was instructed to eat at the institution, draw a weapon from the front tower and report to the front gate. The warden wanted security in place before demonstrators arrived. I already had handcuffs on my belt so I was issued a .357 revolver. I checked the weapon, loaded it and then attached the holster to my belt. The perimeter patrol officer gave me a ride to the front gate. To my surprise, Mr. Branch, the training officer, was already at the gate. Apparently it was a part of his duty during executions. He took the time to explain how I was to sign people in when they entered the gate. There was a list of those approved, mostly departmental personnel. I was told that witnesses would be driven to the rear when that time came.

It was quiet as the evening approached and mostly my duty was directing traffic as institutional employees started to leave for the day. When things slowed down again, Mr. Branch took me over to a fenced in area and showed me the areas were roped off for the protesters. On the opposite side of the entrance was a place designated for those who were in support of capital punishment. Mr. Branch said that later in the evening, Troopers from the Georgia State Patrol, Rangers from Natural Resources and Butts County Deputies would arrive to help with crowd control and security. Then he turned to me, patted me on the back and said, "But you are the man up here."

All the support agencies began to arrive. The Georgia State Patrol brought their mobile command post, a large R.V. specially outfitted for these occasions. They were very friendly and had no problem taking direction from me. The news crews arrived next. I recognized three of the major news stations from Atlanta with their remote satellite vans and tall towers. As I looked around I saw a lot of high ranking officers from the state patrol and the department of natural resources. There were Captains, majors and even a lieutenant colonel. I was used to being inside where it was quiet, but this was a very big event. Being young and ambitious, I was proud to be a part of it. As night fell, the demonstrators started to arrive. One of my duties was to keep the two opposing sides separate. The troopers and rangers took care of the vehicle searches.

There were far more demonstrators against the death penalty and they carried signs for the cameras. Those in favor of the execution talked loudly about their feelings on the execution. They wanted to be heard by those opposing the execution, but were warned if any disturbance started, they would be asked to leave and if it got too bad, they could be arrested and we had plenty of personnel here to do it. It was all mostly orderly and peaceful. The cameras were what everyone wanted to attract. Any chance to get their view heard. What bothered me the most is there was no representation here tonight for Teresa Carol Allen. Even those who stood in favor of the death penalty were more interested in cursing the system than standing for any victims' rights. As I watched in silence, I thought about her and I couldn't help but think about the man that I had escorted to the holding cell just a few hours earlier that would pay the ultimate price for his part in her murder. Regardless of their views, everything was in God's hands now.

The principle staff were assembled inside the Diagnostic Center. Assistant Superintendent Hugh Long was in the front office along with William Hill, assistant to the Georgia State Attorney General, Michael Bowers. He waited by phone with Commissioner David C. Evans at the commissioner's command post in Atlanta. The Superintendent of the Diagnostic Center, Ralph Kemp was in the H-5 execution chamber waiting to give instructions to the witnesses and to give the order to start the execution. Willis Marable, the Administrative Assistant to Mr. Kemp waited in the observation room directly behind the electric chair in the execution chamber. He was in constant contact by phone with both Hugh Long in the front office and Commissioner Evans in Atlanta. Everyone was in place. The execution of Roosevelt Green was in progress.

Marable: "Is everybody on?"
Long: "I'm here."
Evans/Bowers: "We're here."
Marable: "Ok."
Long: "What time are you showing Mr. Marable?"
Marable: "Hold on one....I'm showing 11:35 in about 20 seconds."
Long: "I'm about 25 seconds behind you. .....I have a report that the vans containing the witnesses have cleared the sally port and are inside the perimeter."
Marable: "Ok"
Long: "Mr. Hill has walked in the office."
Evans: "William?"
Hill: "How you doing commissioner?"
Evans: "How you doing? Mike wants to talk to you a minute."
Hill: "Ok."

Bowers: "Hill, stand by right there, ok?"

Hill: "Alright."

Bowers: "Have you got anything on that end to stop this at this time?

Hill: "There are no outstanding stays and no proceedings in any court."

Bowers: "Just stay right there cause I wanna talk to you again before we start."

Hill: "Alright."

Long: "I'm back."

Marable: "Commissioner, Mr. Long, the witnesses are entering the room at this time and are in the process of seating themselves."

Evans: "Everything appear to be orderly?"

Marable: "Yes sir, no problems at this time."

Long: "I show the time now 10 seconds past midnight, now January 9, 1985."

Marable: "You're correct……..All the witnesses for the state have entered the witness Room and are seated at this time."

"At this time, the witnesses for the condemned are seated and we are in the process of bringing in the witnesses for the news media and they are being seated at this time……… all witnesses are present and seated at this time."

"Commissioner, Mr. Long, we are a little ahead of schedule, so we will stand by just a little while."

"Mr. Evans, you copy? We'll stand by until ten after."

Evans: "Yes……you'll have to get your timing down on the witnesses just a little bit."

Marable: "Right sir."

Long: "I show the time is 12:02."

Marable: "you are correct."

Marable: "Commissioner, Mr. Long, very orderly. I see a couple of the news media sketching, a couple of the other witnesses talking to each other, but other than that, it's very quiet.

Evans: "Marable, do you know whether he is going to have prayer?"

Marable: "That I don't know, but he will make the statement. He indicated so when when I asked him."

Evans: "I understand that."

Marable: "But as far as the prayer, we don't know yet."

Marable: "Mr. Evans?"

Evans: "Yes"

Marable: "Mr. Kemp has advised me that judging from what Chaplin Lavelle said, he will have prayer."

Evans: "Ok"

Marable: "Mr. Evans, Mr. Long, its 10 after. Mr. Kemp has left the control room and is in the death watch area. We will be proceeding in a couple of seconds."

Long: "I show the time at 12:10."

Marable: "That's correct."

Evans: "You're a little fast there."

Marable: "Mr. Evans, Mr. Long, the Superintendent has entered the execution chamber and is in the process of adjusting the mike to brief the witnesses."

"At this time the Superintendent is briefing the witnesses to remain quiet and avoid any unnecessary movement and also that medical personnel are available if there is any assistance needed."

"He is now in the process of confirming the witnesses."

"All Witnesses have been confirmed at this time."

"He is instructing the witnesses that we will be proceeding with the court ordered execution of Roosevelt Green, Jr."

Marable: "At this time, the condemned is being escorted into the execution chamber by the execution team."

"He has seated himself unassisted."

"A member of the execution team is now in the process of securing the body straps."

"The remaining execution team members are securing the remaining straps."

"The condemned is sitting very quiet, he is just observing the execution team members secure him to the chair."

"The witnesses at this time...I detect very little movement. They are sitting very still and starring into the execution chamber at the condemned."

Long: "I'm showing the time is 12:11."

Evans: "That's 12:12."

Long: "I'm showing 12:12, I stand corrected."

Marable: "At this time the condemned is secure in the chair and the backboard has been adjusted."

"The Superintendent is affording the condemned the opportunity to make a last statement"

"He has answered in the affirmative."

"Stand by for his statement."

"He is now in the process of giving his last statement."

"He is advising the witnesses that he believes this is a grave misjustice."

"He is being executed for a crime he did not commit."

Marable: "He is primarily stating that we are executing him because he is black."

"He is stating at this time that he holds no remorse to anyone."

"Prayer has been offered and he has answered in the affirmative and that is in process at this time."

"Very little movement from any of the witnesses."

"I do see a few of the media still sketching."

"But other than that, very little movement from any of the witnesses."

Long: "I'm showing the time as 12:14."

Evans: "You're still a little off there, Hugh."

Marable: "Yeah, I'm showing almost sixteen after."

"Prayer is completed at this time. The Superintendent is in the process of reading the essential court order to the witnesses and the condemned."

"The Superintendent is still in the process of reading the court order."

"The condemned is sitting very still in the chair and starring directly into the witness room."

"Very little movement from any of the witnesses."

"The court order has been read to the witnesses and to the condemned."

"The execution team has entered the execution chamber and are in the process of securing the headpiece and the leg band to the condemned."

Bowers: "Hill, William Hill?"

Hill: "Hello"

Bowers: "Hill, this is Mike. Do you know of any reason to stop the execution?"

Hill: "No."

Bowers: "I don't know of any reason to stop. I recommend that we proceed with the court ordered execution of Roosevelt Green, Jr."

Marable: "The leg band has been attached. Two of the execution team members are still in the process of securing the headset."

"The condemned is sitting very still, very little movement from any of the witnesses."

"The electrician has entered the execution chamber and is in the process of securing the electrical wire to the headset."

Long: "What time are you showing, Mr. Marable?"

Marable: "I'm showing.....looks like about 19 after."

"The electrician is now in the process of securing the electrical wire to the leg band."

"The condemned's forehead has been wiped for perspiration. The hood is in position and the leg band is attached. Both wires secured at this time."

"The speaker has been switched off and all the straps are being checked at this time."

"Stand by for the Superintendent's final check."

Kemp: "Commissioner, is there any other word?"

Evans: "Ralph, we have no word of any impediment to carrying out the execution of Roosevelt Green. Proceed to carry out the order of the court."

Kemp: "Very well. On the count of three, depress your buttons. 1...2...3."

Marable: "Commissioner, Mr. Long, the execution is in progress. There was one jerk after that, he seems to have sat upright in the chair slightly. He is easing back down. No further movement at this time. "

"We have completed the first and second phase, we are now into the third phase of the execution. Still no movement from the condemned. At this time He is sitting very still. I detect no movement at this time."

Long: "I show the time is 12:20."

Marable: "Neither is there any exaggerated movement from the witnesses, they are sitting very still.

"His mother is exercising her arms, but other than that, very little movement from the witnesses."

"I still detect no movement from the condemned, I see his hands clinched in fist, he hasn't relaxed those, but there still is no movement at all that I can detect."

Long: "I show the time is 12:21."

Marable: "Commissioner, Mr. Long, it appears at this time that the execution is successful. I have not detected any movement at all from the condemned."

"Ok, at this time, the third phase is completed. The execution is completed the equipment is secured and locked."

"Stand by for the physician's check, as you were, for the first minute of lapse time, started at 12:18."

Evans: ""I believe you should correct that, should be 12:22 or 12:23."

Marable: "Yes, I'm sorry, it's 12:22."

Long: "I show the time also as 12:22."

Marable: "One minute of lapsed time completed, four minutes remaining. We have detected no movement at all from the condemned."

Long: "I'm showing the time as 12:23."

Marable: "Two minutes of lapsed time completed, three minutes remaining."

Long: "The time is 12:24."

Marable: "Aside from the first jerk when the execution first started, I have detected no movement what so ever. Three minutes of lapsed time completed, two minutes remaining"

Long: "I'm showing the time at 12:25. I've been advised that Dr. Dawson's crime lab has arrived and is being transported to the back."

Marable: "Four minutes lapsed time completed, one minute remaining."

Long: "I'm showing the time as 12:26."

Marable: "Commissioner, Mr. Long, the five minutes lapsed is completed, stand by for the Physician's check."

"At this time the physicians have entered the execution chamber. The first physician is in the process of making his check for vital signs."

Long: "I show the time as 12:27."

Marable: "The first physician has completed his check, the second physician is in the process of making his."

"Both physicians have completed their check."

"The superintendent has briefed the witnesses that the court ordered execution of Roosevelt Green, Jr. has been carried out. I have now, 12:28."

Evans: "Willis, any activity in the witness room?"

Marable: "No, the curtains have been closed at this time and the witnesses are in the process of being removed from the witnesses room and to be escorted back up front."

Marable: "The execution team members are entering the execution chamber at this time to remove the body from the chair as soon as all the witnesses have departed."

Evans: "Still no reaction from the witnesses?"

Marable: "Not at all. It was very quiet, very orderly even from the mother. I noticed her moving her arms one time and that was all."

Long: "I'm showing the time as 12:29."

Marable: "Mr. Evans, from what I can tell, it was very clean, very professional."

"They are in the process of removing Green's body from the chair."

Evans: "How soon can you tell us what his exact statement was?'

Marable: "I'll have to play the recording back, Mr. Evans."

Evans: "You don't have anybody there taking shorthand in case the recorder broke?"

Marable: "No sir. He basically told that they were executing the wrong man, it was a grave injustice."

Evans: "What about playing it back for us if you can get it."

Marable: "Ok sir."

"I understand that there was quite a bit of saliva, but I don't see any burns from where I am. The doctors are checking him over very closely now to see if they can detect any."

"Commissioner, Mr. Long, they have removed the body from the execution chamber and he is in the autopsy room at this time. "That completes that part of it." "Stand by for the recorded last statement."

Roosevelt Green: "I would like to say that God is with me and I hope he is with all of you tonight. What you people are about to witness is a grave misjustice.

I'm about to die for a murder that someone else committed and I had nothing to do with. And it seems to me that there is a double standard in our society. I was in the county jail in '77 awaiting trial and a deputy told me that two nigger's lives was not worth that of one white woman's life. To me, at that time, I thought he was just talking out the side of his neck. But, now, tonight, it is evident that black lives are not equal to that of white's lives and Liberty and justice for all is not a synonym of what is about to happen to me now. I would like to say that from deep in my heart that I have nothing against anyone. I have no enemies, period. That I love the Lord and I hope that you all love him, too and that God will take me into his kingdom and...Good bye, mother."

I was intimately involved in the last few years of Roosevelt Green's life. I had never known Teresa Carol Allen, but after seeing Green's trial transcript, complete with her pictures and the details of their crime, I felt a strange almost morbid connection to her and the man who helped to end her life. It was as if the three of us were connected in some way. Green had said that her murder was something "he had nothing to do with." It was absolutely untrue. In his mind, because he had not physically pulled the trigger, he was somehow guilty of a lesser crime. Maybe they didn't discuss it, but her life was over from the moment they kidnapped her, raped her and pulled off on a dirt road in Monroe County. Maybe it was a defense mechanism to claim that he had nothing to do with it. But, the fact that he left her with Moore and the rifle was enough for anybody to reasonably deduce what was going to happen. It was all academic now because she was gone and now so was he.

The vans containing the witnesses arrived at the front entrance and immediately the lights from the cameras flooded the witnesses as they exited the vans. It was a sign to us that the execution was over. Other reporters gathered in front of the news media witnesses to get the story of how it felt to be inside to witness the final moments of a man's life. In the midst of the mass mania around the van, I watched and thought about Teresa Carol Allen and Roosevelt Green. They were now part of the spirit world and I wondered if either was aware of it yet. While I contemplated this spiritual question and the crowd was asking questions, suddenly a set of headlights appeared down the road near the institution. Heads began to turn and the crowd grew silent. The lights moved slowly toward the front entrance. With no fanfare at all outside, Roosevelt Green had died in Georgia's electric chair. I was certain the lights' approaching was the hearse.

The long black vehicle moved very slowly to the front entrance. Not a word was spoken by anyone for a minute or two. Then as the vehicle reached the demonstration area, the pro death penalty side began to cheer. I looked to the opposite side at those who demonstrated against the death penalty and saw that they were bowing there head in silence. A Butts County deputy's cruiser was there at the front entrance. Just before the hearse reached the entrance, the deputy got into the car and turned on his blue lights. He would escort Roosevelt Green on his last trip from the Diagnostic Center and to the funeral home where his body would be prepared for burial. He was free at last.

The show was over and the news media began to pack up there equipment. With the news media leaving, there was no need for the demonstrators and they began to leave as well. Once the demonstrators were gone, the law enforcement personnel began to leave. The

staff from inside the prison was making their way out. Lieutenant Treadwell waved as he passed by the entrance. The last unit to leave was the State Patrol mobile command post. I surveyed the scene and I had an eerie feeling. As I looked down toward the institution I saw a shadow passing through the light. I felt a shudder deep inside as if something touched my soul. Maybe I was caught up in the events of the night or maybe it was seeing the body of Roosevelt Green pass by knowing that just a few hours ago he had been alive to shake my hand, look deep in my eyes and leave me a non-verbal message. Then again, maybe, just maybe, knowing his job was done here, I had witnessed the angel of death departing the diagnostic center.

I was all alone at the front entrance and I suddenly felt a surge of fear. I picked up the radio and called for the perimeter patrol officer to pick me up. I waited in the darkness and silence. My senses were heightened and I heard every noise in the night. Any tree that moved or any movement in the brush caught my ear. After what seemed like an eternity, I saw the lights of the perimeter patrol vehicle. As I entered the vehicle, I must have had a strange look on my face, because the officer asked, "Are you ok, Allen?" I smiled and said, "Yes, I'm fine. Just a little tired." It was a short trip to tower 1 and I thanked him for the ride as I exited the vehicle. The tower 1 officer had already lowered the bucket for my weapon. I placed my .357 in the bucket and waved to the tower officer. My eyes searched the sky in the direction that I had seen the shadow moving, but there was nothing.

It felt good to be in the warmth and safety of my car. I was ready to leave this behind me tonight. Once I drove by the area of the shadow, I looked in my rearview mirror to see if anything was there. Part of my mind expected to see the skeletal face of death looking back, but I saw nothing. I concentrated on the road ahead. I drove away from the institution as quickly as I could. It was a lonely drive home because it was so late and there were no other cars on the road. My mind went back to Roosevelt Green. I wondered where he was lying now. His lifeless body lay on a table waiting to be embalmed. I started thinking about the many altercations we had during his time on death row. There was physical violence, but then there was that long handshake and the stare I received from him. I wondered if there was something spiritual in it all. It felt uneasy. Did Green and I meet at the end of his life for a spiritual purpose? That long last look began to haunt me. Now I had to figure out what it meant and if I had completed a task that God gave me to do at the end of his life. What if it wasn't about Green at all, but his look was intended for me and to search myself somehow.

I was lost in thought when I arrived home. By force of habit, I supposed, my car had found its way to my driveway and there I sat with the engine running. It was almost like I was transported here. I had something new to contemplate. I turned the car off and went inside. I went immediately to Kimberly's room. After being surrounded by death for more than a few hours, I needed to see her. The invisible fragrance of her innocence filled the room. She was only 2 years old and I stood by her bed just watching her breathe. I thought about Leighanne and Tracey and wished they were here with us tonight. I needed to see them, too. I wanted to call them, but it was far too late for that. So I just stood and allowed myself to be filled by Kimberly's essence.

I finally made my way to my room where Sarah lay asleep. Not wanting to wake her, I undressed in the dark, slipped into bed and lay my head on my pillow. I waited in silence,

in the dark with my thoughts. They rushed through my head and made me almost dizzy. I closed my eyes, but my mind was swirling. So I waited with my eyes open and thought about the nights events. Teresa Carol Allen, her parents, Roosevelt Green, his mother and this new feeling that I had been sent a message through Roosevelt Green. My eyes became heavy as I slipped into sleep and the demons came.

Chapter 11

"Do not pollute the land where you are. Bloodshed pollutes the land,
and atonement cannot be for the land
On which blood has been shed, except by the blood of the one who shed it

- Numbers 35:33
(New International Version)

The morning light brought no changes with it. I woke with the faces of Roosevelt Green and Teresa Carol Allen in my mind. It was the same with the other three executions before. Their faces haunted me through the night and then again the following morning. The night before was only broken sleep because I had visions of the day before. As I walked toward the institution, the night was still on my mind. Roosevelt Green was my fourth execution and definitely the most personal. Because I shared the same last name with the family, I felt a kinship to them. I had harbored a secret hate for Roosevelt Green ever since I saw his picture in the paper, after his capture in New York City with that sickening smile on his face. Now in a strange way, I found myself mourning for him. It was a crazy thought and I dare not tell any of my fellow officers. There had been nothing but violence and resentment between Green and me, until that final moment at the holding cell when he shook my hand and stared into my eyes. I had no idea what to do with that feeling. Before I walked into the institution, I glanced skyward in search of an answer.

I asked myself why I was mourning the death of a very violent convicted murderer. My only thought was that somehow through my contact with him, I was standing up for Teresa. Now with him gone, I was mourning for them both. There was now an empty place in my mind and inside me where Roosevelt Green lived. I'd grown used to the hate I carried inside because of the life he helped end. I wondered where he was today. He asked at his last moment that God would take him into his kingdom. If he truly repented for his part in her murder, he was there, no matter what he had done. After all, Jesus told the thief on the cross that he would be with him in paradise. Now that stirred up more inside. My head was swirling with all types of emotions. The chief emotions were anger and pity. There was absolutely no way I could share this with anyone for fear of showing weakness. I was a front line serving officer on death row and having pity for a murderer just would not do. So once

again, I did what I do best; I filed it away deep inside where no one would ever see it and I wouldn't have to talk about it.

We began executions in 1983 and now we had executed four men in thirteen months. It was like someone said, "Go!" and the process jumped forward as if we were making up for lost time. I still believed in the death penalty, but since we carried out four executions and that exchange between Green and I, somehow things seemed different. The other officers in H-house were almost rubbing their hands together waiting for another. All the while I had to play the game as though I was as eager as they. I wasn't turning into a bleeding heart liberal by any means, but being so close to it all and watching these men's faces as they walked through the H-5 execution chamber, in fear, shed light on the reality that men were dying. When their time came, I had an adrenaline rush for several days until it was over because I felt as though I was on the side of righteousness. During that time, I always remembered reading their trial transcripts and the despicable things they had done. But, after it was over, as I was coming down from the rush, I started to think about them as human beings and some with families. It would always take several days before I could look in a mirror again.

I finally reached H-house and entered the cross gate. We all resumed our duties as if nothing significant happened. There was a psychologist that visited H-house 2-3 times per week to talk with the inmates. After an execution, he came daily for the entire week. Fine, I thought, but where was the psychologists for the officers? We were trained to do an unpleasant duty and that was putting it very mildly. The administration didn't seem concerned how this might affect us. I felt a deep resentment because no one ever asked how I felt. I felt cheated somehow. My only defense was stuffing as much as possible in the imaginary file until it bulged at the sides. I assumed if I didn't talk about it, it would go away and I wouldn't have to face it. It was a child's answer on how to handle the issue. Life continued on as usual in H-house. My personal life was a different matter.

Sarah and I continued to grow apart. 1985 was going to be a big year of change for us both. We were living together almost as roommates and only for Kimberly's sake. In a matter of weeks it came to an end. I finally packed some things, held Kimberly in my arms, kissed her and told her how much I loved her. She was only 2 years old and had no idea what was happening. I moved in with my mother and Sarah and I soon began divorce proceedings. We had danced around the subject for over a year and finally we accepted that it was over. I was able to put that part of my life to rest. I was only 25 years old and about to be divorced for a second time. I turned my attention to my career so I didn't have to focus on my personal disgrace.

In less than one month we executed two men. It was a new era in Georgia for the inmates as well as the officers. It appeared the lengthy appeals process was coming to an end for inmates under the death sentence. One month and eleven days later, a fifth death warrant landed in H-house. The unlucky recipient was Van Roosevelt Solomon. Solomon was mild mannered during his stay on death row. I knew nothing of his background or education, but he always presented himself as an educated man. But his stay was relatively short compared to others who had been there for years. He committed his crime with fellow death row inmate, Wilbur May, on June 16, 1979 less than six years before. As with the rest of his fellow murderers, it was another selfish, senseless act.

The victim, Roger Dennis Tackett, was the manager of a self service gas station. Two employees, Linda Rosenfeild and Carol Menfee, were working the evening shift and realized they did not have the keys to lock the station when it closed at midnight. One of the ladies called Roger to inform him of the situation and he came to the station at 11:20 pm to lock the store after closing. The two employees left and Roger locked the station, but remained to catch up on some paperwork so that he could be with his family the next day, which was father's day. At approximately 1:00 am, Linda Rosenfield drove by the station and noticed Roger's car still parked in front. Early in the evening of 16 June, Jill Cindy Rhoda picked her dinner date up at an apartment complex located near the station. She drove her date back to the apartment complex where they argued and her date took her car keys and went into his apartment. Miss Rhoda contacted the police in order to get her keys back. Officer Kendle of the Cobb county police department accompanied her to the apartment complex, but she could not find her boyfriend's apartment. She did remember his phone number and at approximately 1:50 am the officer drove her to the gas station so she could call to find out where the apartment was.

When they arrived at the gas station, Miss Rhoda went to use the payphone. Officer Kendle noticed a green Dodge automobile parked in front of the station with its door open and a loaf of bread on the front seat. As he went to investigate, he noticed a black male, later identified as Wilbur May, open the back storeroom door inside the station quickly look out and then close the door. He found the front door of the station unlocked, drew his weapon and proceeded inside. As he walked through the store, he heard three closely spaced shots, a pause and then another shot. The officer ordered the person in the store room to come out, but got no response. He opened the door and standing near a walk –in cooler were two black males, Wilbur May and Van Roosevelt Solomon. He placed them both in custody and asked what they were doing there. Solomon said that "they were burglarizing."

Officer Kendle had the radio operator call the emergency number listed on the front door of the gas station. He learned that Roger was supposed to be in the station at that time. The officer then broke into the back of the store using a crowbar. When he entered, he found Roger's body. He had been beaten and shot five times. There were approximately twenty to thirty five minutes between the arrest and the discovery of the body. Near the body officers found two guns, one of which still had the hammer cocked. One of the guns, a colt .38 short revolver, had four spent rounds in the chamber. The other, a .38 Smith and Wesson had one spent round. Also discovered near the scene, well hidden, was a van Solomon and his partner were driving. Solomon later gave a statement that he and Wilbur May were driving around because he wanted to show May the Atlanta area. He stated that he didn't know how the van got to the station because he was tied up in the back of the van. He stated that Mr. May made him go into the station and put him in the cooler. He claimed he did not hear any sounds nor did he remember having gloves on. Both he and May were subjected to gun residue test and both were determined to have recently fired a weapon.

We followed the procedure as before with the other four men and every detail was exactly the same. Death watch began in the medical section and in the last eight hours with no stay of execution given by any court, Van Roosevelt Solomon walked his last mile down the corridor and outside for a last look at daylight and finally ending in the holding cell with the

electric chair looming in the next room. Later that afternoon, the administrative assistant to the superintendant, entered Solomon's cell to take his final statement.

Administrative Assistant: "Van Roosevelt Solomon, do you wish to make a last Statement Prior to your scheduled execution?"

Solomon: "Yes, sir." "I wish to make the following statements prior to my death."

"First to the family of Roger Tackett, I send to you, my remorse, for the death of your loved one from the bottom of my heart. I did not kill Roger Tackett and I remorse deeply for his death. To my supporters I send all of my deepest respect. It has been due to your efforts that I have received the degree of justice in my case.

Solomon: "To the world, I suggest that people need to reach out more to help the needy and the homeless. To my family and children I send you all my love and I want you to know that I love you very much and do not be bitter. Work hard, be honest in all life and you will be successful in America. Van Roosevelt Solomon."

I sometimes tried to imagine what was going through a person's mind while they were strapped in the chair, looking into a room full of strangers who were about to watch them die. Did they reminisce about their past life, their loved ones, and their childhood or even try to conjure up any good they accomplished in life or were they too consumed with fear to even recall their past life? I do know that in listening to their statements, I couldn't detect any change in their voices. I concluded that in those final moments, they accepted their fate. Solomon was afforded an opportunity to add to his last statement while he was in the death chamber and strapped in the chair. Even in the last moments of his life, he was defiant.

"I'd like to say to that I give my blessing to all those who seek to save my life, I'd like to curse everyone who seek to take my life."

Then moments later, the superintendent gave the order to push the buttons and the process began to end the life of Van Roosevelt Solomon and he became the fifth man to die in the electric chair. But, the roar of the generator would not be silenced for long. Only weeks later, another execution order was handed down. John Young was only 18 years old when he murdered three elderly people in Bibb County Georgia. The murders were described as a drug induced robbery rampage.

On the night of December 7, 1974, six elderly people were attacked severely beaten, kicked and stomped in their homes in the city of Macon, Georgia. All lived in the same neighborhood, Three of those people pieced together a description of their assailant. The other three, Coleman Brice, Gladys Brice and Katie Davis died as a result of the attack on them. John Young was connected to the crimes by watches and jewelry taken during the commission of the crimes, a fingerprint and statements to his friends that he attacked the people. When asked if he was the one who jumped on those people, he replied: "Yeah man and I'm going to get me some more." When asked if they were white or black he replied: "White." When asked why, he replied, "I don't know the only thing I'm sorry is that they caught me before I got through. "

Young's attorney filed a special plea of insanity before the trial, but a jury returned a verdict against the insanity plea. His insanity plea had no merit because every day that he lived on death row he was calm and maintained relationships with other inmates and even times that I escorted him through the institution he appeared to be as lucid as others and that included staff. He blamed society for being on death row. He said he had a disadvantage in his lifetime because he was born black and poor. He insisted that all he had done was make a mistake and was angry that society wouldn't forgive him. He was afforded the opportunity to make a last statement in his cell and again as he sat in the electric chair. He never demonstrated any remorse for violently stomping three elderly people to death, but insisted that he was the victim. As with Van Roosevelt Solomon, he went to his death accepting no responsibility for what he had done, for the people he murdered and the families he destroyed. Inmates like John Young made it easy for me to support their executions. John Young was executed on March 20, 1985, exactly one month to the day after Van Roosevelt Solomon. We never knew when an execution order would come and after a month with no execution orders, the inmates in H-house seemed to breathe a sigh of relief and we returned to normal operations.

H-house had been a segregation unit before death row was moved to the diagnostic center. It was an older unit and it was decided that a newer, more secure unit was needed. G-house, which was adjacent to H-house, would become the new death row unit. The maintenance department had been busy converting a standard cell house into a more modern unit. After many inspections G-house was released to the security department and ready to be populated. Even with that it was still several weeks away from a move because we were given the assignment of searching the entire unit multiple times to ensure that no maintenance tools or materials were left behind. We had a new unit, but we didn't want to leave anything in the unit with which inmates could forge weapons. Every cell, every corner was searched; every bar and every fence tested and retested multiple times. Finally approval was given by the administration and security experts to move death row to G-house. Each inmate and his property was searched and escorted to G-house under the watchful eye of many officers. The migration was finally completed in the spring of 1985. There were newer more spacious offices for the unit manager, Lieutenant Treadwell, the chief counselor, his subordinates, unit clerk and finally the shift supervisors had their own office.

Shortly after our move to G-House the second shift sergeant resigned to begin a new career. A promotion board would be convened, but it was rumored that Dave Harris, the unit clerk would most likely be promoted. I decided to apply for the sergeants' position to gain experience, but I knew that I would be selected as the new unit clerk. In just a matter of weeks, Dave Harris was promoted to sergeant and became the new second shift supervisor and also the youngest sergeant at the diagnostic center. I welcomed my assignment as clerk and settled into my new office. This position would put me on a fast track to an eventual promotion.

I thought that after the execution of Roosevelt Green, I would have some sort of peace with the awful story of the murder of Teresa Carol Allen. But, it only seemed to open another door in my mind. I didn't feel any relief from his death. I'd silently made the promise to never forget her. Now it seemed like I was serving a sentence of my own because I could not let go of the feelings. His death had changed nothing and I thought maybe that was the real issue of the death penalty. Executing the killers didn't change anything they'd done. If there

was a positive side to their deaths, it was the fact those executed would never be able to hurt another innocent person. Considering those thoughts only caused my dreams to intensify and now their faces came to me in the night and not just the killers, but the victims as well. I started to drink more after work in a feeble attempt to dismiss the faces.

In the summer of 1985 I renewed my friendship with a friend from high school; Hugh Tillman. We were very close and had studied karate together in Forsyth. He married and we drifted apart. Now he was divorced and living alone. I moved in with him and my drinking increased. We both bought motorcycles and began to act like teenagers, riding all through the countryside. I welcomed the freedom that came with each daytime ride. It was the nights that became my enemy because I couldn't hide from the dreams. During the daytime, when I was off duty, if my thoughts clouded my mind, I could drink. Drinking and driving is a really careless thing to do and drinking while riding a two wheel vehicle is even more irresponsible, but I pushed the envelope every day. On this particular Saturday, Hugh and I started drinking early and decided to ride through the back roads of Monroe County. Feeling the wind in my face, seeing the beautiful green trees and drinking alcohol helped me relax and put the faces that haunted me in the back of my mind. But, I became too relaxed and got careless. Hugh was in front of me as we rode down a very curvy road.

My reaction time was slowed because of the alcohol and as I tried to drive through a curve, I wandered too far to the right and my front tire slipped off the shoulder and into a groove. I tried to slowly drive back onto the road, but it was too late. The bike became difficult to control and the last thing I remembered was going over the handle bars before blacking out. When I regained consciousness Hugh was turning me over on my back and removing my helmet. That's when I felt the rattling in my chest as I tried to breathe. I told Hugh, "Oh my God, I'm bleeding internally!" I also felt a slight pain in my left shoulder and I heard Hugh reply, "Breathe shallow, Bobby." I had the over whelming feeling that I was dying and I immediately started to pray out loud, "God, please forgive me, please forgive me." I said those words over and over until the ambulance arrived. I lost consciousness again as the E.M.T.'s loaded me inside. When I woke again, I was in a room with bright lights shining down in my eyes. I heard faint voices in the background. Finally a doctor's face appeared over me and he asked, "Are you in any pain, Mr. Allen?" I shook my head no and replied, "I can feel my chest rattling, am I bleeding internally?" He shook his head as he said, "No, that's just fluid in your chest, but you have a broken left scapula." I passed out again.

I didn't wake again until the following morning. I was in a hospital room and heard the beeping of the heart monitor. I blinked to focus my eyes, looked around the room and there sat my faithful friend, Hugh Tillman. He had the strangest look on his face and I said, "You look like you've seen a ghost." It took him several minutes, but finally he said, "I should be looking at a ghost." I took the bed controls and raised my head up as far as I could. My body was hurting all over like I had been beaten. It took me a minute before I was able to respond, but finally I asked, "What are you talking about." He replied, "Let me tell you what I saw." He pulled his chair closer to my bed and began. "I was looking through my mirror when you came off the road and I saw you go over your handle bars with your arms stretched out like Superman. You began to tumble over and over through the ditch and your bike following right behind you. You finally came to a stop and I thought the motorcycle was

going to crush you." He looked deep in my eyes as he continued, "Bobby, when you stopped tumbling, the motorcycle looked liked it hit a brick wall, as though someone put out their hand out, blocked it and it jumped out into the street." We both sat there for a moment looking at each other. Then he began again, "I went back out to the crash site and there was nothing in that ditch to stop that motorcycle from crushing you. Bobby, you should be dead."

I was out of work for several weeks and had time to contemplate what Hugh told me as I healed. I was living my life recklessly. I drank alcohol in an attempt to block the visions that kept me from sleeping. I wasn't being a father to my three girls and now my behavior had very nearly cost me my life. I accepted what happened as a wakeup call, that God had his hand on me and that I had some part yet to play in my service on death row. I used my time off to do physical therapy in the swimming pool where Hugh and I lived and finally I was well enough to return to my duties in G-house. But, I returned to work with the knowledge that God was watching me. I vowed to stop drinking and opened my mid to discover what plan God had for me. I moved back in with my mother and focused on my job and wanted to be a better father to my girls.

There were no executions through the summer of 1985 so G-house was quiet. I recovered from my motorcycle accident, but what Hugh witnessed out on that road during the summer stayed with me and I returned to my prayer life and listened for God's voice. When I returned to my duties as clerk, I found out that the officer who temporarily replaced me was vying for my job full time. I heard through rumors that he'd gone to Lieutenant Treadwell to say that he could perform my duties and he would always be at work and the Lieutenant could rely on him. I was told that Lieutenant Treadwell became angry and raised his voice to the officer and told him in no uncertain terms that the clerk position belonged to me and he wouldn't discuss it further. It warmed my heart to know that he valued me that much. I had yet another reason to focus on my job because I didn't want to let him down.

My duties took me to the mailroom of the institution at least twice a day to handle outgoing mail for the inmates and to inspect incoming letters and packages for those on death row. Directly across the hall from the mailroom was the legal department for all inmates at the diagnostic center. There was a fulltime attorney, a paralegal and a secretary. On one such trip I looked into the legal office and discovered that there was a new paralegal recently assigned. Her beauty caught my attention and I almost walked into the door of the mailroom. She was absolutely the most beautiful woman I'd ever seen. Her light brown hair was almost blond and fell across her shoulders. Her beautiful eyes were mesmerizing. I had become friends with one of the mailroom employees, Riana. I asked about her and she gave me the story.

Her name was Deborah and she recently transferred from the legal department of the Georgia State Prison at Reidsville and had a four year old daughter. My heart sunk as I asked, "Oh, she's married?" Riana said, "No, she's divorced." When I smiled it must have lit up my face because Riana laughed and said, "Yes." Over the next couple of weeks I made any excuse I could to go to the mailroom. She was very quiet and if we passed in the hallway my heart sank to my stomach. I was overtaken by her beauty. She worked out of her office quite a bit, but also had to go to the counseling department to interview inmates. I tried to find any reason to be in the area she worked.

As Clerk, I did quite a bit of typing and filing in my office. . I maintained files for every inmate on death row, but also for the staff assigned there. The staff in G-house received hazardous duty pay for their assignment in a high risk security area and I was responsible for documenting that and turning those documents into the payroll department. I usually spent the first part of my morning in my office. I was busy with my morning duties when I heard the cross gate open in E-house. Out of habit I always looked to see who passed my office. It was unusual to see civilians enter G-house and on those occasions it caught my attention. Two women walked passed my window and my heart skipped a beat. It was the female attorney from the legal department and her paralegal, Deborah. They were talking as they passed and paid no mind to me, but my eyes followed her down the hallway.

There were side windows that allowed a view through each office all the way down to the corridor of G-house. It was to ensure that there were no blind spots. At the very end of the row of offices was a room used for inmate interviews and that was their destination. I made an effort not to stare, but I wasn't very successful. I tried to appear busy at my desk, but I kept looking at the ladies in the office. They were chatting as they looked though the documents they brought. Finally the inmate they came to see appeared and sat down across the table from them. The meeting was very brief and I noticed they had documents for the inmate to sign. Once that was completed the inmate left the office and as they walked by, Deborah looked over at me, smiled and waved. I froze as though I was acknowledged by a celebrity. As they walked toward E-house to leave, I felt the warmth in my cheeks; I was blushing. I wanted desperately to introduce myself, but in many ways I was still the shy kid from high school and I had no alcohol in me to give me the courage to speak to her. Riana saw my anguish and encouraged me to talk to Deborah. I was twice divorced and everyone knew it and thinking about that only made me more uncomfortable. Riana decided that I needed a push so she told me that a secretary from the typing pool had come to mailroom to talk. The diagnostic center was not immune from office gossip it seemed. The topic that day was the new girl, Deborah. Riana took the opportunity to say that I was interested in Deborah, but I was too shy to ask her out. The secretary attacked right away "But, he's been married two times!" Riana smiled and said calmly, "So has Deborah." With nothing left to say, the secretary left the room.

I didn't know until that moment that Deborah had been through circumstances similar to mine. I took a breath and let out a sigh of relief. The playing field was now level. As I left the mailroom I looked over into the legal office to see Deborah sitting at her desk. She looked up and for a brief second we locked eyes and smiled. I smiled all the way to G-house. In the next week we passed in the hallway several times and exchanged smiles. Riana talked with Deborah and discovered that she was not dating anyone and asked her if she would be willing to go out with me. Riana smiled and said, "She said yes, Bobby." Riana told me that Deborah lived in a trailer park on the next exit after the diagnostic center, only a couple of miles away. That night I drove to the exit while drinking beer. I needed courage to make the call. I'd seen her drive out of the parking lot before and I knew her car. I drove through the trailer park and found her car parked in front of a small trailer. I laughed at myself and the cowardly way I was acting. I had the courage to stand up to men under the death sentence and physically subdue them, but I could not find the courage to call a girl that already said she would go out with me. I decided I wasn't going to let this moment pass by. I drove to a store close to the trailer park. After drinking two more beers, I was ready to make the call.

When Deborah answered the phone, her sweet sounding voice melted my heart. We made a date for the upcoming weekend. In some ways I was still that young, naïve kid that called Deedee, my first wife, years before. I was able to make the call tonight because of alcohol and it was becoming a crutch for my feelings. Whenever I felt unsure of myself or had dreams or thoughts that made me feel uncomfortable, I turned to alcohol.

The following Saturday night we went to dinner in Macon. I was so intimidated by her beauty. I'd had several beers before I arrived at her house to calm my nerves. We chatted on our way to Macon, but small talk was something I wasn't comfortable with. At the restaurant, when the waitress came to our table to take our order, she asked if we cared for a cocktail. I looked over to Deborah and she ordered a bourbon and cola. I let out a sigh of relief and ordered the same. Now I would be able to relax and talk with her. When the waitress brought our drinks, she said it was happy hour and we would receive two drinks. Because I had a few beers before our date, the bourbon took immediate effect. As she told me about her life I was almost in a trance looking at her and once I realized that, I was afraid that I'd been inappropriately staring at her. But she finished talking and was now looking deep into my eyes. I'd heard of love at first site before, but never experienced it until this moment and I realized that I loved her from the first moment I laid eyes on her. Later at her home, we kissed goodnight and it was magical to me. After our kiss, she looked into my eyes and whispered, "You can call me Debbie."

Debbie and I became close very quickly. It was as if we'd known each other all our lives. I eventually met her daughter and she became a part of our date nights. Debbie was attending college classes at night to earn her degree. We were together every free night she had. I found myself smiling every day at work so much that the other officers were asking, "What's up with you, Allen?" I just smiled all the more and replied, "Life is good." I made a trip to the mailroom as often as I could just to see her face. I was dreaming about Debbie when I wasn't with her. I always fell asleep with my stereo on to help me relax. I woke one night to the sound of a Lionel Richie song, "Say you, Say me."

I sat up in my bed and looked out the window in the early morning dark as I listened to the words of this song and it gripped my heart to confirm what I already knew; that I was in love. I was in a restless sleep until the morning light came through my window and I knew that I had to find a way to tell Debbie that I couldn't live without her. We dated though the fall into December. Debbie had once told me that after two failed marriages, she didn't ever want to be married again. That was a stab in the heart, but I was determined. Late one night at her house we were sharing a quiet moment together I knew that I couldn't contain it any longer. As the music played softly I looked into her eyes, told her I loved her and asked her to marry me. She hesitated only a moment, then smiled very sweetly and said yes. It was one of the happiest moments of my life because the woman I loved was sitting before me and about to become my wife. Since we both had been married twice, we decided we didn't need a big church wedding and opted to go before a judge after Christmas.

After we married I never felt so content in my life. I finally found the happiness I'd searched for all my life. Debbie was bound to make our family complete by bringing the twins and Kimberly into our lives. I had a wife now that wasn't resentful of my children and wanted them to be a part of our new family. I focused on my career and was intent on rising as far as I could so I could take care of my new family and provide a home for us all.

Debbie and I chose not to talk about work because she was against the death penalty. We just accepted each other's opinion and for that reason, I never shared my dreams with her. During the first few months of our marriage, I was spared the dreams and I attributed that to my new found happiness and the fact that there had been no executions. The spring of 1986 arrived, G-house was quiet and March marked one year since out last execution. It was the longest lull between executions since H-5 reopened in December 1983. Speculation started to stir among the G-house staff if there would ever be another execution. In June of 1986, those thoughts were laid to rest. An execution order came to G-house for Jerome Bowden. He was one of the mildest mannered inmates on death row. He was always jovial and always a smile on his face. He was easy to converse with during my escorts with him. But, as with all others here, there was a dark sinister side to him that led him to a death sentence and now an active execution order waited for him in the counselor's office.

Mrs. Kathryn Stryker and her mother had not answered their door or telephone for several days. Their neighbors became alarmed and called the police. A deputy sheriff entered the house on October 14, 1976 and noticed ransacked rooms and heard labored breathing. The deputy found Mrs. Wessie Jenkins, Mrs. Stryker's mother, lying on a bed in a pool of dried blood, still alive. The deputy then discovered the body of Kathryn Stryker in the kitchen. The victim's skull was beaten in, leaving her features unrecognizable; and a butcher knife was buried deep in her chest. An autopsy revealed that the base of the skull was fractured by the application of extreme force, such as is found in the victims of car or plane crashes. There was also a large open wound behind the ear through which the doctor could see the brain. The knife wound had caused no bleeding, indicating that the victim was already dead when stabbed. Death had occurred three to four days earlier.

A blow of great force by a nonsharp object had caused the injuries. Mrs. Jenkins had suffered a stroke earlier in September, resulting in partial paralysis that left her bedridden. After she was found on October 14th, she was taken to a hospital where she became unconscious and died several weeks later. Mrs. Jenkins, when first admitted had numerous injuries. The police received information from one James Graves implicating Bowden in the crime and obtained a warrant for him. On October 15th, Bowden, who was informed that the police were looking for him, turned himself in to an officer, was advised of his rights and taken into custody. He made a statement at police headquarters, which was admitted into evidence at trial following a Jackson- Denno Hearing; a court proceeding to determine if a defendant's confession was voluntary or involuntary. The statement arose spontaneously between Bowden and a detective as they sat in a police car while two other detectives were in a house speaking to the girlfriend of James Graves, to whom they had been directed by Bowden. The other two detectives then returned to the car and drove Bowden back to headquarters. When Bowden saw some jewelry that the detectives had found in a stove on the back porch of Graves house, he said it was what he had hidden in the stove. In his detailed statement, Bowden stated that while he and Graves were raking Mrs. Stryker's yard one day, they talked about burglarizing her home. Graves lived next door to her. Graves had been inside and saw things he thought were valuable.

The following Monday, armed with a pellet gun to knock anyone out who might interfere, Bowden and Graves entered the house at about 8:30 am, using a screwdriver to open the door. They surprised Mrs. Stryker in the kitchen and Graves hit her twice with the pellet gun, causing her to fall. Graves then unplugged a television and took it over to his yard.

Meanwhile, Bowden gathered together several pieces of jewelry that he found around the house. Bowden then asked the elderly Mrs. Jenkins about the location of a gun in the house. When she would not tell him, he hit her, "Five or six times" in the face. Bowden further related how he and Graves searched the house then left and went to Graves' house.

They spent time "Laughing and discussing" what they had done. Graves suggested going to a shopping center and snatching purses, Bowden suggested they should "lay low" for a while. After making this statement, Bowden additionally stated that he hit Mrs. Stryker twice and then to, "put her out of her misery," stabbed her once with a butcher knife from the kitchen drawer. When they returned to Graves' house they threw wigs they had worn into the trash and hid the jewelry in the stove. Bowden said Graves later sold the television to a Sammie Robertson and received a partial payment of $10.00. Graves also sold some coins belonging to the victims. A wig was found on a sofa in Graves's house. Jewelry found by the police in the stove included a piece with Mrs. Stryker's name on it and a pin which was identified as having belonged to Mrs. Jenkins. A pellet gun was found under Graves' house.

Sammie Robertson testified that he received a television set from Graves' and gave him $10.00. This television set was seized by the police and the model and serial numbers were compared with the numbers on at a repair shop where Mrs. Stryker had ordered some knobs for her television and the numbers matched. The operator of a coin shop stated he bought some old coins from Graves on October 11th. A strand of hair on the pellet gun was compared with Mrs. Stryker's hair and found to be similar. There were no dissimilar characteristics.

At his trial, Bowden testified on his own behalf as follows: He turned himself into the police and told them he did not participate in the crime. He was questioned by a detective about the crime while they were alone in the car and decided to confess because the detective told him he could keep him from getting a death sentence. Bowden stated that he knew about the crime because police read him a statement made by Graves while he, Bowden, was being interrogated. Bowden denied killing Mrs. Stryker and said he confessed because he was afraid. He testified that he did smoke marijuana has he said in his statement. The district attorney asked him if he had smoked the marijuana "after he went in and killed that woman and beat her mother" and Bowden relied, "I guess it was." The defense sought to show that he misunderstood the question. The state called witnesses to rebut Bowden's testimony that his confession had been induced by promises.

Bowden was only twenty four years old at the time of the murder of Mrs. Stryker. James Graves was sixteen years old and was tried and sentenced to life in prison. Bowden's sister repeatedly declared that Bowden was mentally retarded and would sit on his bed rocking back and forth for hours. I had contact and conversations with Jerome Bowden for five years and never one observed that type of behavior. He was, to be sure, very mild mannered, but he was always capable of carrying on an intelligent conversation with me. I have no medical expertise that gives me the right to diagnosis anyone, but I know human behavior and Jerome Bowden, by all appearances, was no different than any of the other inmates on death row.

The evil that I read concerning the murder of Mrs. Stryker and the assault on her disabled mother demanded justice, no matter what their individual involvement may have been. Any human being, who could even stand by watching that atrocity carried out, was equally guilty of their deaths. It reminded me of Roosevelt Green saying, "All I did was rape her," as if that were a lesser crime. That also applied here.

After a year of silence in H-5 it was time to bring the execution chamber to life again. We removed Bowden from the death row unit and escorted him to the medical section and transferred custody to the death watch officers and we returned to our duties and waited, but a last minute stay of execution was given. The emergency stays of execution were never about guilt or innocence, but about some technicality or a legal loophole that a lawyer had discovered to delay the inevitable. But protocol demanded that he be returned to death row to wait. Office Carter and I were given the assignment of retrieving Bowden from the medical section. When we arrived we discovered that Bowden had been given the news by his attorney. He was laughing and talking with the death watch officers and when he saw Carter and me, he was almost excited to see us.

Bowden joked, laughed and talked loudly all the way to G-house. We retrieved his personal belongings and returned him to the housing unit. Once that was completed, we stood down from death watch and everything returned to standard procedure. I thought about the victims who died ten years before and their families. Mrs. Stryker had died in the kitchen probably instantaneously. Her head bashed open to reveal her brain to the medical examiner. I tried to consider the amount of force necessary to achieve that. The thought only made me shudder. But, her 76 year old mother lay in her bed, suffering for four long days in silence. It was hard to imagine the horror of what was going through her mind. Those four days had to be an eternity for her. In the moments when all those on the outside only seemed to consider the plight of the murderer, I gave my thoughts to the victims and their families. I'd promised myself years before, I would never forget them.

I arrived in G-house the following morning and went directly to my office, as usual and started my daily routine of filing documents. I heard the cross gate open in G-house and saw Lieutenant Treadwell walking his usual fast pace down the corridor. He went in his office and picked up the phone. While talking on the phone, he looked up and motioned me to his office. As I entered his office, he hung up the phone. He asked, "Have the other split shift officers reported yet?" I opened the door and looked down the corridor, but saw only the first shift officers. "No, sir," I replied. Then he continued, "The attorney general's office went to court late last night to appeal Bowden's stay and it has been lifted." The state wasted no time with its appeal. He continued, "When the men arrive, I want all of you to go get Bowden and return him to the medical section for death watch."

This was unprecedented on death row. Never had a stay of execution been given and lifted so quickly. When the split shift officers arrived, Officers Carter, Kindle and I went to get Bowden. The unit was locked down and we pushed the laundry cart inside with us. It was very quiet in the unit and the squeaking wheel of the laundry cart gave an air of eeriness to the scene. When we arrived at Bowden's cell he was sitting on his bunk, his arms on his knees, hands clasped and his head hanging down. He knew why we were here. After a strip search, we signaled for the door to open and heard the familiar buzz of the electronics. The door popped open and I pushed the cart to the door and said, "Time to go, Jerome." He looked briefly in my eyes then started packing his personal belongings. Once completed, we escorted him to the last room by the offices where I had seen Debbie just a few months before. I inventoried his items as he looked on. It was deathly quiet as I wrote on my tablet and then I heard a sniff. I stopped writing and looked up and saw tears in Bowden's eyes. Even with all that I'd read of his horrific crime, I still felt human compassion for his fear. My Christian heart sank in my stomach because Jerome Bowden, no matter what he'd done, was a child of God and in that sense, no different than me. He attended the church services offered in G-house every week faithfully and appeared to be sincere. As I wrote, he continued to cry. With his inventory completed, we escorted him to the medical holding cell and his death watch continued.

His attorneys were unsuccessful in convincing any court to issue a stay of execution. The final step for relief from the execution lay in the hands of the state board of pardons and paroles which had the authority to commute the sentence to life. Each inmate who faced execution had their cases brought before the board, but none had been successful. In the late afternoon of June 23rd, we received word that clemency had been denied for Jerome Bowden and his execution was imminent. The usual entourage from G-house, Officers Carter, Kindle, Lieutenant Treadwell and I arrived at the medical section holding cell. Once the medical procedure was complete, we escorted Bowden on his last mile to the holding cell in H-5. Afterwards, I went to the front gate, my usual post for an execution and waited.

Later that evening, the processes began in the holding cell. The administrative assistant sat in the holding cell to record the final statement. Bowden only had praise for the people who had cared for him while he was at the diagnostic center. He thanked all the staff for taking such good care of him. There was no malice in his voice. He admitted how difficult it was to go through the process that would lead to his death. He wanted the world to know that the "old Jerome Bowden," had died in 1980 when he was saved. He said that person no longer existed and that he was the new Jerome Bowden. Never once did he proclaim his innocence. He blamed no one for his predicament and offered only thanks for being treated so well. While strapped in the electric chair, he did say that he hoped that his death would bring attention to the world of how wrong executions were.

With that, he allowed the Chaplin to pray for him and then the hood was placed over his face. Shortly after midnight on June 24th, 1986, Jerome Bowed became the seventh man to die in Georgia's electric chair. As the hearse drove slowly to the front gate I thought about the previous hours before when I sat in the room inventorying Bowden's personal belongings. The fear I saw in his eyes as tears rolled down his face. He was respectful and there was always a smile on his face. He placed no blame on anyone for his years on death row. A psychologist stated that he was mildly retarded and if that were even remotely true, it made me question what we were doing here. But, whenever any thought of compassion entered my mind for these men, I had only to recall the horrible things they had done to get here. Bowden's case was particularly brutal.

Mrs. Stryker had been so severely beaten that her brain was exposed and her elderly, disabled mother lay in her bed for four long days clinging to life. The human side of me cried out for someone to answer for that horrible crime and tonight Jerome Bowden did. But, the same God that was offered a prayer on his behalf was the same God I prayed to and the same God who had blocked my motorcycle from killing me the summer before. I watched the hearse pass slowly by knowing that the body of Jerome Bowden was inside, but wondered where his soul was at this moment. The deputy's patrol car pulled out in front of the hearse with blue lights on. I watched as the lights disappeared into the night and recalled moments I'd escorted Bowden through the institution and how he laughed as we talked. I didn't recall seeing a mentally challenged man anywhere in his eyes nor did I see the murderer that performed those despicable acts on two helpless women. I was at war with myself. I looked up at the night sky and asked, "What the hell am I doing here?"

Chapter 12

"Moreover ye shall take no satisfaction for the life of a murderer, which is guilty of death: But he shall be surely put to death"

- Numbers35:31
-(King James Version)

With the order of the court carried out on Jerome Bowden the H-5 execution chamber fell silent again. The other inmates in G-house never said anything before or after an execution. The officers sometimes talked about what had happened the night before on the next day. But, at this point, it was becoming routine. The next morning in my office, I thought about that word and said quietly to myself, "routine." Then it occurred to me that using that word where a human life was concerned just didn't seem right. Always when I thought about the inmates though, I thought just as quickly about their victims. With every execution came new memories I added to my thoughts when I inspected their trial transcripts. It was like opening a new file in my mind of information I didn't necessarily want to remember, but would be added to my nightmares just the same.

It was still fresh in my mind that Graves and Bowden had "laughed and discussed" about what they did immediately after it happened. While they were laughing, just next door in the house they had terrorized, Mrs. Stryker lay dead and her poor mother was gasping for breath and would lay in that state for four long days. I shuddered at the thought. There was no way I could begin to imagine the horror of what must have been going through her mind if there was any consciousnesses at all. Then to multiply those times 4 days seemed unspeakable.

I wasn't sure if the tears in Bowden's eyes were for what he had done or for his own situation. Either way, it didn't make it any easier for me to think about it. All I knew of any of these men was what I observed during their stay on death row. Most had murdered while intoxicated or high on some drug. Thinking about those that weren't intoxicated became too terrible to contemplate what was driving them. Anyone able to torture, maim and kill another human being while not under the influence of some foreign substance meant, at least to me, that it was pure evil that influenced them. Again, I was reminded about Timothy McCorqudale's statement when questioned by the police, "I just don't think I could do them

things." In this place that I worked, it was a constant reminder that evil was alive and well on planet earth and given the right circumstances, anyone could be susceptible to its power.

Here in G-house they were sober and somewhat cleaned up from the outside world that influenced them. Then I was reminded of what I felt the first time I walked down the corridor of H-house on my first visit to death row and the cloud that seemed to hang over the unit. The evil I felt when I looked into the eyes of Carl Isaacs. Yes, evil was here and in their lives on the outside. I had gotten used to that and I wasn't sure it was a good thing. I felt somehow saturated by it and almost immune to it. That was a dangerous concept of its own. I didn't want Debbie or my girls to ever know what I dealt with here and never wanted to bring it home to them. So, as always, I buried it inside as deep as I could.

July came and no execution orders in sight. But then we would always be the last to know. We were on the business side of the legal system. We could walk in any morning and there might be an execution order waiting for us. There was no way to anticipate it. Since the executions started in 1983 with John Eldon Smith, I knew that these inmates had to be on edge wondering if any one of them might be next. The length of stay on death row was not a factor anymore. That issue was proven with our first execution. Some of these men had been under the death sentence since the early 1970's. The appeal process just seemed to collapse on some of them. We didn't always see the visible signs of stress, but at night in their cells, they were alone the darkness. I couldn't even imagine what must be going through their minds.

Debbie and I didn't have a honeymoon when we first married. So we decided that in conjunction with my 27th birthday, we would take time off and go to Panama City, Florida. My sister wanted to celebrate with me before we left. It was a tradition between her and I. Debbie knew how close I was with my sister, so she didn't object. Debbie and I both put in for our leave time and we were to leave on a Saturday morning. My sister and I went out the Friday night before. I met her in Macon at the pizza restaurant she was managing. We left from there and went to a local country night club that she visited. We had drinks there and danced for a while. I wanted to go to a club that Debbie and I visited on occasion, so we continued the celebration there. We drank and danced until well past midnight. When I finally left my sister's home, I knew I had no business driving. But Debbie and I were to leave the following morning and I wanted to get home. I took the interstate on the way home and quickly realized that it was a mistake. I remember at one point hitting the curb on a bridge and my truck bounced on the road. I knew I was in trouble, but drove anyway. It was when I had just passed the exit to my mother's home that I saw the blue lights in the mirror.

I remembered thinking, "Oh man, you're in trouble now!" I pulled over to the side of the road. When I looked in the mirror, I saw that it was a trooper from The Georgia State Patrol. I said to myself, "No way you're talking you're way out of this." I heard the tap on my window; I closed my eyes quickly and reopened them like I could wish myself away from here. I rolled the window down and he asked for my license and insurance. The license was no problem, it was in my wallet. The insurance card was somewhere in the glove compartment in all the other junk I had been stashing in there. When I told the trooper where I had to look, he came around the passenger side of my truck and shined his flashlight through the window to observe. *"Smart! Checking to see if I was digging for a weapon,"* I thought to myself. I was too intoxicated to find what I was looking for and he knew it. He returned to

my side of the truck and told me to step out of the vehicle. I complied. He took my license, looked at it and asked the obvious, "Have you been drinking Mr. Allen?" I wasn't going to insult him or me by saying that I only had a couple. We both knew I was way passed that. I simply said, "Yes." He looked in my eyes and said, "You were all over the road." I simply hung my head down and said, "I'm sorry."

He put me in the back of his car. I had left home without my badge wallet that stored both my badge and my state I.D. I was very thankful for that. No way was I going to tell this guy that I was law enforcement. In the last couple of years, there had been a big scandal with the Georgia State Patrol about ticket fixing. It went all the way to the top of the Georgia Department of Public Safety and the commissioner who was also the Colonel and commander of the state patrol. It had cost him his job. I decided I didn't need to say anything about my affiliation with my own department. I waited while he called the tow truck and thought about all the mistakes I had made on this little journey tonight and thought about all the things that I could have and should have done to prevent this. Then I thought about the bump on the bridge and my truck bouncing. I also thought about his comment to me, *"You were all over the road."* That's when reality started to creep in and I realized for the first time that it wasn't just my life that I endangered; I could have injured or killed someone else. A cold chill went down my back when I thought about how differently all this could have gone. Even with the predicament I was in, I felt like I was the lucky one.

Once my truck was gone he took me to the local police department to perform a breathalyzer. Before he took me out of the patrol vehicle, he told me that if I refused the breathalyzer, according to Georgia state law, I would automatically lose my license for one year. Another embarrassment waited there for me. The officer was a friend from high school and had also been a band member with me. I wanted to melt into the floor, but there was no escaping. I had to stand there and bear my shame while they conducted their business. After it was all done, I was able to call someone to pick me up. My shame wouldn't allow me to call Debbie, so I called my mother instead. Always the dutiful mother, she came without question. I felt shame again, waking her in the middle of the night to come pick up her drunken son.

On the trip to my house in Jackson, we barely said a word. She seemed to sense that I didn't want to talk. When we arrived, I thanked her for her help and got out of her car. I stood there while she pulled away. Then I turned and looked at the front door of the home that Debbie and I shared. It was a door I didn't want to enter, but I knew I couldn't stay outside forever. It was almost morning. I still had my keys, so I opened the door and went as quietly as I could to the bathroom to take a shower as though that would cleanse me of any wrongdoing I had done. It didn't take long for Debbie to wake and come to the bathroom. "Where have you been," she asked. "I had a problem last night on my way home," was all I could manage. Her woman's intuition served her well. She knew there was more to come. So I laid it all out for her and watched the tears well up in her eyes. I moved in to hug her, but she put a hand up and said, "Bobby, you smell!" It was another blow to my already wounded ego.

Then she took off her wedding band and laid it on the back of the toilet and said, "I don't want to be married anymore." She turned and went back into the bedroom and said nothing else. It was a devastating blow to my heart. I followed her into the bedroom where I found her sitting on the bed crying. I sat down beside her and searched for the words to comfort or reassure her that it was just a huge mistake and that it would never happen again. I found no words to accomplish that. I felt that I needed to be punished. But, this was more than I could bear. It was almost like the four years and the seven executions I'd participated in and all the horror I had read in the pages of those trial transcripts came to rest on my shoulders at that moment. We both sat in silence for the next few minutes. Finally I was able to speak. I don't remember the words that came, but I was able to assure Debbie that this would never happen again and how sorry I was that she had to go through this. I let her know how much I loved her and that I was sure we had a future together if she would give me another chance. It took her a few minutes, but she finally looked up and into my eyes and then leaned in to hug me. Then she spoke, "We'll find a way to get through this together." I let out a deep sigh and held her close.

Today was the beginning of our honeymoon. She went to take a shower and I was left alone with my thoughts. I felt like I had crossed over some imaginary line into a darker place than where I lived before last night. There was no correlation between what happened last night and my job, yet somehow I felt the darkness close in around me and I couldn't stop thinking about the things I saw on death row. I allowed my mind to wander through the last four years of my life and how things had changed. I knew I was drinking more than usual. Maybe there was a connection between my drinking and my job. The first execution, John Eldon Smith in 1983 was as vivid in my mind as was Jerome Bowden just a few weeks before. At that moment I knew that these memories would never leave me and it would be something I would carry the rest of my life.

The first order of business before we could start our honeymoon, was to retrieve my truck from impound. What a start for Debbie, I thought. What should be the happiest moment of our lives was now tainted by my stupidity the night before. That's how I saw it and I knew that she deserved so much more. She was a saint in my book and I was blessed that she was able to move past it so quickly. I didn't have a license in my possession, but I was told I could drive on the citation I was given. After we retrieved my truck, I drove it to my mother's house to park it until we returned from Florida. Then we were off to Reidsville where Debbie's parents lived to drop off her daughter so we could have some time alone together. .

We enjoyed a week by the Gulf of Mexico. Debbie spent a lot of time in the room reading and relaxing. I stayed out late in the evening just listening to the wave's crash. Debbie had earned the right to spend her time any way she chose and I was alright with that. I had a lot of time for reflection. That wasn't necessarily a good thing. My mind seemed to have an automatic mode that took over whenever I was alone. The murder scenes I read in the pages of the trial transcripts from last four years haunted me. Each victim copied into my mind like a computer and of course, the final scene of the hearse driving by with a warm body in the back.

We returned home and picked up our lives again. I was fortunate enough to receive only a fine and a level 1 D.U.I. school the lasted three nights. I didn't want anyone at work to discover my embarrassment, so I didn't tell anyone at work what happened and prayed that the Peace Officers Standards and Training Council didn't find out. It was the agency that certified all law enforcement officers in the state as peace officers. As days turned to weeks, I breathed a little easier. I figured that if I hadn't heard anything by that time frame, I was in the clear. But, it was just one more thing that I had to file away in my subconscious along

with the dark feelings I had buried about the things I witnessed on death row. Another secret to keep and Debbie and I never talked about it.

In late summer of 1986, Lieutenant Treadwell called me in his office for a private meeting. I held my breath when the door closed for fear that I had been discovered. He looked at me and asked a simple question, "What are your career goals for the future with the department?" I let out a silent sigh of relief. Harris was already a Sergeant and I knew that his plan was to move up the chain of command as swiftly as possible. I had other plans and I let the Lieutenant know. "I thought I might like to become a training officer," I replied. He grinned slightly and said, "Let me see if I can help you with that." He picked up the phone and called Mr. Branch, our training officer. They were discussing a way for me to get started with that. After a brief conversation with Mr. Branch, the Lieutenant handed me the phone. Mr. Branch asked me if I thought I could fire at least a 95 average score on the shooting range. I told him that with some practice I felt like I could. It was the prerequisite for attending the firearms Instructor school.

The next week, I was on the firing range qualifying for the school. As it turned out, there was an opening in a firearms instructor school in the next month. After several rounds, I qualified for the school. I was very excited and couldn't wait to share the news with Debbie. After the D.U.I. incident, we needed something positive in our lives and this was a good start. Mr. Branch sent me all the information about the school. It would be conducted in Savannah. It was a 2 week school and Lieutenant Treadwell was more than happy to arrange the time in my schedule to attend. I talked with a fellow officer who had already attended the school and gave me an idea of the how the schedule would work. The first week was conducted on the firing range. All the students took turns as range master calling the course while the rest fired. It was a much needed chance for me to shoot and become more proficient.

The second week was spent entirely in the classroom learning the finer points of classroom instruction. Again we all took turns in front of the class demonstrating our instructor skills. At the end, we had to prepare a lesson plan on any subject of our choosing and present our material to the class while the instructors graded us. I chose to develop my lesson on the execution process. It was a subject that intrigued the other students and it was material with which no one was familiar. I was the expert in my field with this particular group. At the institution there was a miniature model of the electric chair and Lieutenant Treadwell got permission for me to bring it along for my class. As I taught my class, everyone was mesmerized. No one outside of the Diagnostic Center knew of the execution procedures and my class was a big hit. On Friday of the second week, there was a written examine. After the tests were graded, there was a very brief, informal graduation where we were presented with certificates that made us all certified Firearms Instructors. It was the first step to become a Training Officer for the department. On the drive home I was filled with a sense of pride that I was on my way to my goal.

In the fall of 1986, Lieutenant Treadwell called me to his office for another private meeting. The employee of the year awards were given out every November in Atlanta, Georgia. Lieutenant Treadwell intended to nominate me for "Officer of the year" for the state. It was a huge honor for anyone. Under his direction and guidance, Lieutenant Treadwell had me fill out the nomination form. I included all my martial arts training, teaching and tournament participation. He wanted to highlight any volunteer work I had

done. I discovered that Lieutenant Treadwell had quite a way with words. By the time we were finished with the nomination form, even I was impressed at the way he put my name forward. I also found out that he was being nominated for Correctional Supervisor of the year. He took my form to the Warden's office and I never thought about it again.

Lieutenant Treadwell was determined to help me with my goal of becoming a training officer. In November of that year, I was enrolled in the Instructor Training program that was conducted by the Peace Officer Standards and Training Council; the governing body for all peace officers in the state. It would be an in depth school on how to train other law enforcement officers. I had already been informed by others who attended the school that it was very intense. It was two weeks spent in the classroom.

As the end of 1986 approached, things were quiet and returning to some state of normalcy in G-house. It was a term I used loosely because there was nothing "normal" about this unit. It could be quiet for a week and then something could stir in any of these men and a situation could occur. Also, we never knew when an execution order would arrive. We all just took each day as it came with no expectations.

November arrived and I received orders for the instructor school. The Corrections Academy was now located in Forsyth and they would host the school. The academy was located on the campus of Tift College, a noted women's college. Across the street from the offices of the academy was an abandoned AT&T office and the academy managed to secure that location for the school. I was always nervous the first day of any school I attended. I suppose it was my fear of the unknown. The first day consisted of the students introducing themselves and the agency they represented. There was a wide variety of students; the local Monroe County Sherriff's Office, probation officers from the Atlanta area and several police agencies from the coast of Georgia. The class coordinator was an Instructor from the P.O.S.T. (Peace Officer's Standards and Training Council) main office in Atlanta. There were also many guest instructors from different law enforcement agencies including the Corrections Academy across the street. It was as intense as I was told it would be. The first day was partial orientation and then we went right into the first class. Even on the first day, we were up in front of the classroom getting the feel of how it would be to teach a class. Our first exercise we were given an index card with one word on it and expected to talk for five minutes about that word. I never knew five minutes could last so long. Then we each took turns critiquing each other. Learning to talk in front of a group of people covered the first week.

On Friday of the first week, we were informed there was a break for a week so we could develop lesson plans on any subject we chose and then deliver that lesson to the class in our second week. We would be videotaped during our class and had to develop three test questions from our material. The class had to last for one hour, it would be timed and the class could end five minutes early or it could go over five minutes. One minute off and we would fail the entire class and have to repeat it if we wanted to become instructors. It was tremendous pressure, but this is something I had dreamed of ever since joining the department in 1980. I intended to pass. Once again, I chose the execution process as my subject. It would be more in depth than the firearms instructor version I'd given. We also had to prepare training aids.

I had to make layovers for the overhead projector and I intended to bring the small model of the electric chair as a training aid. I felt confident again because it was a subject that the general public or even other law enforcement officers knew nothing about. I was the expert in this field. With our assignments in hand, we were dismissed with a weeklong break to prepare our lesson plans. In the meantime, I had to return to my duties in G-house and work on my lesson plan at night. I was very excited, yet nervous. The thought of spending two weeks in class only to fail on the last day was a lot of pressure so I kept a strong mental attitude and positive thoughts.

After a weekend off with Debbie I returned to my office in G-house. I had quite a bit of catching up to do. Lieutenant Treadwell was always positive and it kept me motivated. On Wednesday of that week, the lieutenant and I were summoned to the Warden's office. Neither of us had any idea what it was about. When we arrived for the meeting, Mr. Parrish, the deputy warden of security was also present. The Warden, Mr. Kemp, told us that the diagnostic center had made a clean sweep of the upcoming awards banquet. Mr. Kemp had been selected has Warden of the year, Lieutenant Treadwell was selected as supervisor of the year, the diagnostic center was selected as institution of the year and I was selected as officer of the year. It was an unprecedented move. We would all be going to Atlanta on Friday to attend the banquet and receive our awards.

A letter of congratulations was posted on the institutional bulletin board. I also received letters from other department heads congratulating me. The institutional parole chief sent me an official letter congratulating me and made a point in the letter that this award was my agencies "meal of honor" and that I was most deserving. I even received a proclamation from the Lieutenant Governor congratulating me. I was almost overwhelmed. I had no idea that this award was that big of a deal. Debbie decided that I needed to look the part of a recipient and took me to be fitted for a new suit. She was very proud and I was happy that I could do something to make her happy. God knows she deserved it after the rocky start we had. She was a devoted wife and I wanted her to be proud of me. At that time she was the anchor in my life. She kept me grounded when I might otherwise be drinking this all away.

The night of the awards banquet, Lieutenant Treadwell, his wife, Debbie and I drove to Atlanta. I invited my mother, my oldest brother, Don and his wife to attend. We drove separate because we were to go on a train ride around Atlanta before the award ceremony. We were treated like royalty. The city was beautiful at dusk as we had our ride. This was my hometown, but I'd never seen it this way. I had a very warm feeling inside as I rode the train with my beautiful wife. My feeling was that everything was as it should be. We pulled into the station and were escorted to our tables. My mother and family were already seated at our table. There were also other diagnostic center employees seated there. After our dinner, the awards began. One by one, the commissioner called out each category and said a few words about each recipient. Then he called each to the stage to receive the award. Finally, it was my turn.

Outside of my children being born, this was the biggest moment of my life. The butterflies began to stir as the commissioner spoke, "This next award is special. When these guys are doing their job, it's quiet. When Walter Zant found out that Robert Allen was selected as officer of the year, he commented that he remembered him and that he had pulled Billy Mitchell off him on death row." Everyone got a kick out of it, though Mr. Zant had me confused with another officer who resembled me. All eyes were on me as the commissioner continued, "Robert Allen, Correctional Officer of the year." Applause rang out as I made my way to the podium. We shook hands and he presented me with a plaque and we posed quickly for a picture.

The awards continued and Mr. Kemp was presented with Warden of the year, Lieutenant Treadwell presented with Supervisor of the year and finally the diagnostic center was recognized as institution of the year. I looked at my mother and I could see the pride in her eyes as she smiled and it warmed my heart. My brother smiled and said, "Congratulations buddy." It was one of those moments that became locked in my mind and my heart and I knew I would carry it with me always. After all the awards were handed out, my family left for home and the award winners ushered to a local club for drinks and a small celebration. Lieutenant Treadwell and his wife got right out on the floor and started to dance. I'd never seen this side of him. He had a commanding presence always. Debbie and I soon followed and then everyone was out on the floor. On our way back to the table, I got my first taste of the politics and how receiving the award helped. A field training officer stopped me and asked, "Have you ever thought about becoming a training officer?" I was elated but contained my excitement and answered, "Yes, that's my goal." He explained to me that there was a training position open at the Al Burruss Institution in Forsyth. The only issue was that it was a uniformed correction officer's position and not really a training officer's position. It wasn't what I was looking for and I thanked him for the offer. I knew that in the upcoming months there would be Sergeants positions open in G-house and Lieutenant Treadwell had assured me I would get one of those positions.

After a long night of celebrating we finally headed for home. After Lieutenant Treadwell dropped us off at home, Debbie and I crashed. The adrenaline had run its course and we were exhausted. I used the weekend to finish my lesson plan for the Instructors school. Debbie even agreed to sit through my presentation. I had to have it timed out to the one hour mark because I had no intentions of failing the course and I certainly didn't think I could repeat it again.

I made it through the second week of the instructor's course. I delivered my lesson plan on the time allotted and was praised for my teaching style. Although I was nervous, teaching came natural to me because I had taught martial arts for several years. I was going to receive my instructor's certificate and it was a huge relief. It was the main step to becoming a training officer. Now I was watching for any instructor school I could attend. Next was first aid/c.p.r. instructor school with the American Red Cross. In the following weeks I received instructor's certificates in the mail from P.O.S.T. Not only was I awarded with a generalized instructor's certificate, but I was awarded a specialized instructor's certificate for Firearms, defensive tactics, and E.M.S. The E.M.S. was unexpected, but was awarded because of the first aid and c.p.r. class.

Lieutenant Treadwell applied for a Captain's position at the prison in Forsyth. I was afraid he would be promoted and leave before the sergeants' positions became available. Then in the middle of all the changes, he was summoned to the warden's office. When he returned to G-house, he was Captain Treadwell. The commissioner had decided that he was too valuable in his current position on death row. In the time he had been unit manager, G-house had been very quiet with minimal problems even during the executions that were scheduled. I looked on his collar and saw the two silver bars indicating the rank of Captain. I smiled and he smiled back and said, "I'm not leaving, Allen." So the plan was still in place for me to become a sergeant.

H-house, the old death row unit, was turned into a mental health and administrative lock down unit. Captain Treadwell was given command of both units. With that move, four sergeants' positions became available. The promotion board was comprised of all in-house commissioned officers. Two of us from G-house were promoted to sergeant. One sergeant was posted in H-house and I was given the split shift assignment working with Captain Treadwell in G-house. Dave Harris was promoted to Lieutenant at the same time, but was moved back into general population. There was a lieutenant posted in G-house because we now had jurisdiction over H-house. He was Captain Treadwell's second in command I was third behind the lieutenant.

My career was moving forward at an accelerated rate and Captain Treadwell had become my mentor. He was overseeing my career and helping me to move forward. My personal life was getting better, as well. Debbie became the overseer of my personal life. After neglecting Leighanne and Tracey because of my marriage to Sarah, she managed to get me back on track getting my girls every other weekend. I was behind on child support, but she helped with that as well. I was able to become a father again to my children. On the weekends when we had the twins, we also had Kimberly.

My dreams now became nightmares. I just chose not to talk about them. Even though I had moved from the clerk's office, the transcripts I'd read and the pictures I'd seen were forever burned in my mind. Though Roosevelt Green was dead and buried, he visited in my dreams. He and Teresa Carol Allen were with me. It had been six months since the execution of Jerome Bowden. His docile attitude and his tears remained in my mind. If I caught myself thinking about any of them too often, I had to shake my head to clear the thought and get up from my desk.

1987 came with no new execution orders. We wondered whether it would stop as abruptly as it all began. There was no way to know because we were not privy to any of the legal information. I just took one day at a time and dealt with the dreams on my own. A lieutenant in general population had been promoted to parole officer and Debbie knew him from her college classes. He had a mobile home in the institutional trailer park by the lake. Now that he was going to be working for a different agency, he could no longer stay in the mobile home park. Rather than move the mobile home, he decided to sell it. Debbie was all over it. We both would be close to work and the mobile home sat beside the lake and was a beautiful spot.

We moved in and right away we realized that we had made the right choice. On the weekends when we had the girls, they had a blast because we were by the lake. My family also came to enjoy the lake. My mother in particular enjoyed the lake because she was the fisherman in the family. My brothers came on occasion and brought their families to fish. My sister was living at home with our mother and they came often during the week to play cards with us. It was as close as my family had been in a long time. I begin to drink more during the week and in turn, Debbie started to drink more. I didn't see what was happening in my life, it just all seemed rather normal. I didn't realize that I was using alcohol to relieve anxiety and the dreams that came at night. I believed that everything I was feeling, everyone was feeling and like me, they just didn't talk about it.

Late winter gave way to spring with H-5 remaining quiet. Then in May 1987, we received our first execution order of the year. There had been no executions for 11 months. I sat in

my office as I watched Joseph Mulligan make his way to the counselor's office. Mulligan was the first inmate I escorted from Death Row when I was assigned to the first shift. I never forgot my first interaction with him. He told a counselor that the stealing of the counselor's car was justified because the thief, a "young man," as Mulligan called him, probably needed that car. That was my first insight to these men's value systems. I don't know if it was because they all had a narcissistic personality or if they were sociopaths. The longer I worked here, the more I came to believe that these men were influenced by evil. It was all a spiritual matter to me; indeed it was a spiritual battle.

Mulligan was quiet and presented himself as though he were more intelligent than anyone else. He was never a physical threat to anyone while housed in G-house, but according to the trial transcript, he was still a very diabolical dangerous man. The details of his crime told the story of his violent nature. Mulligan became friends with Timothy Helms while Helms was stationed with the Marine Corps in Beaufort, South Carolina. On April 12, 1974, Mulligan talked Helms into driving him to Columbus, Georgia by offering him a fee of $1000. During the drive, Mulligan told Helms that he was going to Columbus to "Ice somebody." Mulligan suggested that they stay at a motel on April 12-13 and registered in the motel under false names. The next day, Mulligan and Helms visited Patrick Doe, an Army captain at Fort Benning and Mulligan's brother-in-law. In the afternoon they joined Captain Doe while he was washing his car and Mulligan and Captain Doe argued. Later that evening, with Mulligan and Helms sitting in the back seat (Mulligan sitting behind the driver seat) Captain Doe drove to the house of Marian Jones Miller, the Captain's girlfriend, to pick her up for a party.

When Captain Doe left the car to get Ms. Miller, Mulligan announced to Helms that he would "Do it in the next two blocks." Following Captain Doe's return to the driver's seat and shortly after the car began to move again, Mulligan held a .38 special to Captain Doe's head, which Mulligan earlier borrowed from the Captain and fired once. He then ordered Helms to grab the now abandoned steering wheel, but Helms was unable to do so before the car struck both a stop sign and a mailbox. When Ms. Miller, who was seated in the front seat next to Doe, Cried out for help, Mulligan placed the gun across Helms' back and shot Ms. Miller as he told her to be silent. After Helms finally brought the car to a stop, Mulligan and Helms wiped it down for fingerprints. As they fled the scene, Helms threw away his bloody shirt and the wallet he had removed from the body of Captain Doe. Mulligan threw Captain Doe's gun into some bushes and his own clothes over a bridge.

The autopsy performed on Captain Doe showed that the bullet had entered his left eye, traveled through the brain and exited the right temple. The autopsy performed on Ms. Miller revealed that she had been shot four times; in the left forearm, the left shoulder, the right upper arm and the mid portion of the back of the skull with the exit wound from the last shot exiting the right eye. The cause of death for both victims was laceration and hemorrhage of the brain and cerebral trauma. Several .38 casings were found in the captain's car along with a bullet. The state crime laboratory indicated that the shell casings and the bullet found in Captain Doe's car had been fired by Captain Doe's .38 pistol. Finally a latent fingerprint had been lifted from the left door window of Captain Doe's car was found to match a rolled print of Mulligan's left middle finger. Evidence also revealed that Captain Doe had filed a divorce action against Mulligan's sister and that Captain Doe had told Mulligan on the day of the murders, that his divorce from Mulligan's sister would soon be final. It was later determined that Mulligan had killed Captain Doe for insurance money.

Even though his fingerprint was found at the scene, he maintained that he was not present at the murder, but was in fact on a bus en route to Atlanta, Georgia. He would carry his denial to his grave. Once again, H-5 was being cleaned and sterilized for possible use. We all had our assigned duties and I knew mine very well. Mulligan's execution date was set for May 15, 1987. The appeal process had been exhausted and no stay of execution had been issued. We carried out the execution preparation has before on all others. We had become proficient at our duties. Mulligan was removed from the death row population; his personal property inventoried and the container sealed. He was escorted to the medical section for his final examination. The fresh new inmate uniform was provided and he was turned over to the death watch officers.

On the morning of May 15, 1987, with no stay of execution granted, we moved him to the holding cell in the execution chamber. As always, Captain Treadwell and I waited in our office until the evening hours. Mulligan chose to make a final statement from the holding cell. His statement lasted over 5 minutes and within that statement he proclaimed his innocence. He blamed the person who was with him on that evening and even had the audacity to blame the victim as well, for his own death. My thoughts here were that he had told the story so many times that he believed everything he said. However, twelve people hearing the evidence of the case believed other wise and that's why we were here. I assumed my post at the front gate with my usual accompaniment of troopers, rangers, sheriff's deputies and police officers. Of course there were the demonstrators for and against the death penalty and the news crews waiting to catch it all. Shortly after midnight, I saw the hearse make its usual slow journey to the front gate. Then it was lights out, shut down the front gate and the part I had come to hate; the ride home in silence. I was becoming numb to it all.

Just days later, we had another execution order handed down to us. I couldn't believe it. After H-5 was silent for nearly a year, we were preparing for our second execution within a week. The inmate was Richard Tucker, Jr. If ever there was an argument for the death penalty, Richard Tucker would be the example. In 1963, Tucker was convicted in the stabbing death of his aunt. He received a life sentence for that crime. After serving 14 years on that murder conviction, he was paroled. I had escorted Tucker many times to the medical section because he had a condition with hemorrhoids. His treatment required him to sit in a bath and soak for a period of time. We had time to talk. He was a quiet man, always very polite and I don't recall him ever being any trouble in G-house. But, as my job required, I had inspected his trial transcript when it was sent out and it told quite a different story of Richard Tucker, Jr.

Just six months after being paroled Tucker struck again. In 1978, Mrs. Edna Sandefur of Albany, Ga., was in Macon, Georgia to visit her ill mother who was in the hospital. She was a 50 year old nurse. As she was leaving the hospital, she was kidnapped by Tucker, forced to drive to an abandoned warehouse where Tucker raped her. After he was finished, he beat Mrs. Sandefur to death with an iron pipe. On September 19, 1978, the badly decomposed body of Mrs. Sandefur was discovered in a secluded area. Two days later, Tucker was arrested and implicated himself in the incident, but blamed her murder on a friend of his.

However, in a later statement, Tucker admitted that he alone abducted Mrs. Sandefur and killed her.

He stated that after the murder, he undressed the victim and burned her clothing in an effort to hide his fingerprints. He took police to the scene of the crime, identified the murder weapon, an iron pipe, and the charred remains of Mrs. Sandefur's clothing. Finally, he took police to where he had disposed of her purse and credit cards. Tucker's confession was tape recorded and played for the jury during the trial. Several witnesses testified that they saw Tucker driving Mrs. Sandefur's car shortly after the murder. A friend of Tucker's testified that he had bragged about "killing a white woman" and that he enjoyed killing and would do it again one day.

An FBI witness identified that Tucker's thumb print was found on one of the victim's credit cards. An expert witness testified that a "medium brown Caucasian pubic hair" was found on clothes seized in Tucker's apartment several days after the murder. Tucker is black, Mrs. Sandefur is white. After all evidence was heard, the jury found Tucker Guilty. During the sentencing phase of the trial, Tucker, who did not testify at trial, took the stand. He claimed that he only pled guilty to stop the police from pressuring him.. Tucker claimed that it was his friend that murdered Mrs. Sandefur and that he only removed the clothing to hide the fingerprint evidence. On cross-examination, Tucker was asked about his denial of the confession and his previous record, which included the 1963 murder of his aunt and two burglary charges, one stemming from an attempted rape, Tucker had pled guilty of these crimes.

Tucker's parole officer was called to testify. Tucker had been paroled only six months prior to this new conviction. The parole officer testified that shortly after his arrest, Tucker had admitted to the murder and that he was the sole perpetrator. This rebuttal testimony was inconsistent with Tucker's claim that his friend had killed Mrs. Sandefur. After a short deliberation, the jury returned with two death sentences, one for malice murder and one for kidnapping with bodily harm. Here was proof that the system had failed. A convicted murderer was given a second chance only to murder again. I'm not sure what the family of Mrs. Sandefur was feeling, but it was an outrage that this woman was murdered when it was a life that could have been spared. However, even Tucker's parole officer testified that Tucker was always neat and well mannered. He said Tucker was a good parolee. Richard Tucker was also a good and well behaved inmate. He was always polite and quiet. So this made me wonder, what was the catalyst that caused someone this mild mannered to become someone who was capable of such horrendous things?

We repeated the same steps we made not even a week before. We removed Richard Tucker from his cell, inventoried his personal possessions and escorted him to the medical section. He was given a fresh inmate uniform and then turned over to the death watch officers at the medical section holding cell. Finally when we were within hours of the execution, and no stay of execution expected, we moved him to the H-5 execution chamber. Captain Treadwell waited in his office while I took up my post at the front gate. We all waited together until we saw the lights of the hearse move toward the front gate. Even though the trip home was now just a short drive to the mobile home park, it was enough to jumpstart my mind. The rest would follow in my dreams as I lay in the bed with Debbie and think of my children.

Just a few short days into the next week, we received yet another execution order. In an ironic twist of fate, the order was for another inmate named Tucker; William Boyd Tucker.

He was another inmate that was very well behaved and friendly. But, as always, the circumstances that put him on the road to G-house and eventually would lead to the H-5 execution chamber, told a different story of another time in his life. Again the trial transcript told of the carnage that lay in the wake of William Boyd Tucker.

During the day of August 20, 1977, Tucker had been drinking heavily and smoked several joints of marijuana. Sometime around 11:00 pm, he went to the local Majik Market, a convenient store, where he drank two more beers and played pinball. After waiting at the store for nearly an hour, Tucker managed to sneak behind the clerk, Kathleen Perry. She was the only one in the store at the time. He stuck his finger in her back and she began putting money from the register into a paper bag. Tucker forced Kathleen into his red Volkswagen and drove to Pierce Chapel road where he killed her by stabbing her four times. Three people were driving on Pierce Chapel road, when they passed by a red Volkswagen with its lights on, parked on the road. The three saw Tucker in the car and a woman's shoe beside the car. Shortly after passing, the three decided to return to investigate. The Volkswagen passed them as they returned to the place where it had been parked. At the parking spot they found a vest with a "Majik Market" insignia on it, a bra and then discovered Kathleen's body about ten feet away, face down, in a ditch. The three left, called the police, then returned to Pierce Chapel road to wait the arrival of the police.

Shortly after the police arrived, they saw Tucker returning in the same red Volkswagen. The three identified both the car and the driver. Tucker was immediately taken into custody. Shortly thereafter, Tucker made an incriminating statement in which he admitted the robbery by intimidation and the kidnapping. In his statement to the police, Tucker said he could not remember what happened after Perry got out of the car, but did remember a knife with long brown handles and lots of blood. At trial Tucker admitted again to the robbery and kidnapping, but said he could not remember the murder.

After further investigation, Tucker admitted that he had forced Kathleen Perry to perform oral sex on him. He was not charged with the crime because under Georgia law, uncorroborated confessions could not be allowed. There were those who testified to Tucker's peaceful nature and that he had been under a lot of stress since the death of his father three months before. His mother testified that drugs and alcohol had become a problem in his life since the death of his father. But, what had made this crime particularly heinous was that Mrs. Perry was a 19 year old newlywed who was also pregnant at the time. I identified with the feelings he had concerning his father. I had been there 5 years before. I also identified with the drinking as a means to cope with a loss that is hard to understand. What I could not understand was the violence that those feelings produced. Especially on a young, pregnant woman who was obviously working to help support her future family. It was these feelings that tormented me as a Christian and an officer of the law. These were the thoughts and feelings that caused my nightmares.

The execution order of William Tucker caused my mind to slip back to 1983 and John Eldon Smith, the first man we executed. William Tucker was one of the few, along with John Eldon Smith that attended the catholic mass services faithfully every Wednesday. I knew that this in no way diminished their guilt, but it did cause me a moment of pause. William Tucker's mother and others had testified that he had never been in trouble with the law. When he stepped across the line, it was a giant leap into capital murder. These thoughts always brought me back to the feeling that something else interjected here. Always the

words of Timothy Wesley Mcorquodale echoed in my mind, "*I just don't believe I could do them things.*" Evil was present in this place.

As the body of William Boyd Tucker passed by me at the front gate I had a revelation. This was the third man we had executed in two weeks and he was now the tenth execution in which I participated in the last four years. I was a supporter of the death penalty, but now having participated in the process ten times, it was no longer an issue that could easily be discussed over a beer at the local pub as I imagined some of these supporters and protesters did on these occasions. It was reality for me. Each face and name was now imprinted in my mind forever.

The news that I wanted to become a training officer had finally filtered through the right channels to the right people, thanks to Captain Treadwell. The Director of Training came to the diagnostic center to visit with both Captain Treadwell and me. I met him at the front and escorted him to G-house. Captain Treadwell was due to retire in the coming months so the director met with both the captain and me in our office. He was here to offer both of us a job. He wanted me as a training officer at the newly opened Georgia Public Safety Training Center in Forsyth, Georgia. The training center was a multi-agency facility. It housed all law enforcement, fire and rescue, E.M.S. academies and advanced training agencies. It was the first of its kind in the nation.

I would transfer to the Georgian Corrections Academy as an instructor. Since the captain was retiring, he would become a contract employee, but would retain his rank. The academy was set up as a paramilitary training facility and the students would be in uniforms as cadet officers. Captain Treadwell would become the commander of cadets. Even though the position would be a promotion for me I was concerned about my salary. In addition to my regular pay, I also received hazardous duty pay for both G-house and The Tactical squad. The director assured me he would adjust my pay accordingly so that I would not lose any money. It was exactly what I wanted. It was everything I had been preparing for. All the instructor schools I attended brought me to this moment.

I discussed it with Debbie and she knew this was my dream and she supported it. The only negative thing about it was that we would have to move out of our home on the lake. Even though I still worked for the Department of Corrections, I would no longer be assigned to the diagnostic center. Debbie never complained and went right to work finding another place for us. I never told anyone, but I was glad that this part of my career was coming to an end. The faces of the inmates and more importantly, the faces of their victims were burned into my mind. Every page I read of a trial transcript would always be there and I knew it. I filed them away very deep inside and never told anyone how they visited me at night in my dreams, but the fact of the matter was, no one in the department ever asked if it bothered me.

In July of 1987, Captain Treadwell retired and both he and I transferred to the Training Center in Forsyth. Debbie and I sold our home on the lake to a fellow officer and moved to Jackson into a nice duplex house. After working in a maximum security prison for seven years, it was like a breath of fresh air. Walking into this new beautiful facility no longer felt like I was walking into a dungeon. I worked in an environment that was warm, relaxed and everyone was very friendly. I had worked close with the instructors and taught classes with some of them. For the first time in seven years, I felt relaxed at work and most importantly, I didn't have to hear the sound of the front gate slamming behind me indicating that I was now locked inside.

I was given copies of every lesson plan the academy taught and there were a lot of them. My first few days were spent setting up my cubicle and filing away lesson plans. The academy staff just recently moved to the training center and everyone was busy setting up their own offices. There was no class in session because of the move. The director of training was a fitness buff and expected his instructors to be in shape as well, so we were allowed time to go to the physical training area, on duty, to work out. It was a marvelous facility complete with a full gymnasium, Olympic size swimming pool, weight room, saunas and my favorite, racquetball courts.

It was everything I wanted and more than I could have dreamed. I was working with friends and doing something I felt I had a calling to do. I taught martial arts for several years and teaching was something I was comfortable with and very good at. Now I was being paid to do it full time. I was also still able to work closely with my mentor, Captain Treadwell. One of the instructors once told me, "Relax, you don't work for him anymore." My loyalty didn't work that way. Captain Treadwell was directly responsible for me being a training officer. I was grateful and I intended to demonstrate that by working closely with him.

I hated moving from our home on the lake, but I believed that this was a career move that would allow more advancement than working in the institution. It was also a move toward a little more normalcy. One of the things I got used to was hiding my feelings. One such feeling was that I was mentally tired of working around so much hostility and more importantly death itself. It was beginning to feel as though I had become infected by it somehow. I also was exhausted from having to hide those feelings from my family. I didn't want my girls to see that side of my life and I didn't want them, Debbie or her daughter to see how ugly life could be.

I turned 28 in July of 1987. I had a new exciting career that I loved and we had a new home. I was working with people that I respected and could learn from. Our life was changing very quickly and Debbie never once complained or second guessed the decision we made concerning my new promotion. Debbie came to me that same month to tell me that she was pregnant. With all that was happening, I felt overwhelmed and not sure I was ready. Debbie wanted to get pregnant, but I thought that while she was going to school and I was focusing on a promotion, we couldn't handle it. But, she was the strength in our relationship and she assured me that she could handle it. I thought now that we were entering a new phase in our lives, that I could put the ten executions behind me and more importantly, the faces of the victims I stored in my mind could now be laid to rest. I just didn't realize how much they had become a part of me and what was lying ahead for me and for my family.

Chapter 13

"I think, "my bed will comfort me and sleep will ease my misery," but then you shatter me with dreams and terrify me with visions

- Job 7:13,14
(New Living Translation)

My new job felt like a breath of fresh, clean air that I had not had since starting work at the diagnostic center. I felt free not working around the worst of what humanity had to offer. But, there was another side to my thoughts; I wondered if I fulfilled my task working on death row. My Christian beliefs were constantly in conflict with the job I had to do. I also thought since I was away from death row, maybe my dreams would subside. My dreams were not so much about the execution of the inmates as they were about what I had read in the trial transcripts concerning their victims and more to the point, the pictures I saw. No execution or victim haunted me as much as that of Roosevelt Green and his victim, Teresa Carol Allen. The whole horrible event was trapped in my mind. In the daylight, when those thoughts or feelings came to my mind, I would have to stop what I was doing and take a walk or talk with someone to change my thought process always careful not to say what was in my mind. One such person was my good friend, Terry Duffey. We had worked together at the diagnostic center and he was promoted before me to the academy. Our friendship continued at the training center and we grew closer. We became work out partners and played racquetball quite often.

I had no control over the nights and the visions that came and I kept that from Debbie. I never knew what form the dreams would take, I only knew that there were key players on the stage of my mind. From the horrific details of what Timothy Wesley Mcorquodale had done to his teenage victim, Donna Dixon, and of course Teresa Carol Allen and the nightmare she had endured at the hands of Roosevelt Green. I was just thankful that the dreams didn't have me waking up with screams and disturb my family, at least not at that time. I questioned if I had fulfilled my Christian duty or if I was even supposed to at that time. I was unsure of my own salvation so how could I possibly help another person with theirs? Those were also thoughts that I filed away deep down where no one could see. It was a part of my life I wasn't ready to share with anyone.

Instead I started to act out in rebellious ways. While I kept the professional side of my life clean and spit shined, my personal life was another matter. On my drive home to Jackson, I was stopping at the store everyday to buy beer and drive slowly home while I drank. I called it relaxing, but deep down I knew it was an attempt to suppress memories. At that time, it was working and it became a daily routine. I began to get attention from my female students. Having any type of relationship with a student was both unprofessional and unethical, not to mention that I was a married man. But, I would get messages from time to time that a student was interested in me. I kept this part of my life from Captain Treadwell, my mentor, my friend, a man that became like a father to me. I don't know why I couldn't talk to him about the memories that held me hostage. He was there with me through it all. Thinking about the young women, the children, who had been abused and killed so horribly made me think of my own girls. That was the truly agonizing part of my dreams.

I gave into the temptation two times with my students. The first time was during an inspection. The dorms that were to house the cadets weren't completed when the academy moved into the training center. The cadets stayed at one of the local motels close to the training center. Each instructor was assigned a week to inspect the rooms at nights and make sure the cadets were not doing anything that would cast a bad reflection on our department. There was a female cadet that made her intentions well known to me. She openly flirted with me during the day. It was on one of these inspections that she made her move. When I arrived at her room, she made sure her roommate was not there. As soon as I walked in the room, I knew I made a mistake. She told me, "I wasn't with my husband until after we were married, but there's just something about you." That was something I would hear on more than one occasion. I didn't know what that was and certainly didn't feel special in any way. But, that very same line would be repeated to me by more than one person. I wondered if I had been given a gift that allowed me to reach people in some way. If I was given a gift, I certainly had no respect for it and if it was God given, then I severely misused it. I left the room that night not only with memories of six years on death row, but now I could add massive guilt to the load I carried. Debbie was now pregnant and she adored me. I had four little girls, including Debbie's daughter who looked up to me. With that feeling now added, I had to stop again for a drink for the drive home. I felt dirty, cheap and had no one to blame but myself. No one had forced me to do anything. I walked into it with both eyes open and made a choice. Now I had to live with the aftermath.

The second time I gave into temptation was with a student who was ten years younger than me. I never imitated anything, but I didn't say no either and that made me just as guilty. I left my wife, who carried my child and went on a wild sexual fantasy with a teenage student for several weeks. During that time, I met Debbie on the road from our home and she motioned for me to pull over. She got out of her car and walked over to me. During our conversation only one thing was highlighted in my mind. She stood there and asked me, "Do you just not like me anymore?" It was a stab through my heart and it went to the core of my being. I answered, "Of course I do, Debbie." After she left, I did some soul searching and I remember asking myself out loud, "Bobby, what the hell are you doing?" I immediately ended the affair and went back home to my family and Debbie graciously took me back when she had every right to never speak to me again. I made a vow to myself I would become the husband she deserved and the father my children and our unborn child deserved. I had no idea who I was becoming. It was as though I was outside of my body looking at a person I did not know. On one occasion, while returning from night firing on the range with the cadets, I pulled my truck over to the side of the road and got out. I looked up at the stars, remembering how my mother taught me to pray outside. I asked God out loud, "Please tell me what you want from me?"

Recommitted to each other, Debbie and I started to attend Lamaze classes at the hospital we chose in Macon, Georgia where our child was to be born. This was all new to me because I wasn't in the rooms when my other children were born. However, the twins and Kimberley had been born by cesarean section. Debbie was going to have natural childbirth. As I looked at Debbie while performing the exercises, I realized how truly blessed I was. I tried to look inward at the person I had become, but I couldn't bear the thoughts of things I had done. Rather than accept it and try to change or figure out what the cause might be, I did what I was most comfortable with and that was to bury the feelings deep inside.

Captain Treadwell finally fully retired. I was happy for him because he deserved it after the career he had. It was time for him to rest. He would still stop by to visit on occasion and it always made me smile. He was the reason I made it this far in my career. I hid so much from him or at least I thought I did. In some strange way I had a feeling he knew more about me than he let on. I wanted to talk to him, I wanted to talk to someone, but I just didn't know how. Looking at Captain Treadwell made me think of my own father. I felt cheated that I lost him at such a young age. I didn't know how to open up to anyone.

Debbie and I visited mother a lot on the weekends. Debbie was close to her delivery date and mother told us that if she walked, the baby would come. So Debbie, mother and I took long walks when we visited. I always enjoyed my walks with mother. Being close to my childhood home was comforting to me. Now Debbie had joined in the tradition. Sure enough, after one of our walks, Debbie went into labor. She never panicked or lost control in any way. I drove us to the hospital in Macon and she sat quietly through the trip. She was quickly prepped for the delivery and I was able to be right there with her. On April 10, 1988, I watched my wife deliver our daughter, Brooke Michelle. Debbie made one small moan as she delivered her. I was the first to hold her. "Miki, "as we had agreed to call her, opened her beautiful eyes and looked into mine. It was one of the most precious moments of my life. After the nurse wrapped her, I gave her to Debbie who looked at me in said, "I'm sorry." She had wanted to give me a son, but I assured her that Miki was perfect, beautiful and I could not be happier with what we made together.

My career continued to move forward. A new Director took over the academy and he was one that new of my martial arts background. Terry Chastain had a diverse background in law enforcement and worked for the Department of Corrections on more than one occasion. He was a very intelligent yet down to earth man. His confidence and professionalism commanded respect. He met with every instructor individually. After our meeting he told me I was exactly the type of person he would recruit for the academy. It was a huge honor for me coming from someone like Terry. In the coming weeks he appointed me the coordinator of defensive tactics for our agency as well as Cadet Commander of the academy. It appeared my career was on the move. I continued to stay close to home with Debbie and our little family. Things were going very well, yet deep inside there seemed to be a hole in my life I couldn't fill. It was something that gnawed away at my subconscious. No matter how well things were going for me, I just couldn't shake that feeling.

Debbie was always the stable one in our marriage. She continued to look for ways to improve our family's situation. She found a mobile home for sale that she thought would fit our budget. Mother agreed to let us park it on a part of her property. It would be an investment for Debbie and I and we would be close to mother. At that time I took mother to any medical appointments. I didn't mind because she had done so much for me through my life. It was the least I could do and I enjoyed taking care of her.

The summer of 1988 we moved to Monroe County in our new mobile home. Even with all that was going on; I still carried death row around inside. More to the point, I carried around the faces of the victims and their killers. My life was stable, yet I still felt troubled. It was a feeling I could not come to terms with. I kept my emotions filed away inside where no one could see. Finally came a day I knew I was in trouble. My mother had a small dog named "Keisha" that was precious to her and was her constant companion. One morning I followed my usual routine and got in my truck heading to work. As I backed up I heard the "bump." It was the sound of my tire hitting something. I stopped immediately and closed my eyes. I didn't want to get out of my truck because I knew what I would find. Finally able to open the door, I looked behind me and sure enough, there lay Keisha behind my tire. I picked her up and laid her gently as I could in the grass. I went to my mother's house to give her the bad news. She was understandably upset, but laid no blame on me. I hugged her and told her I would bury Keisha when I returned home in the afternoon.

I replayed the scene over and over in my mind on the trip to work. All day during the classes I taught, it rolled over and over in my mind. It was like a dream I could not awake from. I went to the bathroom to rinse my face with water, looked in the mirror and said to myself, "This is silly, Bobby!" I returned to my classes with the scene playing over and over in my mind. At four O'clock I was already dreading the ride home. When I arrived, I saw the sheet that mother placed over Keisha's small body. I went right to work to bury the body. Once I was finished I went into mother's house to tell her again how sorry I was, but found I could not speak and started to tear up, finally sobbing uncontrollably. Mother tried to comfort me telling me it was alright. I finally looked out the window and said through my tears, "It was just a damn dog!" I had no idea where my tears came from or the strong emotions that came with them. On the way back to my house a thought came to me, *"I can't get away from death."* It was the first time I admitted to myself that there was a problem. Yet, I still had no idea how to confront the feelings I carried or how to talk about them.

I would get questions from Debbie or my friends from time to time inquiring if I was alright. My standard answer was always the same, "I'm fine." I knew full well that I was not alright. Every evening, alcohol became a constant companion. I'd mix a drink, sit down in front of my stereo with my headphones and disappear in a dream world with my music. My favorite was music from the seventies when my life was far less complicated. It would take me back to my teen years, where I was doing exactly the same thing I was doing now; put on my headphones and escape. Only now I was doing it as an adult and in the process ignoring my wife and family.

Debbie and I continued to get the twins and Kimberley every other weekend. We had such a beautiful family; Leighanne, Tracey, Debbie's daughter, Shannon, Kimberley and now beautiful little Miki. I tried to really enjoy our girls when we were together. I wanted them to live their life and not worry about the evil things of this world that I had experienced. I loved my job; teaching was the one thing where I excelled. At the end of every class there were review slips the cadets filled out rating the class. I always received excellent reviews and that made me feel good to know that I was reaching people and helping them in a career that I felt was about helping people. That was the reason I wanted to work in law enforcement and I tried to help the cadets understand what we were ultimately trying to accomplish; help people.

There were long periods with no dreams. I welcomed those times, yet I knew in the back of my mind they would return. I kept the visions at bay with alcohol and evening dates with my stereo. It worked most of the time. My experience on death row understandably sparked my student's curiosity and they would ask questions. That was usually all that was needed to restart my daytime visions. Sometimes they just came with no stimulation at all. When my memory got jumpstarted by a question, the nightmares were sure to follow. Still I couldn't bring myself to confront them by talking about them. I was grateful for the moments in time when I had even a moment of peace.

Inevitably, the nightmares always seemed to create a hole in my life that alcohol and music would not fill. In those times, I looked for other ways to occupy that space. In 1989 I began another affair with a young receptionist in our office, Crystal. This time, I got more committed than I intended and it caused a problem in the office. Word reached the Director of Training and I was quietly counseled that it could become a problem. It indeed became that in 1989. Almost overnight I went from the golden boy to one who cast shame on the department. I was relieved of my duties as Cadet Commander and everyone turned a cold shoulder to me. The affair caused problems at home and Debbie and I separated yet again. I felt ashamed and could hardly bare to look anyone in the eye at work. I became a loner isolating myself in my office when I was not teaching class.

It was during this time that I took a step that would change my life forever. Stress wouldn't allow me to sleep nights. I stopped having lunch with my coworkers and chose instead to go home for lunch to further isolate myself. It was no longer home to me because Debbie, Shannon and Miki weren't there. I sat on the sofa in the silence thinking how far I had fallen in such a short time. The happy times here with my family were now only a memory and caused a headache. I felt very lonely and sad. I couldn't take it anymore so I got up and went to the kitchen. I stood in front of the cabinet and stared at it for several minutes. Finally I got the courage to open the door and there sat the answer to my pain. I reached in and pulled out the bottle of bourbon and sat it on the counter. I looked at it another minute and then reached up for a glass and got the cola from the refrigerator. Now I had all the ingredients needed to escape the anguish I felt. I quickly mixed the drink before I lost the nerve to do so. I gulped it down and sat down on the sofa and waited. It came; sweet, warm relief moved slowly from the top of my head down to the pit of my stomach and down into my legs and I relaxed.. All of a sudden I didn't feel so alone. My friend, sweet alcohol had arrived to rescue me. I sat there with my eyes closed to welcome the relief. I had to leave in

minutes to return to the training center so I went to the kitchen and mixed another drink that would take me through the afternoon until I was back here again for another dose.

On my drive back to the training center, it all rushed upon me of the imaginary line I crossed. I just instinctively knew there was no stepping back across the line. I was committed. I went to my office to check my schedule concerning my afternoon class. The class was stress management. I gathered my lesson plan and started toward the classroom. I thought to myself, "*Stress management, this should be interesting considering my place in life.*" Thirty minutes into the class, I got a hard slap in the face of just how much my life changed in the last hour. I came to a section of the lesson plan that featured stress in one's life and the negative ways to cope with it. Right there at the top of the list was the answer I had chosen to deal with my stress. Alcohol was mentioned and it talked about the dangers of using it as a stress reliever. But, that wasn't the worst of it. The lesson plan went on to talk about recognizing when you had a problem and reaching out to ask for help.

I felt blood rush to my head and I was certain my face was blood red with embarrassment. To my surprise, no one said anything. I rushed through the class and made the class shorter than it was intended to be. As soon as I dismissed the class, I wasted no time getting back to the office. I was stopped in the hallway by a student who had a question. I slowed down without stopping and told him that I was in a rush and that I would answer his question in the morning. I went directly to my office, put my things away, grabbed my briefcase and left the building before my friend, Terry Duffey or any other instructor could see me.

I made it to my truck undetected. I sat there and lay my head back with my eyes closed as though I had just ran through a twisted maze where at any turn I might be discovered. I finally composed myself enough to start my truck and get off the property as soon as I could. It was only 5 miles home, but I couldn't wait that long. I stopped at the local store and bought a six pack of beer to clam my nerves. I downed one before leaving the parking lot. Once my nerves settled, I drove the long way home which led me down dirt roads that were barely traveled and I could relax and finish the beer. I turned my music on and drove slowly taking in the beautiful pastures of the local farms. Slowly, my friend alcohol took its affect. As I started to relax, I didn't feel so tense about my noon time drink. I justified it away by telling myself it was to, "calm my nerves."

Once home, I took my package into the house before mother came out of her house and saw what I had. The mobile home I shared with Debbie and our children was waiting very quietly. I went directly to the kitchen for a stronger drink. It was there waiting for me on the counter where I left it at lunchtime; my new best friend. Instead of mixing a drink, I took out a shot glass and drank several shots and chased them with cola. I stood there looking out the window toward mother's house. The warm feeling moved over me more quickly this time. Like an express train to my brain. My body started to relax. Now, I could mix a drink and go over to check on mother. She knew that I drank; she just didn't know how it was starting to take over. Once I had the shots, I could now sip a drink and talk to mother.

Whatever misgivings I had about my life, I knew I could take a drink and then things didn't seem so bad. It was just stress and once I was through this rough patch with Debbie, I could regain control and life would be back to normal. That was the first lie I told myself. That was on the surface. Deep down in my soul, I knew it was a lie. Yet, I was determined to make myself believe it. If there was a doubt, I had my friend alcohol that would convince

me. I discovered a dangerous concept. No matter what I felt, the proper amount of alcohol could help convince me of anything.

My lunchtime visits home became a routine. I would always take care to cover my breath with mints. However, I was really surprised that no one suspected anything. If they did, nothing was said. On the rare occasions that I got honest with myself, I knew I was living on borrowed time. I continued the affair with Crystal. It was a distraction from the mess I was making of my life. Debbie had moved into a duplex in Macon. The first time I visited Miki, I was astonished at where my cheating ways and selfishness had led my family. It was an old place and not what I had planned for my family. When I left the small place and started home, I almost came to tears as I thought about my family. I couldn't sleep that night. It required more alcohol than usual to rest my mind. I was amazed how quickly I recovered in the mornings. I still had the presence of mind to prepare my training uniform the night before. I usually arrived early for work and started my day off in my office in solitude. I couldn't stop thinking about my family and where they lived. Debbie was now twice as far away from work. I was just going through the motions at work with no enthusiasm at all. I no longer had the passion for teaching as before. I wondered if my students could see a difference. I was falling into depression.

I couldn't take it anymore. I decided that I had to get my family back. One evening, I took a few drinks of liquid courage and went to visit my family. I stayed late enough for Debbie to put the girls to sleep. Once we were alone, I pleaded my case. I asked Debbie to forgive me and move back home. She paused and looked deep in my eyes before she answered. Then she said, "I forgive you Bobby and you can come visit me anytime you'd like, but I can't come back." It was a dagger through my heart. That's when I knew I pushed her too far. All of my ridiculous drinking and unfaithfulness brought us to the end of our marriage. She just couldn't do it anymore and I saw the hurt in hurt in her eyes. I finally lost my family.

I stopped at the liquor store on the way home. I really needed a drink. I mixed it in my truck in a soda bottle. I took a long drink before I started the truck. I took my usual back way home and cranked up the stereo. Halfway to my house, I started to weep. I was feeling very sorry for myself. But, that wasn't the worst of it. I knew I denied Miki growing up without her father at home. I failed at yet another marriage and I also knew that I finally pushed away the love of my life. The only solace I took was that now maybe Debbie could find someone that she deserved, someone who would treat her like the lady she was.

My depression worsened over the next few weeks and my career suffered for it. Crystal wasn't divorced from her husband and he came to the office to confront her and he made a scene. The only thing that saved me was I had taken that day off. The following day she and I were summoned to the Director's office. There was a new female director and she needed to demonstrate her authority. We were counseled on "brining our personal lives to work." The Director pointed out that we had been seen together in town after hours. I was already on edge and I could feel my blood pressure go through the roof. My temper flared as I told her, "What I do after hours in my personal life is none of your business!" She fired back, "If the training director were here, he'd probably curse you out." I wasn't ready to let it go and I pointed my finger to the Commissioner's picture on the wall and said, "That's fine because I can curse back and not him nor you or the director of training are going to tell me what I can and can't do on my leisure time!" I could sense that she knew this was all escalating and she backed down and dismissed us.

I went directly to my office. I was now an outcast and Crystal was subsequently fired from her position. Probably the only reason I wasn't fired was because I was a state employee with rights. So instead, I was shunned. Nothing positive I accomplished in the past few years mattered. Even my friends at work kept their distance. From that moment forward, I taught my classes when scheduled and spent the rest of my time in my office. I even stopped going to the gym on my down time. When 4:30 pm came, I locked my door and went home without talking to anyone. Word of my downfall spread quickly through the department and even people who had no firsthand knowledge of it all were making comments about me. Those comments were very unkind and made their way back to me. The worst part of it all was I knew I deserved it, but that didn't make it hurt any less.

Finally the former director of the academy, Terry Chastain, who was now the director of field training, saw my misery and offered me a way out. He offered to allow me to swap positions with the field training officer at the diagnostic center. I immediately jumped at the offer thinking it would be a fresh start and back at the institution where I started my career. The only person who seemed sad to see me go was my good friend, Terry Duffey. Whether it was imagined on my part or it was actually there, I thought I could see relief on the faces of the academy director and some of the other staff. The warden at the diagnostic center was Walter Zant, who hired me in 1980. He was promoted to Deputy Commissioner over all facilities in the state, but returned to the diagnostic center. I didn't know what the particulars were of his return, but I was told he was back with a chip on his shoulder. I transferred back to the diagnostic center and did my best to stay clear of Mr. Zant. I thought the transfer would feel like going home, but things were different. I walked the long familiar tunnel to the stairs and into the administrative area. There was no homecoming here. I knew immediately that I made a mistake. Debbie no longer worked here, but everywhere I looked I could sense our past here. This is where we met, dated, fell in love and married.

I walked through control one and down the corridor to my new office. People spoke to me, but it was more out of kindness than respect. I could feel the coldness of the staff. The word of my downfall reached here before I did. There would be no homecoming type welcome here for me and I felt like a pilgrim in an unholy land. The new training office was in the very back of the institution and far away from Mr. Zant and I was grateful for that. A sergeant had been assigned to the office since I was last here. My first day I felt isolated and alone.

Every time I walked through the administration area, I felt Debbie's presence and it only made me miss her more. That, of course, caused me to think of Miki. I could feel the emotion in the pit of my stomach and sometime it would make its way to my throat where I felt a knot growing. When that happened I had to find a restroom very quickly or I knew that I would lose my composure. A splash of water in my face and then the part I hated most, looking at myself in the mirror. I was beginning to hate myself and very quickly had to look away.

I had to make a trip to G-house and it seemed foreign as well. But, as I approached the cross gate, the memories of what I had done here came flooding back. The ghosts were still here. The memory of Roosevelt Green and Teresa Carol Allen were still present in this place. As I passed by the Captain's office I looked over and my mind's eye saw Captain Treadwell there. I needed his gentle guiding hand more than ever, but was too ashamed of what I had done to reach out to him. I conducted my business and left as quickly as I could.

Each new day brought me closer to the cold hard fact that I made a terrible mistake coming back here. I didn't belong here anymore. My training supervisor's office was in Milledgeville, Georgia and he was also a personal friend of mind. He came to see if I was settling in to my new position. And it was good to see a friendly face. We chatted for a bit about the new office and the upcoming training events. Afterwards, I walked him to the front on his way out. We talked a bit about Mr. Zant and I asked him if he had asked any questions about me and my transfer. He looked at me and said something I knew he didn't want to say, but as my supervisor, he knew that he must. "He said you're going to have to keep your pants on." He smiled, but the damage was done. My heart sank to the pit of my stomach. Now I finally understood the meaning of the quick glances I received. I went back to my office as quickly as I could. I didn't speak or look at anyone on the walk back. My face felt hot and I wondered if it was red. Once in my office, I closed the door and sat at my desk. My assistant was out in the institution so I was alone. I stared straight ahead as I contemplated what just happened. My mind drifted back to the first class of cadets in which I taught. The cadets usually had a party the night before graduation. At that time, it was acceptable for the instructors to attend that function. The cadets were staying at a local motel at that time. I attended with two other male instructors. At that time, the cadets were allowed to drink off duty and they had quite a party going on. We were offered beers and accepted.

I was the new kid on the block so I just stood and observed the festive occasion. Everyone was laughing and having a good time. I excused myself to the restroom. When I was finished, I turned around to see one of the female cadets standing in front of me. She was quite beautiful and made her intentions known. I remarked at her beauty, but calmly excused myself and went back to the party. I was new and didn't know how things worked in this environment. I noticed my two fellow instructors were talking with two female cadets. I knew one of my comrades was married. Eventually they both excused themselves and left with the two female cadets. It was no mystery where they went. That became a pattern at all other graduations. It wasn't until my encounter with Crystal that it became a problem. After my outcast, I made a remark to my friend Terry Duffey that I believed I had been used to make an example. He nodded in agreement and said, "Yes, you were."

Now here I sat two years later disgraced and censured. I just instinctively knew that there would be no rebirth of my career. I was the example and I felt that I had been crucified and nailed to a wall for everyone to see. What's more, I deserved it. I did so much damage to my personal life, my wife and children. When I was recruited for the academy, it was explained to me that I was being sent as an example to the cadets of what a correctional officer should be. Now, I was an example of what a correctional officer should never be. I carried a load on my shoulders and it was heavy indeed.

My rides home in the afternoons were none too pleasant. I was trained to leave work and not take it home with me. Now I was haunted by it. At home, alcohol was the first order of business. I fell from premium bourbon to cheap vodka. I was now buying only half gallons because I went through the fifths too quickly. I learned a trick at a party for instructors once. Keep the bottle in the freezer because the alcohol wouldn't freeze and shots would then be readily available. That became my ritual every afternoon. When I walked through the door,

I went directly to the freezer; three shots immediately to get the day out of the front of my mind and bury it inside as quickly as I could. Once that was complete, I mixed a drink and went to see my mother who was always glad to see me and never had a condemning look in her eye. Since I had pushed my family away, she was the light of my day.

I hated to see bedtime come. I knew what was waiting for me in the dark. I knew the dreams would come and the broken sleep. I never slept straight through the night anymore. There were always familiar, unfriendly faces to greet me in my dreams. It was during that time I started to dream about my father and that haunted me constantly. It was always the same dream and it was vividly real. It always began with his death. We buried him and I was devastated by that. But, somewhere in the dream, he was alive again. I was ecstatic that he was here. Yet, I somehow had the knowledge that he was going to have to go back to the grave. He would have to die all over again and it was heartbreaking.

Somewhere in that exchange, I would wake up, usually drenched in sweat and staring into the darkness. I had to get up and go to the bathroom to dry myself with a towel. My bed would be soaked with my sweat. I awoke one morning after such a dream. I was almost dizzy thinking of the dream in the night and the day ahead at the diagnostic center. My mind raced and my heart began to flutter. I knew the remedy for my anxiety. I walked to the kitchen and starred out the window at the morning knowing I had to face it. I didn't try to talk myself out of it. I knew what I had to do to start my day. I reached into the freezer, grabbed the bottle, found a shot glass and took three shots and closed my eyes and waited for the warmth to come. When it came I started to relax and opened my eyes. I crossed another bridge into darkness. But, it was done now. After I dressed, I found a cup with a lid and straw. I mixed a drink and started out the door to greet the day. I had the courage to meet whatever waited for me at work.

I drove toward the interstate. As I sipped my drink I turned on the stereo and the music helped me relax. I looked in the rearview mirror at myself and smiled. I convinced myself that things were going to be alright. I always left home early so I could take a slow ride to work. I was on the last leg of the journey to the diagnostic center. There was a state park on the exit before the institution. I had plenty of time so I decided to drive through the park. There was water flowing over a dam. I parked and let my window down to hear the rushing of the water. Another sip of my drink and I was relaxed. A squirrel was going about his duties looking for food. The morning sun was shining through the pine trees. I closed my eyes and took a deep breath. I wanted to stay here all day, but I knew my duties awaited me.

I cranked my truck and drove to the interstate. As I got closer to the exit where I'd turn off for the institution, a knot appeared in my stomach and I took another sip from the cup. I entered the parking lot and found my assigned parking space. I stared out at the huge institution before me. I put my lips on the straw from my cup and pulled hard until I reached the bottom of the cup. Now I had to get busy attempting to cover up my breath. I kept a large bag of peppermint candy in the truck. I popped one in my mouth and grabbed several more to put in my pocket. My ammunition for the day to hide what a coward I had become.

That became my new routine every morning. I don't know if anyone ever suspected anything, but I was never approached. My brother, Don had once told a friend of his that I walked around with a drink in my hand all the time, but could never tell that I was drunk. I patted myself on the back for my ingenuity. In the back of my mind where I kept those faces from my past; Daddy, the victims from the trial transcripts and the executed inmates, was also the knowledge that I was walking a tight rope and any misstep would see my downfall. I finally reached a point where I couldn't leave the bottle at home. It became a constant companion. I had a clever hiding spot under my seat in the truck. I just needed one stop at the convenience store for a bottle of juice and I could mix the drink before I started home. I usually stopped by the state park on the way home because the fresh air and the smell of pine trees helped me relax.

When I got home I could openly drink like I wanted. I began to feel guilty about the lie I was living. When that happened, it just required more alcohol. I had no social life and I had no interest in exercising at all. All I did was visit mother, drink and listen to my music. The nights were the worst because I knew the nightmares would come with Daddy leading the way returning from his grave, but knowing he had to go back to it. My dream never went that far so I never witnessed his return. I usually woke up, drenched in sweat, before that happened. The next morning, I'd start the whole insane process over again.

The days began to run together. Even though I'd started my career here at the diagnostic center, it felt like I was in a foreign land. Everything was alien to me. I realized nothing changed here. It was my alcohol induced perception of everything that changed. I conducted classes, qualified officers on the firing range, taught C.P.R. all under the influence of alcohol. In the back of my mind, I knew I existed on borrowed time. But, with the proper amount of alcohol I could convince myself of anything.

I was posted at the diagnostic center, but I reported to the training supervisor in Milledgeville. That was how it was explained to me anyway. It was also a set up for disaster. For whatever reason, Mr. Zant decided that I was to report to Mr. Parrish, the deputy warden of security. No procedure was laid out for me and Mr. Parrish never met with me to discuss anything, so I just accepted it and thought no more about. I couldn't settle into my new position. I didn't feel comfortable from the very first day and it wasn't getting any easier. I wanted to take a day off and relax. That's what I told myself anyway. I knew the real reason I wanted off. I wanted a day of uninterrupted drinking and music. I called my supervisor in Milledgeville to request a day off. He approved my leave without hesitation. I was off on the weekend, so I took Monday off to have a long weekend. The Friday before, I told my assistant my plans.

After my long weekend, I reported back to work on the following Tuesday. I was anticipating a normal day. I made my way to my office to check the schedule for the day. I received a phone call to report to the warden's office. It took me by surprise and I wondered if I my drinking had finally been discovered. As I walked to the front of the institution I felt the butterflies began to churn in my stomach. I really needed a drink, but had no time to go to the parking lot. When I arrived at Mr. Zant's office, I was ushered in. When I walked through the door, I knew something was wrong. The major, the highest ranking uniformed officer at the institution was present along with Mr. Parrish, the deputy warden of security. Mr. Zant sat behind his desk peering at me with his icy stare. I was told to take a chair.

I found out very quickly that the major and Mr. Parrish were here as witnesses. It was Mr. Zant who controlled the meeting. He wasted no time, "Where were you yesterday?" My heart sank into my throat as I replied, "I was on annual leave." His gaze continued to cut through me as he continued, "Didn't I tell you that you were to report to Mr. Parrish?" "Yes," I replied. "Then why didn't you inform him of your leave?" I stared back into his eyes,

"I was granted leave and I informed my assistant that I wouldn't be here." He was prepared for the comeback, "Who approved the leave?" I answered, "My supervisor in Milledgeville." He already knew what he wanted to do. It was as though he wanted to make the moment last as long as he could. I could tell he enjoyed my predicament. Then he sprung it on me, the real reason I was here and in front of witnesses, "Then you report to him in Milledgeville." I wasted no time, "Of course." I got up from my chair and quickly left the office.

I was so grateful that the stairwell to the tunnel was so near the warden's office. I felt as though every eye in the administration area was on me. I dared not make eye contact with anyone for fear that I might lose my composure. I wondered if anyone could tell how fast I walked. I wanted desperately to disappear down the stairs and into the darkness of the tunnel where no one could see me. I made my way to the front gate and heard the electronic click of the gate. I was completely paranoid. As I pushed the gate open I was sure that the tower officer already knew what had happened. Normally I would give him a wave as I exited, but I did not look up. I got to my truck as quickly as I could. I raced out of the parking lot as fast as I dared. I knew exactly where my first stop would be. At the convenience store I grabbed the juice and hurried to my truck. My mind was racing and I couldn't keep up with the thoughts. I mixed a strong drink and gulped it down. I needed relief very quickly. With "medicine" in me, I could relax a bit. Before I would go to Milledgeville, I needed to call and make sure my supervisor was there. I went to the payphone at the corner of the driveway. I called his office and they said that he was in Forsyth at the training center for the day. I wouldn't have to drive all the way to Milledgeville. I had mixed a drink for the road. I tried not to let my emotions overtake me because I was afraid I'd violate the speed limit, that wouldn't be a good idea with alcohol in my cup. I decided to set the cruise control.

I arrived at the training center and had to go to the corrections academy office to look for my supervisor. Mercifully, he was working out in the field so I wouldn't have to suffer my humiliation with the rest of the staff. I drove to the area to find him. I already decided what my course of action was going to be. I parked, got out of my truck and found my supervisor, my friend. I started right away, "Who approves my leave time?" I don't know what expression was on my face, but I could see in his eyes that he knew something was very wrong. He answered, "My office does." I shot back, "I was just thrown out of the diagnostic center for taking an approved day off." I reached in my pocket and took out my badge wallet and I.D. and handed it to him. I felt my voice crack as I spoke, "I don't need this shit anymore!" I felt a tear form in the corner of my eye.

He was compassionate and handed my badge back to me and said, "Don't make any rash decisions here."I looked away for a moment to compose myself. I looked down to the ground before I came back to his gaze and replied softly, "Alright." He told me to go home and he would contact the Director of Field Training and have him call me. I returned to my truck and headed home. I took the back way home. I needed the serenity of the open pastures and the peacefulness of the country roads where I played as a child. I let the window down and drove slowly. Of course, I drank all the way home.

Once at home, I grabbed my bottle and took it in the house. At this point, I didn't care if mother saw. Once inside, I took several shots and sat down on the sofa. My head was spinning and not from the alcohol. My mind was racing from the events of the morning. I sat there with the lights out just staring out the kitchen window. I was lost in thought when the phone rang and it startled me. I went slowly to the counter where the phone base was. It was the director of field training. He was an instructor at the academy when I first started. He had me explain what happened earlier. He said he was going to call Mr. Zant and straighten things out. The fact of the matter was, I didn't want to straighten things out with him. I wanted out. So, I stated my position, "I don't want to return to the diagnostic center." Before He could reply, I continued, "Please transfer me anywhere you want, but get me away from Mr. Zant." I waited for his response and it came, "We don't have anywhere to transfer you." I waited for a moment sensing that there was no room for discussion and said, "I can't go back up there today." He said, "Don't go back there today and take the day off."

I hung up the phone. I took three more shots. I sat in silence again and contemplated my next move. I felt trapped with no room to maneuver. The training officer I replaced had a disagreement with Mr. Zant. That was how I was able to make the transition. It appeared to me that Mr. Zant was the one who had the issue. Yet, no one was willing to entertain that idea. I mixed a drink and went over to see my mother. She greeted me on the back deck and asked, "What's wrong?" It was a mother's intuition that sensed something was wrong with her child. She was always very good at reading me. I remembered coming in from work one day and as soon as I got out of my truck she said, "You've been drinking, haven't you?" She could read the expression on my face and know what was going on.

I didn't want to go into details of the day so I simply said, "Just an issue at work, nothing to worry about." It was a lie and I suspect she knew it, but I think she also knew that I didn't want to talk about it. We just sat on the back deck as we did so many afternoons and listened to the sounds of country living; chirping birds, the wind and the smell of Georgia pines. This was my safe haven and had been since I was 13 years old. We found things to talk about and talking with my mother relieved my anxiety. I loved her so very much. I thought briefly about my father and how much I wished that he was here so I could talk to him. But, I didn't hold that thought too long because I knew I would lose my composure, especially today.

I drank through the evening. I tried to sit down and listen to my music, but my mind was racing and I couldn't focus. I gave it up. I went outside to look at the stars and listen to the sounds of the night. Finally I made my way to the bedroom. My mind was still racing and I knew I had a decision to make. I dreaded to see the morning come because I'd have to face Zant. He definitely had the home field advantage. It was his institution. His boss was in Atlanta and warden's are given a long leash to control their institutions. I called Debbie with the excuse of checking up on Miki. She already knew what happened. A friend of hers in the office she worked in at the diagnostic center had called her earlier in the day. She said her friend told her Mr. Zant fired me. My infamy it seems was the topic of conversation throughout the department. I explained the truth of what happened. She also had information that my assistant had been questioned of my whereabouts on my off day that started all of this and his answer to Zant was that he had no idea where I was. That was like a knife in my back because I had specifically told him about my approved leave. I felt like everyone in the department was lining up to take a cheap shot at me. Some people I considered as friends were at the front of the line. My world was crashing down on me and all I wanted to do was disappear.

Later that night, I fell into sleep rather quickly, a benefit of a day of drinking. But, it was restless sleep. When the nightmares came, there was Teresa Carol Allen and 17 year old Donna Dixon, the victim of Timothy Wesley Mcorquodale. The faces of their killers usually showed up somewhere in the night and of course, my father, out of his grave, and all the while I had the knowledge that he had to go back. It was a torturous nightmare and caused me to wake. It usually took me several minutes to adjust and realize that it was only a dream and I usually ended up in tears.

The alarm clock sounded entirely too soon. I lay in bed just staring at the ceiling not wanting to face the day. I finally dragged myself out of bed. While most people were headed for their coffee pots, I headed to the kitchen for the vodka bottle. The memory of the day before was still alive and well. I felt as though I would be the topic of conversation all through the department today. My paranoia was in high gear. In my mind I could see myself walking into the institution while everyone stared at me knowing what had occurred the day before. Then I'd have to face Zant in his office and be raked over the coals for a second time. That thought alone required three shots. Once the vodka did its job, I could take a shower and face the day. In the shower my mind raced with what was ahead of me.

After the shower, I required another shot. I mixed a drink, turned on the TV for company. I needed to hear someone else's voice for distraction as I summoned my courage through the drink in my hand. The warmth of the alcohol surged through my veins. I stared at the TV, but my mind raced. By the time I had finished the drink, I decided I wouldn't be facing Zant today or ever. I convinced myself that my best course of action was to resign because my embarrassment went too deep. I couldn't face anyone in the department today. I got dressed and mixed a drink for the road. I was headed to Milledgeville to turn in my badge and I.D. to my supervisor. I took the cowards way out and decided I would never face Zant again.

I took a slow drive to Milledgeville and nursed the drink I had. Anytime I was drinking and driving, I was always very careful not to speed and I adhered to all the traffic signs. I'm sure every drunk driver thought exactly as I did as we all slowly lose control. I used to tell myself that I was a better driver when drinking because I was more aware of my surroundings. That was the lie I told myself in 1986 when I received my first D.U.I. In spite of that knowledge, I couldn't face my supervisor, my friend and do what I had decided to do today sober.

By the time I arrived, I had the courage I needed. I did the usual routine with the peppermint to attempt to freshen my breath. I looked at myself in the rearview mirror and said to myself, "I hope you know what you're doing." I got out of my truck and headed for the office. I saw several friends as I walked through the office and I felt as though everyone was looking at me. I knew that they were all aware of what had transpired the day before, so I avoided eye contact with them. I needed to get to my friends office as quickly as possible. Mercifully he was alone and agreed to see me. I walked in and laid my badge and I.D. on his desk. He didn't try to talk me out of it; he only asked if I was sure I wanted to do this. I told him it wasn't really what I wanted, but I was very sure that I never wanted to see Mr. Zant's face again. He accepted my resignation and wished me well.

As I walked out of the office, I felt as though a huge burden had been lifted off my shoulders. I actually smiled as I walked to my truck. I went directly to a store to buy a bottle of juice. I had brought along my liquid courage and I needed a big dose of it. Once I'd finished that task, I started home. That was when reality started to move in. I realized that I would no longer have a paycheck coming in. The truck I was driving was not paid for and there would be a payment coming due. The burden that had been lifted from my shoulders was now replaced by yet another.

On the drive home my mind was working overtime. I was trying to process the events of the morning and at the same time, think about what my next move would be. I had succeeded in slaying the giant in my mind; not having to go back to the diagnostic center to face Zant or my embarrassment of the entire situation. But, for the first time in almost a decade, I had no future. I had no idea what the next move was going to be. Once home I put the vodka in the freezer because I knew I was going to need it and sat in silence in the dark. My head was swimming because I had so much information to process. I closed my eyes to block out the sun from the windows and fell into a restless sleep.

I don't know how long I slept, but I awoke with a startling jump. I felt fear as my head cleared and of course, I headed into the kitchen for the freezer. Three shots seemed to be the number that carried the alcohol quickly to my brain offering relief. As I stood there waiting for relief from the reality I found myself in, I marveled at how far I had fallen in the last year alone. Nightmares and daytime visions haunted me. On my downward spiral into obscurity I realized at this moment for the first time, that no one in the department ever asked me if I was alright. I thought surely there had to be some outward sign of the torment I felt inside or had I become so accomplished at hiding my fears and doubts that no one could see past the wall that I created?

I had slept into late afternoon. I needed some human interaction so I mixed a drink and went to my mother's house. I found her sitting on the deck where we usually started our evenings together. I sat for a while engaging in small talk. I finally asked mother to take a walk with me. I needed the freedom I felt when we shared a walk. As we walked down the country road we lived on, I sipped my drink. At this point, mother had stopped commenting on my drinking and just accepted it. Finally I had enough courage to tell mother that I resigned during the day. I never told her the details of my meeting with Zant. Being the loving mother she was, she showed no disappointment and simply said, "I had a feeling that something was going on."

Though she hid her feelings, I knew she was disappointed. I had achieved so much and I knew that she was proud of me. Dusk was falling as we ended our walk. We sat on her deck for a while and chatted. I believed she sensed that I didn't want to talk about what had happened and I was relieved. Sitting in the dark, looking at the stars always comforted me. These times always took me back to my childhood when mother taught me to pray outside. Finally I told her goodnight and went home. I drank and watched television for a while. My eyelids finally started to get heavy and I went to bed. I laid there in the dark not knowing what my next move would be and drifted off to sleep. My dreams would give me no peace tonight. First there were the tortured victims of the killers, then the killers themselves. Finally, there was my father and my eyes opened.

I looked at the red numbers of the digital clock. Not even an hour passed. I couldn't stand the silence, so I went to the den and turned on the TV. I had no interest in the programming; I just needed to hear voices. I lay on the couch and watched the images and thought about my last day of employment and I questioned my decision. Fear was overtaking me. I sat there in misery for quite some time before I realized what I needed to do. Relief was in

the kitchen, in the freezer. I finally got tired of the butterflies stirring in my stomach and made the move. As I poured the object of my relief, I felt a tingle run down my spine and it frightened me. I realized I would exist in a realm of my own making. I had created a make believe bubble outside of reality, but I needed it to survive. I took several shots and went back to the den and the TV. I finally relaxed and focused on the program. I sat there feeling numb, but relieved; I drifted off to sleep and gave myself over to the nightmares that came. I didn't have the strength to close them out.

Chapter 14

"Beloved think it not strange concerning the fiery trial which is to try you, as though some strange thing has happened to you......."

-1 Peter 4:12
(American King James Version)

I woke up on the sofa with my eyes wide open, fully awake and sat up immediately. I felt afraid and my eyes scanned the room trying to get my bearing. I knew the feeling all too well and I didn't attempt to recall the nightmare that woke me. Daylight was the only place I had control because the nightmares came on their own. If I ever allowed the nightmares to become daytime visions, I would have no control and I knew it, so I trained myself to consciously block the daytime visions. I knew the remedy for the fear I felt so I got up rubbing my eyes and started to the kitchen for the freezer. There it was waiting like a devoted friend giving me relief and asking for nothing in return. Three shots and I could start the day. After a shower I ironed my clothes for the day. Today was the first time in ten years that I wore civilian clothes to begin my day. I had to turn in all uniforms and equipment at the central warehouse. I felt very strange knowing my duties for the day. After three more shots and mixing a drink for the road, I gathered my gear and started for the training center. I felt like I was in an alien world because I was on no schedule or commitments for the day. I decided to drive the back roads to town and nurse the drink I had and the view was much more relaxing and appealing than the main road to town. I had to have music because I couldn't stand to be in silence for fear of where my thoughts would take me.

After a stop at the department of corrections central warehouse on the grounds of the training center, I decided to stop by the academy to see my friend Terry Duffey, the only friend I felt I had anymore. Terry had changed offices to the assistant director's office while I had been at the diagnostic center. It was very apparent that he was being groomed for assistant director of the academy and he was most deserving. I felt very strange being in the academy offices as a civilian. Everyone was polite and I was greeted with a smile and treated like one might treat a stray dog, a pat on the head and they went on about their business. But, whether from paranoia or actually sensing the feelings, I felt I knew what they were all thinking about me. Terry was the only one who seemed genuinely glad to see me. We shook hands and he invited me into his office. He sat behind his desk and I in one

of his office chairs. He asked if I was doing alright and it was sincere. I shrugged my shoulders and simply said, "Ok." He didn't press for more information and I was relieved. I was afraid that if he pursued it I would lose my composure. He sensed it and left it there. He did have news he wanted to share with me.

A female warden in Atlanta who had been present at the awards banquet when I was named "officer of the year" in 1986 apparently heard the news about me and was asking about me. I met her once on duty at the front gate at the diagnostic center when she came as a state witness for one of the executions. The butterflies in my stomach immediately started to stir. It wasn't from excitement, but more like embarrassment because I knew I must be the topic of discussion throughout the department. Two and a half years before I was the topic of discussion because I was the golden boy on the rise. Now, I was like a disease that everyone wanted to avoid. But, it was good news Terry had.

Terry began, "She said she hated to see all that talent go to waste." I simply asked, "Oh really?" I wasn't sure what to make of it. I didn't think she knew anything about me other than my name. He continued, "She has a sergeant's position open at Metro." He was referring to the Metro Correctional Institution in Atlanta, Georgia. He continued, "Why don't you give her a call and see what's up, she seemed very interested in you?" He wrote down her number and handed it to me. "Thanks, Terry, I really appreciate it." He smiled as he got up from his desk and patted me on the back as we walked out of his office together and toward the front entrance. "Bobby, let me know what happens with it and take care of yourself buddy," he said. We shook hands and I replied, "I will, Terry and thanks again."

I left the office optimistic. The fear was subsiding and I felt a ray of hope. I got into my truck and of course, I needed a drink to celebrate so I stopped at the store for some juice. Now I had a new feeling to contend with. Hope had been offered and I asked myself why I was drinking? I had no credible answer and that concerned me. It made no difference because I mixed the drink anyway. I started home taking the back roads again. It was a beautiful sunny day and I needed the beauty of the green pastures to help calm me. I looked down at the piece of paper Terry gave me and had a flood of emotions and not just one I could focus on. I parked and went over to mother's house with my drink in hand. She had become used to it and didn't talk about it. I needed to hear her voice because it comforted me. We sat outside on the deck as we normally did and chatted. I told her about the prospect of a job and that I had to call first. I could see the relief on her face as she smiled. We talked for a while as I nursed the drink. I knew what I was doing, but didn't want to admit it. I was gathering courage to make the phone call. I couldn't believe what a coward I had become.

After I finished the drink, I went to my house to make the call. Even after the drink, it took another shot to find the courage and then I placed the source of my courage back into the freezer to wait for later when I knew I would need it. Whenever those thoughts came to me I quickly dismissed them for fear that I would have to accept what was happening to me. I was careful to stay in the shadows of my mind and not allow anything into the light of my consciousness. It was almost like tip toeing on the edge of a spotlight, always being careful not to fully allow myself into the light knowing that if I did, everyone would know what I was. The most important point was that I would know. If I remained on the edge of the light, I didn't have to accept what I was becoming.

I finally found the courage to pick up the phone. I punched in the numbers quickly before I lost my nerve. The operator answered, "Metro C.I., may I help you?" "Yes, I'd like to speak to Warden Mattie Rodriguez, please," I replied. Then the next question, "May I tell her who is calling?" "Bobby Allen," I replied. "One moment please." Now I was committed. I'd given my name and now had to wait in agony. I looked out the kitchen window and saw my mother sitting on her deck and it relaxed me. Finally after what seemed like an eternity the line clicked, "This is Mattie." I felt my heart sink into my stomach. "Hi, Ms. Rodriguez, this is Bobby Allen," and then we were off into the conversation. She told me that she was aware of the situation at the diagnostic center. I didn't go into detail but quickly gave her a synopsis of what happened. Finally she asked, "Why don't you come to Metro and meet with me tomorrow?" I felt slightly relieved and asked her, "Any particular time?" "Let's make it 9:00 am," she replied. I placed the phone on the receiver.

My stomach fluttered with activity. I went directly to the freezer and retrieved my best friend. There was always relief waiting for me and it never turned me away and after my usual dose of three shots, relief came. I sat down on the sofa and closed my eyes. So much had transpired in the last couple of days and thinking about it made my head spin. For the first time in many years I felt very unsure of myself. I found myself wishing I could go back to the academy before the transfer was offered to me. If I could magically go back, I would have stayed, taught my classes, returned to my office, shut my door and just wait for the day to end. But, that was fantasy and I knew it.

I turned on the television and closed my eyes to blot out the day. I slipped into an uneasy sleep. Just as always, there were the demons of my past come to break what little peace I felt. Always, the face of Teresa Carol Allen was there with the hole in the side of her face. Somewhere in there the face of Roosevelt Green would appear. Usually it was him strapped in the electric chair and giving his last statement. Next I would see the imagined face of Donna Dixon, the 17 year old victim of Timothy Wesley Mcorquodale. I never saw a picture of her, but she was there just the same. I felt sadness even in my dreams. The innocence of both these young women haunted me in my dreams and I never met either of them in person. It was no matter because they were real in my mind. Then somewhere in the dream I usually saw Timothy Wesley Mcorquodale standing there as I saw the words form on his lips, *"You know, Officer Allen, I respect you, but if you ever stood between me and that door I'd have to kill you."* Sometimes the words were different in my dream, but the context and the threat were just as real. When Roosevelt Green visited I would be taken back to the scene of him dancing in his cell to the Lionel Richie song, "you are."

They were all always there, but not always the same dream. I never heard the voices of the young women, but they were just as real. Teresa Carol Allen in particular because I saw pictures of her. Sometimes Jerome Bowden was there, happy one moment because of the stay of execution he received, but then crying the next because he was going back to death watch and finally his death in the chair. Then there was the face of Carl Isaacs; the butcher of the Alday family in South Georgia. His was the first face that was trapped in my memory from my first experience on death row; his cold dead eyes and the evil grin as he stared at me.

Finally my eyes snapped open and I heard the voices from the television as I came back to the conscious world. But, they were all burned into my mind. Faces, voices, situations from which there was no escape. I sat up and rubbed my face with my hands and said softly,

"This is not the way it's supposed to be." I sat for a moment gathering my composure. I remembered I had an appointment the following morning with the warden at Metro. I went to the bedroom to get my clothes ready for the following morning. I still had enough pride about myself that I needed to make sure the outside was clean. I told myself that if the outside looked clean and presentable, no one would know what was happening on the inside. The outside definitely did not match up with the inside and I needed to keep it that way.

After everything was done it was time for sleep. I'd already had one dream and I didn't want to be visited again. I went to the freezer in the kitchen. I thought that if I could numb myself enough, I could keep the dreams at bay. I took the usual three shots and walked out on the back porch to wait for the affect. I looked up at the stars and it gave me some peace of mind. The quiet of the night, the cool wind blowing in my face caused me to think about my father. I never wanted him to return to this world of pain, but it was times like these that I really needed to talk to him. Then I remembered the last moments of his life and the pain that I'd witnessed and I quickly dismissed the thought. I whispered into the night air, *"I hope you're happy Daddy."* The vodka was having the desired effect so I went to my bed. I set the clock and closed my eyes.

The alarm sounded and it felt as though I just closed my eyes. I laid there looking out of my bedroom window. The sunlight was coming through. I started to think about the day ahead of me and pondered about the upcoming meeting. It gave me butterflies and I knew the answer for that. Mercifully I didn't remember any dreams from the night. I dragged myself out of the bed and into the kitchen. I had a schedule to keep today so I didn't waste any time; three shots and then off to the shower. The warm water comforted me somewhat or was it the warmth I felt in my belly that was now causing my scalp to tingle? No matter, it was the relief that I welcomed.

Once I dressed, I went to the kitchen. While the rest of normal society was making coffee to start their day, I was mixing a drink in a large insulated cup with a straw. Once that task was complete, I headed out to the truck. I had a spring in my step from the vodka. I started the truck and lifted the top to the console to check for the mints I kept on hand masking my breath. A thought crossed my mind that caused me to chuckle. I'd once heard that no one could smell vodka because it was odorless. I wondered how many people had been discovered drinking holding to that logic. It was a leisurely drive to Atlanta. I was always careful to give myself time to make it early to any appointment and even more so today. I didn't want to risk speeding to draw attention from the police. The stretch of highway between Forsyth and Atlanta was a notorious speed trap. I turned on the stereo and set the cruise control. The warmth of the vodka, the music and the prospect of being offered a job today set the mood and I smiled. I convinced myself it was going to be a very positive day.

I saw the sign at the entrance that read "Metro Correctional Institution" and my heart started to race. I found a parking space, pulled in and turned off the truck. I had plenty of time so I sat there with the stereo on as I sipped my drink. I made sure to bring along the bottle for the trip home. Every scenario I could imagine was running through my mind. I'd met Ms. Rodriguez when I was an officer, but that was on my terms. Today I was in her home court and no idea what to expect. Finally I started sucking air at the end of the straw. The drink was finished and it was time to go inside. I popped a couple of mints in my mouth and stuck several in my pocket for later. I also kept a bottle of cologne in the truck so I sprayed some on before exiting the truck.

I checked in at the front gate and the officer allowed me in the waiting room near the administrative area. I could see that Metro was a much smaller institution than the diagnostic center. Since I'd taught for two years at the academy I was recognized by several officers who worked here and they stopped to say hello. I'd seen a lot of cadets during my time at the academy so I didn't remember everyone's name, but I did remember their faces. That caused a concern. I had taught a lot of these people and now I would be working side by side with them. It was a blow to my pride. I sat as patiently as I could, but I soon found myself wishing I could get in to Ms. Rodriguez's office quickly so that I could get this over with and get back to my truck. This was harder than I thought. Finally I was ushered into her office. She stood from behind her desk and offered me her hand. The captain of the institution was also present for the meeting and I recognized him. He had been a trainer when I attended firearms instructor school in Savannah. I shook her hand first and then shook the captain's hand and I waited for Ms. Rodriguez to sit, then I sat. We exchanged pleasantries first and then she went right into her questions. "I'd like to hear your version of what happened at the diagnostic center with Mr. Zant, if you don't mind." It wasn't really a request it was just her being polite.

I explained the morning's events from the day I was asked to leave the institution. I was very blunt and matter of fact about it. I knew that she probably already talked with Mr. Zant and she finally admitted she had. I wasn't sure of the content of their conversation, but apparently Mr. Zant was willing to talk to me about returning to the diagnostic center. Once she had set the stage, she asked me a direct question, "Before I offer you anything here, I need to know if you'd like to talk with Mr. Zant." The question caused the hair to stand up on the back of my head and I flatly answered, "NO!" I didn't want to offend her, but I was sure I never wanted to lay eyes on Zant again, especially after he ordered me out of his institution. She accepted that response and we moved on with her proposal.

"I wanted to offer you a sergeant's position, but we just filled two positions." She continued, "At this point all I can offer you is a C.O. II position. It was a corporal's rank just below sergeant. I saw it as the only way back into the department, but it would be a voluntary demotion. I thanked her for her consideration and accepted the position. We shook hands and she left me in the captain's hands. He was the one who would set my schedule. I was dismissed and told to report to the central warehouse at the training center in Forsyth to be issued uniforms. My badge was issued to me before I left Metro. I thanked the captain and started out to the parking lot to my truck. I shut the door and sat silently inside. I looked at the silver badge that listed "Correctional Officer" on the bottom along with the badge number. Just a few days ago, I had a gold badge with "Training Officer" on it. It bruised my ego, but none the less I was happy to have a job with the department.

I cranked the truck and drove away from the institution. Before I got onto the highway, I stopped at a store for a bottle of juice. I mixed the drink and got on the interstate. I wasn't sure if I was celebrating the job or nursing my pride. Either way, it didn't matter, I still needed the drink. I turned on the stereo and set the cruise control for the trip home. Just a few miles down the road and I was feeling the affect of the vodka. The buzz in my head allowed me to accept my new position. I started thinking of all that I could accomplish and how far I would go at Metro. By the time I arrived at the training center, I was on a high and looking forward to beginning my new position. I was issued uniforms and I went home to do the tailoring that I always performed on any of my clothing. Wearing a tailored uniform was something for which I was known. I was to report to Metro at eight am the following morning. After my alterations to my uniform, I went to mother's house to tell her the news. I could see the relief on her face and that made me feel relief as well. After moving up the ladder so quickly at the training center, I didn't want to disappoint her again.

The drive to Atlanta took almost an hour so I had an early wake up call. I went home and sat in front of the television while I nursed a drink to calm the butterflies inside. I knew I was going to have problems sleeping. Everything had happened so fast. As I sat in the dark and reminisced about the last few months, I began to understand just how far I had fallen. My family was gone. I was alone and the hardest part of it all was the knowledge that I caused it. Now I spiraled down even further with my career and in these moments when I was alone and looking back at my life, I became fearful. I no longer had the courage to face anything in my life without the help of alcohol. If I felt bad, I wanted to feel better. If I felt any happiness at all, I wanted to feel happier. Then I had to contend with the nightmares. I never knew what was coming each night when I closed my eyes. I knew I had to sleep tonight to be prepared for the following day. I went to the freezer for my relief. The usual three shots and then I went to the bedroom. I lay in the dark waiting for relief to come. I couldn't stand the silence so I reached over for the clock radio and turned it on to a station that played easy listening music. That and the vodka were having the desired effect. I closed my eyes and waited for sleep to come and said a silent prayer that the nightmares would stay away tonight.

The buzzing of the clock sounded and I reached over to hit the snooze button and lay back down. There had been no nightmares and I was grateful, but I could already feel the anxiety starting to build in anticipation of the day. It was enough to keep me from falling back to sleep. I turned the alarm off and headed for the shower. I dressed in the perfectly pressed, fit uniform and stared into the mirror. Two years passed since I wore this as a duty uniform. While at the academy, I'd only worn it as a dress uniform for special occasions. Looking at my reflection was another blow to my ego. But, I was committed now and I went to the kitchen. I stood staring at the freezer. I tried to talk myself out of reaching for the freezer, but in the end I knew I would make that move. I surrendered to the anxiety and opened the door. Three shots and I went to the back porch and stared at the sky.

It was still dark as I stood there waiting for the magic to happen. It came quickly and I started to feel embolden for the day ahead. I was starting my new job off on a cowardly note. Deep in the pit of my stomach I knew that I already failed. I went to the kitchen and mixed a drink in the insulated cup that was the symbol of my courage. I grabbed the bottle and walked out to my truck.

I arrived at Metro and sat in my truck in the parking lot as I stared at the entrance. There was a part of me that wanted to start the truck and go back home to hide. But, the thought of failing before I even started outweighed my fear. I sprayed the cologne, put two mints in my mouth, several for my pocket and went inside. I sat in the administrative area waiting for instructions. I was finally paired with an officer who I had trained at the academy just months before; another blow to my already fractured ego.

It seemed the first day was going to be orientation. I followed him around the institution while he went about his duties. He was very polite and professional and I don't think he ever noticed how uncomfortable I was. He was only out of the academy a few months and yet he had moved up through the ranks very quickly while I was just another correctional officer. As we walked through the institution I could tell the inmates were sizing me up. The discipline at metro in no way compared to that of the diagnostic center. I heard comments from the inmates as we walked. They clearly intended me to hear the comments although they were talking to each other. I heard one inmate say to his buddy, "He was a Jackson last week with a suit on." It was a condescending remark and not accurate at all. I never wore a suit at the diagnostic center, but I received the message he intended to deliver. I heard many more of the same type comments and it only reinforced my feelings of inadequacy. Deep inside, I felt like a miserable failure. I did not want to be here, but I felt trapped. I could not walk away from this opportunity no matter how much my ego suffered. I felt weak and unsure of myself. I sometimes felt as though I was on the outside of my body looking in and I didn't recognize the man I had become. At the diagnostic center I had been a sergeant on death row and Captain Treadwell had put a lot of faith in me. I was officer of the year for the entire state in 1986 and the road ahead seemed to be laid out for success. The academy only seemed to strengthen my career. However, in just two short years, I had fallen several rungs down the ladder. I was just another correctional officer doomed to live out a life in obscurity.

Over the next few weeks I was posted to several assignments around the institution. I was being given a crash course in familiarity with Metro. One such occasion, I found myself in a gun tower at 6:00 am. I remembered sitting there watching the institution bathed in darkness and no movement anywhere. It had been years since I manned a gun post. As I stared into the darkness, a rush of fear and uncertainty flooded over me and I said out loud to myself, *"I just don't want this anymore."* I felt shame and embarrassment at how far I had fallen. I was almost driven to tears as I thought about my predicament.

My personal life was in shambles As well. I was still in an uncertain, loose relationship with Crystal from the academy. I didn't love her and was only going through the motions of a meaningful relationship so I wouldn't have to be alone. Being alone frightened me more than anything because I felt that if that ever happened, I would be trapped in my mind with the nightmares and visions. My mind was my true enemy. I had stopped getting the twins or Kimberly on the weekends I was scheduled to have them. Even though they were only children, I couldn't bear to look in their sweet faces because of the guilt I felt. I still visited Miki at Debbie's home from time to time. That only served to make me feel less adequate as a man, because I still wanted Debbie to come back home but I had destroyed any chance of that happening. However, Debbie still treated me with compassion and tenderness. I suspected she still had feelings for me, but was just too afraid to pursue any kind of relationship with me. The worse part of that was in knowing that I was the cause of it all.

It was during that vulnerable time that my life changed forever. I was drinking every day, working or not working. I could no longer look at myself in the mirror without feeling hate and disgust at what looked back. I drank from the time I woke in the morning until the moment I laid my head on the pillow at night. Sometimes I even woke up in the middle of the night, when the nightmares were more than I could bear, with a rush of fear and I had to drink to go back to sleep. Fear and contempt were the feelings that followed me through each waking

moment of my life and most nights even into my dreams. There seemed to be no escape for me. I was locked away in a prison in my mind from which there seemed to be no escape.

At my lowest point a phone call came that changed my life forever. I was off work that day and lying in the bed staring at the ceiling caught up in self condemnation. I jumped when the phone rang next to my bed. I rubbed my eyes and reached for the phone. It was Deedee, the twin's mother. Deedee had remarried shortly after our divorce and was moving on with her life and she deserved that. I wanted that for her because at that moment, she was the stability in Leighanne and Tracey's lives. "Hello?" She wasted no time with pleasantries and got to the point. She detested me and I knew it. "We'd like to go forward with the adoption of the twins." It struck a nerve in my heart and I sat up in the bed. "Can I call you back, Deedee I just woke up," I said. It was a lie but, I needed to clear my head before I said anything. "Yes, that will be fine," she replied. I hung up the phone. I needed to get to the freezer so I could numb my brain. I couldn't even consider her question sober. I took the usual three shots and waited. Relief wasn't coming fast enough so I downed another three shots and finally calmed down. I walked out on the back porch because I needed some air. When I found my intoxicated composure, I went back to the bedroom and stared at the telephone. Deedee had asked me about this before and I very quickly dismissed it telling her there was no way I would ever surrender my parental rights.

As the alcohol moved through my veins and into my brain, I considered her statement. I was a lousy father and had been a worse husband. It seemed that anything I touched or was a part of was a disaster. A tear formed in the corner of my right eye. I knew that all my girls deserved a family that loved them and more importantly a father that was home for them. I knew the best thing I could do for them was to bow out of their life and allow them to be happy. I couldn't do it sober so I returned to the kitchen and downed another three shots. I stared out the window into the yard where I had spent time with all of my girls. I looked as my mind visualized the happy moments when I was married to Debbie and we had them all for the weekend. Slowly the vision faded away as I realized I was becoming a stranger to my children. I said a prayer that God would allow me to do what was best for them.

Now feeling the full affect of the alcohol, I returned to the bedroom, sat on the side of the bed trying to muster the courage to pick up the phone. I dialed the phone quickly before I lost my nerve. I could tell she was anticipating the phone call because she answered right away. I had to act quickly before I changed my mind or lost my composure, "Ok, Deedee, I'll do what you want." She replied, "Thank you, Bobby." I responded as quickly as I could, "Deedee, please take care of the girls and let them know I'm doing this because I want them to be happy." She told me she would, but I had the feeling that she wouldn't. She continued, "I'll set it up with the attorney and let you know when to meet with him." "Alright," I replied. I hung up the phone without saying anything else.

I lay back in the bed and covered my eyes with my arm. Tears ran down the side of my cheeks. My mind was racing with images of the girls as babies in the hospital and through the years as they grew. I was feeling very sorry for myself and tried to convince myself that this would be best for them. I thought to myself that maybe they could have a normal life and wouldn't have to watch me slowly destroy myself. I couldn't take the silence of the room any longer. I went to the kitchen and mixed a strong drink in the insulated cup. I dressed and took my drink outside to walk in the yard. I couldn't sit still and I needed the fresh air.

As I walked and sipped the drink through the straw, I finally started to relax, but I could not get the twins' faces out of my mind. I instinctively knew that I was going to be haunted by the decision I had just made.

As I walked in the yard I heard a voice over my shoulder, "What's wrong?" It was my mother. Her instincts told her that something was wrong and she was always right. As I walked over to her deck where she sat, I was telling myself that there was no way I could share the decision I just made. I knew she would find out eventually, but I didn't have the courage to look her in the eye and tell her so I lied to her. It was something that was becoming second nature to me to avoid any confrontation with anyone. "I just felt like walking and getting some air," I said. I don't know if she believed me or not, but she accepted my answer. I sat down and talked with her a bit. Maybe it was the effect that mother's have on all their children, but I started to relax just listening to her voice. I don't know if she noticed how evasive I was being or how I avoided eye contact with

In any event, I couldn't do it any longer. I was afraid that the more I drank, the harder it would be to control my emotions. I excused myself and went back to my home. I was off for the next three days and spent the majority of it alone in my home. I watched movies on the VCR just to have the company of another voice. Deedee finally called and told me that the documents concerning the twins were ready. Just talking about it made my stomach hurt. I did my usual preparations of three shots and mixed a drink for the trip to town. I felt uneasy through the short drive. I finally arrived at the attorney's office and sat in the parking lot staring out the window and listening to the soft easy listening music. Nothing helped calm me; not the alcohol, the music or the fresh air. I finally accepted that I was as close to peace as I was going to get. I downed the rest of the drink quickly and opened the door before I changed my mind.

The attorney explained the documents to me, but I barely comprehended what he said. I just needed to know where to sign so I could put this traumatic situation behind me and get out the door. As he looked at me while he explained everything, I wondered what he was thinking. I imagined that he was thinking what a sorry excuse for a father I was. I finally realized that it was my own perception that I was feeling. I felt a lump form in my throat. I wasn't sure if I was going to be able to keep my composure. Finally I heard him ask, "Mr. Allen, do you understand?" I was lost in my thoughts and completely lost touch with reality for a moment. I realized I had been staring at the documents and not completely aware of what he had said. I couldn't bear to listen to the explanation again, so I said, "Yes, I understand."He turned the documents in my direction and showed me where to sign. I completed it all as quickly as I could and turned the documents back to him. Then he explained that I would receive a copy of the documents after the judge signed them. I smiled an insincere smile at him and thanked him. I was already getting up from my chair as I shook his hand. I exited the door as quickly as I could and headed to my truck. I needed a drink more than I ever needed one before.

I sat there feeling numb from the top of my head to the bottom of my feet. I couldn't wait to stop at a store for a bottle of juice. I reached under my seat for my stash, unscrewed the top and took three quick shots directly from the bottle. I choked as it burned going down. Drinking vodka without a chaser was something which I was not accustomed. I just needed relief as quickly as I could get it. I rolled the window down for the fresh air. I cranked the

truck and turned the stereo up. I needed to block out what I had just done so I took the back roads home and drove slow.

The remainder of my off days I stayed alone in my home, drinking from the time I woke up until I lay down at night. I'd walk out on the back porch at night while I was intoxicated to get some air. The stars late at night somehow comforted me. It was as if the darkness shielded me. I'd say a quick prayer in the hopes that God would hear me, but I felt God was disappointed with me. Mother would call me during the day to check on me, but I lied to her and said I wasn't feeling well. I didn't want to be around anyone, especially my mother, because I was so paranoid and thought even just a look from my mother and she would know what I'd done.

My days off came to an end and I knew I had to report for duty the following morning. I took a long hot, soaking bath with a drink in hand. I stared at the ceiling and let the water run over my feet. The water was comforting somehow. I spent about an hour in the tub drinking and listening to soft, easy listening music. I finally got out of the tub and prepared for bed. I'd already ironed my uniform for the next day. I still had enough pride to keep to the image that everyone was used to. But, I knew I was hiding behind a lie. I didn't want anyone to see past the exterior. It took more energy than I expected to keep up appearances.

I went through the motions at work, but I had no interest at all in what I was doing. The Captain had given me an administration assignment to work with the deputy warden of security who was responsible for the disciplinary committee. I assisted him with his documentation in the committee. As the inmates appeared before him, I handed him the particular files and made notes after his findings. It was a promising move on behalf of the Captain and the warden, but I just was not interested in any of it. After my decision about the twins, I felt like a ship on the ocean that lost the wind for the sails and was simply drifting with no direction or purpose. When I wasn't off and drinking, I was thinking about it during the day and counting the hours when I could get to the truck and relive my anxiety.

Once I was off, I couldn't get to the truck fast enough. The routine was now waiting for the parking lot to clear so I could take the bottle and drink three shots then on to the store for juice to mix a drink for the drive home. After mixing the drink, I took a big pull on the straw several times until I felt the warm relief of the vodka going down and then the tingle that followed all the way to my head. It was like waiting for a lover to caress me and allowing me to relax.

My routine was the same every day. My only concern was not allowing my breath to give me away. If anyone ever smelled alcohol on me, that would be the end. I wasn't so concerned about losing the job as I was about not having a paycheck to buy my next fix of vodka. I had no life, I was only existing in a world that I was convinced didn't want me anymore. God seemed so far away and my prayers became words that I just flung into the air because I was felt as though God didn't want to hear from me.

As if I hadn't sunk low enough, on one of my off days I got a phone call from Sarah. She had remarried and was moving on with her life as well. I was the only one who seemed to be not moving forward. In fact, in many ways, I felt like I was moving backwards. Sarah told me that her new husband wanted to adopt Kimberly. She was calling to ask me to surrender my parental rights. It hit me hard, but I took this as divine intervention and not some wild coincidence. I believed that God was watching over my innocent children because I could no longer do it. I closed my eyes and told Sarah that I would do it. She thanked me

for allowing her and Kimberly to move on with their lives and said she would contact me when she had the papers ready.

Sitting in darkness on my off days was becoming the norm for me. I thought about Miki and how long it would be before Debbie asked me to give her up. I didn't love any of my girls more than the others, but Miki was my baby. I stared out the kitchen window into the sunlight, but I wanted no part of it. I wanted to hide in darkness. Everything I loved, everything I worked for was disappearing from my life one piece at a time. I had lit the fuse of self destruction. Every day came closer to the bomb going off and I wondered if that was when the end of my life would come. Probably the worst feeling of all was that I wasn't afraid. I wondered if that would bring peace to me and everyone in my life. It caused me to think about Bruce Lee and his favorite song by the group, Blood, sweat and tears, "And when I die." It speaks of finding peace in death and hoping the time is near. I didn't have a real thought of killing myself, but I wondered if that was the only way I would find peace. I had become such a disturbance in the life of those I loved. I think that was the first time I considered dying as a way out. I wondered if my not being here would be better for my family if I wasn't roaring in and out of their lives like a vicious storm. Blowing in interrupting their lives, disturbing their peace and then off again like a hurricane that blew itself out leaving them in my wake. That's certainly what I had done for Leighanne, Tracey and Kimberly. My only peace with the decision I had made was the hope that they would be happy and have some stability in their lives without me.

It only took a week for Sarah to get papers from the attorney. I was spared having to sit in front of another lawyer having him explain how I was giving my child away. Sarah called me when everything was ready and I traveled to south Atlanta where she and Kimberly were living with her new husband. We met at a parking lot and I was so relieved that she was alone. I wanted to see Kimberly, but I didn't know if I had the courage to see her as I signed away my rights. Sarah was sympathetic and promised me that she would take care of Kimberly. In the years since our marriage we became cordial to each other. She even wanted me to stay and talk to her after we took care of our business. We visited for a few minutes, but I couldn't take it very long. I finally made an excuse that I made plans for the evening and needed to get back home, which was a lie.

It was a solemn ride home and of course, I was drinking. I had never felt so out of place in my life. Three of my children were gone and all I had left was Miki. I tried to cheer myself up by thinking that I would be the best father I could be to Miki, but it really wasn't helping. The thought that my girls would not grow up together made me feel even worse. At Miki's age she would probably never remember anything about Leighanne, Tracey and Kimberly. I finally made it home and went inside alone. Mother called in the next few minutes to ask if I wanted to come over and sit on the deck. I lied again and told her I was about to go to bed early because I had to work the next morning. I did have to work, but there would be no rest for me tonight. I turned on the TV for company and went to the kitchen. I mixed a strong drink and went to the back porch. It was a safe place. The security light was nearby and my only view was the woods. I could pretend that I was alone in the wilderness.

I finally pulled myself away from the darkness to get my uniform ready for the next morning. I was in the bedroom ironing, but I could hear the TV in the living room. Even with the voices it was difficult to stay out of my mind. My mind raced constantly and most

times the only relief came with the alcohol. I could never sleep without powering down my mind with alcohol. If I drank too much the nightmares came with the accusing fingers of long dead demons pointing at me with sinister smiles. Restful sleep was not a part of my life at that time. Now I had new nightmares that added to the arsenal already being used against me; my children. I lay in the bed with my eyes wide open staring into the darkness. I tried to focus on the music and wait for sleep to find me. The time I had to wait always depended on how much alcohol was consumed. If I was lucky, the nightmares would be short and the morning would arrive to save me. I finally closed my eyes and took deep breaths. Somewhere in that process I dozed off.

The alarm sounded and I didn't feel rested at all. I lay there trying to muster the energy to get out of the bed. I dozed off again, but soon awakened with a jolt of fear. I was shaking, but I wasn't sure why. I finally drug myself out of the bed and into the shower. After the warm water hit me, I stopped shaking. But, as soon as I dried off, it returned. I shaved and went to the bedroom for my uniform to get dressed. I stood there staring at the shined badge and hardware on my uniform. I looked at the neatly pressed creases in my trousers and then down to the spit shined boots. The longer I stood there looking, the more I hated it. A thought I had when I was assigned to the gun tower at Metro revisited me; *"I just don't want this anymore."* As I reached for the uniform, I stopped and dropped my hand by my side and stepped backward to sit on the bed.

In my mind I knew I wasn't going to work today. I didn't even try to talk myself out of it. I finally went to the kitchen and reached for the freezer. Three shots and then I went to the living room to turn on the TV. I needed the company of voices as I tried to muster courage to make a phone call. Three more shots and then I went to the phone to do my duty. I dialed the number for Metro and asked to speak to the Captain. At that time of the morning he was in his office so I was put through quickly. When he answered I spoke quickly before I lost the nerve and hung up, "Captain, this is Bobby Allen, I won't be in today because I'm not feeling well." I didn't feel well, but not for the reasons I led him to believe. When he replied I could tell that he was not pleased. "We are having an inspection and we were counting on you to help us get ready for that." I apologized for it, but it wasn't sincere. He said, "We'll see you tomorrow then," and hung up the phone. I said softly; "No you won't."I went to the kitchen for the vodka to continue what I began. Three shots and then I mixed a drink. I went to the sofa, sat down and looked at the TV as I formulated a plan. I really didn't want any of it anymore. I was done with corrections particularly at Metro. I was no longer part of the elite. I was just a correctional officer at an obscure institution. The thought of spending another day there made my stomach hurt.

I relaxed as the alcohol took control. I didn't want to stay at home. I felt an incredible need to escape and get as far away as I could. I didn't want to be around anything familiar that would remind me of the life in which I was trapped. I dressed and packed an overnight bag. I meant to escape today if even for a few days. My heart was racing almost to the point of panic. I grabbed my overnight bag and headed out the door with no clear plan of where I was going. I started my truck and drove the back road to town with drink in hand. It was a cool morning so I let my window down to take in the fresh air as the stereo played. The serene cow pastures helped me relax.

My first stop was the bank to get money out of the ATM for my trip. I had credit cards also, but I wanted cash as well. I didn't want anything interrupting my get away. With cash in hand, I headed south through the country roads with which I was familiar. The soft music, the sunshine, the fresh air, my best friend vodka and the knowledge that I was leaving my life behind for the next few days allowed me to feel at peace. I let the alcohol do its job and I began to relax. I looked up at the sun and said a prayer asking God to guide my trip and protect those I left behind; my mother and my children. I had no plan for how long I would be gone. For now, I just followed the road and listened to the music.

After about an hour, I had to make a decision about my destination. I found a small town in South Georgia. There wasn't much traffic and very few buildings. It was a typical small Georgia town. I found the nearest motel and booked a room for the night. I went to the room and looked around. It was just what I needed, completely unfamiliar surroundings. I threw my bag to the side, turned on the TV and lay back on the bed. I closed my eyes in an effort to block out my life and what I left behind. But, it was torture. The faces of all four of my girls flashed through my mind. I couldn't stop thinking about them or seeing their faces. A single tear rolled down the side of my cheek. I opened my eyes, stood up and went to the sink. I ran some cold water in my hands and splashed it in my face then looked in the mirror. As I stared at myself I reached a conclusion and said softly, *"you'll never run far enough to stop seeing their faces."* Then the realization hit me that maybe I should never be able to run that far.

I mixed a drink and went to my truck. I was still too sober to remain still. I needed to move in a feeble attempt to keep my thoughts at bay. I needed new images to focus on. I drove through the small town and finally came to a small state park. I pulled in to enjoy the scenery. I parked and got out with my cup in hand. The sun felt good on my face and the air was fresh and clean. I closed my eyes and listened to the birds singing. I thought to myself, *"It would be nice, just for today, if I could feel the peace that they seem to have."* Eventually my thoughts caught up with me and I felt compelled to move. So I was back to the truck and on the road again.

Evening came and as the sun set; I took in the peacefulness of small town life. There were very few cars moving through town. It seemed everyone was preparing for the night and I thought I should do the same. I stopped at a fast food restaurant for a burger then back to my room. I left the TV on purposely so that when I entered the room I'd hear voices. I kicked off my shoes and sat at the small table. I took a few bites of the burger and fries I'd bought, but that was all I could manage. I left it at the table and mixed a drink in one of the disposable cups provided by the motel. I downed it quickly and mixed another and lay on the bed to watch the TV.

Somewhere between the drink and the lull of the TV, I drifted into an uneasy sleep. That was to be the order for the night. TV voices incorporated into my dreams or visions, I wasn't sure which. The alcohol was in control of whatever I was experiencing. I saw my father first alive, but with the knowledge that he had to return to his grave. My mother flashed briefly through then it was the faces of my girls laughing and enjoying the outdoors of my home. I finally was at the H-5 execution chamber. I saw the holding cell and through the open door to the right, I could see an empty electric chair. There was a file in my hand so I opened it. There on the first page was the picture of Teresa Carol Allen lying on the autopsy table with that hole in the side of her face. I looked up from the file and my eyes fixed on the holding cell directly in front of me. Teresa Carol Allen sat on the lone bed in the cell. A chill ran down my spine as she looked up slowly from the floor and into my eyes. I couldn't move as I stared at her. After what seemed like an eternity, she said, "You promised me you would never forget." I jumped up from the bed with my eyes wide open and for a few seconds I was unsure if I was awake or still asleep. I was disoriented and then the voices of the TV slowly came into my waking mind.

I reached over to the table and quickly downed what was left of the drink I had mixed. It wasn't sufficient, so I quickly got up from the bed to mix another in the small cup. I filled it mostly with vodka and a small amount of juice to dilute the harsh taste of the alcohol. I downed it quickly, put my hands on the counter and looked down at the sink because I couldn't bear to see myself in the mirror. I considered the dream I'd just had with the face of Teresa Carol Allen. I recalled a conversation I had with Captain Treadwell concerning my promotion to training officer and now his words echoed in my mind, "If I were you, I'd stay right there in that trailer park and make lieutenant here at Jackson." I wondered if those were words I should have heeded. If I'd done that, I might still be working on death row and still be the voice of those who had been killed.

Now I looked up into the mirror and gazed into my eyes looking for an answer that I wasn't sure I possessed. Then I recalled the words of the Lieutenant on death row who told me just prior to leaving for the training center; "Are you sure you want to go there, there's going to be a lot of politics down there." As I studied my face I came to the realization that I had probably made a very big mistake. My place should have been on death row. There had been politics at the training center and I got caught up in it allowing my success to go to my head. The two years I'd been there were all about my selfish goals and when the cards were finally laid on the table; I had a really bad hand. When I was the clerk on death row, I had made a silent promise to those murdered innocent people that they would never be forgotten and somehow I'd keep their memories alive. Now my career lay in ruins behind me and I faced an uncertain future.

I walked outside to the darkness and looked up at the sky as I usually did when I had no answers for my life. All I could manage from my lips were the words, "I'm sorry, Lord, please forgive me." I did what so many spiritual people do when they are on a path that was laid before them. I thanked God for his help, but told him that I have this now. Being the loving God that He is, he allowed me to go my own way and stood back to observe at the mess I created in the next two years after I made that decision. I knew he was still here, but I was ashamed to ask him for help again, especially after I turned away from him to pursue my interest instead of allowing his plan for my life to unfold. In the aftermath of that selfish decision, I allowed the voices of those who died to go silent.

I returned to the room and continued what I started. I had to close my eyes and get some rest. I drank until I passed out. It lasted only a couple of hours and I was awake again. I lay there drinking and listening to the TV. Finally I saw a ray of light shine through the part in the curtains. I forced myself out of the bed and into the bathtub. I wanted to feel the warm water around my body. As the tub filled, I lay back and let my head emerge in the warmth. My mind was at work with only one thing in mind; get away and keep moving. In just one night I found the walls of the motel room as much a prison as the walls of my home.

Now that the tub was filled and the water not running, my mind started racing thinking about the dream I'd had the night before; the faces of my parents and finally the face of

Teresa Carol Allen. I couldn't take the silence because my mind would betray me. I got out of the tub and dressed not even bothering to shave. I had no need for hygiene because I knew I would see no one that I knew. I didn't care what strangers thought about me at that point. That was another line I crossed deeper into darkness because my outward appearance helped me to hide my inner feelings. With that gone, people would begin to see the scared man inside and my illusion would crumble.

That was my routine for the next four days. Drive to find new surroundings and hide from my real life. I didn't contact anyone, not even my poor mother. I didn't stay in one place more than one night because if I did, reality would catch up with me. It was an insatiable drive to keep moving and not look back. On the fourth day a moment of clarity peeked through and I realized I couldn't run forever. I started to drive north and toward home. When I finally reached Macon, I was gripped with fear. I was in familiar surroundings and the illusion was crumbling. I made one final stop before going home. I rented a room, turned the TV on and crashed on the bed. I didn't even bother to bring my bag in from the truck. The vodka was all I required. I closed my eyes and my head was swirling. Images from the last four days raced through my mind. There was only one cure for that and I reached for it. I poured a drink into the small cup provided and downed it quickly. I relaxed a bit and lay back down allowing the voices from the TV to fill my thoughts.

I woke up sometime later not even bothering to check the clock. I never slept more than a couple of hours at a time. At this point, every time I woke up I was gripped in fear. I was still intoxicated and as I lay there, I reached up with my right hand into the air and just said, "Please help me, Lord." Then I passed out again. I'd unintentionally left the curtains open and the next time I woke, the sun was bearing down on my face. I hated the daylight. In the darkness I felt like I was hidden from the rest of the world. The daylight seemed to shine a spotlight on me for the entire world to see. I drug myself out of bed and went to the sink to splash water into my face. I ran the cool water through my hair and rubbed my eyes.

I lay the key on the table and got the only personal item I brought in; the vodka. I squinted at the sun as I made my way to the truck. It was a beautiful morning, but made me nauseas. Nothing of beauty mattered to me anymore. It was darkness that I craved. I just wanted to hide from everything and everybody. I sat in the truck in silence as my mind raced. I started the truck and went to the nearest store for a mixer for my vodka. Once I purchased that, I sat in the truck and mixed a drink. I'd brought one of the small cups from the motel with me. It was the perfect size for a quick rush and I needed it to come as quickly as possible. At this point, it was the only way I could quiet my mind and continue with the day. I started toward home and this time I instinctively took the interstate. After the last four days, I was acting purely on instinct. Trying to formulate any type of plan in my mind caused my head to hurt. I had a pain behind both eyes from the sunlight and I reached for my sunglasses. It suddenly became clear to me that I was suffering from mental exhaustion.

I'd made this same drive many times in the last twenty years. I'd driven a few miles before I realized how quiet it was. I reached over and turned on the stereo. I was so tired I didn't want to think. I needed outside stimulation and I felt that if I didn't get it I would drive the truck into the woods off the interstate just to end the silence. Images, faces flooded my mind and made me dizzy. I wondered if this was the beginning of insanity. Is this how it

starts when one loses his mind? I finally made it to the exit that led home. There was a dirt road nearby and I made my way there. It was one of the roads that I used quite frequently to drive on when I was drinking and listening to the stereo. The soft music mixed with the country road surrounded by trees and my vodka was the only way I could escape. I stopped the truck near an old wooden bridge with a small stream running underneath.

I walked over to the bridge to watch and listen to the water running underneath and it helped me relax. My mind started to wander as the water rushed by. The faces of my girls' appeared in my mind, but this time they seemed distant. I was having trouble focusing on the water. Everything seemed blurry. That's when the first tear ran down my cheek. Then another until both eyes were now streaming. I fought hard not to lose my composure. I shook my head and rubbed the tears from my eyes. I went to the truck and mixed a drink in the cup. I downed it and poured another. I did that two more times until I was satisfied that my mind was numb. I reached in for the half gallon bottle of vodka that was near empty. I threw it as far as I could into the woods.

Filled with fake courage, I drove home. I had run as far as I could and it didn't solve anything. When I turned into my driveway it occurred to me that I was right back where my journey began. I parked and went into my home. Everything was just as I left it, yet it all seemed foreign now. I sat on the sofa and the phone rang. I knew it was my mother and I allowed it to continue ringing so I could gather my thoughts. I had no idea what to say to her. Once it stopped, I waited a few seconds and then reached for it. I had to call her back or else she would come over and I didn't want to face anyone right now. It only rang once before she picked up. "Bobby, are you alright?" "Yes, mother I'm fine," I replied. "Where have you been?" "I just needed to get away for a few days," I said. I wanted the call to be over as quickly as possible so I continued, "I'll come over and explain everything in a little while." She knew I was in no mood to talk and accepted my answer. She heard my voice and that was really what she wanted.

As I walked over to mother's house I could see her sitting on the deck. That was our meeting place and where we both enjoyed spending time together. We'd sat there many nights in the cool night air looking at the stars and talking. It was late afternoon and I didn't really want to talk, but I knew she wouldn't rest until she saw me and had some type of explanation. I didn't bother to sit down because I knew I wouldn't be here long. I continued the excuse about needing to get away for a few days, but there was no way I could tell her what I was struggling with in my mind. If I'd shared that with her, she would know that I wasn't really alright. I talked with her as long as I dared. I told her I was tired and needed to sleep and I would talk with her tomorrow.

I returned home to the sofa. It wasn't long before the gravity of my situation started to weigh down on me. My mind began to awake from the alcohol and started to scream at me. I went to the kitchen, but then remembered that I had thrown out the last of my vodka in a feeble attempt to return to normalcy on my own. It wasn't working. I paced around my home until I couldn't take it anymore. I grabbed up my keys from the counter and I was off to town to find the relief I desperately needed. I drove the quickest route to town. I kept my thoughts at bay the last four days with alcohol and now I found myself almost in a panic. My mind was racing and thoughts came so fast I couldn't keep up with them. My eyes fell to the speedometer and I saw that I was speeding well over the speed limit. I eased my foot off of the accelerator because in my condition, I couldn't be stopped by the police. I wouldn't make it through a night in jail with my thoughts attacking me.

The liquor store was like a long lost friend. I tried to contain myself and not look like I was in a panic. I slowed to a fast walk. I grabbed the object of my relief, a mixer and a disposable cup to go along with it. I made it to the counter and as the clerk was placing my purchase in a bag, I was reaching for my wallet. When I held it before me, I found that I was shaking. I wasn't sure if it was anticipation or the absence of alcohol in my system. I didn't attempt to analyze the feeling; I grabbed up the package and went to my truck. I had my prize and I wasn't worried about appearances. Once inside I closed the door and I caught my reflection in the rearview mirror. I could see sweat running down my forehead from my hair line. I ran my hand across the back of my head and found my hair was completely drenched. I didn't have time to consider anything but filling my cup with vodka and just enough mixer to dilute the bitter aftertaste of the alcohol. I downed it quickly, sat back with my eyes closed and waited for relief. It wasn't coming fast enough so I repeated the procedure and downed another cup. Slowly I began to relax. I started the truck and drove toward home on the dirt roads with stereo on and drink in hand. By the time I made it home, I was beginning to relax, but not as relaxed as I needed to be. I took my package inside, mixed another drink and put the rest in the freezer. I turned on the TV and sat on the sofa. I knew I could not be alone with my thoughts. I needed voices from the TV and alcohol to keep my mind from attacking me. I thought about Metro and the job with which I was entrusted. It made my stomach hurt. I could not even fathom returning there. I said those words out loud that I had thought in the gun tower that early morning, *"I just don't want it anymore."*

I lay my head back on the sofa and closed my eyes. The alcohol had done its job and I was no longer sweating. My mind was being merciful at the moment and images were not attacking me. I could hear the voices from the TV as though they were coming from another room. I was lost at the moment. Not asleep, but not fully awake either. I seemed to be floating. I drifted in darkness listening to the TV. I have no idea how long I lingered there. My body jerked me to consciousness and I opened my eyes. It took me a few moments to focus. There was a commercial on TV that caught my attention. It was from an alcohol and drug recovery center nearby. I'd seen the commercial before, but quickly dismissed it. Now, I sat up, rubbed my eyes and forced myself to focus on the message. It came through loud and clear; *"The healing begins the moment you call."*

I quickly reviewed my life to this point. I was definitely on a downward spiral with no end in sight. My life was in shambles. I felt exhausted and I needed some relief, but had no idea where to turn next. I only knew I did not want to return to metro. I wanted to hide, get away from this life I created for myself. I walked over to the freezer and did my routine. Vodka, mixer and downed the drink. I looked out the window as dusk settled in. I mixed another and went to the back porch. I looked up to see the first stars of the night beginning to appear. That's when I asked the question, *"Lord, are you pointing the way for me?"* I suddenly felt a calmness inside that I hadn't felt in a long time. I finished the drink and went inside. I mixed another before reaching for the phone book. I looked up the number of the facility. I took a drink and then dialed the number hoping that someone would answer. A voice answered on the other end. I had no idea what to say, so I just told the person how I had been feeling. The female voice said, "You've made the first step on your own, now let me help you make the next one and you won't be alone anymore."

Chapter 15

*"Turn to me and be gracious to me, for I am lonely and afflicted.
Relieve the troubles of my heart and free me from my anguish."*

*- Psalm 25:16,17
-(New International version)*

I finished the bottle of vodka the same night I made the phone call. Whether from exhaustion, the vodka or a combination of the two, I slept a little easier in the night. I woke the next morning and got myself ready for the trip. The rehabilitation center was located in Dublin, a small town just south of Macon. I was ready for a change. I needed to be far away from Metro and my home. I had no idea what was going to happen, but I needed a new environment. The facility was located in a wooded area just off of the highway. It didn't resemble a hospital at all. The grounds were well kept and it had a serene appearance. The fear of the unknown caused a knot to form in my stomach. I took my luggage and went to the office. There was of course, paperwork to fill out. Then I was escorted to the rear of the building. It was very pleasant decor with a lounge area, but there was also a long counter at the center. Even though they weren't dressed the part, I could tell that the ladies behind the counter were medical staff. They were very polite and introduced themselves. I was taken to a room very close to the counter. I was told that I would be in a "detox" room for at least two days and I needed to be monitored medically before I actually entered the program. Once my personal property was inventoried, I was sent to see the medical doctor. He asked me about the amount of alcohol I had been drinking. I recounted the last 4 days for him and told him I drank continuously. He prescribed some medication that would keep me from shaking while my body withdrew from alcohol.

I went back to the counter to ask how long I would be here and was told twenty eight to thirty days. Although I had reservations about the length of my stay, at least I would have a break from Metro. At that moment I had no idea how I was going to handle that situation. I only knew I didn't want to go back. I thought to myself, *"Ill cross that bridge when I come to it."* I heard a door open behind me and I turned to see a group of people emerging from a room. They were talking and laughing as the dispersed. A young man came over to me and put out his hand as introduced himself. I smiled and thanked him for welcoming

me. He sat down beside me and asked, "So, what's your drug of choice?" I was confused for a moment, but then I realized what he was asking. I replied, "I'm a vodka drinker," not knowing if that answered his question. It did and he continued the conversation, "So, no drugs?" "No," I replied. He readily told me his drug of choice was marijuana. Now I was beginning to understand. We talked for a few minutes until he saw the group of people moving back to the room they had exited and he smiled and said, "Well, it's time for group," and excused himself.

One of the medical staff came over to me with a stack of books wrapped in plastic and said, "This is the material you'll need while you're here." I took the items to my room and opened them. There were books about alcoholism and drug use. I'd heard the term alcoholic in a TV commercial before, but never thought it applied to me. I wasn't even sure what it really meant. When I attended the D.U.I. school after I was stopped in 1986, there was some mention of addiction, but that was it. I thumbed through the books and realized that I was in a new realm of reality.

I was in a "detox" room for two days, then moved into a regular room. I had a roommate and started to attend groups. There was a combination of open discussion groups and lectures to teach everyone about addiction. During the discussion groups when others talked about their circumstances, I realized I had more in common with these people than I originally thought. The only difference I could see was they didn't talk about nightmares. The alcohol was out of my system, but the nightmares remained. I didn't sleep through the nights and I didn't talk about my nightmares. It was a reservation I couldn't move beyond. I was interviewed by a psychiatrist only once and I was not honest about everything. I was assigned an individual counselor and we met once per week.

During one of our sessions, He told me that he had talked with Mattie Rodriguez at Metro and she told him that there was no one in the department of corrections with more charisma than Bobby Allen. I couldn't believe what I was hearing. I certainly didn't have any idea that anyone felt that way about me. I had such a low opinion of myself I assumed that everyone looked at me that way. But, then I was reminded of what I'd heard several female students say about me in the past; *"There's just something about you."* After the meeting with the counselor, it haunted me. If God had given me any special gift, I did not embrace it. In fact, I often rebelled against God and used it for my own personal gain. Now I sat here in silence trapped in my own thoughts without alcohol to numb my guilt.

I was introduced to Alcoholics Anonymous in the evenings. People from Local groups came into the facility to conduct the meetings. The idea was to get us used to attending meetings in the community. I listened to what they had to say without ever sharing any of my personal stories. I merely went through the motions. One thing I did notice during my stay at the facility was that my body was beginning to tighten up. I told my counselor about how I felt and he explained that alcohol could break down the elasticity in my skin and muscles and that detoxing from it allowed my body to heal itself.

I stayed at the rehabilitation center for thirty days. The day I was to leave, there was a special group so that others could say good bye. As they took turns giving me their comments, I was amazed. Several of them commented of the inner strength they saw in me. As they spoke, I felt as though they were describing someone else. I wished I could embrace what they claimed to see in me. Even going thirty days without alcohol, I still felt as empty

inside as the day I arrived. But hiding my inner feelings was something I had mastered completely. I smiled, thanked them all and went to my room to pack for the trip home.

Once outside and away from my peers, that old familiar feeling of emptiness started to slip over me. I was alone again and not able to rely on the comments of my new friends. I cranked my truck and allowed the engine to warm. I stared out the window for one last look at the beautiful grounds I was about to leave. I drove toward the interstate that would take me home. All of the insecurity, doubt, self loathing and fear began to creep up on me and once again, I was alone. I saw a convenient store to my right and the sign advertising cold beer. I felt a panic coming on as I steered the truck into the parking lot. I sat in the truck several minutes with the air conditioning blowing in my face. Even so, sweat still streamed down over my eyebrows. My mind was racing with everything I learned over the last thirty days. But, the fear was overwhelming.

I turned off the truck and went inside before I could talk myself out of it. I reached into the cooler for a six pack. I stayed there a few seconds to allow the cool air from the cooler to blow into my warm face. I paid at the counter and left the store quickly with my package tucked under my arm as though I were protecting a valuable treasure. I pulled my truck away from the front door and over to the side of the parking lot away from other customers. I looked around to insure that I was alone and popped the top on the can. I stared at the can as though it were going to speak to me. Relief was in the can. Finally I lifted it to my lips and drained the can in a matter of seconds. I was now committed. I sat back with me eyes closed to wait for the old familiar feeling of peace. It arrived sooner than I expected.

While at the rehabilitation center, I'd learned of tolerance. How drinking daily raises ones tolerance level requiring more and more alcohol to achieve the desired effect. That explained how I was able to drink so much vodka before and still maintain composure. It had been thirty days since I drank any alcohol and now my tolerance to alcohol had dropped significantly. In a matter of seconds my scalp began to tingle. Almost immediately my mind stopped racing. I downed another beer before driving toward the highway. As I pulled onto the entrance ramp that would lead me home, I turned on the stereo. I was driving toward an uncertain future. I still had to make a decision about Metro. As that thought entered my mind, I felt the anxiety began to rise and my stomach began to flutter. I reached for another beer.

The more I relaxed, the more I was certain I wasn't retuning to Metro. Then I felt a tug of guilt. Mattie Rodriguez had extended an invitation to revitalize my career. She spoke to my counselor of my charisma. But, working in the department of corrections had taught me one thing I knew to be true; everyone at metro and probably throughout the department would know where I had been the last thirty days. I imagined those who applauded my fall would have a new round of ammunition against me. No one at Metro really knew me accept through reputation, but I thought about the stares I would get from everyone. Real or imagined, it would all be waiting for me.

I decided before I returned home that I was going to resign. I also knew that I would take the coward's way out and resign in writing and never talk with anyone there again. My shame and embarrassment were too great. Then my thoughts turned to what I would do next. The past nine years I had been a law enforcement officer. It was my chosen profession and I couldn't imagine doing anything else, yet my embarrassment was too great to return to Metro. My ego was causing me to make a poor choice and the alcohol was helping me do it. Fear began to creep over me. I reached for another beer. I made no progress the last thirty days or at least I was unwilling to use any of the tools I was given. I was merely hiding at the rehabilitation center.

I finished the beer by the time I arrived home. I went to my house without going to see mother because I wanted to be alone. After thirty days, everything seemed foreign. I sat down on the sofa without turning on any lights. The alcohol was faithful to take me out of reality for a moment. The phone rang and I knew it was mother, so I didn't answer. I forced myself up from the sofa and out the front door toward her house. I knew she wouldn't stop calling until she heard from me. She was already out on the deck when I arrived. I could see the concern on her face as she asked, "How are you?" I lied to her and said, "I'm doing ok." I tried to appear as calm as I could so she wouldn't worry. We made small talk for a few minutes pretending not to notice "the elephant" sitting on the porch with us. That of course was my drinking. She didn't ask any questions and I didn't offer any information. I stayed as long as I could before offering her another lie, "Well, I need to go unpack and settle in." I don't know if she believed any of it, but she let it go. She simply said, "I'm glad you're home." I smiled at her and went back home.

I didn't drink any more that night; I just sat in silence in front of the TV. I finally surrendered, turned the TV off and went to the bedroom. I turned on the radio and lay down on the bed. I lay in darkness and contemplated my next move. The only thing I knew for sure was that in the morning, I would be resigning from the department of corrections for the second time in a matter of months. Knowing that I wouldn't be returning to Metro brought some relief. As I contemplated what lie beyond that, I drifted off to sleep.

The sun shining through the window woke me the next morning. I was both surprised and relieved that there had been no dreams during the night. I took a long leisurely bath because I was under no time constraint. After dressing for the day, I sat down at the table and wrote my resignation to Ms. Rodriguez. I made sure to thank her for the opportunity she was willing to offer me. I owed her that. I gathered all my department issued uniforms and brass and started out the door. My next stop would be the central warehouse at the training center in Forsyth. I was becoming used to this process; resigning. I didn't see the need to wait for the letter to make it to Metro. During the drive, I made an honest effort to not think about alcohol. But, as I loomed closer to Forsyth, anxiety got the better of me. It seemed my embarrassment encompassed the staff at the warehouse as well.

I surrendered to the anxiety and stopped at a store for a 12 pack of beer. I was determined not to drink any vodka as though that would somehow save me. I'd learned at the rehabilitation center that there was as much alcohol in a twelve ounce can of beer as in one shot of vodka. I chose instead to believe a lie that I could somehow control things better if I only drank beer. I knew it was self deception, but it was all I could manage with the task that lie ahead of me. With my package secured, I drove toward the training center. I knew I wasn't ready to face anyone yet, so I drove past the entrance and out toward a small country road that lay past the center. I needed time to summon my courage.

Once I found my courage, I drove to the training center. I chose to use the rear gate because I didn't want to see anyone I knew. I parked, took a deep breath and went inside. I saw a few people that I knew, but it was less painful than seeing my friend, Terry Duffey or

any of the other instructors. I was careful not to make eye contact with anyone. I finished my business as quickly as I could and drove away hoping I wouldn't see anyone I knew. Again I used the rear gate and pulled out onto the road that took me toward home. I was relieved with that task done and felt some relief like a weight had been lifted from my shoulders. I wanted to drive away and leave that part of my life behind me, never to return.

I began to consider my next move. I had to find a job and decided that I would go to the department of labor in Macon and see what jobs were listed. The sun was shining and the beer was keeping me calm. I rolled the window down to feel the fresh air in my face. As I reached that place that only alcohol provided, I was feeling more confident. It was all an illusion, but I embraced it. If I didn't I would start to panic from the fear of the unknown. I finally arrived at the labor office. In the office there were computers that allowed one to search through the jobs available. I wanted to stay in law enforcement if possible and that was the area I searched. There were many listings for correctional officer, but that was out of the question. A knot formed in my stomach as I read through the list of institutions hiring in the area. Many were institutions where I had taught classes. I went through the list quickly. I finally arrived at a listing for other state jobs. One caught my eye in Milledgeville. The listing was for a police corporal for the department of human resources at a youth development center. When I read through the requirements I found that I was more than qualified for the position. I wrote down the position number and took it to a job specialist who would help me to apply for the position.

She explained the procedure for applying and gave me a state merit system application. It was the same application I filled out years before at the diagnostic center for correctional officer. I decided to fill out the application at home. On the trip home I felt a new surge of confidence. If it proved successful, I would still be working for the state. I drank more beer to maintain the confidence. Hope started to creep back into my life. Once I arrived at home, I sat down and carefully filled out the application. When I was done, I went to the post office to mail the object of my new found hope. With that done, I decided to reward myself and went to the liquor store in Forsyth. I'd been such a good customer in the past the clerk knew my name. He remarked about my absences the last month. I told a half truth and said I had been out of town.

I only purchased a fifth of vodka, not the usual half gallon, another feeble attempt at controlling my intake of alcohol. I promised myself there would be no shots of vodka this time, only mixed drinks. I felt confident that I would get an interview for the new position and I had to keep my wits about me if I were to make a good impression. I thought back to Ms. Rodriguez's remark to my counselor. *"No one in the department of corrections has more charisma than Bobby Allen."* Maybe that is why I'd always done well in interviews. It was still something hard for me to grasp.

I managed to control my drinking somewhat in the next week. I was drinking daily again, but I was still able to maintain my composure. I hid my drinking from mother. I didn't want to worry her so I didn't drink in front of her. Before I went to her house, I brushed my teeth thoroughly and splashed my face with after shave. Then I would carry peppermint candy in my pocket. I'm not sure if any of it worked, but the routine made me feel more confident. Alcohol was becoming a crutch again.

I received a letter for a job interview a week after I applied. Of course I decided to reward myself with a congratulatory drink. After my last round with the job at Metro, I couldn't afford to blow this interview. I was able to maintain my composure with the drinking. I attributed my control to not having the shots. However I was once again drinking first thing in the morning and all through the day. The night before my interview, I carefully prepared my clothing. Sharp creases on the trousers, shoes shined to a high gloss and I decided to wear a sport coat. The next morning I dressed and carefully inspected myself in the mirror. Everything seemed to be in place, so I went to the kitchen to mix my drink in a large container for the trip.

The drive to Milledgeville was through the country roads of middle Georgia. I'd driven this route several times as an instructor with the department of corrections, but this was a different mission. I needed to make a lasting first impression because I needed this job. The drive gave me a chance to finish my drink and calm my nerves. By the time I made it to Milledgeville I was prepared. I drove up into the driveway of the facility and parked. There was a single fence surrounding the property, but it didn't resemble a prison. There were office buildings and I could see several houses throughout the compound.

At the main gate was a control center. One walked in from the outside of the fence, but exited on the inside of the gate. The glass doors of the building were locked and electronically controlled by a uniformed officer inside the building. I was "buzzed" in and the officer stood from behind a counter that ran the entire length of the building and asked, "May I help you sir?" I replied, "I'm here for a job interview." There was a clipboard on the counter with a sign in sheet. I printed my name and the purpose of my visit. Once he was sure all the information was filled out correctly, he pointed to a large building and said, "That's the administrative building." I heard a buzzer and I opened the door that led inside the fence.

After a short walk to the building, I opened the door to find a civilian receptionist sitting at the desk. I didn't wait for her to greet me I just stated my purpose, "Hi, I'm here for a job interview." She seemed to be expecting me and asked for my name. She looked at a clipboard, checked my name, smiled and said, "Please have a seat." I walked over to a row of chairs. I only had to wait a few minutes before a uniformed officer opened an office door and called my name. I quickly surveyed him and saw the gold bar on his collar signifying that he was a lieutenant.

He shook my hand and told me to have a seat in front of a long table where I saw another uniform seated. I saw the double bars on his collar. He was a captain and the senior officer. I shook his hand and introduced myself. He smiled and pointed toward the chair in front of the table. It was almost like the promotion board I sat before at the diagnostic center when I was promoted to sergeant. After briefly asking about my qualifications, they began to ask me situational questions and how I would respond to each situation. Most of their questions were based on information I taught at the training center. The questions were designed to gauge how well one could think and react quickly in an emergency situation. They both were impressed with my answers and told me how well I did. The captain explained the type of residents that were housed at the facility. These were juvenile offenders and not old enough to be sent to the department of corrections. I left the interview feeling confident that I would be offered a job.

I received a phone call three days later and was offered a job. I was told to report back to the facility to complete the paperwork. After completing the documents, I was sent to a warehouse in the back of the facility to be issued uniforms. I was issued brass and a badge from the captain. I would report the following morning. I had the usual anxiety when entering a new situation. I didn't sleep well that night thinking about the new job ahead. I was grateful to be employed, but the fear the unknown caused me to be restless.

When the alarm sounded the next morning, I didn't feel rested. After I dressed, I went to the back porch for some fresh air. My nerves had me on edge thinking about the day ahead. I knew the remedy for that and gave in to the temptation. I was about to start another job under the influence. After I poured the drink, I stood there in the kitchen staring at the huge cup. I marveled at the coward I had become. I had no self confidence what so ever. I picked up the cup, grabbed the bottle from the freezer and started out the door.

I was paired with another officer for my first day. The facility was an open campus of many different buildings, not a closed facility like the diagnostic center. It resembled a college campus. There was a police headquarters in the rear of the campus and we were the police force of this little community. We patrolled the campus in police cruisers. If there was trouble anywhere, we received a radio call from the dispatch office and responded accordingly. I realized on the first day this was quite different from the department of corrections. The juvenile residents had no respect for any staff member and they were often out of control. I felt I'd made a poor choice in a career change.

After a week of orientation, I was assigned to the midnight shift. It was a little better because the residents were asleep and the majority of the job was patrolling and making security checks in the surrounding buildings. I quickly developed a routine. I brought my bottle with me and left it in my truck. After making security checks and feeling sure that the campus was quiet for the night, I would make an excuse to go to my truck in the parking lot. I carried a soft drink bottle with me. I would pour half of the drink out so I could mix a strong drink and take it back through the gate. That became my routine. I no longer had a life, I just existed.

To become a certified police officer I had to attend the regional police academy. It was a six week mandatory course. I welcomed it because I would be away from the facility and the residents for over a month. The regional academy was located in Macon at the local technical college. At the end of every week there were tests very similar to the corrections academy. The fourth week was firearms training. It was the usual classroom instruction and then out to the range to qualify. I was very comfortable with this segment of training because I worked a lot of hours on the firing range. I became the top shooter in the class and was given a trophy at graduation for my prowess.

I still drank while I attended the police academy and was able to limit my drinking to the mornings before class. At the end of the day, however, I had my stash under the seat of my truck and picked up my drinking as soon as I left. I was cheating my way through life and I hated myself for it. I had no self esteem at all. My life seemed to be a series of lies that I put together. I had no ambition for the future and constantly thought about what might happen if my drinking was discovered and how I would react. It no longer frightened me as it once did. The thought of getting caught almost seemed like a relief because I wouldn't have to live the lie.

After graduating from the police academy, I returned to the youth facility. I hated every waking moment of my life. My only relief was when I had Miki. She was the only ray of sunshine in my life. I was tortured when I went to pick her up from Debbie's house because it was a constant reminder of how far I had fallen from the life I wanted, but couldn't have anymore. There seemed to be no relief anywhere in my life; not even when I slept. Sleeping during the day was difficult and I was haunted by my dreams. I would wake in the afternoon not feeling rested. My self- loathing thoughts condemned my waking hours. I was living a miserable existence.

Debbie eventually started dating again. As long as I didn't see the man, I didn't have to acknowledge that she was moving on with her life. I suppose that somewhere in the back of my tortured mind, was a small hope that one day we would get back together. At least that was what I wanted to believe. Finally the day arrived, that completed my destruction. The day began like any other. I woke up in the afternoon and started my drinking routine. My dreams kept me lost in the past and often followed me to the daytime. As I sat staring out the window, the phone rang and startled me. I shook my head and answered to find Debbie on the other end.

She was being overly nice to me and it made me uneasy. I no longer trusted anyone least of all, myself. She asked, "How are you doing Bobby?" "I'm ok, I suppose," I replied. It was as close to the truth as I could get. "I need to talk to you about something very important," she said. Immediately my heart sunk into my stomach. I felt I was about to hear bad news. I froze with my eyes wide open as I responded, "Ok, Debbie." She continued, "My boyfriend has a job offer in Tallahassee Florida and is moving there." I closed my eyes as if I were waiting for a guillotine to fall and cut off my head. I took a deep breath and simply asked, "Yeah?" "He asked me to marry him and move to Tallahassee," she answered. I could hear the stress in her voice. She was being as compassionate as she could. I had no idea how to answer so I simply said, "Well, I hope he makes you happy, Debbie." My eyes filled with tears as I fought to maintain my composure. She said softly, "I hope he does, too." She offered me a consolation prize, "Maybe I can meet you half way on your weekends to get Miki."My eyes were still closed as I responded, "That would be very nice, Debbie, thank you." I had to end the call before I broke down, "Thanks for calling, Debbie, I'll be in touch." I hung up the phone without waiting for a reply.

My world as I knew it ended right there. I realized it was really over between Debbie and me and now the only child I had left was moving out of state. The destruction of my family and my life was now complete. I got up from the bed and went to the freezer. I needed a big drink to kill the pain in my chest where my heart used to be. I felt dead with no possibility of a life to come. There could be no shots because I had to work that night. However, I did mix a really strong drink and went to mother's house. At that moment, I didn't care if she knew about my drinking. When I told mother the news about Miki, I lost it and began to sob openly, but quickly recovered. Mother said softly, "I'm sorry."

I was very grateful to be on the night shift. After the residents were asleep for the night, I could park my patrol car and stare into the night. I walked around the campus on foot patrol just to be in the night air. I was becoming reckless with my behavior. I mixed my drinks in a large thermos and brought it inside with me. I was still careful to mask my breath with mints and splash on aftershave. But deep inside, I wasn't concerned with getting caught.

Every other weekend, Mother would ride with me to pick up Miki from Tallahassee. It was a six hour round trip so the first and last day of my visit was travel. In essence I had only one day to spend with Miki. There was nothing I could do about it so I made the best of our time together. That one day became precious to me. But, in between the weekends, I was miserable. That was my life for the next two years. Getting Miki every other weekend and a job I absolutely hated in between and of course, nightmares that plagued me on a constant basis; faces of those from my past that would not allow me to rest and then follow me into my waking moments.

I looked through the employment section of the newspaper every day. It was a matter of curiosity mostly, but one afternoon, it paid off. A women's college in Macon was advertising for a certified police officer for their department. I quickly made the phone call to ask about the position. They were very adamant that one had to be a certified police officer. I made an appointment to talk with the chief of the department the following day. I went to work that evening with a small glimmer of hope that I might be able to escape the youth center. When I awoke each day from my restless sleep, I would actually get physically ill thinking about the trip to Milledgeville and the job that waited for me.

The following day, I said a prayer and took my resume to the college in Macon. I passed by the college many times driving through Macon, but never gave it more than a glimpse before dismissing it and had no idea they had their own police force. I saw the sign that read, "Campus Police," and parked in front of the building. I walked in the office and behind a desk sat an officer in a white shirt. White shirts typically indicate a supervisor. As I approached his desk, he rose and introduced himself as the chief of the department. I made the appointment the day before, so he was expecting me.

I gave him my resume and he scanned over it briefly. "I see that you worked for the prison system," he enquired. I replied, "Yes, I worked in that department for several years." He continued, "I've had many calls from correctional officers asking about the job, but this position requires that you be a certified police officer." I called his attention to my resume and replied, "If you look closer you'll see that I attended the regional police academy two years ago and there is a copy of the certification in my resume." He looked closer at my resume this time. Then he raised his eyebrows and said, "I see that you are a certified Training Officer." I smiled and said, "Yes and I've kept my certification current." He continued, "Well, that will prove to be very useful here." I felt a tingle deep inside at his comment because it indicated that he was interested in hiring me. He rose from his chair and said, "Come with me, please."

He took me through the maze of hallways to another office. He wanted me to meet his supervisor. We chatted for a few minutes about my past work history. No matter whom I talked with, when I mentioned that I worked on death row and participated in ten executions, it always caused a pause as they looked at me. This gentleman was no different and remarked, "That must have been quite an experience." I smiled and replied, "You have no idea." That was my standard reply to any comments about death row and it was very accurate. There was no way I could explain to anyone the things I'd participated in and witnessed there. What I could never talk about to anyone was my time as the clerk and the files I'd read concerning the deaths of the innocent victims that lay in those pages. He looked up from my resume and handed it back to the chief, nodded and finally said, "We'd be glad to have you." He shook my hand and the chief and I returned to his office. He gave me all the new hire paperwork that accompanied any new position. "Please complete this and return it to me as quickly as you can." I replied, "I'd like to give my present job a two week notice if that's alright with you?" He smiled and nodded his head, "Of course."

I left the interview feeling invigorated. I was finally going to escape the confines of the youth center and I was ready for the change. Once home I sat down and immediately filled out the paperwork. I also wrote out a letter of resignation for the youth center. I couldn't wait to be done with this portion of my life. That night at work I submitted my letter of resignation to the shift supervisor. He read through the letter, looked up from the page and said, "I'm sorry to be losing you, Allen." As we shook hands I explained that I needed a change in my life. I almost counted every minute of the two week notice and was overcome with anticipation. On the last day I said goodbye to the officers with whom I worked. A few of them became my friends and I was genuinely sorry to lose their friendships, but I was so ready for this next phase of my life. I had to make a trip to the youth center during the day to turn in equipment. My badge, gun belt, and handcuffs I gave to the captain. Uniforms I turned in to the warehouse. I felt a glimmer of relief as I walked out to the parking lot for the last time. I had no feelings of remorse as I drove away. I looked in the rearview mirror and said quietly to myself, "Goodbye and good riddance" and drove away with a smile on my face.

The college gave me a voucher to purchase uniforms from a law enforcement supply store in Macon. The uniforms from the youth center had been a tan shirt and brown trousers and I was never issued new uniforms. They were used uniforms that were recycled. My new uniform colors were dark blue trousers and a light blue shirt. I was issued a silver police badge, collar chevrons and a standard .38 caliber revolver. The chief made it clear that he intended to take advantage of my training experience. He instructed me to maintain firearms certification for the small department.

I awoke early on the first day I was to report for duty. I prepared my uniforms the night before and always tailored them to fit. The trousers and shirt had creases in all the right places. I wore my patent leather dress black shoes that I'd worn as a color guard when I taught at the corrections academy. I put on my gun belt and inserted the .38 in my holster. I walked to the full length mirror to check myself. Everything seemed to be in place. I walked to the back porch for some fresh air. I had the typical first day anxiety that comes with any job. I knew where relief was and as I thought about it, I closed my eyes and shook my head as I said quietly out loud, *"NO!"* I could feel my pulse quicken. I opened my eyes and looked up to the sky and said desperately, *"Please, Lord help me."* But, I had already stepped over the line by acknowledging the image in my head. I closed my eyes again and when I finally reopened them, I was already on my way to the kitchen. I reached into the freezer and there it was waiting for me like an old friend. I grabbed the bottle and went through my mixing routine. I knew that once I reached this point, there was no turning back. I took the cup and headed out to the back porch. I sipped from the straw of the large thermal cup. Slowly the feeling moved over me and I started to relax. I grabbed the bottle, my cup and headed to my truck. Before I made my way to the college, I looked into the mirror and said to myself, "Smooth, Bobby, very nice!"

I arrived at the college and went through the usual routine of mints and a splash of aftershave. Confident that I had properly covered my tracks, I headed to the office. The chief was behind his desk and called me over. He had some information in a packet for me. There were codes to the combination locks on the office door and codes to all the buildings

that I would be inspecting at night. He took me to the office door first to demonstrate how it worked and then had me perform the task. Next we walked around campus for a tour of the buildings which took about thirty minutes. We returned to the office and he had me pull a chair at his desk to sign some documents. After we completed that, he sat back in his chair and looked at me. He asked, "Have you turned in your notice at the youth center, yet?" "Yes, I've already completed my two week notice," I replied. He paused for a minute and then continued, "I thought I smelled alcohol on your breath earlier." My heart dropped down in my stomach and I had to fight to keep my composure. I wasn't sure if I had succeeded. I sat there in uncomfortable silence for what seemed like an eternity. He didn't even ask me to explain. I was now dealing with a real police officer who had experience on the road.

He said, "I can't have you drinking on duty and carrying a firearm in case you have to shoot somebody." I held his gaze without replying. I knew I was drinking and there was no way I could convince him that I wasn't so I didn't insult his intelligence by denying it. I felt like my new job and my career in law enforcement was going to end right here on my first day. In what I can only say was a moment in time that God intervened, the chief simply said, "If you need help, we'll get you some help, my friend." I swallowed and it felt as though a bolder was going down my throat. The chief asked, "Do we understand each other?" I was locked in a gaze with him that I could not break. I opened my dry mouth and managed to say, "Yes, sir.

The chief excused himself and said, "I'll be right back." I sat in silence in the office afraid to move. My mind took me back several years to my father's face. It was there before me as clear as anything in the office. It was a time when someone daddy knew had been drinking and was involved in a serious car accident. The officer who investigated the accident and the ambulance personnel all agreed that they could not understand how the man was not killed, let alone escaped without injury. As daddy opened his mouth to speak, my eyes focused on his words, *"God always takes care of fools and drunks."*

Daddy had wisdom to explain things that seemed unexplainable. Since I was alone I said quietly out loud, *"You're absolutely right daddy."* There was no logical explanation for why I wasn't fired and on my way home unemployed. As I sat there my hands began to shake. It was an incredible rush of adrenaline; my body's reaction to fear. The events that just transpired ran quickly though my mind again. I wanted to escape, just run away. But, I tried that solution before and it solved nothing. I stood and walked around the office waiting for the chief to return and what else he might have to say about my behavior. When he returned, he continued my orientation and never mentioned it again. He gave me my shift assignment and released me for the day. The chief was the only one assigned to the day shift. All other officers worked the evening and night shifts. I was to report the following day for the evening shift.

I returned home and took off my equipment and uniform. I sat down in the den in silence as I reviewed the morning in my mind. I was alone, but as the images raced through my mind, I suddenly began to feel embarrassed and I could feel the warmth in my face. I humiliated myself in front of my new boss. I knew it would be an image that would follow me and the reminder I would have every time I saw the chief's face. I rubbed my eyes and waited as long as I could, but finally the emotions were too much. Even with the memory of the morning still fresh in my mind, I headed to the freezer. I had to have relief to make

the images disappear. My friend was there and after the proper amount of consumption, my mind relaxed. I turned the TV on to block out the remaining thoughts of the morning.

My new career began with a black mark against me. I started the evenings out with a partner because the shifts were overlapped. I was apprehensive for the first few nights because I wasn't sure if the chief had shared my secret with anyone else. But, as the days went by, I saw no indication that I was being treated differently. I relaxed and settled into my new position. It was a welcome relief from the turmoil I'd left at the youth center. In fact, most nights it was downright boring. The job was mostly walking the campus and checking doors in the main buildings where the classrooms were located. Although I was armed, I felt more like a security guard than a police officer.

As time went by, I got more comfortable and started to drink again before work. It only took a few weeks and I was brining my alcohol to work in a giant squeeze bottle with a straw. I'd leave the vodka in the truck until my partner was off duty and then I'd bring the mixed drink in the office. Sometimes students would stop by the office and talk. On one such occasion I had another close call. I was sitting at the chief's desk and the student sat at the officer's desk. As we talked I held my squeeze bottle and sipped from it. Suddenly she said, "I bet I know what's in the cup you have." I was becoming a master at masking my emotions, but inside I felt a chill run down my back. I knew I had to answer or my silence would be an admission of guilt. I simply replied, "Oh yeah?" Then she dropped the bomb, but I expected it. She continued, "Alcohol." I smiled and tried to dismiss it with humor, "Very funny." After a few seconds I told her I had to make my rounds to get her out of the office. We both left the office and I was sure to keep my distance from her. She walked away and I locked the door behind me and started my rounds. All I could do was wait to see if she would report this to anyone.

I was on edge the next few days waiting for the chief to confront me. If he asked about drinking again, I knew it would mean the end of my job because he already discovered my secret. Three days passed with no word from the chief and I deduced the student had not reported anything to anyone. I sat in the office looking out the window wrapped up in my own thoughts. As evening fell, I walked outside and looked up at the sky. I had no idea what to say to my God. I had been spared yet again and I asked, "Why do you save me, Lord?" There was no answer so I lowered my head almost in shame and walked away. I felt both unworthy and grateful at the same time.

The days passed by without incident. My life became boring, but it was comfortable because I had a routine. Mother and I continued to drive to Tallahassee every other weekend to pick up Miki. I drank during the trips and that added to my already over burdened guilt. I was drinking and driving with my mother and my child in the car. I couldn't bring myself to face Debbie sober. I was still in love with her and now she was the wife of another man who was also raising my child. The weekends with Miki were bitter sweet. I was so thrilled to have her, but my guilt was compounded by the thoughts of Leighanne, Tracey and Kimberly. Miki would grow up not knowing her sisters. I took comfort in that she had Debbie's daughter as a sister.

At least she would not be alone. Leighanne and Tracey had each other, but little Kimberly had no siblings with her. In the years since our divorce, Sarah was taking Kimberly to church with her. Sarah always professed to be a Christian, but while we were together

we had both fallen away from our faith. Sarah, by the grace of God had returned to her Christian roots and Kimberly would grow up in the light of Jesus Christ. Sarah would give her something I could not.

I could not remember the last time I had an entire night's sleep without visitation from the memories that plagued me. The players were always the same even if the circumstances were not; my father, Roosevelt Green, Timothy Wesley Mcorquodale and all the other men that died in the electric chair. The other key players came to visit as well; Donna Dixon, the victim of Timothy Mcorquodale and always Teresa Carol Allen. Even if they never spoke during my dreams, their presence was enough to haunt me. The rest I acquired would depend on their involvement in the dream. I would awake from the dream, but soon dragged back to the plane of existence where they lived.

I kept in touch with some friends in the Department of Corrections and they would call to check on me from time to time. I had several friends at the Milledgeville office where I resigned my position a few years before. One such call came with an interesting offer. One of the training officers from Milledgeville had been promoted to Deputy Warden of a nearby institution. The department of corrections instituted a new paramilitary program called "Boot Camp." Several institutions were converted to these new programs. It was a last chance for rehabilitation before being sentenced to hard time in a state prison. The residents of the institution were placed on probation for five years with the first ninety days incarcerated at the boot camp. If they completed the program, they were released to serve their probation under the supervision of a probation officer. If they failed the program, they would be sent to state prison for five years. It was a very bold innovative program.

My friend told me the new deputy warden was looking for experienced officers to staff the institution and my name was put forth for consideration. It was a chance to go back to state employment with benefits. My friend told me she would make the phone call on my behalf if I were interested. I was definitely interested. It seemed God was giving me yet another chance for a fresh start. I'd started the job at the college with a strike against me on the first day of employment after the chief smelled alcohol on my breath. I was excited and asked my friend to make the call.

The institution was located in the small town of Eatonton. It was renamed a "Probation Boot Camp." The residents of the Boot Camp were classified as "detainees" and not inmates. On my next off day from the college, I made the trip to Eatonton. It was an hour long trip, but a very pleasant drive through small country communities. As I drove into the parking lot, I realized just how small this institution was compared to the massive diagnostic center. I parked and walked to the entrance. I identified myself and gave the name of the deputy warden. I only had to wait minutes before he appeared. We shook hands and he invited me to his office. I handed him my resume and he scanned it quickly. "Everyone from the Milledgeville office speaks very highly of you," he said. I smiled and replied, "Well, that's good to know." It was nice to know that some in the department of corrections still liked me.

After a short conversation about my experience, he offered me a job. I was surprised how fast things were moving and I gladly accepted. He stood and asked me if I could type. I told him I'd been a clerk on death row and had some typing skills. "I going to send you over to the personnel office and I want you to type your application so we can expedite things" he said. After typing my application I turned it into the personnel manager. She smiled and said, "We'll be in touch as soon as this is processed." I left the institution feeling invigorated. I drove toward home with a smile on my face. I looked into the mirror and said, "You've been given another chance, don't blow it!"

In just a matter of days I received a call from the personnel manager to come in and complete the usual pre-employment paper work. I didn't wait for my next scheduled off day; I called in to the college to ask for a day off. I went to the institution and completed all the paperwork. Afterwards, the deputy warden wanted me to meet the warden. When I entered his office, I recognized him immediately. He was the deputy warden of care and treatment at Metro when I was hired there. My heart skipped a beat; I wasn't sure if I'd be well received. But, thankfully he did not remember the details of my employment. The meeting turned out to be just a formality. We shook hands and he welcomed me to the institution. After our brief meeting, I was sent back to the deputy warden. He informed me when I was to report for duty and asked me if that would be sufficient time to work a notice at my job. I told him I could make it work. I went home and immediately wrote out my resignation letter for the college. I wanted to move forward as quickly as possible. The next day I reported for work early so I would have time to talk with the chief before my shift began. I told him about the job offer at the institution in Eatonton and laid the letter on his desk. He acted as though he was sorry to see me leave, but in reality I believed it was a relief for him. I believed that I was a burden for him because I'd begun my employment with the suspicion of drinking on duty. There was really no suspicion I had been caught with alcohol on my breath. I was a liability for him and his department and I knew it.

Nothing changed while I worked the two week notice because I continued to drink. I started a lie in my mind. I was going to drink until I started my new job and then I would stop and change my life with this new position. I still attempted to cover my breath with mints and aftershave before every shift. I told myself that I did I didn't want to disrespect the chief with my disobedience in the last few days. When I considered what I was thinking I finally admitted to myself that it was insanity. My disrespect had began on my first day on the job and continued through the few months of my employment. My last evening of employment the chief made a gesture of kindness to me. He told me that if I wanted to change my mind, he could just tear up the resignation letter. I smiled and thanked him, but I realized it was an empty offer. I could almost see the relief on his face when I turned him down. But, I respected him all the more for attempting to make me feel like I was a valuable member of his department.

The next day I went to the college to turn in my uniforms, weapon and gun belt. I thanked the chief for the opportunity he gave me. We shook hands and I turned the page on another sad chapter of my life. The family I'd been entrusted with; Debbie, the twins and Kimberly was gone. Miki was far away from me and I sometime wondered if she would be better off without me. She had a chance for a new life with her mother and her sister. I began to think that I might just be a barrier in the way of her happiness. But, I also felt that if she were gone, my sanity would be gone as well. She was all that I was left of the life I had, that I wanted, but was now far out of my grasp.

After a few days off, I reported for duty at the boot camp. Just about every officer knew me from the academy. The shift supervisors, the commissioned officers, remembered me from the training center. They all went the extra mile in making me feel welcome. Since it had been more than two years since I'd worked for the department of corrections, I was informed that I would have to attend the academy in Forsyth. That was going to require quite a bit of humility on my part. The last time I was there, I was an instructor and the coordinator of defensive tactics. I had written lesson plans for several of the classes. I'd also made training films that were still used in the class curriculum. Now I was going to be a student all over again. My first day was familiarizing myself with institutional policies. Once I completed that, I was given the rest of the day off and told to report for the split shift the next day. My hours were 8 am to 4:30 pm Monday through Friday with weekends off until I completed the academy.

Since I had to wait for a new class to begin at the academy, I would be working in the institution as an uncertified officer. I was assigned as a trainee to work several different posts with certified officers. This was the beginning of my test in humility because I had trained most of these officers at the academy. Now they were the instructors. The night before my first day at the boot camp, I stood in front of the mirror trying to condition myself for the day to come. I wanted to start the new job sober. I promised myself while at the college I would do that and failed miserably.

I had the usual first day anxiety so I didn't sleep well the night before. I wasn't exactly job hopping, but I felt out of place at my last two law enforcement positions. I desperately wanted and searched for a place where I could belong again. Nothing seemed to fit like it did when I was at the diagnostic center and an instructor at the training center. But then again, my personal life had been turned upside down as well. Every time I thought about what I lost in the last three years only served to remind me how I failed. I could find no comfort anywhere; in the jobs I'd had, with my family and not in the arms of another woman. The only peace I had was in the bottle of vodka that I relied on. Even that wasn't true peace. It was only a way to block out the demons of the past that tormented me. It was simply a momentary reprieve from the life I created for myself.

The clock went off to remind me that my first official day of duty arrived. I got out of the bed with my stomach turning flips with anxiety. I showered, dressed and inspected myself in the mirror. As usual everything was in place. The outside was immaculate, but my mind was quite different. But, that was always the goal. Spit shine the outside so no one would know what was happening beneath that first layer. I walked outside to see the morning sun peeking on the horizon and breathed in the fresh air. I'd become familiar with this routine in the last three years; the day beginning with anxiety over a new job. I desperately wanted it to be a month in the future when I would have the academy behind me and working a post. I didn't want to be the new guy again. Yet, here I stood going through the motions again. A chill went down my back signaling my anxiety level increased.

I paced around the house, walking outside to inside trying to quell the uneasiness inside. The more I walked the more agitated I became. My mind was now racing with anticipation of the day ahead. I was trying to rehearse every situation the day might present. I knew I was going to get the same question from whatever officer I worked with today and that was familiar with my career; *"Why did you leave the training center?"* I searched my mind for an excuse that I would give everyone. The more I thought of an answer I would give, the faster my heart raced until I was about to hyperventilate. I hadn't even made it to the boot camp and I was working myself into a panic. I felt a bead of sweat roll down from my sideburn. As I wiped it away, I looked over at the refrigerator. The answers to this situation lie in the freezer. I closed my eyes and quietly said, *"No!"* I opened my eyes and walked outside again as if the sunlight would rescue me from myself. I checked my watch and it was time for me to leave. I went back inside for my keys that lay on the counter in the kitchen. I picked them up and took a step toward the door and stopped. I couldn't resist any longer, I turned to the freezer and grabbed the bottle. I quickly mixed the drink in the large squeeze bottle. My task complete, I picked up the bottle and started toward the front door.

A few sips from the squeeze bottle and I was already beginning to relax. I stashed the vodka bottle under the seat and started my journey. Vodka was going to be a part of my new career. It was an hour drive to the boot camp so I had time to finish the drink and formulate a response to the questions I anticipated from the other officers. As the vodka took effect, the excuses came faster and easier. By the time I pulled into the parking lot of the institution, I was relaxed and prepared for anything the day would bring. After a splash of after shave and a peppermint I was ready. I looked in the mirror and I actually had a mile on my face. Since I had admitted to myself that drinking was going to be part of this job, I didn't have to lie to myself. I found a strange peace in that simple truth.

It was intake day at the boot camp. The new detainees were arriving from the county jails. The officers in charge of the intake were dressed out in black B.D.U.'s like I wore as an instructor at the training center. The uniform was topped off with a campaign hat, like state troopers wear. Once the detainees were dropped off the whole act began. It was just like I remembered Fort Jackson on intake day at basic training. The officer's were barking orders at the new arrivals in an attempt to disorientate them as they were acclimated to their new home for the next 90 days. These detainees were young and the purpose was to "shock" them into a new reality so they would conform to rules and regulations and learn to live in society as law abiding citizens or they would spend the next 5 years at a state prison with hardened inmates.

Most detainees appeared to be teenagers who more than likely had been part of a gang. Only now, they were alone to face the consequences of their decisions and had no gang around them to protect them. Many broke down and cried during intake. The reason for the process was to break them down so that they could be built back up over the next ninety days under our direction. It was a very impressive course of action. We would be teaching teenage boys how to become men and reenter society. I was very impressed with the process and wanted to become a part of it. Over the next three weeks I began each day the same. Since I had surrendered to the fact that I would be drinking each day, I woke up in the mornings without fear of the day ahead. I knew on my way to the boot camp I would prepare myself mentally with the assistance of alcohol. Each afternoon after work, I drank on the way home to wind down. Though I was drinking daily, I was able to keep myself miraculously in control. However, none of what I did affected the nights as I slept. The faces of the dead came haunting. Ultimately my sleep was interrupted and I woke drenched in sweat.

Finally after two weeks on the job, a new class was beginning at the training center. Just the thought of returning to the training center caused me anxiety. I reported to the training center on a Sunday afternoon as scheduled. The other cadets sat scattered throughout the auditorium, but I knew what was coming so I sat down close to the front. Finally the instructors entered the auditorium and one yelled, "On your feet!" The sound of the folding seats slamming shut filled the room. I was now participating in a process that Terry Duffey and I had developed. As an instructor, I had been the one ordering the cadets to their feet. Now, I was the student. I recognized all of the instructors and as some passed by; they looked at me out of the corner of their eye. In the first few minutes, I realized how difficult this was going to be.

All the instructors wore black B.D.U.'s sharply pressed with their trousers tucked in their boots. The senior instructors wore black campaign hats. There on the stage was my friend and former partner, Terry Duffey. He was now the Assistant Director. The session was under his supervision as the senior instructors moved about the room. It resembled intake day at the boot camp, but now I was the student. I didn't expect any special treatment and none was offered. All the instructors, my friends, treated me with the courtesy and respect just as they did with every other student and they were very professional. After a roll call and filling out paperwork, we were given a break. I walked out into the huge atrium area where I had performed cadet inspections for two years. I stood in the corner by the wall in an attempt to blend in with everyone else. I hated this already and I still had a month to go before graduation.

A small group of instructors walked over to me and shook my hand. They seemed genuinely glad to see me. Terry Duffey kept his distance and I understood why. He was an administrator here and had to maintain the appearance of objectivity. In what I assumed was an attempt to help me relax, one of my instructor friends smiled and said, "Now, don't think you're not going to have to crack open the books just because you used to teach here." I was grateful for his kindness and simply smiled and replied, "I understand and I'll do my best." I'm sure that those who knew me best sensed my uneasiness and were trying to help. I just wanted to get this all behind me and return to the boot camp.

We finished up the evening being assigned a dormitory room. All cadets were required to stay in the dorms for the duration of the training course. We would go home every Friday afternoon after the last test of the day and return on the Sunday evening to prepare for the week ahead. The rooms were semi-private so I introduced myself to my roommate, put away my clothes and walked around the training center in solitude. I needed some time to reacquaint myself with my surroundings. It was very ironic seeing the training center from a student's perspective. I wanted to keep a low profile while I was here. In retrospect, I suppose I seemed rather unfriendly to everyone, I felt uncomfortable with my new role.

The following morning we assembled in the atrium to be divided into sections and class leaders were selected just as Terry Duffey and I had organized three years before. I wasn't sure if the instructors wanted me as any type of leader and I didn't want any of that responsibility. I just wanted to be a student. I tried to blend in with the group of students. Thankfully I wasn't selected as a section leader, but I was selected as a squad leader. It was a very small leadership role and I wouldn't have to report to the administrative staff. I accepted it without objection.

Once we had our section assignments, we were to report to the warehouse to be issued cadet uniforms. I'd visited here several times in that last three years, having uniforms issued and then turning in uniforms after I resigned the position. I was embarrassed to show my face there because I knew everyone. My roommate and I drove to the warehouse in my vehicle. I parked, got out and I stood there looking at the warehouse office. I sighed and dropped my head for a moment. My roommate asked, "Are you alright, Bobby?" I looked over at him and said, "Yes, I'm fine," as we started for the main entrance. I hadn't shared my experience with him. I wasn't sure I was going to, but I also wasn't sure I could go an entire month holding everything inside. I dismissed it for the moment and just concentrated on what I came here to do.

I didn't engage in conversation with any of the warehouse employees, my former friends. I already knew what the instructors were looking for. They were here to ensure that our cadet uniforms fit properly. I was here for two years doing the same thing with past cadets. I just wanted to get it over with and leave. When we finished, we were instructed to return to the main building, change into a uniform and wait in the atrium area. As I waited in the atrium, in my cadet uniform, I saw employees from other agencies pass by, some of who had been coworkers and friends. I don't know if it was real or just my imagination, but as they passed by they seemed confused that I would be in a cadet uniform. I finally decided that it was my own discomfort that I was feeling. It was only the first day and here I was embarrassed to be seen. I told myself it was going to be a long month. Once everyone returned to the atrium, we were taken next to the gym to be issued tee shirts and sweat pants for our physical and defensive tactics training. We passed by the basketball floor where I had taught many hours of defensive tactics. The memories of the years I taught flashed by in my mind as I waited in line to be issued gear. The butterflies in my stomach were in full flight. I found that being here was going to be harder than I imagined. Nothing I had done to prepare for this moment was working. I knew it was my ego and pride working overtime that gripped me.

After being issued training gear and putting it away in our rooms, we went directly to classrooms to begin our training. As the instructor taught the class, I recalled comments from the previous day; *"Don't think you're not going to have to crack any books just because you used to teach here."* However, as the class proceeded, I discovered that he was wrong. Even though it had been almost three years since I taught the material, I recognized every part of it. I didn't tell any of my classmates that I was once an instructor. I kept a very low profile, especially during classroom instruction. I could have commented on any topic and easily answered any question that the instructor asked. I pretended to take notes on the subjects that were taught, but I remembered the material so well that it really wasn't necessary.

Gradually I settled into my role as a cadet and the first week went by rather quickly. I stayed at home the entire weekend, drinking to hide my discomfort. I had just three weeks to go and it would be over.

Sunday came sooner than I wanted and it was time to prepare for the second week. I still felt uneasy about returning and to combat my anxiety, I mixed a drink at home and took the bottle with me. I knew there was no way I could take the bottle into the dorm room, so I stashed it under my seat as I'd always done. Just knowing that relief from my fears was in my vehicle in the parking lot brought relief somehow. Even into the second week, I still felt uneasy. Each class seemed to drag by because I was so familiar with the material. In this second week we had the restraint class and instructed in the use of handcuffs and leg irons. This was one of my areas of expertise and I was the author of the lesson plan. There was also an instructional video starring me and a fellow instructor who was now director of the academy. As the video played I became nauseas.

I sat in my seat like a statue and my heart beat increased until I was sure it was going to jump through my chest. From the corner of my eye I could see a fellow student look at me and then back to the video. Finally he made the connection. He pointed to me and said, "Hey, that's him!" My heart sank into my stomach as each of the students began to realize that I was one of the stars of the video. There was murmuring until finally the instructor said, "Quiet down." The cat was definitely out of the bag now. When the video finished and the light were turned on all eyes were on me. We were dismissed to the atrium for a break. Several of the cadets came to me about what they'd seen. There was no way I could hide it any longer so I confessed. "I was once and instructor here at the academy." I could tell that they were curious for an explanation, but I offered none and they seemed to sense that I wasn't going to give one. From that point on I was very self conscious. I became paranoid and felt as though everyone in the training center was staring at me and knew by now that I had failed as an instructor. Every time I saw a classmate look in my direction, I felt as though I was the topic of their conversation. It was more than I could bear. When we were dismissed for lunch, I walked at a fast pace to my truck. Once inside, I started the engine and turned on the air conditioner on high. I felt sweat roll down my cheek and lay my head back and closed my eyes.

I wanted to be anywhere but here, but I knew no mattered how much I prayed or wished nothing would change. I finally opened my eyes and realized my past caught up with me and there was no escape. I knew what would alleviate my stress and it was just an arm's length away. Under my seat was the answer to my fears. Suddenly the irony caught up with me. I was at the crossroads again and faced with a decision that was a potential game changer in my life. The irony was the first time I was faced with this dilemma, I was here as an instructor teaching a class on stress management. Now, I had returned as a student and about to cross the line again. I realized that if I followed through, there would be no return. I had come full circle.

I fought as long as I could, but finally my fears overwhelmed me. I looked carefully around the parking lot to make sure no one would see me. I finally felt safe enough to reach under the seat to retrieve my relief. There was some watered down juice still left in the squeeze bottle I'd brought with me. I quickly poured the vodka in the bottle and returned it under my seat. I shook the contents of the bottle to mix it. I knew what I was about to drink was going to be strong and taste horrible, but it wasn't the taste I was seeking. It was the relief that would follow. I closed my eyes and drank it down as quickly. The burning that followed almost caused me to vomit. But, I was determined to find the peace I needed. I opened a peppermint and popped it in my mouth. My chore complete, I closed my eyes and imagined the small stream on the country road. My stomach was settling down and once I was sure the vodka was going to stay down, I opened my eyes. I positioned the air condition vent so that it blew directly in my face. I was trying to compose myself. I splashed on some after shave and returned to the main building. I was feeling much less anxious. But, I still had the second half of the day to go.

Nothing else was said about the video and with the help of the vodka; I was able to make it through the afternoon feeling clam. Finally the day ended and I walked as fast as I could to my room to change into civilian clothes. Then out to my truck and quickly left the training center. The need to flee was very heavy on my shoulders. I made a quick stop at the local store for a mixer. I mixed the drink and started to my mother's house via the country roads. I gulped down the drink to start the process. As that old familiar feeling slipped over me I realized this was my path for the next three weeks. I visited with my mother as long as I dared. I had a curfew at the training center and made my way back. I was relaxed, yet fearful that I might be discovered. My roommate was out when I returned and went to the shower in an attempt to freshen myself and went directly to bed. It wasn't long before my roommate entered, but I pretended to be asleep. I was afraid that if we talked, I'd be discovered.

I was able to maintain my composure through the remainder of the week, but I still felt paranoid. It became increasingly difficult not to drink to alleviate my uneasiness, but I made it through the rest of the week. When Friday came, I was completely stressed out from forcing myself not to drink. When we were finally dismissed for the weekend, I reached for the vodka as soon as I made it to my truck in the parking lot. I continued drinking through the weekend. I wondered what my friend Terry Duffey would think of me if he knew how I was surviving the stress of the academy. Guilt consumed me thinking how I failed our friendship especially after he helped me out with the metro job. Sunday arrived much too soon and I would start another week living a lie.

It was firearms training week and there would be several days of qualifying rounds on the range. I was completely engrossed in my drinking now and felt I could not maintain my composure if I didn't drink. I reminded myself that I had carried a gun on duty before while I was drinking and that I could handle it for the few days while we were on the firing range. But, that didn't stop me from hating myself for doing it. I loaded my pockets with mints and kept a bottle of after have handy. Daytime qualifications went by without incident and my shooting was better than my time at the police academy. Our final qualification round was night fire. I thought I was home free and that's when I became careless. One of my classmates had been a probation officer which was a division of the department of corrections. I wasn't sure why she was going through basic correctional officer training and never asked. I was concerned with my own situation and getting through the academy. No one had to quality for night firing it was for familiarization only. So we were dismissed from class and given instructions to report to the firing range at a designated time after dark. We had free time so I drove off campus. I was ready for it to be over and had a drink before I returned.

As we waited for each group of shooters to finish their rounds, we stood in groups talking. I noticed the former probation officer keeping her distance from me. A set of headlights pulled up in front of the range and out steeped Terry Duffey and two instructors who were also friends of mind. Terry came to me and asked, "Can I talk to you inside for a minute?" There was a building where the range master called commands from an intercom system. I had sat there many times giving those commands. Now it all seemed foreign to me. The two instructors and I sat in chairs while Terry sat on the counter.

I could sense the tension in the air, but I still wasn't sure what was going on. Terry said, "I've heard that you're shooting better now than when you were an instructor here." I smiled and said, "Yeah, I've improved somewhat since then." I guess he figured he'd broken the chill in the office and got to the point. "We have a report that you smell like you've been drinking." My heart sunk. I'd had plenty of practice at disguising my emotions and I hoped that my face had not given me away. I simply replied, "Ok." Terry looked at me and asked the question that he was obligated to ask, "Have you?" "Of course not," I replied. He continued, "Well here's what we've come up with," I was sitting like a statue afraid that any movement would betray me. Then he said, "We can call the Monroe County Sheriff's office out or we thought we'd have you blow into a hat or something like that." If the sheriff's office came, that would be the end. I would be discovered without a doubt. I said a quick silent prayer in my head that he would choose the latter.

He looked at his colleagues, my friends, and asked, "What do y'all think?" one spoke up and said "Yeah, just have him blow into something." I got the impression that they were trying to give me a way out. Terry looked around on the desk and found and empty clear, plastic bag. He handed it to me and said, "Blow in this, Bobby." Thankfully, I just had a peppermint before they drove up and hoped it lasted long enough to disguise my breath. I blew into the bag then held my breath as Terry smelled and then handed it to each of the instructors for their opinions. They immediately wrinkled up their noses, shook their heads and said, "No, there's nothing there." A chill ran down my spine as I felt like I'd just been given a reprieve from a firing squad. They each shook my hand and told me they'd see me tomorrow.

Once we were dismissed I went directly to the dorm. I was just spared personal and professional humiliation. If I were discovered, there would be no returning from it. Once I arrived at the dorm parking lot, I got out and stood beside my truck staring at the night sky. It was beautiful, as usual. I looked up, but could find no words and felt so ashamed for my actions. I thought about my friend, Terry Duffey, how I looked into his eyes and told a lie. So there was more guilt and personal condemnation added on to what was already there. I knew there was no way I could continue to drink for the duration of the academy and so I was left to experience the full force of my guilt and shame.

Because of stress the nightmares and deranged dreams returned and all I could do was deal with it with a sober mind. I dreaded the nights when I had to lay my head on the pillow and simply wonder who would visit that particular night. There were visions of my children from different periods of their lives, smiling and sometimes reaching for me, yet always just out of my grasp as I reached for them. My father from moments of my own childhood, but knowing he had to die and be buried all over again. The murder victims came reminding me of my promise not to forget them and sometimes the faces of the executed accompanied them.

Finally the last week of training arrived and I was ready to embrace the end. I needed to get away from the training center and the memories of my past life here. More importantly, I needed to drink to quell these haunting nightmares. But I had one last pain to endure. During one of the classes the door opened and there was the face of my former commanding officer, friend and mentor; retired Captain Bill Treadwell. I had not seen him since his retirement from the academy. I wasn't sure how much he knew of my fall from grace and I had no idea how he found out that I was here. But, in true Captain Treadwell form, he made a grand entrance to the class. He asked the instructor if he could speak for a few minutes and of course, the instructor agreed. He began to tell the story of my career making sure to highlight accomplishments and training expertise. He called me an "Instructor's instructor." He told them of how much he relied on me on the death row unit. Before he left, he walked up to me to shake my hand and as he did, I saw a tear in his eye and his voice began to crack. He was emotionally touched and it was a side of him I'd never seen in all the years I worked for him.

After he left, even one of the students commented on what he'd seen and how it touched him. I was both gratified by the display of my captain and fellow classmate, but also felt shamed by it because I let Captain Treadwell down. He had gone through so much to help me rise to the level I attained with the department before my fall. He was the man directly responsible for me being chosen as Correctional Officer of the year in 1986. We met at the dining area when the class was on break and he didn't show any signs of disappointment. He was just glad to see me and happy I was back with the department. We sat as two old friends sharing a cup of coffee and catching up on life in general. Since the loss of my own father, Captain Treadwell was in many ways like my father. He guided me in my personal life as well as professional. Without his guidance my life, personal and professional, had suffered.

The classes came to an end and we began to practice for graduation. Terry Duffey came to the auditorium to take everyone through the process of what we were to do. This was the graduation ceremony that Terry and I had developed just a few years before. I'd seen the graduation from an instructor's point of view and now I was seeing it from a student's view. I was elected the class representative to deliver the student address and so I spent the last night preparing my remarks. With everything completed, all that was left was the ceremony the next day and I was ready to have this all done and return to the boot camp. The four weeks I'd attended the academy had been a very humbling experience. When I was suspected of drinking, it was downright humiliating. I still carried guilt in my heart for lying to my friend, Terry. It was just one more rock to put on the load that I carried on my shoulders. The worse part being that I created it all.

There was quite a crowd for graduation; family and friends of the cadets who were about to become certified Correctional Officers. When the moment arrived to recognize the honor graduates, I was selected as the top shooter and presented with the Corrections Academy's "Top Gun" award. I later found out that I had missed being the top academic student by only few points. It was a high honor to have outscored over one hundred cadets. I delivered the class remarks being very careful to give honor to those who had instructed us throughout the training session. I knew the entire training staff and had been colleagues with most of them so the respect I spoke about in my speech was genuine. When I was done, I received a standing ovation. It was a very heartwarming moment for me. The last segment of the graduation was for the class to stand and take the oath of office. Once completed, we became sworn peace officers of the state of Georgia.

Once the ceremony was over I went directly to my dorm room and changed into civilian clothes. I turned in my key and headed to the warehouse to turn in my cadet uniform. With that completed I had officially completed Basic Correctional Officer Training. I was free again and able to concentrate on my new career that lay ahead and able to put an uncomfortable portion of my life behind me. Yet as I cast off the burden of the training program, old ghost and memories returned to visit. They had been hidden somewhat behind the stress that I created at the firing range. Now released from that, they came to the forefront of my thoughts. I turned again to my coping skills. I turned on the stereo, rolled down the window and drove toward the country roads that brought peace even if it was only temporary. I pulled over to the side of the road, closed my eyes and took a deep breath of the country air. I could hear the wind gently blowing though the trees. I opened my eyes and reached under my seat and pulled out the bottle. I put it to my lips, turned it up then sat back and waited for that old familiar feeling. The whirlwind was about to begin again.

Chapter 16

"Amid disquieting thoughts from the visions of the night,
when deep sleep falls on men, dread came upon me and trembling,
and made all my bones shake. Then a spirit passed by my face;
The hair on my flesh bristled up.

- Job 4:13-15
(New American Standard Bible)

With the stress of the academy behind, I turned my focus to the future. But, haunting me was the fact that I began on a lie to my friends at the academy. It was more guilt to add onto an already troubled conscience. A letter of commendation was placed in my employee file for being top shooter and an honor graduate at the academy. I began this tour of duty with kudos from the warden and the deputy warden. It seemed like I was on a fast track to promotion again. Within only a month, I was selected as the senior drill instructor. My duty schedule was now Monday through Friday, 8:30 am to 4:30 pm with weekends off. My primary responsibility was orientating the new arrivals to the structure of the boot camp and teaching them drill and ceremony. They were as trainees at military basic training.

Mother and I continued to drive to Tallahassee to get Miki every other weekend. Now that I was off on the weekends, I could spend my time with her. I gave up the trailer I was living in and moved in with mother. Being with Miki was both a blessing and a curse. On the one hand I was blessed to still have my youngest child, but when we were together it made me realize what I gave up; my other three girls. I was also saddened by the fact that Miki would grow up not knowing her sisters. It was a burden I was cursed to carry and one that I brought on myself. I sometimes wondered how God viewed me in all of this. Did he see me as the failure that I saw myself? I prayed less and less because I was overwhelmed with guilt from my choices in life.

My personal shame only served to give way to the failed promise that I'd made myself to be a voice for the murder victims of my death row years. The faces of those that affected me most occupied my waking thoughts less, but came to visit more often in the night; Roosevelt Green's victim and my namesake, Teresa Carol Allen and the teenage runaway victim of Timothy Wesley Mcorquodale, Donna Dixon. Sometimes I'd see Roosevelt Green dancing

in his cell. Timothy Wesley Mcorquodale being told that he'd stuffed Donna Dixon into a small chest after breaking her arms and legs. I'd hear his faceless claim; *"I just don't think I could do them things."* Then a change to the scene of him walking beside me and saying, *"I like you Mr. Allen, but if you ever stood between me and that door, I'd have to kill you."*

The nightmares came more frequently and I slept less. I awoke with the faces of the victims and their killers burned into my mind to begin my day. The only relief from that torture was a drink first thing in the morning. I'd given up trying to fight it. If I didn't have that drink in the morning, I wouldn't make it out the door because I would be stuck with visions of my dreams from the night before. Once I had my composure, I could make the 1 hour drive to the institution. I always had the vodka bottle with me no matter where I went and work was no different. I thought I was being very clever covering up my breath, though at times I thought I could see other officers looking at me strangely. I wasn't sure if it was reality or just my paranoia deceiving me. I became suspicious of everyone and was very careful to keep my distance from people when I talked to them for fear that my breath would betray me.

When I finally made it to my truck at the end of the day, I could feel relief slide over me and I took a deep breath and exhaled as though I had just run a marathon. The lie I was living was taking its toll on me. Of course to compensate, I reached under the seat for the only relief I had anymore. I always waited for the other officers to leave the parking and then I would take a drink in preparation for the ride home. Once I felt that relief, I'd start the truck and head for home. Once there, I changed into civilian clothes and headed back out the door. I knew that mother knew I was drinking, but she didn't know to what extent. I risked drinking and driving to hide the truth of my life from my mother. Driving the country roads close to my home gave me the only peace I knew at that time. I hated to see the sunset because I knew the night was coming for me and I had to return home to my bed which had become my enemy.

I walked into my bedroom and became nauseated at the sight of my bed. I'd plug headphones into my stereo, continue drinking and allow the music to sooth my mind. I drank until my eyes became heavy, then unplug the headphones, turn the music down low, lay back and hope that sleep would find me before my mind could betray me. It was a few hours at best and then I'd wake up covered in sweat. Sometimes I'd remember the dream, sometimes not, but I always recalled the faces in my dreams. I closed my eyes again until the alarm sounded and always before I was ready. Then my routine started all over again. I drank myself to sleep, drank to begin my day and all the hours that I could in between. The only time I didn't drink was when I was at work and I even considered bringing alcohol in like before at the college and the youth center. However I never got that brave because I worked very closely with other officers and I knew I would be discovered.

That was my life for several months. Each day was identical to the one before and I was beginning to wonder how long I could last. My only break came when I was selected to attend a boot camp training program at the academy. It was an advanced class that lasted a week. I was back at my old stomping ground again, but not under as much scrutiny as the basic training class. But, once again, the instructors of the class were former colleagues of mine. I knew I had to accept the fact that this was my place in life now. Men and women I'd once worked alongside with as equals were now my superior officers. It was another blow

to my ego, but I was actually getting used to the idea. Even coming to terms with that fact didn't alleviate my embarrassment. I saw the way they looked at me, but I stopped trying to guess what they might be thinking. I just relied on the alcohol to cover up any insecurity I felt.

I survived another class at the academy and returned to the boot camp to continue my duties as the senior drill instructor. To break the monotony of my life, I started going to a night club in Macon on the weekends. It was a change of scenery, nothing more. I didn't feel comfortable there, but it was a chance to be around other people because I had cut myself off from any contact with people other than my mother. I existed in an invisible cage that I wasn't even aware that I created. I worked, returned home to drive the country roads and went to the nightclub on the weekends I didn't have Miki. I only slept on a reprieve from my nightmares and it was broken sleep at best. I was a prisoner in my own mind and almost like a pressure cooker with no relief valve, yet ready to explode.

Finally came the day there was no place for the pressure to go and I lost control. No sleep, nightmares and a steady diet of alcohol and very little food had me on the edge. In the spring of 1993, on my drive from work I recognized Crystal's car, the young receptionist from the academy. I'd given up my family to be with her, but destroyed that relationship as well. Her ex-husband was driving her car and I assumed they were together again. It drove me insane because I'd given up everything to be with her and now she had her family back and my family was gone forever. The woman that I loved was now another man's wife and he was raising my only child. I'd never felt so small and insignificant in my life. I felt as though I was standing on an empty stage with the spotlight on me and for the first time in my life the stage was bare and no one wanted any part of the life I created and I felt totally alone.

I went home and drank myself to oblivion. Images flooded my drunken mind all through the night. Faces from the last twelve years of my life visited me. The executed men, the victims I'd read about, the sweet innocent faces of my children, my brothers and sisters, my poor mother watching me plunge into a sea of despair and finally Debbie, the woman I loved, but abandoned. My mind was swirling as one by one the faces appeared and then vanished only to return again in the dark. Finally the alarm rescued me from the torture I was imagining. I opened my eyes and stared at the ceiling. The thought of putting on a uniform today made me sick. I was also still intoxicated from the night before and there had been no restful sleep. When I sat up in the bed, I felt the contents of my stomach rise up in my throat and I hurried to the bathroom. Thankfully mother was still asleep. Once my stomach settled, I returned to the bedroom to get dressed so I could leave before mother was awake. In my condition I couldn't stand the thought of mother questioning why I wasn't going to work. I needed to be alone.

I grabbed the bottle and headed out the door. I could still feel the effects of the alcohol, but I needed more in order to calm my nerves. I turned the bottle up in the truck several times. Finally I felt calm enough to start the engine. I drove away not even sure of where I was going. I chose the country roads to begin my journey. I finally reached the old wooden bridge over the creek and I pulled over to the side of the road. I took the vodka bottle and sat down on the bridge and allowed my feet to dangle over the edge. The cool morning air felt good on my hot face, courtesy of the vodka. Listening to the water rushing under the bridge eased my anxiety. I imagined myself in a small raft riding the current passed the trees on either side of the banks and disappearing out of sight around the bend. I wanted to disappear from everything and return when the pain was gone. But, I knew that was a childish wish and not reality. I turned the bottle up several times and returned to the truck.

I wasn't going to work today nor was I returning home. I checked to see how much cash I had in my wallet and decided that I could disappear for several days. I wasn't sure I would ever return to work or home. That insatiable need to get away that I'd experienced two years before had returned. I felt exhausted from the decisions I needed to make about my life or what was left of it. So I took another drink then started the truck. I drove toward Macon with no clear destination in mind. Then I begin to think about what I witnessed the day before; the ex-husband driving Crystal's car and the two of them getting on with their lives while I was alone in my misery. I continued to drive and drink with all my emotions on fire; shame, guilt and finally anger. I wanted someone to pay for what I was feeling. Self hatred only took me so far. I needed to hold someone accountable.

I chose the only person, besides myself, that I could blame and that was the young Crystal. The farther I drove and the more I drank only served to fuel the fire I was feeling. By the time I reached Macon, I was seeing red. It was almost as if I was outside of myself watching a mad man control my actions. I stopped at a local department store and bought a large kitchen knife. When I returned to the truck, I turned up the bottle yet again. I decided that if my life was over, hers would be too. I started the truck and begin to drive to downtown Macon. I was focused on drinking and when I finally had a conscious thought, I was already at the office where she worked. It was still early morning and I drove to the rear of the parking lot and parked facing the office so I could watch everyone enter. My head was now swimming with hate fueled by alcohol. I picked up the knife and squeezed it tightly in my hand. As I thought about what I contemplated, I almost laughed out loud. It would be poetic justice for me to die in the same electric chair where I walked so many to their deaths. When I looked up, I saw *her* car pull into the parking lot. There was no one else around. I put my left hand on the lever of the door. I watched her get out of the car and walk to the steps of her office. My eyes were now burning into the back of her head. I pulled the lever and the alarm went off because the keys were still in the ignition.

I jumped at the sound of the alarm and it was enough to jolt me back to reality. I shook my head and looked around. I closed the door and begin to tremble from the reality of what I was contemplating. A shudder went up my spine. I waited until she entered the office before I started the truck. I drove away as quickly as I dared. I got on the highway and drove south where I knew a cheap motel was located. I stopped first to buy more alcohol. I felt mentally exhausted from the events of the morning. I paid for the room and as soon as I opened the door, I fell across the bed and closed my eyes. There were no words to describe what I felt. I had just come dangerously close to what I despised the most; a man that would take another human life for selfish reasons.

I immediately formed a picture of Teresa Carol Allen. I felt shamed at the thought of her knowing what I planned. I lay there for several minutes afraid to open my eyes for fear that all those murdered victims would be staring at me in disgust. I once made a promise to myself to be the voice for those who no longer had a voice. Just an hour before, I lined up to be counted in the ranks of those who selfishly sought their own will. Hate reached a new high only this time it was directed at me. I rolled over on my stomach as if hiding my face would somehow make the faces of the dead stop looking at me. My emotions caved in on me and I began to sob out loud. I had no idea who I was anymore.

When I finally opened my eyes my only peace was that I couldn't remember any dreams from my sleep. But, there was no restful sleep because I passed out. I was still afraid to open my eyes for fear their faces would still be there. My head was aching from the alcohol and the evil of what I did in the early morning hours. I was nauseated and full of fear because of my actions. Yet, being aware of that only gave way to the proof that I was going insane because all I really craved was another drink. I lay my right arm across my face as though I were hiding. I finally forced my eyes open and gradually peered under my arm to see the ceiling. I looked around to ensure that no one was there, but knowing full well I was alone. I was genuinely afraid ghosts might be in the room watching me with condemnation. When my eyes focused, I got up from the bed and reached for the new bottle I bought before renting the room. I turned it up several times hoping to ease the pain in my head, my stomach and in my mind. It only served to make my body numb, but it was enough and I was grateful for it.

I turned on the TV in an attempt to drown out my thoughts. I was feeling sick again and decided to make a trip to the vending machine to put some sustenance in my empty stomach. I forced down the peanut butter crackers I bought. I couldn't remember the last time I had a full meal. I'd been operating on alcohol and a bite here and there when I was feeling sick. I knew I was losing weight, but I was willing to pay the price in an effort to keep my demons at bay. Once the crackers were down and I could tell they were going to stay down, I went back to the vodka. I made a trip to the motel office and paid for the room for several days while I was able to walk without stumbling. The next few days were a blur because all I did was drink, pass out, wake up and drink only to pass out again after I got the vodka down. I hadn't called work or mother to let her know where I was.

I lost track of time because the vodka stopped working and my dreams returned with a vengeance. I was in a strange state. Not sure if I was awake or dreaming. Every year of my time on death row flashed through my mind and I watched as though I were in a nightmarish cinema, but unable to turn away. It all began with my first visit to death row and I saw the ghoulish smile of Carl Isaacs that seemed to go from one ear to another. One scene gave way to another without any pause in between. I open my eyes briefly, took another drink and then I'd be right back in the vision as though I'd never left.

I saw the catholic priest talking with John Eldon Smith, our first execution, just before we walked him to the holding cell. That gave way to escorting Alpha Otis Stephens to the H-5 execution chamber. There we saw the electric chair looming under sheets like a ghost waiting with open arms to take him to his death. His comment had lingered though the years, *"Just sit me down and burn me now."* Next here was Roosevelt Green, who seemed to be my arch nemesis because of the name of his victim, Teresa Carol Allen. The image of him lying on the floor, hands cuffed in front, head rocking back and forth, smiling with the same evil grin as Carl Isaacs and saying, *"I love it, I love it."*

Jerome Bowden smiling, doing his little dance as he packed his belongings because of the stay of execution he'd just received only to give way to the image of him crying the next day as we took him to H-5 and executed him. Ultimately the faces of the victims came next. The innocent teenage women sexually abused, murdered and tossed aside like trash. 17 year old Donna Marie Dixon raped and strangled then her body broken to fit into an old trunk.

Lastly, there was the face of Teresa Carol Allen lying on an autopsy table with a hole in her face. I'd lost my composure the first time I saw the picture in the trial transcript thinking about my own girls.

They all came to visit me through the night and into the days as the dreams went on in between the drinking. Finally I sat straight up in the bed as the last face went through my mind and said, *"Jesus Christ!"* The alcohol wasn't taking me away as it usually did; it seemed to be aiding the visions. I looked around the room, covered in sweat. I rubbed my eyes and looked at the almost empty bottle. I was disoriented and couldn't get my bearings. I picked up the bottle, took a drink and reached for the phone. I dialed the front desk. A few rings and I heard, "Front desk." The question I asked made me feel very foolish, but I had no choice. "Can you tell me what day this is?" Evidently they were used to this type of question because voice on the other said with no hesitation, "Yes, sir, it's Thursday." I hung up the phone without responding. I was out of touch with reality for three days and my nightmares persisted while I drank a half gallon of vodka. I checked my wallet for cash and found only a twenty dollar bill. I had no choice but to go home.

I finished the vodka and tossed the empty bottle on the table. I drug myself from the bed and into the bathroom for a bath. It was the only way I could compose myself for the journey I had to make. I was no longer concerned about the job, but I felt so bad for my mother. I hadn't talked to her in three days. She didn't deserve what I put her through, but there was no way I could make her understand how cursed I was with guilt, shame and degradation. It now totally consumed me and I had no control what so ever. After my bath, I dressed and left the room. I was still intoxicated, but there was no one I could call to help me. I knew that vodka was the last thing I needed, but I had no courage of my own and relied on what was manufactured in a bottle. I drove north toward home and stopped at a liquor store that had a drive through. I wasn't sure I could walk into a store without staggering. Once I received my prize, I started home.

I took the back roads so I could drink and prepare myself to meet my mother. I drank as much as I dared. The lines on the road begin to blur and I strained my eyes to keep the truck on the road. Taking the back roads home was the safest bet because I knew if any law enforcement stopped me, I'd end up in jail, where I deserved to be. I was only a shadow of the man that I was 7 years before when I walked across that stage to accept the correctional officer of the year award. I looked in the rear view mirror at my reflection and turned the mirror away so I couldn't see myself. That's when I made my decision. I had one more stop to make before I went home. I pulled into a store and parked. I sat there for several minutes to get my bearing. I looked over at the vodka bottle, but quickly decided that if I drank any more I wouldn't be able to walk in the store without staggering. I rubbed my hands over my face, got out and walked slowly into the store. I walked over to the medication shelf and found a bottle of sleeping pills, paid and returned to the truck.

Now I reached for the vodka bottle and took several drinks before I started the truck. I had everything I needed for the mission I planned in my mind. Once home, I pulled into the driveway and parked. I looked around the empty yard where I had played with my children when they visited; all that was gone now. Miki was all that was left and I hadn't seen her in more than three weeks. I looked at the vodka bottle and the bottle of pills I'd bought and decided that I made the right decision. I destroyed my life and I thought the best thing I could do for everyone was to simply fade away. The thought of going to sleep tonight and

waking tomorrow morning to start it all over again made me feel sick. I opened the door and staggered inside. Mother knew I was drinking, but I put my alcohol in a bag in an attempt to show some measure of respect. I almost laughed when that thought came because at this point in my life, I had no respect, especially for myself. It was a drunken attempt to spare my mother's feelings.

Evidently mother had not heard me drive up because when I pushed the sliding glass door open, I heard her get out of her recliner in the living room. She came to the kitchen as quickly as she was able. She asked, "Bobby, where have you been?" I just shook my head and she continued, "Your job has been calling for you." All I could manage to say was, "I know, mother, I'll call them tomorrow." That was a complete lie because I had no intention of being here tomorrow. I went to my room and she returned to the den. I took the instruments of my doom out of the bag and sat on the side of the bed looking out the window. Outside the window I saw the security light attached to the tall pole where I practiced martial arts as a teenager. Life was so much simpler then and it was my age of innocence. Now my life seemed like one big mess I created and from which I could not return. I sat in my room all day drinking from the bottle I'd bought and now watching as the evening fell. Mother checked on me only once when she came to ask if I was hungry. I told her no because the thought of food made me nauseas.

After a day of drinking alcohol, I developed the nerve to reach for the bottle of pills. I felt as though God was a million miles away, but I still couldn't bring myself to begin my plan without asking for forgiveness. I murmured a short prayer and then opened the bottle. It took three hands full of pills before I could get them all down. Then I just continued to drink waiting for the end to come. I decided I wanted to be outside where my mother taught me to pray. I stopped in the kitchen and poured the rest of the vodka in a cup. Then I went to the deck where mother and I had spent many nights talking and sat on a bench. I was fading in and out of conscience as I sat there with my head down. Finally mother came outside and asked me a question, but I couldn't understand anything she said. I mumbled something, but could form no words. I heard her pick up the cordless phone and return to the deck with me. I felt like I was in a tunnel listening to the echoes of someone talking. I did make out her saying "Please come help me because I can't handle him."

It seemed as though an eternity passed since I took the pills and I faded in and out of conciseness with only brief moments of clarity. In one of those moments I heard two voices talking. I looked up to see my sister standing there with the phone in her hand. She was talking into the phone as mother asked questions. I closed my eyes and only heard voices this time, but no idea what was being said. When I opened my eyes again there were three people standing there, but only two were talking. Now I wondered who else they called to join the end of my life. I picked up my head as far as I could and tried to focus my eyes. It finally came clear to me that the third person wasn't part of the conversation, but was only here for me. Finally my eyes focused to see Teresa Carol Allen looking at me with a sad frown on her face and I was out again.

When the next moment of clarity came my sister was standing beside me saying, "Come on, Bobby." She reached for my arm and I stood up and followed because I had no will of my own. I looked around to see if *she* was still here, but I could only see my sister and mother. I sat down in the car and was out again. I came to several times briefly on the trip and would lift up my head only to black out again. The next moment of consciousness, we were parked in front of a large building. The driver seat was empty and I looked in the back seat to see my mother sitting behind me. I opened my mouth to speak, but found words very hard to form. It was important for me to know so I mustered all the energy I could and asked mother, "Where is she?" Mother replied, "She's inside checking you in." She thought I was talking about my sister. My tongue felt as thick as brick, but I continued, "No, mamma, where is Teresa?" She thought I was just delirious, but I persisted. "Please tell her I'm sorry." My head flopped back against the head rest as I passed out.

I have a vague recollection of being lifted into a wheelchair and wheeled inside the building. When I could open my eyes, I knew where I was. It was a mental health center that I'd driven by many times on trips to Macon. Next we were in an elevator going up. I was finally taken to a small room filled with several hospital beds. I was in and out with no idea of the time that passed. It became apparent to me that my suicide attempt was not going to be successful because my sister and mother had interfered and gotten me to the hospital on time. A nurse came over and lifted a pill cup to my mouth and said, "This is for your depression." I swallowed without even asking what I was taking. The last thing I saw before slipping into unconsciousness was the figure with long dark hair standing at the foot of my bed. This time she had a very warm smile. My last words were, "I'm sorry." She faded away as my eyes closed.

I woke up with my head pounding. I barely had the strength to keep my eyes open. A nurse nearby noticed my eyes were open and came to my bed. "Bobby, do you know where you are?" It took me a moment, but I finally said, "I'm at charter hospital." It took me another few seconds to ask, "How long?" She replied, "You've been here two days." Apparently I'd been asleep the entire time because I had no recollection of the time. My eyes were hurting so I closed them again and drifted off to sleep. It was another full day before I would open them again and able to stay awake. My throat and mouth felt parched and I was able to sit up slightly and ask for some water. The nurse supported my head and allowed me to sip water from a straw. I still felt disoriented and drifted in and out of consciousness. When I opened my eyes again the doctor was standing there observing me. "How do you feel, Bobby?"I replied, "Groggy." He continued, "That will pass in a few days, in the mean time we're going to take care of you." All I could mange was a nod of my head.

On the fourth day I was able to sit up and eat a little food. I felt like I was able to stay awake and I asked if I could take a bath. The nurse helped me to my feet and into the bathroom. I allowed the water to run slowly as I lay there. The warm water felt good on my body and it invigorated me. I was there when the doctor made his rounds and he was upset that they'd left me alone. He opened the door enough to let his head in and asked, "Bobby, are you ok?" I assured him I was, but he insisted that the door be left open. Once my bath was complete, the nurse helped me back to my bed. I looked around the room and saw other patients. It became clear to me that I was in a detoxification ward. As I lay back my mind started to wander. I recalled that I'd seen Teresa Carol Allen at mother's house and at the foot of my bed when I arrived. I wondered if she had really been there or if my drugged mind caused me to hallucinate. On top of all my shame and guilt over my children, I recalled the promise not to forget about *them;* those who could no longer speak for themselves.

Dreams, nightmares or visions, they all came to me at some point; my father, the victims, the murderers themselves. Yet, Teresa Carol Allen and Donna Marie Dixon were the special ones to me. They'd both endured torture, rape and finally murder and both were just teenagers. I thought, maybe they were special because I had four girls myself. While I was contemplating this, another nurse came to my bed and said, "Ok, Bobby, it's time to get out of bed and walk around, doctor's orders." She helped me to my feet and we walked together to the day room where all the other patients were sitting. They were very polite to me and introduced themselves, but I wasn't in the frame of mind to socialize. The nurse sat with me and I had a feeling that was doctor's orders too. They didn't want me walking around alone because I was a suicide risk. The nurse seemed to sense my discomfort and said, "You're a miracle, you know?" I looked at her and said, "I don't feel much like a miracle today." She smiled and said, "When they brought you in, we weren't sure you were going to make it."

I didn't say it out loud but I thought to myself, *"That was my plan."* I stood up and walked to a window. The sun was shining, there was a beautiful lake just below and a breeze was making ripples in the water, but none of that mattered to me. All I could feel inside was what a miserable failure I was to myself and everyone I loved. Everything was gone. Leighanne, Tracey, Kimberley and I wondered how I could possibly be a father to Miki now. The more I thought about my life, the more I wanted to get out and finish what I'd started. As I looked out at the beautiful day, I wondered what God thought of me in all of this. I felt ashamed to even think his name. As I did, I closed my eyes and said the only thing I could, "I'm sorry." It seemed as though that had become the motto of my life. I felt empty and thought all I was doing in life was taking from people and contributing nothing. That was as much as I could take and I said to the nurse, "I'm tired, I'd like to go lay down now." It was the truth. I was mentally and physically drained.

As my strength returned in the next few days and I was allowed to attend groups. Our days always started with a group meeting with the doctor. The doctor had a file for each patient and went through the group addressing each patient. Nothing was done privately. We were encouraged to talk about our feelings openly. However we each had an individual counselor and would meet privately with that person. In the evenings, we attended meetings of Alcoholics Anonymous and Narcotics Anonymous. There were arts and crafts groups, and outside activities as well, but I had no motivation to attend any of it. Most groups I stared out the window and just listened. The group leader would attempt to engage me and I would only say enough to convince the doctor that I was improving. It was a lie, but I wanted to get out of the hospital as soon as I could. When I was allowed to go outside, I looked up into the sky and attempted to pray, but felt as though my prayers were dying in the air. I felt abandoned by God, but the truth was, I had abandoned him.

Mother talked to my supervisor at the boot camp and amazingly I still had my job. But, I wanted no part of it. I had no zest for life in any form. I went through the motions and after thirty days, I was released from the hospital. Mother picked me up at the hospital and took me home. Everything was somehow foreign to me. I received a check from my insurance company while I was in the hospital and as soon as I unpacked, I went to the bank and directly to the liquor store. I didn't like my reality, so I decided to alter my reality with alcohol. My first day home, I was drinking as though I'd never stopped. After taking that first drink, I drove to the wooden bridge where my journey began a month ago I relived

the last month in my head. I bought a weapon and planned to kill someone. When I found I didn't have the nerve to do that, I tried to kill myself. I'd failed at that as well, but I was afraid to try again. I sat at the bridge and drank into the late evening.

When I returned home, the lights were out which meant mother was asleep. I was thankful for that because she wouldn't have to see me arriving home drunk, yet again. I sat in the truck drinking and listening to the soothing music on my stereo. The darkness and the alcohol somehow hid me from reality. The daylight was now my enemy because each new day meant I had to face what I had become. I sat drinking and contemplating my next move. I had no clue what my next move was. I decided that I was done with law enforcement. I could no longer put on a uniform each day and pretend to be something I didn't believe in anymore. My head was swirling again. I finally came to with mother shaking me. I'd gotten out of the truck and was lying on the ground with my foot propped up on one tire. I couldn't respond to her and finally she gave up and I slipped into sleep again. The chill of the night air woke me again. I laid there a few more minutes and finally found the strength to pull myself up. I staggered inside and down the hall to my bedroom, collapsed on the bed and fell into a deep sleep hoping not to awake again.

In the early summer of 1993, I was terminated from the boot camp and my life became a series of drunken days and nights. Over the next few years I went from one dead end job to another just to have enough money to drink. I could stay sober long enough to get a job and work several weeks until I got a few paychecks. My drinking had progressed to binges. Once I started, I wouldn't stop until I lost any job I had and the money ran out. Then usually I would check myself into a state funded psychiatric unit in Macon. The days of going to the country club style psychiatric hospitals were over when my insurance ran out. They would treat me for the alcohol withdrawals that I now experienced, but nothing more. I became a familiar face in the unit. Each counselor who facilitated the groups would tell me the same thing. "Bobby, there's something in your past that keeps you from facing reality and nothing will change until you face it and talk about it." I could never bring myself to talk about my nightmares or how I abandoned my children. The fear associated with it all made it impossible to talk about. It seemed easier to silence it with alcohol. But inevitably, the fear would return no matter how much I drank.

Sometimes the nightmares were so severe and come so frequently that I'd mix alcohol with sleeping pills in my attempt to end it all again. That would only ensure a trip to the emergency room followed by a longer admission at the state psychiatric unit. After a few days of avoiding the real issues in my life, I'd be discharged to start it all over again. Through the years I owned firearms, but never had the courage to use one on myself. I also went from one relationship to another. A psychiatrist once told me that before I could love anyone, I had to love myself. There seemed to be the problem; I hated myself. So how could I possibly return any affection someone showed me?

Sometimes I'd pick my head up from self pity and manage to stay sober for a few weeks. But inevitably the nightmares would call and I'd start down that long, dark path where alcohol led me. It was during one of those sober periods that I was looking though the newspaper and saw a name in the obituary that was like a knife in my heart. My mentor, my friend and my Captain, Bill Treadwell had succumbed to a heart attack. The last time I saw him was at the academy during my basic training class. I was grateful that he passed

without seeing what a mess I made out of my life, but saddened that I didn't have a chance to say goodbye.

My vehicle was repossessed because I could not hold down a job and therefore could not make the payments so I had no way to get Miki and I wondered if she thought I abandoned her. I was also not paying child support. Debbie had the child support enforcement unit searching for me for nonpayment. In the spring of 1995, I was using my sister's car and I got stopped for my second D.U.I. I went to jail overnight and that alerted the child support enforcement to my location. I knew that when I went to court that I'd probably go to jail for non support of Miki. While I was waiting for court, Debbie called me at mother's house. She wanted her new husband to adopt Miki. Debbie told me that Miki asked if I was dead because I hadn't seen her in a couple of years. Debbie was kind enough to tell her that I was sick. It broke my heart and I was completely defeated, so I surrendered. I agreed to surrender my parental rights of the only child I had left. I lost my composure and simply said to Debbie, "Please take care of her."

My second D.U.I. came 9 years after my first one. When I went to court, my license was suspended, I was fined a hefty sum and had to serve two days in jail. But, as I suspected, the child support people were on to me. I decided that since I had no money to pay my fines or pay child support, I would opt for serving time rather than pay the money I owed. There would be no more child support charged after I signed the papers concerning Miki, but I was still being charged for back child support. I was given a 6 month sentence in the county jail, but because I was on a work program, I would only serve three because for every day I served, I was given a day off my sentence. It actually gave me time to clear my head, sober up and I started exercising with weights. I lifted three times a day, for three months. By the time I was released, I was huge. I'd been sober, but the nightmares continued.

I was out of jail with no vehicle and in desperate need of a job. There was a pallet plant close to home and I was fortunate enough to get a job there. My only mode of transportation was a bicycle, but I felt blessed to have it. I started drinking beer after work and was able to control it enough to maintain the job for several months. Eventually though, it caught up with me and I quit yet another job. The nightmares persisted and I still was unable to talk about them. The alcohol led me again to the state psychiatric center for several more trips over the next three years. But, in 1998, with the help of AA, I was able to get sober and hold a job down for four years. I also started my martial arts training again. It was my therapy and in 2001 I earned my third black belt at the age of 42. Once again, however, the nightmares caught up with me and I turned to alcohol.

My poor mother watched me fall so far down over the years to a useless unproductive man, but she refused to give up on me. On one occasion as I lay on the sofa, drunk, I asked her why she did it. She simply replied, "Because you're my child." After watching me self destruct for years, my oldest brother, Don, went to my mother and told her, "Let's put him in Milledgeville." That was the location of the state mental hospital. My brother went through his share of bad decisions with alcohol and drug use and mother was there for him as well so she told him, "No, I didn't do it to you and I won't do that to him." No matter what I did, how much I hurt and disappointed her, mother remained faithful to stand by me. Yet, I could see the toll it was taking on her and it broke my heart that I did this to the one person I knew would never give up on me.

In 2001, while I was sober and in my right mind, mother gave the inheritance she was planning to leave me and signed over her property and the mobile home we lived in. I was receiving phone calls from creditors of my past and one attorney told me they were coming after my assets. I couldn't bear the thought of mother having to move from her home, so I signed it over to the one person I thought would never turn on me, my sister Rachel. She assured me that I could always live there even after mother's passing. It would turn out to be one of the biggest mistakes of my life.

In 2004, Rachel took my mother's checkbook on the premise of helping her take care of her finances. After a few days, my mother decided that it was a terrible mistake. She called and asked for her checkbook and Rachel refused. Our mother called a childhood friend of mine who was a magistrate judge, Buck Wilder and told him the circumstances. He called Rachel to speak on my mother's behalf. Rachel came immediately to mother's house and she was furious when she walked through the door. Mother was sitting in her recliner and I was lying on the sofa watching TV. Rachel threw the checkbook hitting mother in the head. Before I could get off the sofa, she was at mother's chair and pulled her foot until she slid down in the chair. Then put her hand around mother's throat while screaming at her. I finally got to the recliner and pushed her away and asked, "What the hell is the matter with you?"

She continued to scream and I called the local sheriff's office. Rachel went to the back deck and started to throw mother's patio chairs into the yard. Two deputies arrived in minutes. However, instead of talking with me and mother, they listened to Rachel's rant. When it was all over, I was forced to leave the house. One of the deputies drove me to Forsyth, but I returned in a few hours despite the warning not to return. It was the most ludicrous display of law enforcement I'd ever seen. The deputies didn't seem to care that Rachel destroyed mother's patio chairs or had wrapped her hand around mother's throat. I was labeled as the perpetrator and forced to leave. Rachel informed mother that she was to move out of the house. I heard mother on the phone asking my oldest brother, Don, if he would help her move. It was more than mother could bear and over the next couple of days I saw a marked change in her. She had no energy and seemed to have no will to do anything. At one point she was so weak, I had to help her to the bathroom. While we were walking she told me, "Bobby, thank God you're here because the rest of them don't seem to care." I could tell she was defeated.

The next morning when she awoke, I helped her to her recliner. She wanted to sit there to gather her strength. Mother always conducted her medical task at the dining room table; checking blood sugar level and giving herself insulin shots. I was lying on the sofa watching TV when she asked me to help her to the dining room table. Once we were there, I told her, "Mother let me know when you're finished and I'll come help you, don't try to get up by yourself." She nodded and said, "Alright." I returned to the den and lay on the sofa to watch TV. In just a few short minutes I heard a loud "thud" and ran into the kitchen. Mother was sitting up on the floor holding her head with her right hand. "Bobby, I have smashed my brain!" I immediately helped her to the den and into her recliner.

The longer we sat there, the more strange she acted. She began to slur her words. I thought maybe she had taken too much of her pain medication because she was so upset. It was something she had done in the past. I said, "Mother, lay back and just rest." I helped her recline her chair. I returned to the sofa. She closed her eyes and lay back. I watched her

for over an hour and finally noticed that her breathing was labored. I got up and prepared a warm wash cloth to wipe her face. As I did so, I noticed her eyes moving under her eyelids. I shook her, "Mother, wake up." There was no response. I attempted that several more times. Now I was afraid and called my brother, Rusty, who lived behind us and said, "I can't wake up mother." He came right away. We both sat there trying to wake her and then finally I decided to call the ambulance. The EMT's wanted to know her medical history and I filled them in, but they could not revive her and finally decided to transport her to the hospital.

Rusty followed them to the Monroe County Hospital. I stayed home and prayed it was nothing serious, deep inside I knew that wasn't true and everything around me suddenly seemed alien. I laid on the sofa with the TV on and fell asleep. The telephone woke me up and I was surprised to see the sun coming through the window. I grabbed the phone like my life depended on it before it could ring a second time. It was my sister-in-law, Darlene, Rusty's wife. "Bobby, they had to life flight your mother to Atlanta and she's there on life support." My stomach immediately went into knots. It was too much to handle. She sensed I was speechless and continued, "I'm on my way up to pick you up and take you to Atlanta."

I dressed as fast as I could and waited. She was there in minutes. We started our journey to Atlanta which would take about an hour. On the trip she explained to me that mother's heart stopped at the hospital in Forsyth and after they revived her, the helicopter was called. On the flight to Atlanta her heart stopped again, but was revived yet again. By the time Rusty made it to Atlanta, the doctors said she had irreversible brain damage. That's when I knew that the fall in the kitchen the day before had done the damage. I recalled seeing her on the floor holding her head and saying, *"Bobby I have smashed my brain."* I closed my eyes and fought back tears and felt it was my fault. I thought, *"If only I had stayed in the kitchen."* Darlene saw how upset I was becoming and said, "Bobby, I know your mother loved you very much." I begin to sob lightly.

When we arrived at the hospital, I ran to mother's room and found her connected to many tubes and lying there with her eyes closed. I couldn't take it and I cried out loud as I sat on the side of her bed holding her hand. My oldest brother, Don arrived next then Rachel and her husband. Rachel didn't speak to me and I wondered what was going through her mind in light of the way she treated mother at their last meeting. Two doctors came in and asked us to excuse them while they did some test. We all walked outside the room and waited. They were there minutes, but it seemed like an eternity. Finally the door opened and the doctors appeared. Apparently they had performed an M.R.I. before everyone arrived because the doctor spoke about it now, "I'm very sorry, but there's no activity in her brain and there is no response to pain stimulation anywhere on her body." We all looked around at each other then the doctor continued, "When she hit her head, it caused a hemorrhage in her brain and she bled out into her skull." Don spoke next, "Is there any chance of surgery or that she will recover?" The doctor looked at him with a grim face and said, "No, I'm sorry there is just too much irreversible brain damage." That's when the second doctor spoke, "She just isn't here anymore, guys."

We walked back into her room and Don cried out loud and said, "I want this stuff off of her." In just a few minutes a nurse came in and asked if we were ready. I sat on her bed and leaned in close to her ear and whispered, "I'm not ready for you to go, Mamma." I knew it

was selfish, but I could not comprehend a thought of the only person in the world who never gave up on me not being here anymore. I squeezed her hand and Don said, "Go ahead." The nurse disconnected the ventilator as we waited. I looked up and saw the heart monitor was slowing down and Rachel cried out, "She just blinked her eyes!" The nurse assured us that it was a reflex action. As the sound of the monitor slowed even more, I caressed her hand and when I looked at her face I could see her left eye opened slightly. Rachel cried and hugged her husband when the monitor finally stopped and that's when I knew that my mother, the one who gave me life, my best friend, my protector passed on while she was looking at me.

That's when I was reminded of what she told me as a child years ago while I was angry at her; *"What if mamma died right tonight and you remembered all the rest of your life that you were mad at her."* As tears streamed down my face I said to her, "Mamma, I was never mad at you." I leaned down and kissed her on the forehead and lay my head on her chest. I was reminded of the song by Amy Grant: "I will remember you."

The rest of the day didn't seem real. I stood outside with Darlene as my two bothers talked to each other. My sister made the arrangements for mother to be picked up by the only funeral home in Forsyth. Darlene talked on the way home, but I wasn't up for conversation. She dropped me off at mother's house and told me that she'd talk to me tomorrow and to call her if I needed anything. I walked into mother's house and just stood there in the kitchen and stared at the spot where she fell. Everything seemed different because I knew mother would never come home again. I walked back to her room. I opened the closet doors and looked at all of her clothes. Then I lay down in her bed and buried my face in her pillow. I inhaled deeply and started to cry because I could smell her there. I stayed as long as I could and finally returned to the den and lay down on the sofa. I fell asleep with the TV on.

When I woke, it was night and it took me a moment to focus my eyes and realize the day's event were real and not a dream. I looked over at the recliner to which mother would never return and that caused my heart to ache. I lay there looking at the ceiling and listening to the TV in the background. I reminded myself of Mother's routine every morning when she got out of bed. I'd hear the bed squeak and then her feat would touch the floor. There was a pause while she put on her slippers and then she'd shuffle down the hallway to the kitchen, make her coffee and sit at the dining room table to check her blood sugar and administer insulin. The same routine she'd performed the day before only I had to assist her. That's when I heard it.

I heard the bed, the pause and then her shoes shuffling down the hall. I felt as though my heart stopped. I sat up and went into the kitchen, turned on the light and looked toward the hallway. There was nothing there. I went back to the den and resumed my place on the sofa. It only took a few minutes and I heard the routine again; the bed, the pause and the shoes shuffling down the hallway. I immediately shot up and returned to the kitchen only this time I walked down the hallway, turning on lights as I approached mother's bedroom. I switched the light on as I looked around. I spoke softly into the air, "Mother?" I felt a little foolish, but I also knew what I heard. I had no sleep that night and I heard her walk through the house all night long. Each time a brief pause before it repeated again.

As the footsteps continued through the night, I drifted off to sleep. When I woke again it was daylight. It felt very strange to be here without mother. I felt like a stranger in the house where I'd grown up. My whole world seemed foreign on this day. I'd experienced the same feeling when I lost my father, but I had mother to help me through it. But, now I had no one because my brothers and sisters rarely talked to me. My children were gone and for the first time in many years, I was totally alone. I knew God was there, but my faith was very weak and he seemed a million miles away. I forced myself off the sofa and into the kitchen. I poured a cup of coffee and went out to the back deck. The sun was beautiful and the cool morning air felt good, but I took no joy in it because I had none. My world fell apart the day before when the nurse unplugged the ventilator.

I returned inside and sat down at the dining room table looking at the chair where mother sat every morning. I turned and looked out the sliding glass doors in an attempt to find some peace and as I did; I saw the tall walking stick I carved for mother from a tree. She used it every day as she walked to the mailbox. Now it stood propped in the corner as a silent reminder of who was missing and I knew it would never be used again. Mother and I watched a TV show together about a psychic who claimed to talk to the dead. He said that he and his mother made a deal that whoever died first would send a message to the one left behind to let them know that they were alight. As a joke, mother and I made a similar agreement. I learned the lesson when my father died that though we all know death is coming; we are never prepared for it. I had time to prepare for my father's death, but it didn't make it any easier when the time arrived. Mother, on the other hand, was yanked away in one day and I was left to process it alone. Now, I sat there looking at mother's walking stick and missed her all the more. I needed something, but there was nothing to comfort me. Finally I said, "Ok, mother, I need my sign." I looked out the door from the dining room table to see the breeze blowing though the pine trees that mother and I loved so much. I got up from the table and returned to the coffee pot. I poured a second cup and stood there looking out the small window over the kitchen sink and that's when I heard it. Something hit the floor with a thud. I looked behind me and saw mother's walking stick on the floor. It fell from the corner that it occupied. I walked over, picked it up and looked around. The sliding glass doors were closed and there was no window open.

The room was still. I carefully returned the stick to its resting place and I smiled. The footsteps from the night before, the walking stick falling on the floor left me with just one conclusion. Mother stopped by her house to let her son know she was ok. It was a moment meant only for mother and I and I never shared it with anyone.

Our family arrived and the next two days were a blur for me. We had family visitation the night before the grave side service we decided on. Twenty two years after Daddy died, mother would finally be laid to rest next to her husband. She was faithful to visit his grave every week and I took her most times while I had a vehicle. We kept the marker on the grave cleaned and fresh flowers. I was an emotional wreck during the service and unable to keep my composure. My brothers and sisters had their spouses with them, but I had no one so my sweet daughter Kimberly came to sit by my side. When it was all over, I stood at the grave marker and looked at the inscription my mother chose when we laid daddy to rest; "Together Forever." I said a prayer that they were indeed together on this day.

With mother gone, I was alone in the house and it didn't seem like home anymore. I spent my nights on the sofa with the TV on just to hear other voices. There were no more footsteps, but her bedroom was as she left it and I visited it each day. I'd stand there as long as I could until I started to cry and then I had to leave. Rachel came by to check on me and we rode to the cemetery to view mother's grave. I knelt down beside mother's grave and said

"I wasn't ready." My sister thought I was referring to my life situation and said, "I told you, Bobby, that one day she'd be gone." But, that wasn't my concern. I was trying to infer to her that I wasn't ready for mother to leave. I knew she wouldn't understand so I let it pass.

In the coming months my sister decided that she would sell mother's house and allowed me to stay with her. I still wasn't working because I couldn't stay sober. If I got my hands on any money, I drank it away. It finally caused a huge problem between us. We became very angry with each other and in the heat of passion; I said something that I would regret the rest of my life. I said, "You know that you killed mother." I was referring to the last argument they had the day before mother died. It struck a nerve with her and she became unhinged. The sheriff's office was called and I was arrested for disorderly conduct. At my arraignment, my childhood friend, Buck Wilder, was the judge to set bail. He was very professional and didn't make eye contact with me and I was very embarrassed for my friend to see me like that. He released me on my own recognizance and I had to walk away from the jail because I had no one to call. No one wanted anything to do with me. I walked 5 miles to mother's home. Though the property now belonged to my sister, it was the only way for me to be close to mother. I went to the detox center in Macon for five days, but I had no intention of staying sober. When I was released, Rusty picked me up from the center, but made it very clear that I could not stay with him.

I had very little money and it wasn't enough to buy alcohol so instead a walked to the dollar store in Forsyth to buy a bottle of mouthwash. There was 26% alcohol in the mouthwash and it was enough to get me intoxicated. I returned to mother's house, but all the doors were locked. I slept the next few nights in an old shed that my father and I built when I was a teenager. Finally on the third day, I couldn't take it take it anymore. I had no home and felt as though I had no future. I found and old rope in the shed and went to mother's house. On the side of the house was a satellite dish. I hung the rope around the dish and connected the other end to my neck. I sat down in a chair and leaned forward so that the noose tightened on my neck and waited.

I don't know how long I was there because I passed out. The next thing I remembered was my brother pulling the rope off my neck and I fell to the ground. I tried to get up, but was so intoxicated that I stumbled and fell to the ground again. Next I saw a sheriff's deputy standing over me and I also saw the ambulance in the yard. I heard Darlene tell the deputy that I recently lost my mother. That made me lose control and I started to sob very loudly and yelling out for my mother. I was in and out of consciousness and I barely remember the ride to the hospital. When I finally awoke, I was in the emergency room and I felt warm blankets around me like a hug and I was able to fall asleep. I was awakened by a nurse and there was another deputy standing there. I recognized him from my days at the training center. He said, "C'mon Bobby, let's take a ride." I lay down in the back seat of his patrol car and stared into the night through the back window. I rose up only once to peer out the side window to gather my bearings. I found that we were on the road that led to Milledgeville. It was the same route I'd taken to work at the Youth Center for two years. That's when I realized where he was taking me; to the state psychiatric hospital where Don had wanted me committed a few years before. Surprisingly, I felt relieved because I had nowhere to go. My family had completely turned their backs on me and I was now homeless. When we finally arrived at the hospital, I sat up and waited for the deputy to open the door. I was escorted to a waiting room. I sensed compassion in the deputy as he said, "Good luck Bobby."

After about an hour, I was escorted to one of the wards in the hospital. We passed through many locked doors only to have them locked behind us. I was finally turned over to the nursing staff. While waiting, I looked around the unit absorbing my surroundings. I had no concept of time from the moment I put the rope around my neck until now. The lights were low and I saw no other patients so I assumed everyone was asleep. My body started to shake. The alcohol I'd ingested from the mouthwash was wearing off. I also started to sweat profusely. The nurse filling out my paperwork saw my condition, smiled and said, "We're going to give you some medicine Mr. Allen." Once she completed the paperwork, she disappeared behind the counter and returned with a small paper cup and a cup of water. I didn't even ask what it was; I just accepted that it would bring relief. Next she took me to my room and I lay back on the bed staring at the ceiling waiting for the medication to take effect. After a few moments my shaking eased off. My eyelids became heavy and as I drifted off to sleep I whispered to myself, "Well, you finally made it." I was at the hospital that housed the most mentally unstable people in the state of Georgia.

I woke to the sound of people talking in the hallway. It was early morning and finally the door opened and I heard someone say, "Good morning, it's time for breakfast." I sat up in bed, still a little groggy from the medication. I walked out into the hallway and saw people walking toward a room so I followed as well. When I turned the corner I was in a large day room and I heard a television in the background. I sat down in a row of chairs that faced the TV. Finally a staff member said; "Line up for breakfast." I followed everyone else out into the hallway where we were escorted to the cafeteria. I wasn't very hungry, but I forced myself to eat some food and drank some milk. Afterwards we were escorted back to the day room. The hallways were now busy with what I surmised were doctors and medical staff because I saw many white lab coats. I sat down and focused on the TV because I had no idea what to expect. Finally my name was called from the nurse's counter. I was taken to a room where an oriental gentleman was seated in a white coat. He didn't speak, but was looking into a file, which I assumed was mine. I learned that he was my doctor.

In a few minutes he looked up from the file and introduced himself and lightly shook my hand. He asked me to recount the day before for him. I explained it all to him. He asked, "Were you really trying to kill yourself?" I looked directly in his eyes and said, "Yes, I most certainly was." He wrote into the chart. He looked up and said, "Have you ever been diagnosed with depression?" I told him about my drinking problem, but that I had never been diagnosed with anything else. After reading more in my file he said, "I believe that you are suffering from major depressive disorder." Then he began listing off medications he was going to prescribe for me. He was ordering a nerve medication, an antidepressant and a medication for mood disorder. Finally he said, "Let's try these and see how you do over the next week." It was fine with me because I knew the alternative was living on the street.

Through the next week I was given daily medications and attended group sessions with a counselor and other patients. The medication I was given made me very sleepy. I found myself falling asleep in front of the TV quiet often. I felt numb and as if I had no feelings. The only exception was when I thought about mother. That would usually bring me to tears. In the second week I spent a lot of time staring out the window. I stood there with my hands in my pocket looking at the beautiful day outside. The sun was shining, the clouds were white and fluffy and I could see birds flying in and out of the trees, but found no peace in any of it. As I stood there I begin to contemplate my past life and all those I'd hurt or used. I had a vague recollection of the pedestal I was put on with the department of corrections. I thought about Captain Treadwell and all he helped me accomplish. I recalled the slow painful death of my father and how I sat there watching him slip away. The faces of my children flashed before my eyes and how I'd given them away one by one. The final blow was the death of my mother and I still blamed myself for that. The torturous thoughts came to mind as I replayed over and over what I should have done. When she slipped away in that Atlanta hospital, I felt my life end right there. There was no one left and I asked myself, *"What the hell are you hanging around here for?"* As I stared outside at a world I felt I didn't belong to anymore, a single tear fell down my cheek because that's all I had left in me. I recalled the words of a song by the group Genesis, "In too deep." It was about searching through life and crying for help, but falling on deaf ears. I felt that no matter how hard I cried out, no one could hear my anguish.

Those words summed up where I was in my life. I'd had everything. My family, the career I wanted the love of my life as my wife and four beautiful children. My place in life seemed to be set. But, then I thought about the faces of the dead that came to visit me in the night. The promise I made to never forget. I sometimes wondered if others who worked on death row ever shared my visions. As I contemplated my sorrow, a nurse noticed my distress, walked up to me and locked her arm in mine. She said in a very compassionate voice, "C'mon, Bobby, I've got some medicine that will help you feel better." I looked over at her and she smiled. I dropped my head down and allowed her to lead me to the nurse's station. In a moment she returned to the counter and handed me the small pill cup and said, "This will help you calm down." I tried to smile only to find out that I didn't have the strength for it. I took the medicine and returned to the day room. In just minutes I was falling asleep in the chair.

That was my routine for the next several weeks; medications, groups, meal time, sleep and repeat it all the next day. On one occasion, I met with a therapist alone. She wanted to know my thoughts of the day I tried to hang myself. I explained to her that I simply wanted to slip away so that all the pain would stop. She looked at me and asked, "are you a Christian, Bobby?' I answered, "Yes." Then she pointed out something I had not considered in my emotional pain, "Well then we don't know if death stops the pain, do we?" It shocked me and I looked into her eyes and said softly, "No." I was caught up in the moment when I'd tried to kill myself looking for peace that might never come. Then I thought about all the anger, shame, guilt and depression that I would have carried across the void with me. If I'd been successful, it might well have been an eternity of pain from which I could not escape.

I turned 45 years old in July of 2004 at the state psychiatric hospital. The medication didn't seem to be working. It only served to make me sleepy during the day and very little sleep at night and they were the worst. I lay in the bed with the thoughts of my past life running through my mind like a movie that I could not turn off. When I did fall asleep it was from mental exhaustion of the tiresome mental images that flooded my mind. Then I was shocked awake by the memories of all the death I'd seen in my life with the most recent being my mother sitting on the floor, holding her head and saying, *"Bobby, I have smashed my brain."* It was in those moments that death seemed preferable to anything I felt here. But, then I would hear the voice of the therapist in the back of my mind saying, *"We don't know if death stops the pain."*

After 30 days I was told one morning by a counselor that I was being discharged. There was no warning and no one asked me if I felt stable enough to leave. It was simply a matter of resources had come to an end for me. I was being discharged to make room for others. I was shocked to reality in a harsh way and I asked the counselor, "Where am I supposed to go?" He said as he walked away from me, "You'll be released at the outpatient center in Macon and then you can try to stay at the Salvation Army." I stood there in the middle of the hallway feeling helpless. I saw a door in the hallway and almost punched it in an effort to get someone's attention. I had been warehoused for 30 days, medicated and had only one session with a therapist and now I was being turned out on the street. There was no compassion to be found here. I was just a name on a sheet of paper whose time had ended.

I was loaded into a van with others who were being released. I was familiar with the route because I had driven it many times while I was working at the Youth center. When I saw the Macon city limit sign, I started to feel nauseated. We arrived at the outpatient center, they opened the door and we all got out. As the van drove away, I stood there at the main entrance of the facility and never felt so lost in my life. I was totally alone with no family, no future and nowhere to go. I was close to the Ocmulgee River and was familiar with that area so I walked there to sit in the small park beside the river. I sat there and watched the sun set over the city. The bridge nearby was known to be an area where homeless people congregated. I'd crossed over it many days in my vehicle and remembered saying on many occasions, "How can they live like that?" Now I made it to that point in my life and was about to find out.

I brought an overnight bag to the hospital and everything I had left in this world was in that bag and it wasn't much. Two outfits and one of those was a set I'd received at the hospital. As night fell I took my bag and walked across the Spring Street Bridge to find a secluded place to be alone. I stopped in the middle of the bridge to see the full moon shining down on the river. At any other time in my life, it would have been a beautiful site that I would stop to see and say a prayer to my Lord. But tonight, I was lost. I recalled the scripture of Matthew 18:12;

"What do you think? If a man owns a hundred sheep and one of them
Wanders away, will he not leave the ninety-nine on the hills
And go look for the one that wandered off?"

I started to cry and I said, "Please Lord, come find me." I heard voices on the bridge and looked around to see others walking on the opposite side of the bridge. The darkness was bringing out the nightwalkers. Prostitutes, those searching for the next drug fix and I knew it was time for me to go. I walked to the end of the bridge and found a spot in a small grove of trees. I'd never been homeless before and I didn't know what to expect from the streetwalkers. I hid myself as best I could and lay down with my head on the bag. I was grateful that it was summer and I wouldn't be cold.

I slipped in and out of an uneasy sleep. Images flashed through my mind all night. The images of the deaths I'd been involved with in my life; H-house, G-house, the holding cell

and the electric chair lurked in the background. I recalled once looking at the death mask that covered the faces of the condemned as they sat in the electric chair and seeing a stain on the inside. I didn't know if it was saliva from the jolt of electricity or tears. I saw the image of my father alive again after 22 years in the grave. But always I had the knowledge that he must return. It brought an uncontrollable sadness and sometimes tears. The face of my mother in her casket was the newest addition to my torture. It had only been three months since I witnessed that. I was jolted awake and sat up. I was shaking but not from the temperature. The visions had been all too real and I rubbed my face and said, "Jesus Christ!"

I heard the chirping of the birds in the trees. Next I saw the sun rise over the skyline of the city. I sat there with no plan for the day. I took the discharge paperwork out of my pocket that I'd received from the hospital. I saw a name of a counselor on the paperwork that the hospital didn't bother to tell me about. The address was the outpatient center where I'd been released. The day was beginning and I heard traffic noise from the street above me. I waited until 7:30 am and then started the short journey to the outpatient center. I arrived just as the doors were opening. I checked the form for the office number of the counselor. I finally found the office I needed and walked into the waiting room. I gave the receptionist my name and told her who I was there to see. I was the only one in the office so I didn't have to wait long.

The counselor came to the waiting room and ushered me to his office. He had a kind face and a pleasant way about him and that was something I desperately needed at that moment. I told him I was released from the state hospital the day before and handed him my paperwork. He reviewed it and asked me, "Where did you stay last night?" I looked away from him and said softly, "Outside in the park." When I finally made eye contact with him again, he smiled and said, "We'll have to do something about that." He explained to me that he would sign me up for a program to help people with mental health issues and he could help me get housing. But he was very clear, "It's going to take a little time." My hope faded away as quickly as it rose. He continued, "In the mean time I'm going to take you to the Salvation Army so you won't have to live on the street." He wrote some notes down, stood up and said, "Come with me." I followed him out to his car. He drove me to the Salvation Army's men shelter about a mile away. He shook my hand and told me to stay in touch with him.

Everything was happening so fast. I'd been at the state hospital for 30 days and allowed myself to get comfortable. Then overnight my life was turned upside down again. With no regard as to where I would go, they discharged me. I'd been on medication for an entire month and released with no medication. The shelter manager informed me that I could stay free at the shelter for 5 nights, but then it would be $10.00 per night after that. However, I was glad to be off of the street even for one night. I lay in my bunk that night with my mind racing faster than I could keep up. Exhaustion finally gave way to sleep. I tossed and turned all night long. When the morning returned, my eyes were open and I was almost in a panic because I was about to start it all over again. The desk attendant came through turning on lights and telling us we had 30 minutes to clear out. I asked if there was someone I could talk to and the attendant told me that I could wait next door for the social worker to arrive. I decided to wait because at least I wouldn't have to walk the streets all day.

I walked in the office next door and the receptionist told me to sign in on the clipboard and have a seat. I was given an application for assistance to fill out. The waiting room was

already full with people seeking help. After I completed the application, I sat down and tried to focus on the TV in the corner in an effort to keep my mind from racing and worrying what to do next. After about an hour, I was called to the window and escorted to the social worker's office. She smiled when I walked in, shook my hand and pointed to the chair in front of her desk. She had my application in front of her and was looking over it as she spoke, "How can we help you Mr. Allen?" I took a deep breath and let out a sigh and said, "I don't know, all of this is new to me." She looked up from the application and I continued, "I've never been homeless in my life and I have no clue how to survive out here."

She looked back to my application and asked, "Do you have any health problems?" I replied, "I have no medical health problems, but I was recently diagnosed with Major Depressive disorder." She continued reading then put her hands on her desk and looked up, "We have a 6 month spiritual program for men here, would you be interested in that?" I felt immediate relief in my knotted stomach and replied quickly, "Yes!" She picked up her phone, made a call and gave my information to someone. When she was finished she said, "Go next door and ask for Mr. Charles, he's the director of the men's program and he'll talk with you." I thanked her and went back to the building where I'd stayed the night. The desk monitor said, "Just have a seat and be patient, Mr. Charles will be with you shortly."

I dared not move from that spot. I didn't want to miss seeing the director because I didn't want to spend another night on the streets. Finally after 2hours, he came through the door. He introduced himself and shook my hand. He took me to a small office where he explained the program to me in detail. It was a 6 month Christian spiritual program. I would attend the Salvation Army church twice weekly; Sunday and Wednesday. I never knew that the Salvation Army was an organized denomination of the Christian church. I'd heard about them all my life, but mostly just around Christmas time. I had assumed they were a social services group, but never imagined that they had a church. I would be assigned a "ministry assignment" to work 40 hours a week. It wasn't called a job because there would be no salary paid. Instead, I would be given a "gratuity" of $20.00 per week for personal needs. Room, board and meals would be provided at no cost. To someone in my condition, it was a true blessing. I had no home, no job and no money. Once all the paperwork was completed, I was assigned a bed with a locker in a 5 man room. He also gave me a clothing voucher for the Salvation Army thrift store next door. I was able to get 5 sets of clothes and I needed them because I had very little of my own.

The remainder of the day I sat in the day room watching TV. As other members of the program came in they introduced themselves and were all very kind. I'm sure it was because they had stories similar to mine. As I watched the TV my mind was working overtime. I was grateful to be off the streets, but now I was already starting to wonder what I would do after the 6 months were over. I'd been through so much in the last few months since mother died; it was hard for me to stay focused in the moment. After dinner, I was called to the front desk to meet with the shelter manager. He was a very kind Christian man and offered his hand to introduce himself. He smiled and said, "I'm Harrell Johnson." I returned the smile and said, "I'm Bobby Allen." He continued, "Bobby, I need a night desk monitor next door at the women's building and I'm wondering if you'd be willing to help me out?" The thought of being alone and away from everyone appealed to me and I answered, "Yes, I would." He smiled very big and thanked me. He told me to get some rest and I would go on duty at 11:00

pm. I tried to sleep, but the adrenaline was surging though my veins from the day's events so instead I sat in the day room. At 11:00 pm, I was taken next door by another program member and briefly trained on what to do. There wasn't much to it because all the women were in bed for the night. Once I was alone, I walked outside to get some fresh air. I took a deep breath as I stared into the night and contemplated my future.

Chapter 17

"And I will give you a new heart; I will give you new and right desires, and put a new spirit within you. I will take out your stony hearts of sin and give you new hearts of love."

- Ezekiel 36:26
(The Living Bible)

Because I worked nights I had very little contact with the other program members. I didn't reach out to any of my family to let them know where I was because they all turned their backs on me. My world became very small. I stayed at the compound around the offices and the two housing units; the men's and women's dorm areas. I only left on Sunday's and Wednesday's when I had to attend church and sat in the very last row. I wanted to stay in my own little world where no one could betray me ever again. But, I couldn't escape from myself and that seemed to be where most of my problems began.

It was difficult to sleep during the day and my dreams became twisted and evil at times. Not only did I have the faces from my past, but now I was having dreams about doing evil things to my family. I had bitter resentments deep in my mind. Rusty turned his back on me and Rachel sold the home I once owned after promising me that I would always have a place to live. Those resentments followed me into my waking hours. I remember many days plotting ways to kill Rusty and Rachel while I was in the shower. It frightened me because I was planning details of how to get there, carry out my plan, but had no plan to escape. I decided my life was over and when I took their lives, I would lay down mine before being captured. My dreams haunted me daily for well over a month and I thought I would lose my mind.

My thoughts were active even while I was at work at the women's unit. One night I followed my usual routine and waited until I was sure all the women were asleep. It was raining and I decided to walk outside to feel the cool breeze. As the rain fell it took my thoughts back to my childhood and how I would lie in my bed at night listening to the rain fall on the roof and it seemed to purify everything. Watching and listening to the rain brought relief tonight. I closed my eyes and prayed to God that I might find peace. I prayed for death tonight if there was any chance of going to heaven. I needed relief from the storm that was in my mind and wasn't sure how much more I could take. That's when I felt it. I had the overwhelming feeling that someone was watching me. I looked around, but no one was there.

Then I felt a peace roll over me like a warm blanket. That's when the voice came. *"You have a message to write for me."*

The events of my life began to flash through my mind and for the first time in several years, I didn't feel alone. I heard the whisper in my ear, *"I'm here and you are not alone."* I felt like my mind was wiped clean and in that instant, the resentment and hatred left me. I didn't see my life as a tragedy any longer, but instead I saw a life blessed with new opportunity. God spared me so many times in my life like the motorcycle accident where I should have been killed. The overdose I attempted with alcohol and sleeping pills and finally the rope I'd put around my neck just recently. I completely let go and turned my life over to God that night and said a prayer into the night as I looked into the sky. "Lord, if anything that I've been through can help me witness to another poor, grieving, lost soul please show me the way."

On the next Sunday in church, I sat a little closer to the preacher. I opened my bible and followed the scripture from which the message came. For the first time in many years it didn't seem that my prayers were be carried away by the wind. I felt a real connection to God. I discovered that he was the same God in the valley as he was on the mountain top. He was there all along, but I had turned a deaf ear to him. He woke me out of my despair that night he whispered in my ear, *"I'm here and you are not alone."* I purchased a type writer from the thrift store and started to put my thoughts on paper to see where God might lead me. The shelter manager, Harrell Johnson, became a close friend and my spiritual mentor. He would come to the women's shelter at night and spend hours talking to me. The first time he told me he loved me almost brought me to tears because it was the first time since mother died, that I felt genuine love from another human being.

As my spiritual life grew, I got to know the senior pastor of the church. The Salvation Army is a quasi- military organization. The clergy are given military style rank and wear uniforms. Their seminary is a two year college and when they graduate they are given the rank of captain and ordained as ministers. Their commands are called "corps." They oversee not only the church, but a social service division that helps people in the community with things like food, clothing and overnight housing shelters for men, women and children. They follow the true meaning of what Christ intended his people to do; help others in need. By the end of the six month program, I'd become close with Captains Johnny and Rebekah Poole. They were the most compassionate people I'd ever known and I aspired to be like them.

Since I completed the six month program, it was time for me to start looking for a job. I had no idea how I would accomplish that because I had no vehicle. But, instead of stressing over it, I prayed about it and trusted God. He saw me through much worse times in my life and I knew that he would bring me through this. He did in a very big way. Mr. Charles, the program manager, talked with Captain Poole about me working for the Salvation Army. There was a truck driver position open and my name was submitted. Captain Poole came by the women's shelter one night to talk with me. His only question was if I was in good health since the driver job would require lifting.

I assured him I was and the next day I was taken to the central warehouse where donations were processed. I filled out an application and in just a matter of days; I was working for the Salvation Army as a truck driver. My duties would be driving through the city picking up donations.

I felt closer to God than I had in a very long time. My spiritual life was growing and I felt peace in my life. My nightmares came less frequent and I was grateful for every minute of peace I had, though I was still unable to trust anyone enough to share my dreams. I wanted more of what I was experiencing so I stopped by Captain Poole's office one day to talk with him about joining the Salvation Army church. I'd been a Baptist all my life, but I felt compelled to serve in a more proactive way. He explained it to me in very clear terms; "Be sure that you have been called to serve because if you haven't, you're going to be miserable." I thought about that for a minute and realized it was a big step I was taking. Then he continued, "On the other hand, if you have been called to service and you don't answer the call, you're going to be equally as miserable." I felt firm in my conviction and told him so. He smiled at me and then we prayed together.

While I was waiting to be join the church, my call to service was confirmed in a very big way. Mr. Charles told me that he received a phone call from my daughter asking about me and she wanted me to call. He smiled as he gave me the number. I had no clue which one was trying to get in touch with me, but I was overjoyed no matter who it was. I went directly to the chapel, got on my knees at the altar and thanked God. It was a direct intervention from him because I hadn't told my family where I was. I went to the front desk and stared nervously at the phone. My breathing was quick and my heart was racing. Finally I picked up the phone and dialed the number not knowing who would answer the phone. When she answered, I recognized the voice right away as Tracey. We started talking as if we had never lost contact. Tracey was now married and informed me I had grandson and granddaughter. My life was blessed beyond words. Tracey, her family and her sisters, Leighanne and Kimberly came to my induction into the Salvation Army. Becoming a member of the church meant that I would become a uniformed soldier. I'd been in uniform in one way or another almost all of my adult life. It felt good to be in uniform now in the service of Jesus Christ. After so many years of being lost, I found a place where I belonged; where I could give back instead of take. I felt I found a home.

As time passed, Captain Poole gave me more responsibility. I was promoted within the church to recruiting sergeant. There was also an employee apartment on site and I was allowed to move there. In September of 2005, Hurricane Rita plowed through the Gulf of Mexico and into Louisiana right behind Hurricane Katrina. The Salvation Army command in Atlanta called for Captain Poole to join the disaster team that would be deployed to Lake Charles Louisiana, but sent me instead. I was there almost two weeks. When I returned home Captain Poole told me he received high praise for sending me and was told that I performed my duties exceptionally. The Salvation Army was receiving so many donations from all over the country for the hurricane ravaged area that they opened a regional warehouse in Atlanta.

I was sent there in the second week after it opened with two program members to take over the operation of the warehouse. This time when I completed my mission Captain Poole received praise from top officers in Atlanta for my performance. One of the top commanders in Atlanta told Captain Poole that if he could afford to pay me, he would hire me away from the Macon Corps.

The command needed someone from Macon to go to Lake Charles for an additional week, but this time they asked for me specifically. Captain Poole told me I was making a name for myself with the Salvation Army. I felt I was doing what God wanted me to do;

serve him by helping others. When I returned from my third week at Lake Charles, I was promoted to assistant warehouse manager. The warehouse manager ran the day to day operations of the warehouse and I handled all the scheduling and paperwork. My spiritual walk with God was growing, but always in the back of my mind I was haunted by my past. The nightmares were decreasing, but at times, I had daytime visions of the past. I still couldn't talk about my dreams and visions with anyone. It was my secret and I felt compelled to hold onto it.

I became a trusted member of the church and Captain Poole continued to give me more responsibility. I became a Sunday school teacher and a member of a prayer team. My first experience with the prayer team involved a church member and her granddaughter. She was just a baby and had developed a severe staph infection in one of her legs. It was so bad in fact that they were going to have to perform surgery. Captain Poole asked my fellow soldiers and me to go to the children's hospital and pray for the little girl and her family. When we arrived at the hospital, we were informed that we could not go to the room because only family was allowed. When we returned to the men's unit, we decided that we could still pray for the child and her family and we went to the chapel. The four of us joined hands and each said a prayer that God would guide the surgeon's hand or indeed heal the baby so she would not have to have surgery.

The next day we received word from the grandmother that a miracle occurred. The doctors prepared the baby for surgery, but when she was taken to the operating room, the surgeon found no evidence of a staph infection and released the little girl that day. God heard our prayers. It was a true miracle of our Lord and I was privileged to be part of it. On the following Sunday, the grandmother brought the baby to church and stood before the congregation to give a testimony of what occurred. It was the first time I was involved with a healing. I read of the miraculous healings in the bible and heard many stories of others who witnessed the events, but never imagined that I would be involved with one.

I felt fulfilled in all my duties with the Salvation Army. Yet, inside I always felt something was missing. Almost like there was a hole that I could never fill. In my most honest moments, when there was no one around, I knew it was those haunting dreams and visions I could never talk about. So I pushed them as far down inside as I possibly could. For so many years I lived a lie that if I could keep the outside cleaned up, no one would think that anything was wrong on the inside. I was living a good life with a future and I wanted to hold onto it. But, at night when I was alone, sometimes the dreams would return and I begin to wonder if one of these nights, they would completely consume me.

Tracey picked me up on my days off to spend time with her family and I was grateful for the time I had with them. I also began to think about having a relationship again because I didn't want to be alone the rest of my life. I began dating Mary, a girl who worked for the Salvation Army at the women's unit and also attended our church. It was nice to share company with a female companion and not just hang out with the men. I had friendships with men in our church and cherished those relationships. I became very close with Mary and I liked the fact that she was a member of the church and was serving God at the Salvation Army as well. But, things were happening too fast and I started to feel uncomfortable. The nightmares returned in a big way. Rather than find a doctor that could help, I turned to alcohol once again to numb the feelings. Captain and Mrs. Poole were out of town for the weekend and I locked myself in my apartment and attempted to drink the nightmares away. Mary knocked on my door that Saturday night. As soon as I opened the door, she could see that I was a wreck. We talked for a bit and I asked her to leave. I wanted to continue the drinking. She left, but reported to the Captain what was happening.

Captain Poole and his wife came to my apartment when they returned on Sunday night. I looked at the Captain and practically begged him not to fire me, but did not mention my nightmares. He asked me if I was able to walk over to his office and talk with him and his wife. I assured him I could. He told me to get cleaned up and meet him next door. When I walked in his office I received compassion I didn't deserve. He assured me that he wasn't going to fire me, but wanted me to get some help. They both prayed with me and told me to get some rest and they would talk with me on Monday morning. I lied to the Captain and told him I didn't have any more alcohol in my apartment. I continued to drink through the night. I slept on my sofa with the TV on and the bottle close by. I needed the distraction of the TV and alcohol to block the demons that appeared in the night.

The following morning, I got on the phone right away to search for a local psychiatric hospital where I could sober up and get some medication before I left the Captain with no alternative but to terminate me from my job. I found a hospital that would accept my insurance and it just happened to be where I'd been 26 years before as I sat and waited with family for the twins to be born. Then I was there again 9 years later to watch Miki being born. I chuckled at the irony of it all; how far I had fallen and the downward spiral of my journey. Mr. Charles took me to the hospital and walked inside with me while I registered. Then he smiled, shook my hand and left me in the care of the nurse. After signing the paperwork, I was taken to the psychiatric floor and found myself once again staring out the window wondering if this journey would ever come to an end. Even after all I accomplished with the Salvation Army, the love I was shown, the patience of my God, I wondered if it may all end with my death.

The first couple of days I was detoxing from the alcohol. On the third day, I called Mary. She was given orders, by the Captain, to give my apartment a thorough cleaning because I made such a mess out of it on my drunken weekend. While cleaning, she came across some of my financial statements and discovered that I was in major credit card debt from my past. Apparently it was more than she could handle because she told me I could forget about any relationship. So once again, I was abandoned and left alone by someone that claimed to love me. I was left to my misery and my nightmares, but still unable to talk about them. The new psychiatrist prescribed an anti-depressant and medication for my anxiety. It was as if the last few months of progress exploded in my face and came crashing down. I was lost in my suffering alone once again.

I was in the hospital for a week and when I made it back to my apartment everything seemed alien to me. With the help of medication I was able to function at a bare minimum. I performed my duties at the warehouse like a programmed robot. After work I went home and sat in front of the TV. I attended church and was heartbroken each time I saw Mary. After about a week of going through the motions, the nightmares returned again and I chose alcohol over the medication because it worked faster. I returned to my old routine of three shots and the demons were at bay. But, I was more like a zombie, than a functioning member of the Salvation Army.

I went to the hospital two more times after that, but this time I wasn't able to break the cycle. Captain Poole was going to transfer me to Columbus, Georgia, but I couldn't stay sober long enough to get there. Finally, when he had no other options, he terminated me from employment. He was very compassionate about it and I knew it was because I left him no other option. My last phone conversation with him he said, "We've got to get you some help, Bobby." After my last stay in the hospital, Mr. Charles picked me up and took me to his office. We sat down and he came directly to the point, "Would you like to go to Jacksonville or Tampa?" I asked him what was there and he said, "Salvation Army Adult Rehabilitation Centers." I thought for a moment and said, "Jacksonville I suppose because I won't be so far away from my family." He picked up the phone and called the number immediately.

I talked with someone in the Intake office and was scheduled to leave in two weeks. Mr. Charles told me I could stay in the shelter until I left, but I was too ashamed to face any of the men in the program who worked with me. I had helped Don's wife, Martha, get a job at the women's unit. I asked her if I could stay at their house until I left for Florida and she was more than happy to help. I had one final paycheck after being terminated, so I used that money to continue my drinking for the next two weeks. I respected my brother and sister-in-law enough to not drink in their house. I started to wonder if I would ever be sane and in my right mind ever again. I was too ashamed to attend church and just remained at my brother's house waiting to be accepted to the rehabilitation center. My mind still raced through most of the day and it was so exhausting. All I was able to do was drink and watch TV to occupy my mind. I was somewhat apprehensive about traveling alone to a brand new city, but I begin to realize that it was probably what I needed; to start fresh in a place where I didn't know anyone.

Finally I was accepted at the rehabilitation center. Captain and Mrs. Poole graciously bought a bus ticket for me and my sister-in-law drove me to the bus station. She hugged me before I boarded the bus. It was the first human contact I had with another person in weeks because I shut myself off from everyone. In my state of mind, I didn't think anyone wanted anything to do with me and how could I blame them? I boarded the bus and begin my journey to a new city and hopefully a new life. I felt some relief as I left Macon behind, but I was also leaving my church behind. I had not been on a commercial bus since my army days so I sat back and tried to enjoy the beautiful scenery of coastal Georgia as we drove through many small towns. I looked out the window as dusk came and tried to keep a positive frame of mind. I closed my eyes and lay back, but was unable to sleep. Night had fallen when I heard the bus driver announce, "Jacksonville, Florida." I rubbed my eyes and looked out the window. It was not what I expected for a coastal city of Florida. I saw skyscrapers as we exited the interstate and the lights of the city reflecting off of the St. John's River. I could tell that the entire city was built on either side of the river.

As the bus drove into the terminal, I could tell we were in the heart of the city I claimed my bags and walked inside. The intake coordinator told me the number of the city bus that would take me to the rehabilitation center. I walked outside and found a bus stop in front of the bus station. I checked the schedule posted at the bus stop and discovered the buses stopped running for the night. Because it was late night, I could see the city coming to life with the "nightwalkers." It reminded me of my first night on the street in Macon. I returned to the lights of the bus station and sat down on one of my bags outside. I figured that the lights would deter anyone approaching me for handouts. I checked my wallet and found I had just seven dollars and still had to pay for the bus. However, it didn't take long for a man to get bold enough to approach me; a tall bald black man. He didn't appear to be a street person because he was clean cut. He smiled very big and asked, "How are you tonight?" I returned his kindness and answered, "A little tried, but otherwise, I'm fine." He asked if he could sit down on a piece of my luggage and I nodded in the direction of the bag and said yes.

He asked where I was from and when I said, "Macon," his eyes brightened as he said, "Bibb County." Now we had something in common. I could already see where this was going, but I decided as long as he was cordial I would be as well. He made some small talk about Macon and when he figured we had made a connection, he made his move. "Could you spare a little change?" I shook my head and said, "Sorry, I only have seven dollars and I don't know when I'll come into more money." I regretted it right away. But, he seized the opportunity and persisted, "Let me get two of them." I replied right away, "No, I just told you I can't spare anything." He must have been desperate because he tried again, "Let me get one of them." I looked him directly in the eye so he would know that the game was up. "Sorry, I can't spare anything." I saw the look of defeat in his eyes and he sighed very loud. I told him the baggage he was sitting on contained my suits. He misunderstood and asked, "Did you say you have soup in there?" "No, they are my SUITS," I replied. He immediately walked away and I decided that sitting outside the bus station wasn't a good idea.

I gathered my bags and returned to the safety of the bus terminal. I sat down in a seat and lay my head back and kept my foot on my luggage. A security officer walked up to me and said "Let me see your bus ticket." I stood and showed him what I had and he said, "This is just a receipt." I replied, "Yes, I just came in from Georgia about an hour ago." He asked me, "Do I need to pull the video?" I was tired and agitated from the exchange outside and said, "Do whatever you need to do, I told you I just arrived." He studied me for a minute and then rudely said, "Sit down right there." He pointed to the seat I had sat in. "What a jerk," I said to myself as he walked away. Then I looked around as he questioned several more people some of which, he asked to leave. Then it hit me that a lot of the street people probably came in here at night to get off of the street.

I drifted in and out of sleep though the night and finally the sun came shining through the window where the buses parked. I wasn't sure what time the city busses started to run, but I'd had enough of the security officer's hospitality so I gathered my luggage and went outside to sit on the city bus bench, but lying on the bench was a homeless person with a blanket. However, it was either this or return to the wrath of the security officer. I sat down on the bench and listened and watched the city come alive with morning traffic as people started their day. Finally my companion on the bench sat up. He looked at me, but made no comment. I took the two one dollar bills out of my wallet for bus fare. That got the attention of my friend on the bench. I was waiting for him to ask for money, but all he said was, "The bus only cost $1.25." I smiled and thanked him for the information. Finally I saw the bus coming down the street so I stood and waited. The door opened and I stepped in, paid my money and asked the driver to inform me when we reached the rehabilitation center. As we pulled away from the bus station, I could see the man who sat with me the night before walking across the street toward the bus station. It appeared he had been up all night on his quest for money. It caused a shudder down my spine and I said a silent prayer, *"God, please don't let me ever fall that far."*

The bus drove across the river on a huge bridge. To my left I saw a football stadium and the sign out front flashed "Home of the Jacksonville Jaguars." As we drove up to the bridge I saw a huge ship docked on the side of what appeared to be a shipyard. I only saw the river briefly in the dark, but it was quite beautiful with the morning sun shining down on it. I looked down the river toward the huge buildings and saw several other bridges in the city. I was nervous about what the morning would bring because everything was happening so fast. Yesterday I was in Macon, which was familiar territory through most of my life. Overnight I'd been thrown into a foreign land with no idea of what lay ahead. I felt the butterflies in my stomach start to stir when the bus exited off the main road at a sign that read, "Beach Boulevard." I'd been told by the intake coordinator that the rehab center was located on that road. After traveling about a mile through many traffic lights, the bus stopped and the driver announced to me; "Salvation Army." I gathered my luggage and stepped off the bus into a steamy summer morning. The rehab center lay in front of me and it was much larger than the center in Macon.

I entered the building into a lobby, gave my name to the front desk attendant and discovered he was expecting me. I was introduced to the intake coordinator and spent the next few hours signing paperwork and touring the facility. Later I was assigned to a five man dorm room similar to the rooms at the Macon facility, but the room was much larger. This facility housed 120 program members compared to Macon's 40 man unit. I was given a schedule of my duties and an overview of the program. I had the day off to rest and acquaint myself with the facility. I lay down and studied the program paperwork. This was a 9 month program with ministry assignments like Macon. However it was a much more organized program with classes and each programmer was assigned a counselor that we met with once a month.

Just like Macon, there would be church services on Sunday's and Wednesday's. There was a Salvation Army Major, a fulltime Chaplin who would discuss spiritual needs. When evening arrived, I went to the dining hall and was overwhelmed with the food choices. It was like going to a very nice restaurant. After dinner I attended my first class which was orientation to the program. There was a curfew and all program members had to be in their rooms by 10:00 pm and lights out followed at 11:00 pm. I lay in the dark with my eyes open trying to gather my thoughts. So much happened in the last 24 hours and I was almost overwhelmed. Probably from mental exhaustion, I fell asleep and tossed and turned through the night. Finally at 6 am, someone opened the door and turned on the lights. The new day was beginning and after breakfast, there was morning devotionin the dining hall followed by daily announcements by the General Supervisor, a civilian employee and the administrator, Major Fredrick Macintosh, the manager of this facility.

I was initially assigned to the donation center, where people drove in to drop off donations. On our downtime, I got to know my fellow programmers and they explained the entire operation of the Salvation Army in Jacksonville. I soon discovered this was a multimillion dollar business. There were five thrift stores throughout the city. The main store was located next door to the main building. In the back of the thrift store was an enormous warehouse that processed incoming donations. There were six trucks that traveled through the city daily to pick up donations. People donated vehicles, boats, campers, RV's and every month an auto auction was held. It was more organized than anything I'd seen since being involved with the Salvation Army and these centers were located throughout the nation.

I sat in front of the donation center and stared out into the busy traffic on Beach Boulevard. It was one of the main strips to the Jacksonville Beach that was only 9 miles away. It was a beautiful day, but my mind started to wander as usual. I was in a strange city where I knew absolutely no one. The thought of being here, separated from everything I knew for the next 9 months seemed over whelming. All I could think about was home. But, then that thought brought anxiety as well. I didn't really want to return there because heartache was there. I was out of place in Macon and now out of place in Jacksonville. I didn't really belong anywhere. I wondered if I would ever have a "normal" life as other people did.

Within the first month, the general supervisor moved me to the front desk as a monitor. I knew that Captain Poole talked with the new administrator about me by phone. I thought maybe he informed the Major about my administrative skills. I worked the front desk for the next several months and attended the classes that were very informative, but it wasn't anything I hadn't heard many times before. We were also required to attend outside AA meetings. Once again, none of it was new to me. All the classes centered on addiction issues and the spiritual road to healing them. All the psych hospitals I'd been to and the detox centers I'd attended told me the same thing; that if I'd stop drinking my life would improve. Initially they appeared to be correct. Life did improve for a time, but then the nightmares would return and drinking was required to silence them. That would eventually lead to destroying whatever life I was building for myself. I knew that at some point in my life I would have to talk about the nightmares, but that would make me withdraw back inside my shell where I felt safe.

My sixth month at the center, the residence manager resigned to move to Georgia. I was selected as his replacement. At that time, the rehab center allowed its program participants to be employed while finishing the program. I was hired and given a private room. I managed the entire center at night as I completed the program. After completion of the program, I was given more freedom, but I still had to attend outside AA meetings like members of the program. I was required to live at the center in order to manage it and also had to pay rent. My meals were still provided and that alone enabled me to save money. I became very comfortable in my employment except where the administrator was concerned. He'd spent many years in the Navy and retired before becoming a Salvation Army officer. He was a pastor, but he brought that discipline from the service to his operation of the center. I didn't know what to expect from one day to the next. That stress triggered my dreams again and I started to lose sleep.

Even though I was an employee, I was still required to see a counselor once a month. My counselor was the program director. Bill Nichols was also an ordained minister and his guidance made it easy for me to trust him. However, I never shared my nightmares with him, but we did become friends. He was kind and in his eyes I could see he genuinely cared about people. He helped me understand things about myself. I learned more about my failed relationships from him than anyone was ever able to convey. When he left the Salvation Army for another job, we stayed in touch and remained friends. I didn't have many friends and I had damaged the relationships I'd had with my family and people who wanted to be my friends, like Captains Johnny and Rebekah Poole. They remained friends with me through some of my darkest days and now Bill Nichols became that type of friend.

I completed my first year in Jacksonville and was becoming more familiar with the part of the city where I lived. That mostly was the 9 mile stretch from the rehab center to the beach. Jacksonville Florida is a huge city. It covers the entire county of Duval and I didn't dare stray too far for fear that I'd get lost and not be able to find my way home. I was content with my job at the center, but I couldn't really see a future here because I felt like it was a dead end job. When Bill Nichols left employment to take another shelter management job in the city, the intake counselor was promoted to Assistant Program Director. The Intake job was offered to me and I jumped on the chance. It was an administrative job, with daytime hours and weekends off. There was also a pay raise involved with the job. The most important perk was that I could live outside of the center.

My first week on the job was very intimidating. There were so many small details to the job. But, my main duty was brining new people into the program. It took me several weeks to learn the job, but I finally settled into my new position. Within the month, I was able to move downtown to a small studio apartment and it was nice to go to my own home and relax. However, Major Macintosh still kept his watchful eyes on my duties and was very quick to point out any discrepancies. He had no problems embarrassing me in front of a group of program members or other staff. At one point I was so unnerved by his actions that I was ready to walk away from the job. But, I knew that would probably mean moving back to Georgia and that wasn't an option for me.

Moving out of the center alleviated some of my stress and being home was a blessing because I could relax, unwind and put it all out of my mind. Work was a different story, because whenever Major Macintosh walked through my office door, my stomach would tighten because I never knew what was going to happen. His praise was few and far between and when he walked in, I always prepared myself for the worst. A teenage female church member was assigned to help out in my office as an intern. It was awkward at first, but we soon found common ground to carry on a conversation. The computer in my office had sensitive, private information on it and no one was allowed to use it except me. One afternoon, my young intern wanted to show me something online and stood behind me about to log on. I didn't even know how she knew my password and just as she put her fingers on my keyboard, Major Macintosh walked through my door. It set him off on a tirade. He asked. "How do you know the password?" Through her stunned expression she replied, "The bookkeeper told me how to find it." He was looking for a way to point a finger at me and I was sure I'd be fired. She was taken out of my office and put in the secretary's office. Over the next few days I was given the cold shoulder and I avoided the Major like a plague. But, one afternoon he caught me in the hallway and told me that people were talking about me and the young intern. I knew it was a lie otherwise I would have heard it through the grapevine at work.

That was it for me. Major Macintosh, an ordained minister, was now accusing me of having an inappropriate relationship with a teenage intern. I never asked for any type of help in my office. I felt like I was just called a child molester by my boss. I was quiet the next few days and hardly left my office. I wanted out of here, but I had no job prospects and I didn't know enough about the city to even begin to look for another job. Stress always triggered the nightmares. I wasn't sleeping much at night and when I went to work in the mornings I felt like I'd had no rest. After a week of no sleep and haunting nightmares, I knew where relief would be found. I went to a local liquor store and bought a small bottle at first. It had the desired effect. But, that only led to a bigger bottle the following night. Within a week, I was bringing it to work with me, closing my door and drinking from the bottle. It was especially helpful when Major Macintosh came through the door with his rants.

Two weeks later, I was too drunk to report for work. An ambulance took me from my apartment to the emergency room and I was fired immediately. One of my secretary friends from work came by to see me at the hospital. She was in tears and apparently everyone had the opinion I tried to commit suicide. I drank for another week going from one hotel to the next throughout the city. The alcohol betrayed me again. Each night I passed out and had the faces of my past flash through my mind to remind me that they were still with me. I finally ran out of money and went to the only place I could; the detox center in downtown Jacksonville. After the third day, I was able to keep some food down and not shake quite so much. I also received a message from the Rehab center. There would be a bed waiting for me at the center if I wanted to return. I knew that I would return because I was out of resources. After five days, I was stable enough to be released and a friend from the Salvation Army church in Jacksonville gave me a ride to the center.

When I was dropped off, my perception of the center changed and I felt like I was behind enemy lines. In my job as intake counselor, I had brought most of the residents into the center and now I was just another resident on their side of the fence. My pride was bruised beyond repair. My mind raced constantly and I had trouble controlling my emotions. For no reason, I would burst into tears. The first few days I had almost no sleep. It was difficult to function during the day. I was assigned to the communication room where donation pick-ups were scheduled. I had trouble talking to people on the phone. Every new resident had a meeting with the Chapin, a Salvation Army officer. On the fifth day, it was my turn. When I walked into Major Robert Summer's office, he shook my hand and invited me to sit down opposite his desk. He placed his hands on the desk, looked at me over the top of his glasses and asked, "Is there anything you want to say?" I replied, "Not especially." I was still in a fog from my last week of drinking and just wanted this to be over. But, he had other plans, "Well, I've got some things I want to say to you." He pointed his finger at me and then unloaded on me, "I'm as sure as I'm sitting here that if you had died while you were out there, you would have gone straight to hell!"

I was dumbfounded. There was no compassion found here. He continued, "I'm really concerned of the damage you've done to the Salvation Army!" I couldn't believe I was listening to an ordained minister. As he continued his rant and making his points all I wanted to do was get out of the office. I almost made a move for the door, but then realized I had nowhere to go. This was a man I looked up to and had been in this very same office many times to have him pray for me. I sat there in silence like a scared school boy in the principal's office being scolded. When he finally reached the end of his rant, He took a deep breath and let out a long sigh. Then he had the unmitigated gall to tell me, "Let me pray with you." My jaw almost hit the floor. After accusing me of damaging the Salvation Army, telling me I was going to hell, demonstrating no human compassion whatsoever, he wanted to pray with me. It sounded more like a chore he had to perform than an attempt to help me. As he prayed my eyes remained open and his words meant nothing to me because that's all they were. There was no feeling at all in his jabber and his words bounced right off me. When he was done I immediately got up and walked out of his office without any exchange at all.

Everything that Captains Johnny and Rebekah Poole taught me, that I believed as truth about a church that wanted to help people, that I wanted to be a part of was just destroyed by this heartless Salvation Army officer, Major Summers, who masqueraded as a pastor. I'd once believed that I could help people as a law enforcement officer and had that myth destroyed as well. I took off that uniform. I thought I'd found another way to help people with this new uniform I wore, but now that was gone as well. I vowed to never again put on a Salvation Army uniform. I was done with uniforms. All I wanted to do was run away from here and these people, who stood behind the cross, promoting the name of Jesus Christ, but in the end, it was all about perception and money.

Over the next few days I had no sleep. My nerves were raw and I could barley function. I found a friend to help and I finally made an escape. He took me to the bus station downtown and I bought a bus ticket to Macon. I had to get out of Jacksonville and as far away from the Salvation Army as I could. I drank on my trip to Macon. After days of with no sleep, nightmares attacked me at will and I needed to escape. I looked out the window as we made the trip to Macon and wondered what my next move would be. I had no plan other than to get away from the confines of the Salvation Army. Evening gave way to night and I looked at the stars in the sky. The night sky always seemed so peaceful and as my mind relaxed from the alcohol, sleep finally came. They were all there waiting for me. Teresa Carol Allen, Donna Dixon, My mother and father. Even the murderers appeared. Their faces were blank, but gazing at me as if they had a question on their mind. I remembered saying; "I have no answers tonight, I don't know what I'm going to do." Finally the voice of the bus driver on the speaker said, "Macon, Georgia." It snapped me into consciousness. I sat up and looked around to see who was watching me, but the faces were now gone.

I got off the bus and claimed my luggage. I was standing in the same bus terminal that I'd arrived at 31 years before when I was home from the Army. But, tonight there was no one waiting and no one to call. I was feeling the effects of the alcohol. I tried to pick up my bags, but staggered instead from the weight. I managed to drag the luggage to the end of the street. I saw a motel across the street and headed for the safety of the lights. Thankfully they had a room on the bottom floor. It took me a minute to get the key in the lock and once inside; I locked the door and collapsed on the bed. When I closed my eyes images raced through my mind. I didn't give them a chance to capture my attention. I pulled myself off the bed and got the half empty bottle out of my bag and turned it up to my lips. I chocked from the burning in my throat, but I kept it down. I lay back and waited for the alcohol to take me.

When I awoke again, I had no idea of the time. I went to the door and opened it to see the morning sun shining. I took a deep breath of fresh air before staggering back into the room. I needed a bath to bring myself to life. Once that was completed, I knew the next order of business. I dressed and headed out the door. I was on my home turf again and I knew the location of the nearest liquor store. I was still intoxicated from the night before and walking was a challenge. I'd been around enough to know that if I staggered into the liquor store they would refuse to sell me anything. I stood outside the liquor store trying to get myself together. When I felt reasonably sure I could maintain my balance, I walked inside. I was paranoid and I was sure that everyone in the store was looking at me; even the customers. I had to conduct my business quickly or else I would be discovered. I picked up a half gallon of vodka because I knew I wouldn't be able to make it back out that day once

I started drinking. When I had my prize, I walked outside and let out a deep sigh of relief. Now, I had to make it back to the room.

I walked as steady and slow as I could and made sure the bottle was tucked safely under my arm. I made it to the sidewalk and only had about a block to go to the motel. I felt relieved and then my feet betrayed me. The bottom of my shoe caught on the concrete and I tripped. My head broke my fall and I could see the warm fluid as it ran down my eye. But, my first concern was the bottle. I reached over to my side like I was searching for a child I dropped. When I found it, I smiled and said out loud, "Thank God it's plastic!" I staggered to my feet and continued my journey. I walked past an elderly gentleman and I assumed from his facial expression that I looked like I just lost a fight. But, he said nothing, only looked at me with a frown. I finally made it to the breezeway of the motel and I sat down in the shade to compose myself. I knew I couldn't stay here because if I did, someone would become suspicious and call the police. I had wrinkled clothes on and blood running down my brow into my eye. I said to myself, "Move, move!" I stood up, started walking and made it to the room. After several attempts at the lock, I finally opened the door. I carefully set my bottle on the table and fell on the bed. The coolness of the air conditioning felt good on my warm face and I drifted off to sleep.

I had that terrible feeling of emptiness when I woke after the alcohol was processed through my body. It was usually enough to have me wake suddenly. I lay there staring at the ceiling trying to focus. Once that was accomplished, I turned my head to make sure that the bottle was safe. It's amazing how an inanimate object can become like a living soul once it consumes your thoughts. Nothing else mattered at that moment, but making sure that I had more alcohol to stop me from feeling anything else. After a few minutes of silence, I couldn't take the racing thoughts of my past any longer, nor did I have the strength to consider what lay ahead of me. Considering both would take me to a panic if I remained in silence. I turned on the TV first just to hear another human voice and then I went for the vodka. I decided that I would mix this time so that I could maintain some sort of composure. I put the bottle down and went to a vending machine for anything that would cut the taste of the vodka. Then I returned to the room and mixed several drinks in the small plastic cups provided by the motel.

Once my nerves calmed, I sat with my back on the headboard of the bed with the remote control in my hand. As I flipped through the channels I tried to formulate a plan. I would be out of money if I stayed too long at the motel. I hadn't told anyone that I was home again. I thought about Captain Poole and his wife, but I couldn't bear the thought of them seeing me like this after they'd done so much to help me. The next person I thought of was my sister-in-law, Martha. That was the only other person I could think of that wouldn't pass judgment on me. I needed several more shots of courage before I could pick up the phone. I waited until I was sure that she was at work before I made the call. After I dialed the phone I closed my eyes and prayed that she would be working. I was relieved when she answered the phone. I briefly told her of the problems I'd had in Jacksonville and asked her if she could help me. She told me she would be by the following morning to pick me up.

I felt much needed relief. That was one item checked off of the list. At least I knew that I wouldn't be out on the street. I continued to drink all afternoon. I'd pass out, wake up and start it all over again. Most of the time, alcohol did its job and kept me safe from the visions

of my past. Then there would come a point where drinking too much invited visitation from those very same faces. I never knew what the trigger was. I knew that stress played a role, but sometimes my mind just would not let go of the thoughts and feelings. This night was lining up to be one of those nights. Whenever a face surfaced, I woke up and my first reaction was to grab the bottle to keep it at bay. But sometimes they refused to be silenced and required my attention and wouldn't accept no as an answer. I followed my usual routine of three shots and lay back down to sleep again, but peace would not find me tonight.

I was standing in H-2 and saw Carl Isaacs with that gruesome grin spread across his face. Cold, dead eyes void of any feeling. One of his victims, Mary Alday just 27 years old, raped on her own kitchen table, then shot and left naked on a red ant bed while the men in her family lay dead in the rooms of their mobile home. Sometimes there was no method to the madness, just faces that stared at me. Reading those trial transcripts had turned out to be a huge mistake on my part, not to mention seeing the dead faces of their victims. At times they all returned to me as a collage of faces with no story at all. Even the faces of my parents were sometimes mixed in with the faces of murderers and victims and that was the real torture. I wanted to reach out to my parents, talk to them, but they were always just out of my reach. In those tortured moments, I would wake up in a cold sweat.

I sat up in the bed, bathed in my own perspiration and heard the knocking on the door. I shook my head and staggered to the door. It was Martha come to pick me up just as she promised. I opened the door and almost fell into her arms. She helped me back to the bed. She asked, "Are you alright, Bobby?" I shook my head as I bent over and put my face in my hands. As she gathered my bags she saw the bottle on the table and asked, "Is this really necessary?" I unequivocally told her, "Yes!" She saw the shape I was in so she put the bottle in my bag and continued to pack my things. Once that was completed, she helped me out to her van. Then she returned to my room and retrieved my bags. She was very kind and gentle with me. After what I'd been through with the Salvation Army in Jacksonville, I needed it.

She drove me to her home and helped me inside. She sat me down in her den and went to prepare a room for me. I told her, "I need to go see the Captain." She just said, "No, we can't go see the Captain today." In the meantime my brother, Don, walked in and sat down in his chair and asked, "How's it going?" I was unable to answer, but I saw the look of disgust on his face as he got up and left the room. It seemed like an eternity since my sister-in-law left the room and now that I saw how my brother felt about me, I needed to get out of the room. Finally she returned and took me to her main living room and lay me down on the sofa she prepared for me. The cool sheets felt good to my warn skin and I passed out again.

I lay there for several days drinking until finally the vodka was gone. I was unaware how much time passed. When I came to my senses, I heard the TV on in the den. I couldn't bear the silence any longer so I went to the den to find my brother sitting in his recliner. I asked, "Do you mind if I watch TV with you?" He kept his eyes fixed on the TV and never acknowledged that I was standing there. I had my answer and returned to the living room, took out my laptop and pulled up some music. I lay down on the sofa and closed my eyes to try and find some peace.

I woke up the next morning shaking from the last few days of drinking; my mind and body screaming at me from the lack of alcohol in my system. I heard my brother outside

with the weed eater. My sister-in-law was in the kitchen. I took the opportunity to go out the front door where I wouldn't be seen. I managed to slip passed my brother and walk up the road to a nearby store where I bought a fifth of cheap wine. I needed to silence the screaming in my mind. I went behind the store and downed the entire bottle of wine and waited for my body to stop shaking. In a few minutes, I was able to walk again. I started walking toward town to find a liquor store to finish what the wine began. A truck pulled up beside me and stopped. I looked over to see my brother sitting behind the wheel and my sister-in-law next to him. She asked, "Where are you going Bobby?" I lied and told her, "I'm going to the emergency room to get help." She got out of the truck and helped me inside. As my brother drove to town, she sat there with her arm around me the entire time with the most incredible look of compassion I'd seen in a long time. It almost brought me to tears because I felt so alone.

She sat with me in the emergency room until I was checked in and told me to call her if I needed anything. I was taken to the detox center where I'd been so many times before. After five days I was medically stable and released. I called my sister-in-law who took me directly to see Captain Poole and his wife. I tried to explain what happened in Jacksonville with the Majors Macintosh and Summers, but I could tell it was difficult for them to believe that a Salvation Army officer could behave in such a manner. Captain Poole allowed me to stay at the center as a program member. It was going to be another difficult transition just as it had been in Jacksonville. I'd once been an employee here, too. But, I was out of money and out of options. I tried to blend in with the program members as best I could, but I was very uncomfortable. After a few days, I had to be taken to the hospital again because I couldn't stop shaking. The doctor in the emergency room prescribed medication for anxiety. It allowed me to settle down and perform my ministry assignment. Even though this was home, I felt like a stranger. It was as if I didn't really belong anywhere. My sister-in-law worked next door in the women's unit and stayed in touch with me. My brother on the other hand, had no interest in me. He asked my sister-in-law why the Salvation Army was helping me again. It was a sign that he had given up on me. I didn't blame him because I didn't know why people were helping me either.

I was at the Salvation Army through Christmas of 2007 and even after being there several months, I still felt out of place, but I needed a place to recover from my time in Jacksonville. Captain Poole allowed me to put my uniform on and rejoin the church, though none of it felt the same anymore. That was reaffirmed for me when Captain Poole said he heard from his supervisors in Atlanta. The very same officer who wanted to hire me to work for him in Atlanta now asked Captain Poole, "Why would you work with Bobby ever again?" To make matters worse, that officer walked up to me, shook my hand at an event and welcomed me back to Georgia. That was all the betrayal I could handle. I'd faced it in Jacksonville and now at home in Macon. I apologized to Captain Poole for the trouble I was causing him, but he was willing to take the heat for my sake. But, I wasn't willing to cause any trouble for him and his wife. In January 2008, I received my tax forms from Jacksonville and went immediately to have my taxes prepared. When I received my check just a few days later, I cashed it in downtown Macon and went directly to the liquor store. I knew that I wasn't going back. I rented a room and did what I always knew would work temporarily. I drank until the voices and faces in my mind went away and stopped torturing me.

Captain Poole and his wife put their own reputations on the line to help me and in return, I tried to give the Salvation Army another chance. Now that I was aware of how the command staff in Atlanta really felt about me, I was finished with them. These were people who were supposed to demonstrate the love of Jesus Christ and the only evidence I ever experienced was from Captain Poole and his wife. They were true Christians in every sense of the word and I couldn't stand by and see their reputations destroyed because of me. I had no idea what I was going to do next. I stayed two nights in the hotel and finally had to be rescued by ambulance because my alcohol level was so high. After I left the hospital, my sister-in-law was kind enough to take me to the rescue mission in Macon. I could not get in touch with any feelings at all. I just wanted it to all be over, but I was too much of a coward to attempt another suicide attempt. After a few months at the mission, I couldn't handle being in Macon anymore. I saved some money and bought a bus ticket to Jacksonville. I had made a friend in Bill Nichols and decided to return there for help. Mr. Nichols was now the shelter manager of the rescue mission in Jacksonville. The mission had a similar spiritual program as the Salvation Army and Mr. Nichols took me in.

2008 was the beginning of my decent into a hellish existence for the next seven years. I went from shelter to shelter, from one failed relationship to another. I went through many small towns in north Florida trying to find a place to belong and I hurt many people along the way. I was using relationships to stay off of the street. I would stay with someone for a few months and then ultimately, my night terrors would resurface to haunt me and I was off and running again. Medication didn't work, but alcohol always helped keep the faces away if even for a few days. I could only go for a few days without alcohol and if I couldn't get to it, I'd end up in the emergency room in whatever town I happen to be in. I couldn't talk about the nightmares, but I had no problem telling anyone that would listen that I wanted to die just to keep the faces away. That would always lead to a trip to a psychiatric unit for several days where they would pump me full of medication, keep me for a few days on observation and then release me.

In my misery, I attempted overdoses on several occasions only to wake up in the hospital to find out that I hadn't succeeded. Sometimes I'd be close enough to death that I would awake on a ventilator. Nurses, doctors, counselors, mental health technicians would tell me how lucky I was. I would look at them and ask, "How am I in any way lucky?" I wasn't living, I was existing in a fish bowl of life just swimming around and around always with the same view until I felt it necessary to get off of the merry-go-round. Then I would buy alcohol and sleeping pills. Next I'd find an empty lot or deserted building and drink until I had the courage to swallow all the pills and pray, "God, please forgive me, but I can't do this anymore."But God had other plans. I'd wake up in an emergency room with no idea how I got there. If I didn't have money to buy alcohol and pills, I'd steal them and try again to carry out my plan. The psychiatrist that saw me in the psych units most of the time had tunnel vision where I was concerned. They'd see my use of alcohol in the chart and tell me, "If you'd stop drinking, you wouldn't have these troubles, Mr. Allen" That usually brought on a laugh from me and I'd say, "Ok, doc whatever you say." I couldn't make them understand that the alcohol was all that kept my demons at bay. I was such a regular at one psych unit that the doctor would tell me, "You can't continue to come here." I was told on one occasion that if I came to the hospital again, I'd be sent to the state hospital in

north Florida. I smiled at him and asked, "You think that scares me?" Since it didn't have the desired effect he was looking for, he looked up from my chart he was writing in and I leaned forward, look directly in his eyes and say, "Give it your best shot, doc!" He shook his head and continued to write in my chart.

Late at night when I was outside looking at the moon and the stars, drinking up the courage to swallow pills, I'd have a moment of clarity and reminisce about the respected and decorated law enforcement officer I once was. This particular night was no different. I looked around at my surroundings; trash lying everywhere as I sat in my dirty clothing. It caused me to laugh as I took another drink. Once I had the nerve, I swallowed the pills and hope that I would succeed this time. After I finished the alcohol, I lay back and wait for darkness to take me. As I drifted off, this time I heard the words to a song in my mind.

A song by the group Audio Adrenaline and it touched me. The song was based on the scripture: Matthew 18:12. I'd forgotten what the love of Jesus Christ was like when that promise was made. I wasn't alone tonight. My eyes blurred, and before I lost consciousness I said, "Thank you, Jesus, please forgive me." I woke up yet again to the sound of air and the awful taste of plastic. There was some type of breathing machine in my mouth. It was hard to focus and I thought there were other people in the room. I heard someone clear their throat. I tried to turn my head, but it felt like it weighed a ton. I slipped out again. The next time I woke up, there was a doctor in the room with me. He was dark skinned and spoke with an accent. He looked down at me, placed his hands on either side of my face and he almost seemed in tears as he said; "I'm not your doctor, but I wanted to come by to say I know what you're going though." I tried to respond, but all I could manage was to nod my head. He smiled and said," I know, my friend, it's a mother fucker is what it is." He tapped my face slightly and walked away.

It was the first act of compassion I'd received in a long time. Most of the psych units I visited were only concerned with how many times I'd been there. Their compassion had long since gone. Their job was no more than a paycheck and the patients on the ward were just names on a chart. Meeting with a psychiatrist was only to start medications and they never made eye contact with me. They'd ask what medications I had been on in the past, write in my chart and then simply say, "You can go." Never a question about how I was doing or what brought me there. There were groups during the day, but no individual counseling at all. Each day was the same and at the end of five days, I'd return to the psychiatrist. I sat on the opposite side of his desk as he looked up from the chart and say, "You go home today." Write in my chart, dismiss me and in a matter of hours, I was escorted to the door and released whether I had anywhere to go or not. Then I was free to roam the streets. In my despair, I'd start the whole process all over again.

In 2012, I found a small Christian program in north Jacksonville out in the country away from the city. It was a beautiful campus and reminded me of home. I could walk out in the fresh air and smell the aroma of trees and freshly cut grass. I became closer to God than I had been in several years. Because I was a clerk on death row, I had many useful office skills. Wherever I stayed, I was usually assigned to their office or front desk. I was comfortable talking to strangers and in my heart; I wanted to help people. This new assignment allowed me to do just that. The assignment was almost like my job as intake counselor at the Salvation Army. I conducted phone interviews with program applicants and was soon given the authority to approve their entry into the program. The director of the facility

only wanted to be notified. I wasn't being paid, but everything was provided for me. I felt at peace for the first time in many years. My nightmares were less frequent, but I was still unable to sleep through the night.

The facility had a yard sale on Friday's and Saturday's to help raise money to support the ministry. I was given management of the event. I met many people from the community and started to make friends. I was attending church on a regular basis and studying scripture under a theologian. I learned more about the bible in the next year than I ever had before. In 2013 while managing the yard sale, I met a Christian lady, Day Bennett. She began attending church with me and we became very close over the next few months. Late that summer, she developed breast cancer and was to undergo a double mastectomy and reconstructive surgery. Day was self employed as a housekeeper and would miss several weeks of work. She asked me to move in and help her through what was going to be a very difficult time. The surgery went well and in a few weeks, we received word that she was cancer free. The scare with her surgery brought us closer together and we made a mutual decision to marry. After a short honeymoon to Charleston, South Carolina we returned home. Day would still need several weeks to recover so I took a job as a plumber's helper to help out in the meantime. She finally healed enough to return to work and we were happy for several months.

I had back trouble for years and now performing manual labor aggravated it to a new level so I made an appointment with a back surgeon. My MRI showed significant damage to my lumbar region and the doctor recommended surgery. I was very concerned because I never had any type of surgery before, though I didn't let anyone know how I felt. Hiding my fears from people was nothing new for me. The surgery was scheduled quickly and I spent several days in the hospital. Day stayed by my side as much as she could. But, because she had been out of work for many weeks healing from her own surgery, she had to return to work. The nurses had me up and walking the next day after surgery. I was discharged with a back brace and it would take many weeks to heal. I lost the job that aggravated my back because I could no longer perform the duties.

I was taking pain medication on a regular basis so I spent a lot of time watching TV and my past finally caught up with me. I was watching a documentary of infamous murderers of the past. There was a segment that suggested that the brain of a mass murderer and other killers might be dysfunctional. Charles Whitman, the clock tower sniper at the University of Texas killed 14 people and wounded 30 others. After he was killed and an autopsy was performed and it was discovered that he had a brain tumor. It caused me a moment of pause as I considered the murderers I'd worked with and if their brains were somehow different. Then I began to consider my own situation. I wondered if there was something abnormal about me. So much had happened in the past few months I hadn't thought about my past. I knew that watching this program was a mistake and I turned it off.

Now my mind was racing and I couldn't be still. I walked around the house and finally outside for some fresh air. But, my memories wouldn't leave me alone. I woke a sleeping giant. I picked up my cell phone, and then laid it back down. My breathing increased and I was feeling panicked. I had that overwhelming urge to get away. I got into my truck and started driving with no clear destination in mind. As I drove into north Jacksonville I turned

on the stereo and tuned it to a station that played easy listening music. Seeing people drive and walk down the street going about their day only made me feel more alienated. I drove passed a liquor store and my attention was immediately drawn to it. I closed my eyes briefly and said, "NO!" I continued to drive, but my attention was back on the liquor store. I only made it another block before I gave into the urge and turned the truck around. I pulled into the parking lot and sat there as if I could talk myself out of it.

I bought a fifth of vodka and a bottle of juice. I returned to the truck, drove to the end of the parking lot and parked where no one could see me. I stared at the bottle and knew right away that relief was only a drink away. Because the bottle was in my hand, I knew there was no turning back. I poured half of the juice out and filled up the bottle with vodka. I raised it to my lips and gulped half of the bottle down. Then I lay back, closed my eyes and waited for peace to find me. In a matter of seconds I felt the effects move to my brain. I started the truck and continued to drive. The alcohol didn't have the same effect as usual. As I drove into downtown Jacksonville I began to feel incredibly sad. I thought about the documentary I'd watched just a few hours before. Tears rolled down my face as I thought about the people in Texas that day. They were going about their lives until a madman interrupted. I said to myself, "My God, those poor people!" Then I started to think about those with whom I was intimately affiliated; cold blooded heartless killers and the innocent faces of the victims staring at me from their pictures within the trial transcripts. I sobbed openly and I couldn't stop. Before I realized how far I'd driven, I was on Beach Blvd., driving by the Salvation Army Center where I'd worked. I continued toward the beach thinking that the sound of waves crashing against the shore would relieve my anxiety. Suddenly the thought hit me that I was to pick up Day's grandchildren today at school. There was no way I could drive them home in my condition. I pulled into a parking lot. I held my cell phone in my hand, but realized I couldn't talk to Day on the phone. I took the cowards way out and texted her instead.

I typed, "I'm sorry, I can't pick your grandchildren because I am in a very dark place today." In a few seconds I received the reply, "Then come to me and let me help you." I left the conversation there and began driving again. In no time I drank half of the bottle I bought. I wasn't going to be able to drink the images in my head away today. I had no idea what was different, but I felt very strange. I was now driving toward town and not really aware of my surroundings. I felt that something was very wrong. It was a feeling I never had before. In an instant I saw a flash of light and I was standing in front of the holding cell in H-5 and saw Captain Treadwell standing to my right. It was all too real.

I turned my attention back to the holding cell and there was Roosevelt Green. His stuck his hand through the bars and Captain Treadwell shook his hand, then he offered his hand to me and I took it. He said, "I just want you to know I always tried to be the best man I knew how to be." It was the scene I'd been a part of almost 30 years ago. I let go of his hand, turned to leave and I almost walked into the face of Teresa Carol Allen. I jumped and in an instant I was back in my truck driving toward home on the interstate. I had absolutely no recollection of how I got there. My head was pounding as I turned off the highway. The last thing I remembered was crashing into the mailbox and my truck was in the ditch.

When I woke up, I was in the emergency room. I was looking at the ceiling and I heard someone clear their throat. I looked over to see Day sitting next to me reading a magazine. I was in and out of consciousness. When I came to again, we were in her car driving toward

home. I still had no idea what was going on. As we drove up to the house, there was a Florida Highway Patrol car parked in the driveway. My heart sank into my stomach. We got out of the car and the trooper walked to me and asked, "Are you Robert Allen?" I nodded my head and replied, "Yes." Then he continued, "Your truck was reported in an accident on Beach Blvd. today, is there any reason why you didn't stop?" I told him that I couldn't remember. He was very polite and showed compassion and said, "I'm not going to take you to jail, but I will have to write you some citations."I thanked him and Day said," Why don't you go inside, get cleaned up and get some rest." After I showered, I took my sleeping meds and lay on the bed. I just wanted to shut out the entire day. I fell into an uneasy sleep, but thankfully there were no dreams. I woke up to find Day lying next to me and she told me what the trooper told her. I hit a car on Beach Blvd., got out of the truck, then returned to the truck and drove away. Thankfully no one was hurt. I was charged with making an illegal turn and leaving the scene of an accident. Day looked into my eyes and said, "Whatever is wrong, will face it together." It was relief beyond words because I had no recollection of the day after texting her.

The next day, Day took me to see a new psychiatrist. He was a young Middle Eastern man and he took the time to listen to what I had to say. He actually seemed to care about what I was going through. After I explained what happened the day before, He suggested I be hospitalized for observation and to adjust my medications. He called the hospital to reserve a bed for me. Day drove me and stayed with me until I was checked in. The psych ward at the hospital was very state of the art. It was much different than the state run facilities that I'd been going to. The staff was compassionate and much more professional.

I met with my doctor the following morning. He was different from the others. Other doctors I'd seen were too busy writing in a chart to even look at me. When that happened, my wall went up and I had no interest in sharing anything about my past. This doctor was different. He sat at his desk, looked me in the eye and had nothing in his hands. I felt his compassion as he looked at me. Then he said, "Mr. Allen, I want to help you, but I can only do that if you will trust me and be completely honest with me." I looked in his eyes for several seconds to make sure what I was seeing was genuine concern. I felt a connection with him that I'd not felt before. Finally I said softly, "Alright."

I took a deep breath and begin to tell him the things I witnessed, the transcripts I'd read and the pictures I'd seen. I told him about my namesake, Teresa Carol Allen and how she'd been found so close to my home. I explained the level of intimacy I'd experienced with her killer and walking him on his "last mile". I shared about watching the hearses pass by me at the front gate and each containing the body of a murderer I'd walked to the holding cell only hours before. Then I explained the dreams, the visions, the nightmares and just recently the flash back I had on Beach Blvd. I admitted to him that I didn't feel any regret from participating in my part of the execution process, but that once the killers were dead, how they and their victims shared my thoughts and dreams. I told him of the promise I'd made to be a voice when they had none. I just never quite figured out how to express the feelings that I held inside. I've no idea how long I talked. It was like opening a floodgate; once it started to flow, I couldn't stop. When I finished, I was covered in sweat. I had never talked to anyone about the details I shared with this doctor today. I felt relief deep down in my soul that I had not felt in a very long time. My chest didn't feel quite so heavy. When I

made eye contact with the doctor again, he had that same compassionate look he had when we began. All the years I kept my feelings and thoughts to myself was because I was afraid of what people might think of me, especially my friends and colleagues. I was never afraid when I worked on death row nor was I afraid of the men I was charged with securing.

The doctor smiled and said, "Thank you for your honesty." He typed on the keyboard in front of his computer. Then he turned to me again, "Robert, I believe you have Post Traumatic Stress Disorder." Then he continued to type on his keyboard. I'd heard of P.T.S.D before, but it was usually attributed to veterans returning from combat. The doctor turned back to me, "It appears that you have been misdiagnosed for many years." He typed again and then said to me," I'm going to start you on some new medications for your nightmares, depression and anxiety which will also help you sleep." Every doctor I'd seen would only address my drinking issue. Not one had ever taken the time to actually talk to me about how I felt and ask me to talk about my feelings. There was a doctor in Lake City, Florida that was only concerned with how I many times I came to his facility. His answer to my issue was not to come back.

Later that day a nurse had me sign for my medication, gave my first dose and explained what I was taking. I was prescribed Prazosin for nightmares, Serequel for anxiety and sleep and celexa for depression. It was the same medications soldiers returning from war, with P.T.S.D., were prescribed. Later that night, I was given my first dose of Serequel and Prazosin and told that the Prazosin would take a couple of weeks before I noticed any change. But, whether from the medication or just the knowledge that relief was coming, I drifted off easily to sleep. I had dreams, but no nightmares. Instead, I dreamed of precious memories of my past, with my parents and my beautiful children. I dreamed of Sunday's when all my brothers and sisters would meet at our parent's home for an afternoon cookout. I had a deep, restful sleep. I was in the hospital for 5 days under observation then discharged with prescriptions and an appointment to see the doctor in two weeks.

When I returned home, things were never the same with Day and me. I went to court for leaving the scene of an accident and was fined four hundred dollars and when we left the courthouse she told me, "I'm very angry with you." That was the beginning of the end of our marriage. In just a few short weeks, she told me that she wasn't happy anymore. She filed for divorce and I returned to the ministry in North Jacksonville. I applied for disability a few years before because of my back and was denied. I had a new mental health diagnoses, a new doctor and I found a new attorney who specialized in disability and my case was reopened. I stayed at the ministry for a few months, but eventually I was given the cold shoulder there as well. I was told to find another place to go, but I couldn't bear the way I was treated by the ministry leader, so I packed my clothes and left with nowhere to go. I'd met a Christian friend through the yard sale and he paid my fine for me and gave me some spending money. Other friends at the ministry witnessed how I was treated by the ministry leader and gave me money as well.

I was out on the street again for the first time in a few years. I bought a tent and lived in a wooded area in North Jacksonville for a few weeks. I would go by the ministry on occasion to check my mail and finally received what I had been praying for. I had a hearing with the disability review board. When that day finally came, I cleaned up as best I could and traveled downtown by bus. I met my attorney there and he prepared me for the hearing. When we appeared before the judge there was a vocational expert for the government meant to discredit my claim. My attorney waited very patiently for him to finish and then proceeded to take his testimony apart. He knew all the right questions to ask. His final question for the vocational expert is what I believed sealed my case for me. He asked, "With the type of mental disability that Mr. Allen has and the many times he's tried to commit suicide; what job do you think he'd be able to focus on and maintain?" The expert sat there in silence for a moment and finally said, "None."

I left the hearing feeling optimistic about being approved. However, it would take several weeks or months for the judge to rule on my case. I returned to the tent and sat there in silence as I contemplated my future. I knew I could not stay here in a tent for months. Finally I packed up my belongings, left the tent and took the bus to downtown Jacksonville. I knew of a ministry there that operated a shelter and also a Christian program for men similar to the ministry where I was previously. I was not meant for life on the streets and I was ready to surrender to anything that offered compassion. The cross on the outside of the building reminded me that Christ offered the peace I was searching for. I walked in the front door ready to surrender to any compassion that would be offered to me and I found it.

I was interviewed by the manager of the shelter. He offered the kindness that I was not given at the last place where a cross was displayed. These men were the genuine article. It was a ninety day program of studying the bible and attending lectures. During the interview I briefly told him of my past in law enforcement and the skills I possessed. Once again, I was given an assignment on the front desk. I felt genuine love and concern in this place and I welcomed it with open arms. I made many new friends and even became a part of a prayer group each evening. We prayed for each other and the men and women participating in the program. Day by day, with my new medications and living in a Christian environment, I found peace I had not felt in many years. I could close my eyes each night without fear of the dead coming to find me in my sleep.

I was performing duties that allowed me to help others again. I always felt as though my calling was to help others who had been neglected by family, friends and society. People, like me, who were victims of an illness that they didn't ask for nor understand. As we checked in men each night for the overnight shelter, I witnessed the power of alcohol, drugs and mental illness held over people. I saw younger versions of myself in these forgotten men and how life had beaten them down and some had given up. I remembered I once made a promise to be a voice for the murder victims who could no longer speak for themselves. I had failed miserably in that promise. But, I knew that I could pick up that torch again in the cause of these lost souls.

For three months I talked and prayed with anyone who expressed a desire to listen or seek help. By helping them, I was helping myself. On my off time I started to go outside and pray to God again as my mother taught me so many years before. That empty place deep in my soul that I tried to fill with a career, money, women, and alcohol was now filled with the Holy Spirit. I felt love and compassion for people again and I had no enemies. My disability case was no longer a concern for me. I had many friends praying for me and I knew that the outcome was in God's hands and I didn't need to stress over it. However, I did make periodic calls to my attorney to check on the status of my case. Finally after several months, I was told that I had been approved for 100% disability. My prayers were answered.

I immediately went outside, looked up into the beautiful blue sky and the billowy white clouds and gave thanks to God. Within a week, I received a letter from social security to fill out the paperwork for my benefits. At the office, I was informed of my monthly benefits and would receive back pay for the last two years. I was granted Medicaid which meant all my medical services, including medication, would be provided at no cost to me. By focusing on the daily work God had given me to do, he now provided for me for the remainder of my life. I received my first monthly installment and back pay in June of 2015. I was able to move out of the shelter and into my own apartment where rent was based on my income. Now I was free to pursue whatever God called me to do. I pray every morning and then listen for what I am called to do for the day. Every night I study the bible and end my night with prayer of thanks for the life God has given me.

Day and I remained better friends after our marriage than we ever were while we were together and we remain close today. Sadly, Deedee, the mother of our twins died in 2005 when cancer returned and invaded her body. I had a brief reconciliation with the twins and Kimberly. Kimberly has a family and children of her own today that requires my absence. They are all loved by her mother and her husband. Tracey and I remain close and talk and text on the phone often, but her sister resentments me and choose not to have me in her life. Miki's mother, Debbie made contact with me on Miki's behalf, but it was not to be. The times I did talk with her though email or social media, she was very bitter toward me because I left her while she was so young. She has other sisters and a family that loves her, so I leave that situation in God's hands. I pray for all of them each and every day and knowing they are all happy is the most important thing.

The murderers' with whom I worked so closely all faced their fates. Billy Mitchell, the friend of Roosevelt Green, was executed in the electric chair on September 2, 1987. His last words were in defiance to the chairman of the State board of pardons and parole, who denied his request for clemency. While strapped in the electric chair, he proclaimed, "Tell Wayne Snow to kiss my ass," then went to his death. Timothy Wesley Mcorquodale, the killer of Donna Marie Dixon was executed in the electric chair on September 21, 1987. His last statement was to his father whom he encouraged to stay strong in Christ. Carl Isaacs, the killer of the Alday family and in whose face I saw evil for first time on death row, was executed on May 6, 2003 by lethal injection. 30 years after he committed those horrible murders. All of his accomplices' sentences were commuted to life in prison.

I have been invited to speak at several criminal justice classes at various colleges on the topic of the death penalty. I also appeared on a national radio program on two occasions to talk about the death penalty in America. On one such program, I shared the air with a former death row inmate from Georgia who came within hours of execution, was spared, his sentence commuted to life and he became a free man. Only God could bring a former inmate and officer together to openly talk about the death penalty. I still have mixed emotions about the death penalty. I do believe there are some individuals who can no longer function in society and must remain behind bars if not executed.

But, I am also a Christian who knows God can change the heart of any man and I did see people change during my time on death row. I leave the death penalty to be debated by society and I offer my views and opinion when I am asked to speak. It's a difficult topic because I observed firsthand, in pictures, the devastation that men can heap upon their victims and the faces of the killers that often demonstrated no remorse for their actions; usually blaming society itself or the imagined discrimination of their skin color, but never taking any responsibility for what they'd done. When I consider that topic, I'm always taken back to 1985 and hearing the words of Roosevelt Green, strapped in the electric chair as he proclaimed; "I'm about to die for a murder that someone else committed and had nothing to do with." Even at that pivotal moment in his life, about to meet God face to face and yet refusing to take responsibility for his own actions on that fateful night in December 1976.

Sometimes my medication fails me and a face from the distant past sneaks in and interrupts the peace I've found. In those moments I call out the name of Jesus Christ and peace returns. I hope to share my memories with others in uniform and about the dangers of not talking about what haunts them at night. I know from experience they are out there because for many years, I had no idea that I wasn't unique. The feelings aren't fear or cowardice, but being witness to death over and over again and remembering the faces of the innocent. I hope to reach out to share my experience and let others know; "You're not alone."

Teresa Carol Allen was more than just another victim. From the day I walked into the Diagnostic Center in Jackson, Georgia thirty six years before, she and the monster who raped and helped end her life, Roosevelt Green were like a mission I needed to complete. Seeing the picture of her lying on that autopsy table made it all too real for me. I promised myself the day I saw that picture that I would visit the site where it all began and then pay my respects at her grave. I bought a BMW convertible with back pay and decided that this was the day. I let the top down and drove north on interstate 95 until I reached the Georgia state line, then I exited and drove north on the beautiful country roads of South Georgia. It was a beautiful southern summer day and I passed by old abandoned buildings that gave character to the countryside. I finally arrived in the small town of Cochran, Georgia. I knew what I wanted to see, but had no idea how to find it. I decided to start with the local newspaper. I stopped in a drug store to ask for directions. There was an elderly lady standing nearby. I asked her about the newspaper and she very kindly offered me directions. I had a hunch so I asked her, "Are you a native of Cochran?" She replied, "Yes, all my life." I continued, "Do you remember the Teresa Carol Allen murder?" She immediately said, "Oh yes."

I explained who I was and that I was on duty the night Roosevelt Green was executed. She recalled the incident like it had happened yesterday. She went on to tell me that everyone in town still talked about that horrible day. She said that no one locked their doors in town before that, but her abduction and murder changed the town forever. I took a chance and asked, "Can you tell me the location of the store where it happened?" "She pointed to a building across the street and said, "That's it, but it is a beauty parlor now." She gave me the name of the owner. I thanked her, returned to my car and drove across the street.

I walked in and asked for the owner, Miss Betty. I introduced myself and explained who I was. It caught the attention of everyone in the building. She told me that Teresa Carol Allen's brother lived across the street from her, but didn't talk about his sister and I could certainly understand why. I told her I intended to write a book about my experiences on death row, but that was not why I was here. I explained this was very personal for me. She went on to say the cousin of Teresa Carol Allen's boyfriend worked in the shop as well. I talked briefly with him and he gave me the phone number of his cousin. Afterwards I walked around the store trying to image what it was like thirty years before. The trial transcript gave a brief description of the store, but I was unable to visualize it. I thanked them all for their time and walked outside. I took several pictures of the store because I wanted to remember that this place was the scene of a horrific moment in time for an eighteen year old girl who now shared my mind.

I had one more stop to make to fulfill my promise. I took out my cell phone and entered the address of a church in my GPS and started the car. I felt butterflies in the pit of my stomach as I drove the country road. After only a few miles I reached my destination. It was a small quaint building with a cemetery adjacent to the church. I walked among the headstones looking carefully at each one. I stopped to look into the blue sky and heard birds singing in the nearby trees. I closed my eyes and took a deep breath of fresh air. It reminded me of the summers back home when I was a child and had no knowledge of the evil in this world. I opened my eyes and continued walking and finally found the object of my search. It was a family plot, but only one grave occupied the space. I saw my own last name on the headstone and it gave me chills. There was a pair of praying hands at the top of the headstone and a marble slab. I knelt down and touched the headstone and said, "I'm sorry it took me so long to find you." The fact that she was actually under that slab was all too surreal. I thought about her all these years, but never saw more than a faded picture on the pages of a trial transcript. As I knelt there staring at her headstone, the words of a song formed in my mind, "Oceans, where feet may fail," by Hillsong United, a Christian group. It was about following the Holy Spirit no matter where he led.

That's when I finally realized after all these years that she had been right where she was supposed to be, in the arms of her savior. Her memory started my journey years before and finally brought me to this place in time. She, Donna Marie Dixon, the Alday family and all the other victims were all at peace. This simple, beautiful song held the key to my redemption through the Lord Jesus Christ. I finally found the purpose of all my suffering; to reach out to those like me, to witness that everyone's redemption waits with open arms. I smiled as I looked down at the headstone and said, "It's time for me to begin!"

The End

CPSIA information can be obtained
at www.ICGtesting.com
Printed in the USA
BVOW07s1048260218
509110BV00024B/826/P